CONTENTS

PART TWO
The System Perspective

Effective Structured Techniques

From Strategy to CASE

C. PAUL ALLEN

Prentice Hall

NEW YORK   LONDON   TORONTO   SYDNEY   TOKYO   SINGAPORE

First published 1991 by
Prentice Hall International (UK) Ltd
66 Wood Lane End, Hemel Hempstead
Hertfordshire HP2 4RG

A division of
Simon & Schuster International Group

Typeset in 10/13 pt Sabon and Syntax
by Keyboard Services, Luton, Bedfordshire

Printed and bound in Great Britain at the
University Press, Cambridge

Library of Congress Cataloging-in-Publication Data

Allen, C. Paul.
  Effective structured techniques: from strategy to
  CASE/C. Paul Allen.
    p. cm.
  Includes bibliographical references and index.
  ISBN 0-13-155763-7 (paper): $36.00
  1. Management systems--Design and
  construction.   I. Title.
T58.6.A435   1991
658.4'032--dc20   91-17530
                                                   CIP

British Library Cataloguing in Publication Data

Allen, C. Paul
  Effective structured techniques: From strategy to
  CASE.
  I. Title
  004.2

  ISBN 0-13-155763-7

---

2 3 4 5   95 94 93 92

PART THREE
The Strategic Perspective

Contents

PART FOUR

The Enterprise Perspective

PART FIVE

The User Perspective

PART SIX

The CASE Perspective

PREFACE

There are many structured methods and automated software tools that proffer instant panaceas to the well-known problems of systems development. The reader seeking such an instant off-the-shelf solution, or wall-to-wall methodology, will be disappointed by this book: there are no miracle cures. Let me explain then what I *have* sought to achieve with this book.

Since 1974, I have known both the dizzy heights of success and the depression of failure in systems development. Looking back, much seemed to hinge on effective application of structured techniques. I have had to learn from my mistakes in applying structured techniques 'in anger'. There is no one book that I have followed. This book is an attempt to consolidate my experience and produce a compendium of what has worked and what has not worked.

In my role of consultant and instructor with YOURDON™ I've visited dozens of DP shops and addressed many groups of people, involved in the systems development process. They have ranged from junior programmers to senior managers. Despite their different attitudes and backgrounds, a common thread of interest unites them: the problem of developing effective software in an increasingly complex environment. Most appreciate there is some value in applying structured techniques, otherwise they would not have called me in! A great many are also familiar with the established books on the subject. However, most also recognize that there is something 'different' about their own situation. Increasingly audiences want to know how best to apply structured techniques to their own particular problems and cultures. In the discussions that ensue ideas are generated. This book represents an effort to collect together the best of these ideas.

Parts One and Two of the book describe a set of proven structured systems development techniques based on an established literature. The major focus then switches to fresh ground in applying these techniques in a way which is:

☐ Effectively geared to company strategy, to produce quality systems 'on time and within budget' (Part Three).
☐ Supported by effective data administration (Part Four).

☐ Conducive to user communication through integration with prototyping tools (Part Five).

☐ Supported by a recommended blueprint for CASE (computer aided software engineering) tools (Part Six).

An organic lifecycle is developed as a framework for coming to terms with these issues in a way which can be effectively planned and controlled. An underlying theme of the book is the need to harmonize with the evolution toward object orientated technology.

I have sought to clarify what things mean firstly by looking at how they are used and secondly by formal definition. A large part of the book is devoted to developing examples from three case studies, each of which is fully documented in the three appendices. The first appendix attempts to explain some of the jargon of structured techniques by reference to an everyday example. Appendices 2 and 3 reflect differing approaches to requirement specification for different system types. A detailed glossary is also included.

Finally, I have found that success in systems development depends heavily on a range of human factors which I have only touched on: talent; thorough business knowledge; enthusiasm; enlightened management; strong leadership; hard work and humour (which though listed last is often the most precious of assets). Nevertheless, this book rests on the assumption that effective structured techniques should foster and not discourage such vital elements.

It is customary at this point to cite an audience for the book. Simply stated, the book is intended for anyone involved in systems development, especially defining user requirements: for managers, users and developers from both commercial and real-time environments. However, a central theme is that effective structured techniques are little more than a rationalization of common sense. From that point of view, any reader should be able to use the techniques presented. However, it is not my wish to mislead you into thinking that the learning process will be effortless. The real benefits only come with practical application, and with thinking problems through in your own environment.

ACKNOWLEDGEMENTS

Many people have contributed, both directly and indirectly, in many ways to this book. To try to list everyone who has influenced me in one way or another through my career and thus helped shape this book is an impossible task. Nevertheless my special gratitude goes to the following:

- [ ] First and foremost to my wife and children for enduring my distraction for the best part of a year.
- [ ] To those whom I have attempted to teach, whose questions and insights have proved that learning is very much a two way process.
- [ ] To those who have helped me to shape many of the ideas of this book 'in anger' on live projects.
- [ ] To David C. Lee of GEC-Marconi Software Systems for a thorough and constructive review of the manuscript.
- [ ] To Robert Chaundy of Bookstyle for his painstaking work and tolerance in copy editing the manuscript and designing the book.
- [ ] To Bo Nielsen of Hewlett-Packard (Denmark) for valuable insights on systems strategy.
- [ ] And last but by no means least, to all at YOURDON^{TM} (past and present) who have helped provide both stimulus and sounding board for my own thinking. In particular: Phil Sully (for reviewing the manuscript with such insight), John Bowen (for his personal support), Mike Brough, Rick Marden, Viv Lawrence, Peter Davies, Sami Albanna, Steve Bodenheimer and Lew Sherry (for knowingly or unknowingly each contributing at least one good idea), and to Julian Morgan (for supporting the development of a course which led initially to my writing this book).

PART ONE

Introduction

The value of modelling tools as a vehicle toward the development of more effective systems is widely accepted and yet the software crisis remains a fact of life. Three reasons for this are poor choice of modelling tools, poor application of modelling tools and lack of effective CASE support. This part of the book begins to address these problems by setting out the pattern for the remainder of the book and by introducing some of the more central concepts, including the organic lifecycle.

However there is a more fundamental problem which we will seek to address in this part of the book before progressing further. This problem is perhaps more cultural than logistical: for modelling tools to work we need (a) the right cultural conditions and (b) an appeal to natural problem solving patterns. Too often both are missing. Chapter 1 deals with the first point; Chapter 2 with the second.

CHAPTER 1

Overview

☐ ☐ ☐ ☐ ☐ ☐ ☐ ☐ ☐ ☐ ☐ ☐ ☐ ☐ ☐ ☐

A book is a machine to think with.

I.A. RICHARDS
Principles of Literary Criticism

1.1 Introduction

The power of yesterday's mainframe computer is available today on a single integrated circuit. Rapid advances in hardware, using conventional engineering techniques, have resulted in enormous computing potential. Software is the mechanism that seeks to exploit this potential, but that all too often fails to meet our expectations:

- ☐ Software is delivered late and over budget.
- ☐ Maintenance of software is difficult and time consuming.
- ☐ Software quality is often suspect.
- ☐ Customer requirements are not fulfilled.

An abundance of statistics and horror stories lend prolific testimony to what has been commonly termed the 'software crisis'. Paper titles such as 'Some Computer Related Disasters and Other Egrarious Horrors' (Neumann, 1985) and 'The Star Wars Defense Won't Compute' (Jacky, 1985) are typical. The reader will be relieved to learn that it is not my aim here to add to the library of software crisis literature. Suffice it to say that many users are programming their own local PC-based systems not because of a desire for new technical skills, but as a result of disillusionment with the efforts of systems developers.

This chapter begins by briefly considering the history of structured techniques and the advent of computer aided software engineering (CASE) tools as a response to the software crisis. The problem is then expressed in terms of a lack of effective systems. This is a book primarily about using modelling tools to establish requirement definition, with the aim of producing effective systems.

However, I suggest that, everything else aside, there are three essential conditions for the development of effective systems before we can even start considering the use of modelling tools. That is, effectiveness must also be achieved in terms of:

- ☐ Lifecycle.
- ☐ Working methods.
- ☐ Mind-set.

Certain problems and needs in systems development that I come across virtually every day as a consultant prompted me to write this book. Therefore, after establishing the ground rules, it seemed appropriate to characterize the parts of this book with respect to a wish-list. The wish-list is really a summary of the most prevalent of those problems and needs. Each part of the book represents a response to each of those wishes. However, the reader will find that just as the wishes are interdependent, so the same is true of the parts of this book.

Ideally therefore this book should be read cover to cover. Pressure of time often dictates that we are unable to do this with any thoroughness, especially in one go. I also realize that certain parts of the book will appeal more strongly to certain categories of reader. I have, therefore, included a chapter-by-chapter summary at the end of this chapter for those readers who wish to be more selective.

1.2 A historical perspective

Various sets of structured techniques have evolved during the 1970s and 1980s as a response to the software crisis. Such techniques recognise that, 'Clearly it pays off to invest effort in finding requirements errors early and correcting them in, say, one man hour rather than waiting to find the error during operations and having to spend 100 man hours correcting it.' (Boehm, 1976). Structured techniques seek to avoid the maintenance backlog by the use of modelling tools to build systems that accurately reflect user requirements. This is done by dealing with software as an engineered product that requires planning, analysis, design, testing, implementation and maintenance. Perhaps the most common and salient engineering feature of these various techniques is the principle of determining requirement definition before creating a software design. This principle, to determine *what* you want to build before determining *how* it is to be built, is a contemporary echo of Louis Sullivan's advice to architectural engineers, at the end of the nineteenth century, that 'form forever follows function' (Sullivan, 1896). Indeed, it was upon this premise that the Bauhaus school of design was esablished in 1919, and upon which good general engineering practice has always thrived.

Model making has a history reaching far beyond the Egyptians, who made use of burial models. Most industries use models, full-sized or scaled; for example, in the aircraft industry, models of various sizes are utilized for wind tunnel testing; the theatre uses models of stage settings as a means of testing workability cheaply, and so on. One result of using structured techniques in the late 1970s and early 1980s was that those great tomes of text, known as systems specifications, notoriously difficult to administer, began to disappear. They were replaced by the product of structured analysis and design: the structured specification. This consisted of models: a set of various diagram types supported by a data dictionary, with minimum accompanying narrative explanation. On small, well-defined applications this proved generally successful. However, problems like payroll and purchase ledger soon became replaced by more sophisticated user demands for larger and more complex systems. The result was that the structured specification started to grow top-heavy. 'A picture is worth a thousand words' we are often exhorted, but if your picture has a thousand words written on it then this becomes self-defeating. In short, the structured specification became as unwieldy and inefficient to administer as its unstructured ancestor.

The response to the administrative problem, was the advent in the mid-1980s of computer aided software engineering (CASE for short). PC-based CASE products, incorporating graphics editors with integrated data dictionaries to automate the mundane and time consuming administrative burden of manually driven structured techniques, exploded onto the marketplace. More technical sophistication is delivered with each release of a vendor's product: witness today's advanced windowing facilities, shared data dictionaries, networked products, code and database generation and object oriented knowledge bases.

1.3   Toward object orientation

A yet more recent trend has seen a move away from traditional structured techniques toward object orientation. It is not my aim here to add to the rapidly rising groundswell of literature on object oriented analysis. Object oriented programming is a fact of life; however, this is not the case with object oriented *analysis*. Like teenage promiscuity everyone seems to be talking about it but very few people seem to be really doing it, and those that are are only experimenting. The view here is that we should build upon the best of what we have learnt to do well, whilst learning from our mistakes in systems development. The last thing that the beleaguered MIS manager needs is some new revolution: he or she has heard it all before and is justifiably frustrated by all the industry hype.

The reader looking for a revolution in systems development will therefore be disappointed by this book: there are no new object oriented notations. We will seek to build upon better application of what we have in fact learnt already. There will be no new silver bullets. However, this does not mean that we can ignore the trend toward object orientation: to repeat, object oriented programming is a fact of life. What I have therefore sought to do is to provide some salient pointers as to how the tools and techniques recommended in this book can be applied toward object orientation. The approach is very much evolutionary and not revolutionary.

1.4   The concept of effective systems

The technological advances of CASE have eased the administrative problems of using structured techniques but the promised improvements have been generally disappointing. Systems produced are not as effective as we would wish.

In many ways the software crisis is a crisis concerning system quality, which, though notoriously difficult to define, can be judged by applying various factors which are weighted according to environment and then averaged. Try this for your own environment with respect to the following factors:

- ☐ Accuracy of business function.
- ☐ Reliability.
- ☐ Speed.
- ☐ Flexibility.
- ☐ Portability.
- ☐ Security.

However, debating the merits of such a list, which is always going to be relative to the needs of a particular environment, is not the issue here. Another way of viewing the software crisis is to consider it in terms of productivity. This can be simply expressed as follows:

$$\text{Software productivity} = \frac{\text{System quality}}{\text{Time invested}}$$

Poor system quality results in user dissatisfaction and a maintenance backlog. Too much time invested results in inefficient systems development. Together they yield a low return on investment. This is the 'bottom line' of the software crisis.

The formula is a simplification of the real problem in that in practice not only is productivity determined by each variable but also the variables are not as separable as implied. A frantic rush to meet a deadline inevitably compromises quality. Conversely, the need to ensure system quality causes slippage in the delivery date.

Most people would agree that better automobile production methods have resulted in better cars. However, although it seems obvious that the quality of a car and its means of production are interdependent, we have more difficulty applying the same thinking to software development. Indeed one of the basic problems that we seem to be up against is that very often sets of structured techniques are presented as either *descriptive* or *prescriptive*.

Descriptive techniques literally describe a set of modelling tools that can be used in conjunction with various heuristics to engineer better quality systems. The problem with this approach is that it fails to recognize efficiency of the development process itself as a major factor in determining a system's effectiveness.

Prescriptive techniques, in contrast, concentrate of the means of production: sets of recommended activities for each phase of a project with milestones are presented as *the* way to engineer systems. The problem with this approach is that it presents developers with a fixed set of tools to be employed rather blindly, in standard ways, without considering whether a tool is appropriate for a particular job, and usually with a paucity of guidelines on meaning.

This book takes the view that the effectiveness of a system is determined by both its quality and by the efficiency of the development process and that the two are intimately connected. Developers need effective toolsets but they also need techniques: help in choosing the right tool for a particular job and in how to apply it for that job. Broadly speaking therefore tools and techniques for their use are considered together, rather than trying to separate the two artificially as often seems to be the fashion.

Although this book centres on the use of structured techniques this is inevitably something of an oversimplification of the real problem. Clearly there are many factors at work here. Perhaps the most prevalent of these are the closely related problems of producing effective estimates and reducing system maintenance costs. Because of reasons of scope these issues have not been covered separately or in any depth. However, we will find throughout the course of this book that both these problems surface again and again, inextricably linked with the more fundamental problem of effective modelling in requirement definition. Indeed, looking ahead somewhat, Chapter 12 contends that an effective CASE environment needs to address all these problems not individually but as aspects of the same underlying malaise.

For example, if I were recommending techniques for cultivating plants, I could not do this by considering the plants in isolation. I would need to suggest the right conditions for healthy growth: soil type, climate, position and so on. It would be no good planting a palm tree on the Yorkshire Moors, unless, presumably, I were willing to erect some sort of glass house around it! Similarly the tools and techniques recommended in this book rely on certain conditions if they are to stand any chance of success. Three of the most critical conditions can be summarized as follows:

- ☐ Effective lifecycle.
- ☐ Effective working methods.
- ☐ Effective mind-set.

Let me characterize each in turn.

1.5   Effective lifecycle

Structured techniques treat software as a product that must be engineered, like any other (including hardware), in terms of classical steps:

- ☐ Planning.
- ☐ Analysis.
- ☐ Design.
- ☐ Testing.
- ☐ Implementation.
- ☐ Maintenance.

Traditionally the steps were performed in sequence with a deliverable, including an outline proposal for the next step, to be signed off before the next step could be sanctioned. This gave rise to the so-called 'waterfall model' of systems development. This proved attractive in theory: quantifiable steps lending themselves to a well-planned and easily controlled approach to system building, along the lines of classically established engineering. Mostly, however, it proved unworkable in practice for various reasons. For example, it was usually impossible to do a complete analysis job in terms of a rigorous requirements definition, before considering at least some of the design. This was partly because users or customers were reluctant to commit themselves to *what* the system was going to do before considering *how* it would look, and partly because it was only by getting to grips with the design of an application that developers were fully able to understand requirements. Similar problems occurred throughout the lifecycle.

In short, the traditional lifecycle was unable to cope with iteration. 'Build one to throw one away. You will anyway.' (Brooks, 1975) is a lesson that Fred Brooks learnt in the 1960s during the development of the OS operating system. It seems to have taken considerably longer to permeate through to the system building community as a whole. Indeed, there are many organizations still using, and struggling with, the original waterfall model as a basis for systems development. Generally speaking though the lesson does seem to have been learned, often through bitter experience. What was needed was an approach that recognized the reality of the situation as opposed to the myth of the waterfall model, as depicted in Figure 1.1.

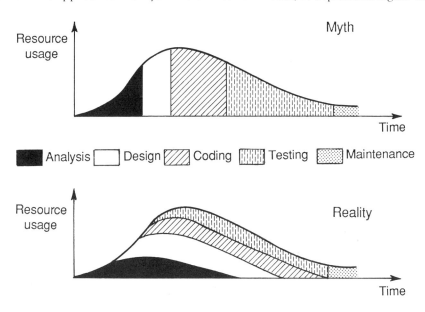

Figure 1.1 Myth and reality in systems development.

Various lifecycles have been proposed and tried in order to come to terms with the iterations of systems development, whilst retaining the original framework of the waterfall model. The most popular of these seem to be spiral models deriving from the work of Barry Boehm at TRW (Boehm, 1986). The spiral process depicted in Figure 1.2 is a set of repetitive steps whose iterations are intended to converge to an 'operational prototype'. Each iteration involves four basic steps, corresponding to each of the four sectors on the diagram. Effectively what we have here is an extended feasibility exercise as a prelude to the later steps of the waterfall model: design, code, etc.

The reader will find that the tools and techniques employed in this book relate much more to the spiral model of systems development than to the original waterfall model: systems strategy, analysis and prototyping are seen as iterative activities which are performed at project level with the aim of reducing uncertainty regarding the requirements definition for a system. I refer to this as an 'organic'

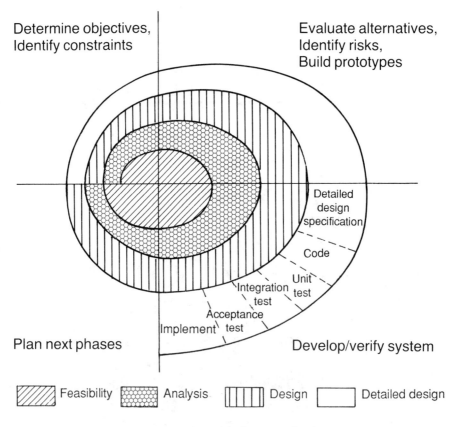

Figure 1.2 A 'spiral' model of systems development.

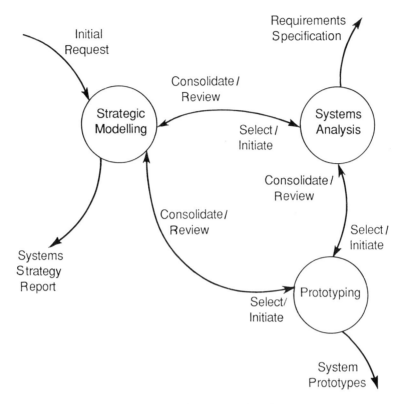

Figure 1.3 The organic lifecycle.

approach, as depicted in Figure 1.3, as it is founded upon growth. That is, projects do not start with a 'clean slate' every time: they need to be selected and initiated in the context of what has already been learnt, which itself is subject to subsequent review as new found knowledge is consolidated. It is 'Strategic Modelling' that forms the fulcrum for selecting, initiating, reviewing and consolidating requirements definition with respect to the needs of the organization as a whole. All other systems development activities (from external design to implementation) are also ultimately controlled in this way; however, for reasons of scope these are not shown.

The organic approach suggested here shares an important feature of the waterfall model in that it aims to produce deliverables: for example, in Figure 1.3 the items 'Systems Strategy Report', 'Requirements Specification' and 'System Prototypes' all represent deliverables. It is necessary to have such deliverables not only as evidence of progress but also as evidence of management commitment. However, the organic approach is inherently different in that it views the underlying models as living documents. In particular, we will require a framework within which systems development can be co-ordinated and carried out with reference to overall business objectives. Therefore the systems strategy report must not only be created quickly (weeks rather than months) it must be reviewed and maintained on a regular basis to keep pace with change. Indeed, a basic premise of this book is that all projects should be short-term (weeks, rather than months).

The organic approach provides flexibility in that all three of the activities in Figure 1.3 can be operating concurrently and in that they can be initiated on a short-term project basis as required. All activities are selected and initiated from Strategic Modelling except Prototyping which may also be initiated from Systems Analysis. The same concept also applies to all other systems development activities. Feedback from each activity is reviewed and consolidated often for use by another activity. The vehicles through which this is achieved are the *project profile* and *system profile* which are discussed in some detail in Section 6.10.

1.6   **Effective working methods**

As a rookie systems analyst I can remember being baffled by a phrase that my more senior colleagues would often employ in the aftermath of long discussion meetings with users: 'X was just playing politics' they would say with a unique combination of exasperation and resignation. In a nutshell, I came to find that what users were doing was protecting their own interests against the changes implied by a new system by putting up obstacles to its development. In general, people do not like change, even where the change is for the corporate good. Let me give you some examples.

One company, involved with servicing many different types of financial contract from mortgages to trusts and bonds, found they were losing custom to those companies which presented their clients with an integrated financial service en-compassing all products. Instead of having to be switched from one departmental clerk to another over the 'phone, a client was assigned a 'guardian angel' who would deal with *any* query or change on a general but personal basis. The guardian angel would have a wide but not particularly deep financial knowledge. Ninety per cent of the time he or she could deal with the query at source; for the remaining 10 per cent it would be necessary to consult via a specialist in, say, pensions or bonds. Nevertheless the personal service was retained. Although the change implied by the new client servicing system was obviously for the common good there was much departmental resistance from product managers who saw the change as reducing their own spheres of influence.

Again, giving life assurance salesmen laptop computers to automate production of proposals in the clients' homes is popular from a corporate viewpoint and from the sales manager's viewpoint but is likely to provoke resistance from the new business department manager in that a large part of that department's work, proposal checking and entry, has been removed at a stroke.

Another more general example that promoted much resistance in the early 1980s was the shift from batch to online processing that removed much of the data preparation function.

Tackling such resistance can be very difficult and time consuming causing budget overruns and missed deadlines. Moreover, although they have responsibility for establishing requirements in a conflicting user community, systems development people do not have the matching authority to resolve political problems. Sometimes compromises can be forged by the politically astute systems analyst. More often than not, however, the project starts to spin its wheels like a car trying to get out of a mud patch. Eventually interest wanes, the budget blows, frustration rules, and the project gets abandoned.

Such problems require that one senior business manager, known as the *executive sponsor*, takes responsibility for the project in terms of:

☐ System definition.
☐ Implied organizational changes.
☐ Resource provision.

The role of the executive sponsor is thus distinct from that of the *project manager* whose responsibility is for the day to day running of the project itself.

At project inception the executive sponsor organizes a 'working group' consisting of all interested user managers plus the project manager and systems developers as appropriate to the stage of the project. User members of this group are responsible for ensuring the system is satisfactory from the point of view of their specific business areas.

Note, the term 'project' here is used in a general sense and might centre on any activity from conducting a systems strategy for a whole organization to designing or prototyping a small sub-system. The specific size and make-up of the working group will vary depending on the type and stage of the specific project. However, the roles of executive sponsor and project manager are essential to any project.

Again, responsibility and authority go hand in hand. It is absolutely vital that the executive sponsor has the authority to make decisions. This means that if necessary he or she is able to 'pull rank' on user managers who are playing politics. Sometimes, at strategic level for example, this will entail that the executive sponsor is the chief executive or the managing director. Clearly this is a new departure for some companies where such individuals are used to playing a backseat role. The development of effective systems requires effective leadership.

Effective leadership requires new ways of working. If political problems are to be resolved and effective systems developed we shall need effective ways of working together.

Traditionally, most interaction between participants in systems development is conducted at two levels. Firstly, there is the interview level where the analyst elicits user requirements in a one to one situation, and then goes away and writes up notes which are formally agreed. Systems developers then synthesize the notes into a specification, which is agreed using the second level of working, which involves a group meeting of all interested users and senior developers. Typically, the specification is walked through page by page, with agreements and change requests noted. A second meeting then resolves the changes and the specification is deemed accepted.

The major problem with this approach is that it makes no use of group dynamics; it neither encourages positive questioning nor promotes creative thinking. All the spadework is done in isolated one to one sessions at the first level. The second level involves a group, but here one of two things normally occurs. Either the group operates very much to rubber stamp the spadework and users feel inhibited about raising what are often genuine doubts at a late stage, thus compromising deadlines; it is indeed ironic that such meetings are often called *acceptance* meetings thus implying by their very name an embargo on creative thinking and discussion by the group. Or the group meeting degenerates into a political debâcle as intimated earlier. Part of the problem is that normally there is a lot of discussion in the early stages of the project at the 'kick-off' meeting and in initial interviews, and there is also a lot of discussion in late stages of the project at acceptance meetings but that very little genuine communication takes place in the intervening period.

A more effective approach is to utilize workshop environments alongside traditional interviewing techniques. All project participants are assembled in one place at various times to establish objectives, to agree what is needed and how it will look. To structure the session and to maximize the potential of group dynamics a *session leader* is appointed to keep everyone on course. This should be a person trained to facilitate discussion and guide participants through the various activities. It is vital that participants understand the objectives of the session and an agenda should be supplied for all participants in advance of the session to facilitate this. Other documentation should be produced on the spot, as problems are identified and points resolved by a *session administrator*, again trained for the role. Ideally some form of electronic whiteboard should be provided to assist in this process, with each participant issued with a list at the close of the session. This list would typically show all points agreed and problems to be addressed with action points for resolution.

One of the advantages of this approach is that it lends itself particularly well to using the diagrams of structured techniques as a communication and specification vehicle. Diagrams can be drawn and developed interactively on a whiteboard to reflect the perceptions of the group as a whole. Also included in the session documentation would be all diagramming products of the session.

This way much of the time consuming cycle between writing up the discussion and formally agreeing it is removed, although it is recognized that there will always be problems resulting in action points for resolution before the next meeting. Also, although group sessions save calendar time, they are heavy in actual usage of man hours. Therefore, traditional interviewing, which minimizes user time and involvement, should not be ignored; that would be to throw the baby out with the bath water. Moreover, very detailed work, such as establishing exact business rules of specific processes, is usually better approached through one to one communication. Therefore, we need a prudent balance between the two approaches of interviewing and group sessions.

Group sessions should be well-planned and budgetted for (time is money) and held at regular intervals *throughout* the project. Indeed, successful use of the diagramming techniques described in this book depends very much on the group dynamic approach. Because of the scope of the book, I have really only touched on the issue here, let me, therefore, make two points for further reference.

Historically, practical use of group dynamics has its roots in the work of Bennis (1965) and more latterly Doyle (1976). There are four basic principles:

1. Traditional meetings with the most senior individual as chairperson do not lend themselves very well to problem solving. Hence the need for a session leader.
2. Decisions agreed should be consensus decisions with which all participants can identify. There are no losers. The documentation produced is a group product, in which all have a stake.
3. The agenda itself is produced by the group as part of the documentation; this avoids negative feelings that the meeting might be biased before it is even started.
4. Documentation should be produced on the spot and not as minutes after the session. It is openly displayable as 'group memory' using a whiteboard or other visual aid. Hence the need for a session administrator.

Finally, IBM initially applied these principles to the field of systems development in the form of Joint Application Design (JAD). The IBM user organization GUIDE has in fact published several papers on the subject; the reader is referred to GUIDE (1986) for a detailed account.

1.7 Effective mind-set

It has been realized since Kant, writing over two hundred years ago, that we attribute meaning to observed activity by relating it to a larger image that we supply from our mind. The observed activity is only meaningful to us, in fact, in terms of a particular image of the world or *Weltanschauung* which we normally take for granted. (Because I shall frequently have recourse to use this appropriate but ungainly word I shall abbreviate it to the colloquial 'mind-set' from here on!)

An example will serve to bring the term 'mind-set' into sharper focus. Last night I asked my eldest son why he only wrote a single page for his homework on a recent school visit to York. 'Because the teacher asked for at least a page' came the reply I had walked into. Here the same purposeful human activity, writing, is viewed according to two mind-sets which make sense to two different perspectives: my concern for my son to get the most out of his homework; and my son's concern to get the homework out the way as quickly as possible to permit the much more important activity of watching the World Cup on television.

Typically, we cling tenaciously to mind-sets which make what we observe meaningful. Newton and Einstein are celebrated as the greatest scientists precisely because they forced the establishment of new mind-sets, based on revolutionary frameworks which turned existing mind-sets upside down. Both were able to establish hypotheses which survived severe tests, and hence became public knowledge.

In system development there is a traditional mind-set which I believe has had much to do with holding the industry back and is an underlying cause of the software crisis. As humans we seem to have a hankering after simple, hard, unquestionable truths whether they be embodied in the laws of physics, Marxist analysis or belief in the literal truth of the Bible. A prevalent attitude of delegates on many of the courses on structured analysis and design that I have taught is the seeking of some secret recipe to be followed in the pursuit of effective systems. Similarly there is often an attitude amongst senior management to view systems development as a production line. In a banking environment, for example, the mind-set might be dominated by a desperate need for the bank to match the dealing systems of the competition. This is perceived as the base-line by which all these well paid technical specialists will be judged. Producing a good dealing system is viewed rather like rolling a new car off a production line. This traditional mind-set perceives structured techniques embodied as a CASE tool as a panacea for all ills: something you can lift off a shelf and plug in and, hey presto, you roll the new system off the production line. After all, the opposition bought the Xyz CASE tool to develop a state of the art dealing system, so why don't we just jump on the bandwagon?

Unfortunately the nature of software conflicts with this mind-set. Requirements are not predefined: the hard part is not so much in creating the product as in determining what you want to create in the first place. There are often countless political obstacles to gaining this understanding. Furthermore, perceptions of both users and analysts change, and the business itself changes with time. There is something inherently different with software that makes engineering it both challenging and frustrating.

We hear much talk today about investing in information as an asset, in exploiting software for competitive advantage and so on. Tom Peters, for example, makes the following observation. 'The ability to take action close to the market – and fast – is the first requirement for competing. Therefore both information availability and the authority to move forward to the front line are musts' (Peters, 1987). Does the traditional mind-set assist in this vision?

Let us return to the analogy of car production. Ford, for example, spent over a billion dollars on engineering before the first Taurus rolled off the production line. In other words, several thousand people spent over ten million total hours 'deciding' what kind of car to build. But someone had to start the process and seek the help of others in assembling and co-ordinating what proved to be a winning team.

Although the example is deliberately extreme, the point is that although research is something we take for granted with manufactured items like cars, this is not generally true of software. Activities such as prototyping are all too often seen as game-playing, unproductive and time-wasting. The traditional mind-set is embedded in Oscar Wilde's definition of a cynic as 'someone who knows the price of everything and the value of nothing': it wants software to be engineered but does not wish to incur what it sees as the burden of research. It sees software as plannable-in-advance and engineered through a series of simple steps, without the need for any scouting ahead in the form of research to see what users actually require. The result is systems which are ineffective in that they need continual change because they fail to match requirements, because we did not research the problem effectively. The irony is that we still do our research, but in actually using the delivered system rather than as a consciously planned exercise.

The organic approach to systems development goes against the grain of the traditional mind-set: it sees research as a useful and productive activity. Indeed, large parts of this book are devoted to system reconnaissance and prototyping work which are seen as critical to the success of systems development and in coming to terms with the software crisis. This involves a shift in gear from the traditional mind-set to viewing research activity as work which should be carefully planned and controlled: like any other project work in fact.

1.8   A wish-list

We have seen that despite the technological breakthroughs of CASE the software crisis still persists. Some of the blame for this might be attributed to ineffective conditions in terms of lifecycle, working methods and mind-set. However, a cynic might say that structured techniques are to blame: no longer can we blame their failures on administration.

In my role as consultant not only do I see structured techniques employed *successfully*, but as 'agony aunt' I hear many problems voiced by systems managers. Consideration of some of these throws a little more light on the problem. Here is a problem/wish-list that typifies four of the most common:

1. *Problem*: 'We can not pick our way through the minefield of different terms and modelling tools used by all the different method houses.'
   Wish: 'We want something simple and yet flexible. Our organization needs a minimum of different modelling tools with a maximum of choice in the way we choose to employ them according to the needs of different applications.'

2. *Problem*: 'Our systems do not integrate and we are continually fixing the many interfaces between them, and all too often new development work is abandoned before we have had a chance to develop anything useful. Because of pressure to produce results we are driven by short-term response to user demands, developing each system by considering its immediate business priorities and cost without considering its impact on other systems.'
   Wish: 'We need to move toward a long-term response to user demands. I want each system to be developed by considering its benefits in an open-minded way in relation to the needs of the organization as a whole.'

3. *Problem*: 'It's been bad enough to deliver so many systems late and over budget, but with users asking for so many changes after implementation we just haven't the resources to keep pace with their demands. Now internal users are starting to develop their own PC-based applications. We tried one set of structured techniques but the diagrams were too abstract for my own staff, let alone the users.'
   Wish: 'I need to *involve* my users in defining requirements, not just as passive observers but in a way that commits them actively to the systems development process itself.'

4. *Problem*: 'Even though we have spent a lot of money on a CASE tool to

facilitate development there have been few tangible results. The software has actually constrained the way we have worked in that there are many features which, though irrelevant to our own applications, are mandatory as far as the CASE tool is concerned. Rather than the CASE tool supporting the method we seem to be putting a lot of effort into satisfying the dictates of the CASE tool. Although this is to the liking of some of my more technically minded staff who are quite happy to while away the hours poured over a screen in some corner, in effect we seem to have bought a lot of superfluous functionality.'

Wish: 'We need a CASE tool that cost effectively supports the way we want to work.'

A closer look reveals that the failures we are faced with here fall into two categories. Firstly there are failures concerning structured techniques themselves, exemplified by Problem 1. The requirement can be summarized as:

☐ The modelling toolset provided must be simple yet flexible.

The remaining three points concern *application* of structured techniques and can be summarized as:

☐ Structured techniques must be applied strategically.
☐ Structured techniques must be applied in a way which encourages user involvement in defining requirements.
☐ A CASE tool is required which cost-effectively supports the techniques.

The remainder of this part of the book focusses on the requirements for effective modelling and recommends an outline modelling framework and toolset. Each subsequent part takes a different perspective as follows:

☐ Part Two: *The System Perspective* characterizes the modelling framework and toolset in more detail with respect to system requirements.
☐ Part Three: *The Strategic Perspective* applies the approach enterprise-wide with respect to business objectives.
☐ Part Four: *The Enterprise Perspective* ensures effective administration of the approach enterprise-wide.
☐ Part Five: *The User Perspective* integrates the approach with prototyping techniques.
☐ Part Six: *The CASE Perspective* recommends a blueprint for supporting the tools.

Broadly speaking this is a book about identifying a suitable set of structured techniques and applying them to build *effective systems*.

The book starts by looking at the system perspective. This appears illogical: from a lifecycle point of view it would obviously make sense to start with the strategic perspective and gradually push forward from there. However, there are two important reasons for this:

1. The general approach applies a set of existing tools and techniques, known collectively as 'event partitioning'. This approach is best understood initially with respect to *system* requirements.
2. The reader will find that a basic premise of this book is that systems only exist in relation to other systems. Ultimately this means that enterprises should also be considered as a special case of systems.

Therefore, I have found it expedient first to define the recommended modelling tools with respect to the system perspective.

The central argument of this book is that all too often in the past modelling tools have been applied in abstract isolation at system level: the strategic and user perspectives have been, at best, unco-ordinated with systems analysis and design. At worst they have been ignored altogether. Firstly, this results in systems which do not meet corporate objectives because they fail to meet the needs of the strategic perspective. Secondly, it results in systems which fail to satisfy the user because they do not meet the demands of the user perspective. Finally, it often means that CASE support for both user and developer is fragmented with respect to the different perspectives. The situation is illustrated graphically in Figure 1.4.

The major objective of this book is to integrate the strategic, system and user perspectives toward the development of effective systems. Let me now explain (in outline) how I have sought to achieve this chapter by chapter. I hope this will provide the reader with a rough map of the terrain that lies ahead.

1.9   Summary: chapter by chapter

Chapter 2

This chapter outlines a proposed toolset and modelling framework to be used throughout this book. The requirements for effective modelling are discussed with respect to some common dilemmas of system development.

Simplicity and flexibility are vital characteristics for any set of structured techniques, but are all too often lacking. In particular this causes problems that the techniques are actually meant to help with: in communication with customers and users.

The principle of encapsulation is universally acclaimed (surfacing again today in

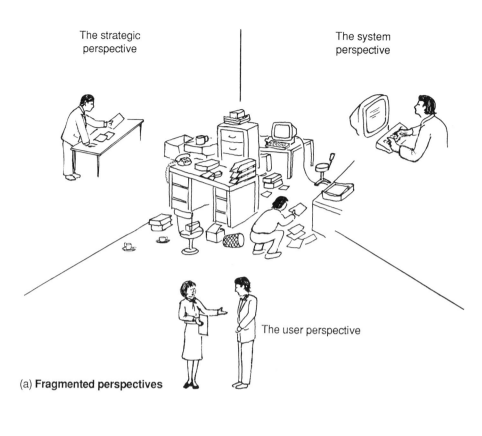

The strategic
perspective

The system
perspective

The user perspective

(a) **Fragmented perspectives**

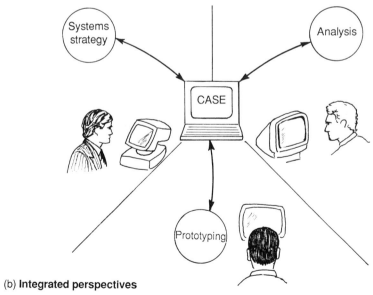

Systems
strategy

Analysis

CASE

Prototyping

(b) **Integrated perspectives**

Figure 1.4 Perspectives in systems development.

the form of object oriented techniques) and yet is often poorly applied. The need is for an approach which applies encapsulation not only at system level but also at enterprise level.

A suitable toolset must appeal to natural problem-solving patterns and encourage encapsulation. A natural problem-solving approach is outlined in terms of the following stages:

- ☐ Determination.
- ☐ Exploration.
- ☐ Understanding.
- ☐ Organization.
- ☐ Specification.
- ☐ Verification.

Event partitioning (EP) is introduced as an approach which has the potential of meeting our requirements. The toolset of event partitioning is introduced inform-ally by using a culinary example. Finally, recommendations are made concerning the employment of models for effective user communication.

1.9.1   Part Two: The System Perspective

Chapter 3

Event partitioning starts out by *exploring* system environment with the goal of establishing system scope. The tools of the *environmental model* are introduced:

- ☐ Statement of purpose.
- ☐ Context diagram.
- ☐ Event list.
- ☐ Data dictionary.

Examples from control and information systems are covered.

Chapter 4

The graphical tools of the *behavioural model* are introduced:

- ☐ Data flow diagrams (DFDs).
- ☐ State transition diagrams (STDs).
- ☐ Entity relationship diagrams (ERDs).

Event partitioning works by first developing an *understanding* of system require-ments using the environmental model as a base-line from which preliminary versions of DFDs, STDs and ERDs are constructed. This is where the approach gets its name: the system is literally partitioned using events. Techniques are described for *organizing* the preliminary models for presentation and review.

Chapter 5

The textual tools of the behavioural model are introduced:

☐ Data dictionary.
☐ Process specifications.

These tools are used primarily for *specifying* system requirements, on the basis of our organized understanding of system requirements in terms of DFDs, STDs and ERDs. The data dictionary is also used to ensure integration of those diagrams, as well as in all phases of model building.

The key concepts of views and extensions are explained and the contents of a typical functional specification are described. Since this will often include elements of external design, as well as the models previously described, a brief overview of design tools is provided.

1.9.2 Part Three: The Strategic Perspective

Chapter 6

The strategic perspective is presented as an imperative for contemporary systems development, for *determining* systems to be developed. Broadly speaking this involves developing systems which support corporate business objectives in a way which is both flexible and responsive. Most importantly the activity of systems strategy is not a one off exercise, but it should be seen as an ongoing activity which seeks to steer systems development in the right direction to meet these objectives.

The assertion that 'structured techniques are not strategic' is examined. Indeed, it is acknowledged that the often tried architectural approach is inappropriate on the grounds of inflexibility and lack of response. Nevertheless, it is argued that there is hope: tools of event partitioning can be adapted to deal with the demands of the strategic perspective. An alternative framework for systems strategy is presented for employing these tools in terms of global modelling and systems reconnaissance.

Chapter 7

Global modelling is clarified with respect to the strategic perspective. The basic idea is to create a strategic model of the enterprise in a way which avoids the pitfalls of the architectural approach previously considered. This means keeping to short timescales and maintaining senior management interest. We are creating a broad platform upon which requirement definition work can be effectively scoped, planned and budgetted for, with respect to the needs of the organization as a whole.

Appropriate tools of event partitioning are adapted to deal with this requirement in terms of:

- ☐ Enterprise statement of purpose.
- ☐ Global ERD.
- ☐ Global context diagram.

Note that as well as giving a continuity with system modelling in terms of existing tools there is the added benefit that there are no new tools to learn here.

Proposed systems are scoped in terms of high-level data and processing, and statements of purpose are generated. Other information from system reconnaissance, including the proposed development strategy is combined with this to form '*system profiles*': base-lines from which requirement definition work can be initiated, in the form of either *event partitioning* (as described in Part Two) or *prototyping* (as described in Part Five), or, indeed, sometimes both.

Chapter 8

Systems reconnaissance is research work which is often sadly lacking because the traditional mind-set does not perceive it as productive. The view taken here is that it is vital *project work* initiated from the system strategy the aim of which is to provide advanced information on those areas, drawn from the global model, about which we are least certain. In essence it seeks to raise useful questions and to provide tentative early answers. Two basic types of system reconnaissance are clarified – local and global.

Local system reconnaissance aims to 'lift the cover' off a proposed system identified at global level to provide more detailed information as to the most appropriate systems development strategy. For example, would it be better to purchase a package or develop inhouse? If the latter, is prototyping likely to be useful or should we attempt a behavioural model in some detail first?

Global systems reconnaissance seeks to test the hypotheses of the global model on an enterprise-wide basis. Is the partitioning into proposed systems broadly sensible? Are there better alternatives? Relevant outputs are fed back for review to systems strategy. The tools used are again adapted from event partitioning:

- ☐ Global DFDs.
- ☐ Global event lists.
- ☐ Global entity STDs.

Either way, whether employing local or global systems reconnaissance, the reconnaissance models constructed here will be assembled as part of the appropriate system profile.

1.9.3 Part Four: The Enterprise Perspective

Chapter 9

Underpinning all development work, from strategy to prototyping, is the enterprise data model (EDM). This consists of:

☐ Enterprise entity relationship model (EERM).
☐ Entity state transition diagrams (ESTDs).
☐ Enterprise database model (EDBM).

The first two are requirements models which are essentially based upon ERD and ESTD already described. The EDBM has a very simple notation which is explained. Again this has the advantage that there is really very little extra notation to learn.

Two key issues are discussed. Firstly, administration of the EDM: this is a critical area, the significance of which often seems to be neglected with disastrous results. Secondly, mapping from EERM to EDBM: this is required to give a foundation for the prototyping work discussed in the next part. Also, although it is perhaps on the edge of the book's scope, the reader will need some direction as to 'what happens next'.

1.9.4 Part Five: The User Perspective

Chapter 10

Prototyping is presented as a tool for *verifying* system requirements. Structured techniques and prototyping are commonly misunderstood as representing divergent philosophies. Certain misconceptions which foster this view are considered. It is argued that the two approaches are in fact complementary. Three aspects of prototyping are identified:

1. Essential: which seeks to reduce uncertainty about requirement definition.
2. User interface: which aims to reduce uncertainty over how a system should appear to a user.
3. Technical: which centres on removing uncertainty regarding system performance.

We will be concentrating here on the first of these where the emphasis is very much on data content and function as opposed to dialogue style or system performance.

A basic framework is established in terms of an essential prototyping skeleton, before further distinguishing four different categories of essential prototyping – primitive, event, decision support, and object oriented – which are discussed in detail in the next chapter.

Chapter 11

Primitive prototyping. Primitive prototyping seeks to build a foundation for later work by confirming a chosen portion of the EERM. Primitive modules are constructed to create, read, update and delete tables mapped from the chosen portion (see Chapter 9).

Event prototyping. Event prototyping aims to reduce uncertainty over event responses from the behavioural model. Typically, this might involve constructing menus which will mirror portions of the behavioural model. The principle is that the user reviews the prototype rather than some illegible textual specification written in a so-called structured language. Event prototypes will normally be serviced by primitive prototypes to update and access stored data.

Decision support prototyping. Decision support prototyping seeks to verify the underlying EDBM as flexible enough to meet a wide range of potential *ad hoc* enquiries from all levels of management, particularly the executive level. It thus provides a strategic sounding board.

Object oriented prototyping. Object oriented prototyping represents the natural future convergence of primitive and event prototyping. One of the major aims of the principle of encapsulation (introduced in Chapter 2) is to localize functions around their required stored data structures. We consider how this can be practically achieved by means of an example.

Results from all classes of essential prototyping will need to be consolidated and the results fed back to the systems strategy for review, and eventual filtering to requirements definition. We are aiming to establish the details of requirements definition by communicating with the user through prototypes, rather than textual specification. However, this must not be seen as an excuse to avoid 'hard specification'. This will still need to be documented as part of the behavioural model.

1.9.5 Part Six: The CASE Perspective

Chapter 12

In this chapter some suggestions are made as to how current CASE tools can be applied to the task of creating requirement definition for effective systems. A problem with using such tools is their stand-alone nature. Whilst applying leverage at certain points in the lifecycle, they do not lend the integrated support that is required for real gains in productivity.

On the other hand truly *integrated* products under the banner of ICASE tend to be highly focussed toward specific implementations and hook the purchaser in to proprietary methods. This can involve great expense and attendant risk, particularly as such products are very much in their infancy. Moreover, ICASE stands currently at least very much within the traditional mind-set.

Despite industry hype, a more flexible ICASE with an open architecture capable of supporting the requirements of the organic lifecycle stands some way off. A more cost-effective approach is to mix and match various products within an organic environment centering on a common CASE repository.

Two particularly important features of such an environment are reusability and the 'people dimension'. Reusability is important not only in terms of delivered software components but also in terms of project planning and control. The 'people dimension' involves a cultural change which is often underestimated. A viable environment therefore should facilitate cultural change via suitable user interfaces.

Finally, we enter the area of possible future trends with respect to object orientation. The tools and techniques of the organic lifecycle lend themselves particularly well here without the need for new notations. The key CASE issue becomes holding an effective object orientation of the behavioural model within the CASE repository; upon building an object oriented view of what we already have. The real benefit comes with eventual generation into an effective object oriented implementation.

CHAPTER 2

Effective modelling

□ □ □ □ □ □ □ □ □ □ □ □ □ □ □ □ □

The meaning of a word is its use in language.

LUDWIG WITTGENSTEIN
Philosophical Investigations

2.1 Introduction

Effective systems depend on effective modelling techniques. The aim of this chapter is to introduce a modelling framework and toolset that will stand us in good stead for meeting the demands of producing effective systems. Above all else the technique can be characterized as *organic*, as intimated in the previous chapter.

We have already seen that simplicity and flexibility are of prime importance in determining effective modelling principles. However, there is clearly more to it than that. I shall try to sharpen our focus in a threefold manner:

1. By first considering some of the dilemmas that structured techniques are commonly faced with.
2. By citing the principle of encapsulation as a guiding light.
3. By introducing two key distinctions between:
   (a) the use of models for specification and verification;
   (b) system and enterprise models.

I once heard someone characterize structured techniques as 'like taking a PhD in the totally obvious'. Many a true word is often spoken in jest. In order to meet our requirements the modelling principles must fit naturally with ordinary human problem-solving patterns. Town planning is illustrated as a case in point, before establishing a general modelling framework for the development of effective systems.

The tools of event partitioning are identified as lending themselves particularly well within this modelling framework. The toolset is introduced by means of a culinary analogy before considering which tools to apply at each stage within the framework.

Finally, I have included some salient pointers on the topic of getting the best out of the tools as vehicles for user communication; it is usually upon this that success or failure hinges at the end of the day. (This involves a brief consideration of prototyping – a subject dealt with in its own right in Part Five of this book.)

2.2 Modelling dilemmas

'The problem with structured techniques is . . .' How often have we heard sentences start like this, whether in a formal classroom situation or in conversations with friends? The dilemma we are faced with is no doubt a complex one. At the same time both developers and users seem to like and loathe the idea of modelling systems. Managers see it as a drain on resources and as a gateway to better productivity. There is a certain ambivalence which we as humans often seem to express when faced with complexity. All too often structured techniques provide us with a convenient scapegoat when things go wrong. And let there be no doubt that harnessing the potential of cheaper hardware by building more effective systems is above all *complex*. What exactly are we asking for from a toolset? There is a certain polarity in our demands, which present us with three particular dilemmas (amongst, it must be said, many others) which are of interest here:

1. Realism versus abstraction.
2. Pragmatism versus rigour.
3. Clarity versus creativity.

The toolset chosen must be able to maintain equilibrium between these often conflicting forces. Let me give some examples of each dilemma by citing some appropriate assertions and counter-assertions.

Realism versus abstraction

Assertion. The objective is to establish the 'true needs' of users in terms of a requirements specification. This document is intended to provide a clear view of the system that is independent of implementation technology.

Counter-assertion. Unlike their professional counterparts in systems development, many users are unable to deal with the abstractions involved in building and understanding models. Like the house purchaser who only has a layman's view of the architect's drawings and becomes aware of what he really wants only after he has moved in, the user is unable to make an intelligent decision on system requirements until the system has been delivered.

Assertion. CASE solves the user communication problem.

Counter-assertion. Despite what the salesperson might tell the chief executive, CASE tools will not interview your users for you. On the contrary, the technical niceties of CASE tools can sometimes be a distraction to those systems analysts who, rather than sitting down with users, might prefer to shut themselves away in some corner at a workstation happily experimenting with the graphics capabilities of a CASE tool.

Pragmatism versus rigour

Assertion. Building models of user requirements is easier and cheaper than setting up the real thing. Using simple tools to foster communication changes to user requirements can be dealt with efficiently: errors that would be costly to fix later on are simply fixed by changing a definition here and inserting a line there.

Counter-assertion. There are many variants of 'structured analysis': a spectrum of methodologies proffer their own solutions to the software crisis. The situation is made yet more complex by a growing proliferation of attendant CASE products, plus a veritable tangle of conflicting terminology from competing methodology houses.

Assertion. CASE solves the complexity problem.

Counter-assertion. The advent and development of CASE tools has now gone a long way to automating many of the previously burdensome administrative tasks. However, if the toolset itself is large and complex we are still left with the complexity problem.

Assertion. System modelling is an engineering discipline which calls for rigorous definition. Any models must be truly verifiable; that means they must be no less testable than a suite of programs. And that means using some form of implementable textual tool (for example, structured language), as the prime vehicle for modelling user requirements.

Counter-assertion. Textual specification does not lend itself easily as a user communication tool, especially if used in isolation. The requirement for 'rigour' too often leads to 'rigor mortis': projects grinding to a halt under the burden of overspecification.

Assertion. The requirement for rigour implies a narrow toolset to be used in a narrow strictly defined way.

Counter-assertion. The systems developer is increasingly faced with a spectrum of different applications from commercial information processing to real-time embedded. Where projects fail it is easy to blame the toolset. However, the cause of failure is often to be found not so much in the toolset itself, but in the fact that the choice of techniques and tools was unsuitable for the particular problem.

Assertion. CASE satisfies the requirement for rigour.

Counter-assertion. A good CASE tool should support a toolset, not *vice-versa*. Although this statement may seem obvious there are many CASE tools around that contradict it. This situation is exacerbated by the quest for rigour which causes

CASE tools to become hard-wired to rigid methodologies, which may not be wholly appropriate to handle the particular needs of the organization. Where large investments have been committed to using such a CASE tool there is 'no turning back'.

Creativity versus clarity

Assertion. The 'start point' is some sort of problem definition for a particular system.

Counter-assertion. The very idea of starting out with an established problem *definition*, does not encourage us to question the scope of the system. There is a tendency amongst most analysts to 'dive in' and start specifying a system without fully considering what it is all for in the first place.

This might be acceptable for the development of stand-alone systems, particularly where an existing system needs to be replaced by a technically more efficient system but with similar functionality. However, increasingly we are asked to improve functionality and that means questioning assumptions at the outset.

Assertion. Limited budget and resources dictate that systems analysts should concern themselves with clarifying requirements, rather than seeking out new business solutions. That means articulating an assumed requirement rather than finding out what that requirement should be.

Counter-assertion. A major feature of many large companies today is the sheer proliferation of data in all its many forms from computer disk files to filing cabinets full of forms. The same item of data is often duplicated across many application files; in a financial services company it is not uncommon for example to find the same customer's address contained separately in marketing, life assurance, trust management, pensions and banking files. The result is a jungle of interface programs and files, the maintenance of which is a constant drain on valuable company resources, both human and computer. In such cases problem definitions themselves are difficult to formulate: they *are* the issue.

In order to tackle such problems it will not do simply to seek to reorganize existing applications because it is the very way in which processes and data were grouped into programs and files within applications that is actually *causing* the problem. Analysis of these systems, if it took place at all, was very much geared to making optimum use of the, often limited, technology of the day. What is needed is a fresh look at system requirements across the company, enterprise wide.

2.3   **The principle of encapsulation**

Such common dilemmas are symptomatic of the general complexity of software engineering. It is important therefore to have a principle for managing complexity. The approach of *information hiding* proposed by Parnas (1972) provides an early example of such a principle in action. Parnas's method presents design guidelines for achieving module independence. The *Dictionary of Computing* (Oxford, 1986) defines information hiding as 'A principle, used when developing an overall program structure, that each component of a program should encapsulate or hide a single design decision. The interface to each module is defined in such a way as to reveal as little as possible about its inner workings.'

Tom DeMarco's advice (1978) to systems analysts to 'partition to minimize interfaces' is in effect to apply this principle to the problem of requirement definition. It has been a guiding beacon in structured systems development for over a decade. The simple logic of this principle is that the more complex the interface between processes in a data flow diagram, the more difficult it becomes to understand one process without having to understand the others. The processes reflecting business requirments should be as independent from one another as possible.

More generally where there are breakdowns in *any* type of system these are often associated with interfaces. Therefore, the fewer interfaces – the fewer breakdowns. DeMarco acknowledges that the principle is no more than a rationalization of this common sense statement. For example, I can recall one systems development exercise where different teams within the DP department were allocated different tasks (data analysis, systems analysis, package evaluation, database design, programming), where users were widely scattered geographically, and contract consultants and programmers were brought in to handle specialist problems. Whilst the complexity of the system presented a challenge, it was the logistics of project organization that proved the final downfall.

Another way of saying this is that the number of committee members is inversely proportional to the time taken to reach a decision.

With respect to software, the fewer interfaces between processes in systems analysis the greater the chance of developing a maintainable systems design to implement the business requirements. In structured design we see the principle applied again in the ideas of Meiler Page-Jones (1988) with respect to program structure. Program modules should be 'highly cohesive' but 'loosely coupled': broadly speaking the more like autonomous 'black boxes' the modules are and the less traffic flowing between program modules, the greater the chance of a maintainable design.

The second, closely associated principle, is that of clustering processing and data. Data should be structured in such a way that its use is localized to as few processes as possible. That way the data itself becomes much simpler to manage, and there is less need for interfacing between different processes to ensure data integrity. Where data is shared across different processes, reusable routines are created to avoid interfaces.

We see the two principles effectively merging more recently in the form of object oriented analysis. The basic idea here is to encapsulate data with its associated processing and control mechanisms into packages called 'objects'. An object is 'an abstraction of data and exclusive processing on that data, reflecting the capabilities of a system to keep information about or interact with something in the real world' (Coad and Yourdon, 1990).

From a practical viewpoint the analyst's greatest enemy is the inevitability of changing requirements: if those parts of the requirement that are most volatile are encapsulated within their own objects then the changing of those requirements becomes less of a threat. Object orientation opens up the possibility of reducing the threat of change by localizing it. Therefore, the approach is attractive from a management as well as a technical viewpoint.

The real pay off, however, comes with reusability. Again there is nothing new here. The discovery of subroutines was one of the very first programming short-cuts: Donald Knuth (1973) reminds us of a subroutine for Sin X, written in 1944 for the Mark I calculator! However, reusability is not only about processing. Data analysis founded on normalization theory (Codd, 1970) recognizes the criticality non-redundant shared data: in other words 'reusable data'.

Encapsulation therefore must foster the identification of reusable system components. Again, this surfaces more recently in the form of object orientation. Objects consist of 'attributes' and 'methods' (or processes) for using attributes. An object can 'inherit' attributes and methods from another in the same classification structure. Also, an object can use 'services' of another object by sending 'messages' requesting certain methods to be performed on certain attributes.

One author puts the attractions of object orientation thus: 'The ultimate promise is the development of "software chips", myriad standardized, generic facilities out of which application software can be built. Between the promise and the pay off, however, stand some formidable challenges. Object oriented approaches alone are not enough to achieve dramatic gains in reusability, extendability and generic modularity' (Constantine, 1989).

Finally, the object oriented approach to managing complexity holds the ultimate promise of efficient estimating. By quantifying phases of development, in terms of the time taken to develop objects, an empirical database can be gradually built up to provide a base-line from which future estimates can be gleaned. Indeed we shall return to this concept in Chapter 12.

The view taken in this book is that, despite what we might sometimes read, there is, in fact, nothing revolutionary about object orientation as an approach to systems analysis. (If there is a revolution it is in system and program design.) The contention is that object orientation is in fact a refinement of some of the best existing concepts of structured techniques and that it would be folly to discard what amount to huge investments in established practice. In this sense the reader will indeed find the approach of the book organic: we should build upon the best of what we have learnt whilst learning from our mistakes. This is what the remainder of the book seeks to do. We shall see that the real leverage of object orientation comes in the areas of prototyping and CASE which are discussed later in Parts Five and Six of this book. For now, let us return to the fundamental issue of making practical the principle of encapsulation.

2.4 Specification versus verification

The general validity of the principle of encapsulation is one thing; applying it is another. One of the greatest obstacles to success here is the common mistake of equating specification with verification. Indeed, this is often at the root of some of the modelling dilemmas previously discussed. It is important therefore that the distinction is made plain at the outset. Firstly, let us consider three of the most widely accepted principles of structured systems development:

1. *Abstraction*: assist understanding of requirements (or design) by representation of aspects into simplified, generalized forms.
2. *Hierarchy*: assist understanding of complex requirements (or design) by 'divide and conquer' into a set of smaller components, each easier to understand and solve. The result is expressed as some form of (inverted) tree-like structure.
3. *Formality*: provide means of rigorous, fully testable requirement (or design) specification.

The three principles surface again and again throughout history as methodological linchpins. Structured programming (Page-Jones, 1988) provides an early example in terms of modules (abstraction), structure charts (hierarchy), and couples and module specification (formality). More recently object oriented analysis (Coad and Yourdon, 1990) advocates objects (abstraction), classification structures (hierarchy), definitions of services, attributes and messages (formality).

Formality is not the issue here. Ultimately we require formality both in terms of requirement definition (otherwise we do not know exactly *what* we are going to design for) and in terms of design (otherwise we do not know *how* to exactly implement the system).

Abstraction and hierarchy, though widely acknowledged as basic principles, are unfortunately much more open to misunderstanding. There is, for example, the rather prevalent assumption that the models you show a user in order to *verify* requirements are exactly equatable with models used to *organize* and *specify* requirements. Sometimes indeed they are, as evidenced by most of the graphical tools that we shall use throughout this book. However, there is no unwritten law that says this must be so. We shall, for example, see that textual specifications and certain diagramming types and conventions are often best left transparent to the user.

Encapsulation involves organizing and specifying requirements for maximum re-usability and maintainability. This may well involve the analyst looking *widely* across different user perspectives and *deeply* into processing logic. The particular view that an analyst chooses to take may therefore be complex. Such a representation of requirements will probably be inappropriate for individual users. To verify requirements we would like to have more limited views: representations which are relevant to the needs of a particular user. Users may justifiably ask to see what the system looks like rather than dealing with abstractions. This may well involve extending requirements into sketches of a proposed design or prototypes of requirement.

The distinction between specification and verification is one that we will need to be particularly mindful of. If specification seeks to provide rigorous answers, it is verification that seeks to ask the right questions in the first place.

2.5   System and enterprise requirements

Again, the general validity of the principle of encapsulation is one thing; applying it is another. The toolset chosen must not only encourage the principle, it must also foster its application. Let me illustrate the point by example.

Today's successful factories function with a mechanical precision that as recently as the early 1980s did not seem possible. Most operations interlock so tightly with their neighbours that an entire production line can seize up if a single machine breaks down.

Until the Japanese taught the industrial world otherwise, production lines were deliberately kept loosely connected. The mind-set of the day called for 'buffering' operations by providing storage space between each pair of adjacent operations in the production line. The logic was that if a machine broke down the adjacent operations could continue working by emptying and filling their respective buffers.

Despite the apparent sense of this arrangement it also resulted in difficulties. For example, if a particular machine developed a fault which went undetected for some time, faulty products would continue to be assembled. This would continue until eventually the problem actually surfaced further downstream in the production line. Often, the problem did not manifest itself for days or even weeks because older material in intervening buffers had to be exhausted before the offending articles made their presence felt. The bigger the storage the higher the effective cost of the production fault.

Until recently such problems were accepted with resignation. Things only changed when the competition forced producers to strive for levels of quality and efficiency achievable only by an excellence of integration across the entire production line. The lesson to 'partition to minimize interfaces' was learned the hard way. Similarly encapsulation will need to be applied not only within systems, but more importantly across the enterprise itself. An appropriate modelling framework and toolset must be capable of supporting both system and enterprise requirements. The system lifecycle (shown previously in Figure 1.1) is illustrated with respect to enterprise-wide requirements in Figure 2.1. Examples of the latter will be data

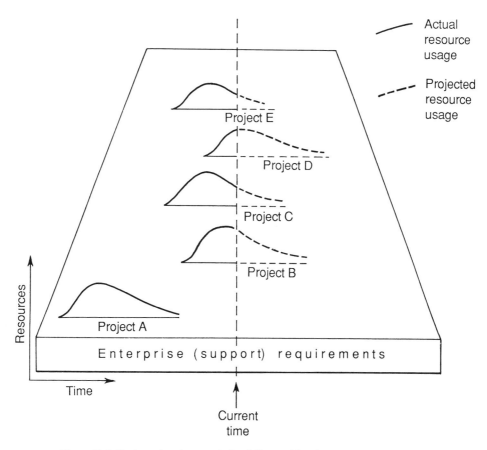

Figure 2.1 System developments (at different lifecyle points) supported by enterprise requirements.

structure and resources (such as people and hardware). Since these are obviously sharable across systems their planning and control becomes a critical issue.

It is therefore imperative that any candidate toolset has the potential for continuity between system and enterprise modelling. This also requires an effective approach to modelling: a modelling framework, which appeals to natural problem-solving patterns, is needed. This means acknowledging systems as existing within other systems. For example, my word processor is powered from a socket which exists within a ring main of my house. The ring main is part of a collection of circuits for the house as a whole. The house circuits are part of the street circuit . . . and so on. Similarly, a system is part of a bigger system which is nested within another system and so on until we reach a system known as the enterprise itself. The enterprise might exist within another enterprise . . . and so on. But if this is a little abstract, let me give you another example.

2.6   A town planning analogy

Imagine that you were asked to plan a new town. What are the steps that you would go through? Experience suggests you would determine the problem before building a solution: in systems development parlance, determine requirements before building a design. Intuition and common sense suggests the usual human problem-solving pattern would go something like this.

1. *Determine* the requirement: what sort of a town are we talking about, in 'ball park' figures, in terms of population, number of shops, dwellings and factories, transport and communication facilities? Also, what physical constraints are we faced with in terms of geological structure, rivers, climate and so on? Draw up global plans and documents, review and agree feasibility with the government.

2. *Explore* the requirement: what are the boundaries of the town to be? Are there any conservation areas, how are we to interface with existing transport systems? Are we responsible for building the whole town or just one suburb of a larger town? Create high-level maps showing proposed site of new town in relation to surrounding area. Invite local people for discussion and feedback with a view to government sanction to continue project.

3. *Understand* the requirement: what are the components to be? How many shops, public houses, churches and so on? What sort of leisure facilities and green areas? What sort of drainage system? What are the most appropriate architectural styles? Use much more detailed diagrams to explore specific issues with experts.

4. *Organize* the requirement: what is the layout going to be? Are we going to organize it so that all shops are centrally located or distributed in pockets? Should the bus and railway station be positioned adjacent to one another? How should we organize for efficient traffic flow and convenient access? Create a portfolio of different diagram types (power, roads, drainage, etc.) for presentation and review with all interested parties.

5. *Specify* the requirement: what are the exact dimensions of each component part with respect to the layout? What building materials are going to be used? Exactly how many cars will the multi-storey car park accommodate? Construct detailed documents for review and agreement as a basis for construction with the experts.

6. *Verify* the requirement: test the specification by reviewing detailed documents with experts. Where there is uncertainty provide physical models to test our previous understanding, organization and specification. Such models can be many and varied. On the one hand there will probably be 'toy-town' models to give a general impression of how the town will be organized. At the other extreme there might be mock-ups of bridges to test structural reliability.

The six steps are illustrated graphically in Figure 2.2. This approach gives the town planner the ability to meet the potentially conflicting demands cited above. For example, toy-town models and maps provide realism with no sacrifice in ability to use, say, graphs and tables alongside plain text to articulate abstract requirements. Also, the principle of encapsulation becomes one of mere common sense: for example, of course, we would like to site shopping facilities with minimum of impact on through traffic flow; one is clearly encapsulated as far as practicable from the other.

Notice in particular that the approach works very much outside-in: the components of the town are considered in relation to the requirements for the town as a whole which in turn are considered in relation to the needs of the surrounding environment. As intimated above, systems are considered within systems: they are considered in context. I am suggesting it would be helpful to harness such a natural problem-solving approach to the problem of requirement definition for effective systems. An outline of such an approach is given in the next section. However, we must remember that the town planner has many advantages not available to the system developer.

First and foremost, whereas problem determination is *relatively* straightforward in town planning this in itself is often one of the biggest issues in systems development. That a satellite town of 30,000 population for, say, Glasgow needs to be built may be relatively obvious, except to certain protest groups: the problem is clear even though there are severe disagreements. However, although at first sight it

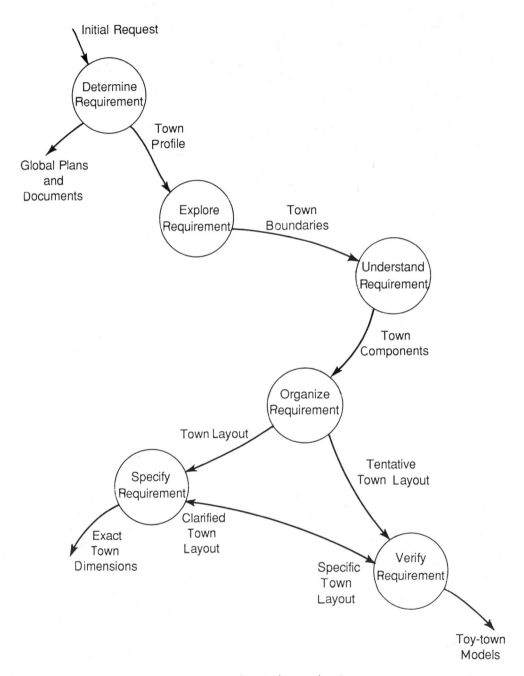

Figure 2.2 Phases of town planning.

might seem simple, exactly what *sort* of stock control system is to be built may be a matter of great debate: the problem itself is conceived differently by different parties.

Secondly, despite the problems of scale and diversity, the town planner is working within a field with an established history. Although fashions change, there are certain things that history has taught the town planner not to do. A large part of the problems of systems development are connected with its relative lack of history, and because technology has changed and is changing so fast.

Thirdly, and most importantly, the town planner has recourse to established modelling tools: for example, that a cross on a map represents a church is common knowledge. In contrast the systems developer is often faced with a diversity of possible diagramming tools and textual conventions that can be used. Again we see that the toolset chosen should be simple, flexible and powerful. A modelling toolset is supplied in Section 2.8 after first considering the approach in outline.

Finally, we have all seen the results of no planning: towns which sprawl in an untidy mess. Perhaps even worse, witness the results of poor planning or over-planning. A modelling framework alone does not guarantee quality results. Certainly it is not a recipe for success. Different problems call for adaptability, skill and innovation. No less so in software engineering. Indeed, it is no accident that the word 'engineer' has its roots in the French equivalent 'ingenieur' which literally translated means 'ingenious one'.

2.7   **The modelling framework**

The approach recommended here is essentially outside-in in that it recognizes that systems are best understood as existing within other systems. It recognizes the same six basic phases of modelling activity in requirements definition: *determination*, *exploration*, *understanding*, *organization*, *specification* and *verification*. Each phase is analagous to the phases of town planning as mentioned above. It is important to understand that they do not constitute a prescription to be performed in sequence. Rather, these phases are iterative, providing a framework for development as illustrated in Figure 2.3 and as summarized below.

Determination

Establish the initial terms of reference for the system with regard to the needs of the organization as a whole. The rationale (or 'statement of purpose') for the system must be justified with respect to corporate business objectives. Broadly, this is one part of strategic modelling known as *global modelling*.

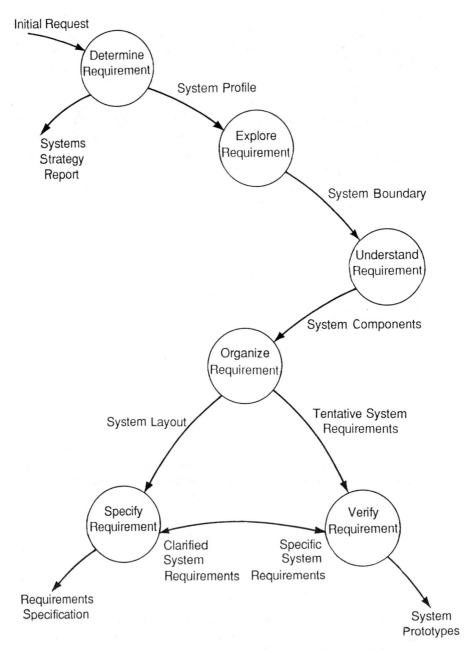

Figure 2.3 A modelling framework for systems development.

Exploration

Examine the system interfaces, raising often thorny questions as to what is part of the system and what is not. The main aim here is to obtain consensus between the various parties as to what the system is for before committing further expenditure on detailed matters of specification. The purpose of *environmental modelling* is to explore and agree the scope of the system by focussing on external requirements in terms of interfaces and events. This will involve much discussion between management, users and analysts in order to obtain concensus.

Understanding

Once broad concensus has been reached a preliminary model is constructed by the analyst of what is actually required to support the system, from a business point of view – that is, independently of implementation technology. Events from the environmental model are used to drive this activity, hence the term 'event partitioning' (see below). This model is very much an analyst's thinking tool to get an 'early' idea of what is actually involved in the system in terms of diagrams for data structure, processing, and control of dynamics.

Organization

Having gleaned an understanding of what the system is going to do in some detail the analyst then organizes the preliminary model into convenient sections for review with users. This is the first step in *behavioural modelling*.

Specification

After review with users, the more complex parts of the system must be analyzed and textual support ensured for all diagrams. A complete behavioural model must specify data structure, processing, and control of dynamics.

Verification

Check that user requirements have been understood completely and correctly. This may be done by 'walking through' the textual specification, threading through test cases where appropriate. It may also be done through the use of *prototyping*.

Notice that the first activity operates at enterprise level whereas the remaining five activities operate at system level.

The middle four activities of this approach are sometimes known collectively as 'event partitioning' (EP for short). EP provides an effective framework which closely matches the heart of the natural problem-solving approach. For more detailed exposition, particularly of the method, the reader is referred to McMenamin and Palmer (1984), Ward and Mellor (1985), Kowal (1988) and Yourdon (1989).

2.8 The modelling toolset

EP recognizes that 'all systems have some functional and some data and some time-dependent behaviour . . . Thus we could imagine a three-dimensional space in which the X-axis represents increasingly complex functions within a system, and the Y-axis represents increasingly complex information, and the Z-axis represents increasingly complex time-dependent behaviour' (Yourdon, 1986a).

The EP toolset can be visualized with respect to this three dimensional space as follows:

☐ X-axis: data flow diagrams (DFDs)
☐ Y-axis: entity relationship diagrams (ERDs)
☐ Z-axis: event list
☐ $X–Y$ plane: entity-process matrices
☐ $X–Z$ plane: state transition diagrams (STDs)
☐ $Y–Z$ plane: entity state transition diagrams (ESTDs)

Underwriting this toolset is the data dictionary for textual definition, the term 'model' referring to a diagram(s) plus supporting data dictionary. The toolset provides the following features.

Specification and verification. The former is provided by constructing rigorous models. The latter involves using the toolset to ask questions; indeed the question mark is probably the most useful piece of notation employed in practical work.

Simplicity. Simplicity stems from the fact that, apart from simple matrices, only three basic diagramming types are used: data flow (DFDs), entity-relationship (ERDs) and state transition (STDs and ESTDs). Each diagram type uses only four symbols. This provides the important advantage that the toolset is easy to learn and simple to use.

Flexibility. Flexibility is provided by the potentially wide application coverage. Any system can be considered and 'weighted' according to each dimension. At one end of the application we might model decision support systems with the emphasis on ERDs; at the other end of the spectrum the dynamic control of domestic appliances

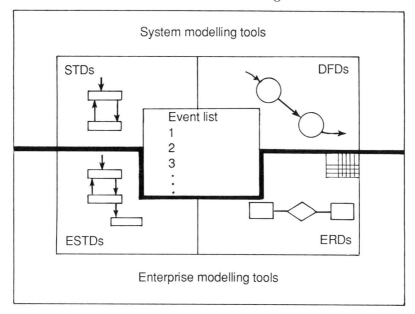

Figure 2.4 The recommended toolset at system and enterprise levels.

might best be modelled using STDs. With the increasing emergence of wider application portfolios flexibility has become of paramount importance.

Encapsulation. Encapsulation is provided by guidelines for the clustering of the three types of behaviour to form cohesive packages, not only at system level, but more importantly at enterprise level. This requires rules for the integration of different diagram types.

Finally the toolset provides the necessary support for modelling at both system and enterprise levels, as shown in Figure 2.4.

The formal notations used are discussed in Chapters 3 and 4. However, let me first illustrate EP with respect to a culinary analogy.

2.9   A culinary analogy

Imagine the scene in the kitchen of your local tandoori restaurant. The restaurant opens and the staff are waiting for the first customer. A customer comes in and is

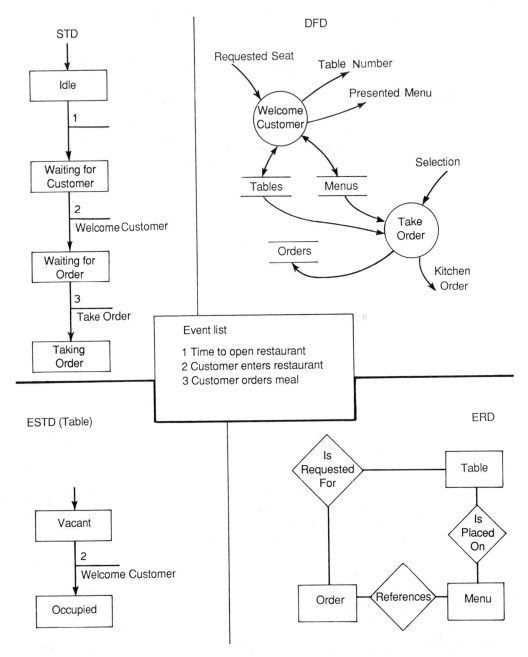

Figure 2.5 The 'Morgan Tandoori': an initial view.

shown to a seat. The customer orders some dishes from the menu. The waiter takes the order to the chef. The chef prepares the meal . . . and so on. Part of the job of the waiter can be visualized in terms of the EP toolset as shown in Figure 2.5. The reader is asked briefly to examine Figure 2.5 before reading further.

I suggest that most readers will find the meanings of those symbols intuitively obvious, if only from their knowledge of restaurants. There is really no magic here. However, a more formal analysis follows.

STEP 1

Event list:	Event 1: Time to open restaurant
STD:	State change: Idle to Waiting for Customer

STEP 2

Event list:	Event 2: Customer enters restaurant	
DFD:	Function:	Welcome customer (show customer to seat: present menu)
	Data flows:	Requested seat
		Table number
		Presented menu
	Data stores:	Menus
		Tables
ERD:	Entities:	Table (Waiter needs to look to see which ones are vacant and suitable)
		Menu (given to Customer)
	Relationships:	Menu *is placed on* table
STD:	State change: Waiting for Customer to Waiting for Order	
ESTD:	Entity state change of table: Vacant to Occupied	

STEP 3

Event list:	Event 3: Customer orders meal	
DFD:	Function:	Take order (Compile an order of selected menu items for this table and remove menu from table)
	Data flows:	Selection
		Kitchen order
	Data stores:	Menus
		Orders
		Tables

ERD: Entities: Menu (for selection of items)
                             Order (created by waiter)
                             Table (for requesting of order and removal of menu)
                  Relationships: Order *references* menu
                             Order *requested for* table
                             Menu *is placed on* table

STD: State change: Waiting for Order to Taking Order

ESTD: No entity state change

A complete model of the 'Accept Customers System' is included in Appendix 1, The Morgan Tandoori. The reader will find this also includes a *context diagram* (a single bubble DFD used alongside the event list for modelling system environment) and is recommended to read Appendix 1 before progressing beyond this chapter.

2.10 Modelling and user communication

The quality of a system reflects the business knowledge that went in to developing that system. The user represents the most accurate and thorough source of such business knowledge. The essence of modelling is to communicate the user's business knowledge in such a way that system requirements are accurately defined.

In what has become one of the classics of structured techniques Tom DeMarco made the following observations on the effect of structured analysis on the user–analyst relationship:

□ 'Users are not dummies. Some of the methods they work with are far more complicated than structured analysis. Years ago, it was fashionable to look down on users because they had so little knowledge of EDP. Nowadays, the user areas we are automating are much more complex, and the users are correspondingly more high-powered.'

□ 'Users are inclined to have little patience with jargon. If you refer to one of your drawings as Third Normal Form Structured Decomposition Hierarchy, they are liable to decide they have no business looking at it since they are not experts in such things. If you refer to it as a Picture of What's Going On Here, they will examine it constructively and help you to get it right.'

□ 'Users need only have a reading knowledge of structured analysis. There is no need for them to learn how to write structured specifications (although many users do become adept at marking them up).'

(DeMarco, 1978)

Over a decade on, DeMarco's words still ring true. Have we really progressed? Let me explore some of the points he was making in a little more detail.

The criticism that structured techniques fall short as a means of communication between analysts and users is one which seems to be gaining momentum. Indeed, I have often witnessed puzzled looks from baffled users during reviews of structured specifications. Certainly some of the structured language specifications I have had the misfortune to review would confuse the most experienced technician, let alone an end user. Badly drawn and over complex DFDs, ERDs and STDs can appear very daunting even to the most technically minded of audiences.

Whilst acknowledging that there is indeed some truth in this criticism I think it embodies a somewhat patronizing view of users which greatly underestimates the intelligence of the average user. There are indeed methodologies which seem to employ a proliferation of different modelling tools each with its own complex structure, requiring an 'expert' to navigate its intricacies. Such a scheme may help to protect the ego of the analyst but is by definition self defeating.

Perhaps this is reflected in the very use of the term 'user' which in ordinary language is often employed in derogatory descriptions like 'drug user'. In contrast the term systems developer or software engineer has a quasi-professional ring to it. Indeed, if you ask most developers what they do, they do not describe the industry: 'I work in insurance'; 'I'm in retail'; 'I work in the car industry'. The usual answer is 'I work in software development (or computers)'. This again seems symptomatic of the culture gap between developers and users which again demonstrates the attitude that users are not really equipped to deal with the abstractions of diagramming.

Do we really want to argue that the average user is not bright enough to under-stand the passage of information represented by a data flow between bubbles on a DFD; or that a box on an ERD represents an important grouping of data; or that a system can change from one observable state to another, represented by an arrow between rectangles. And yet this is indeed what is often argued.

I am suggesting here that too often the complexity of these diagrams is over-exaggerated. All too often it is presented as a stock excuse for failures in system development, which reflects a deeper psychological malaise. Certainly there is often a double-edged internal voice at work here. On the part of developers, this internal voice says, 'The user will hold me in higher esteem if I show that I have skill in manipulating the models; my skills are not for the uninitiated'. On the part of the users it says, 'developers are paid to analyze, and that involves knowing how to use the diagrams so let them get on with it – I've more important things to do'.

I believe most people would agree that the modelling framework and toolset of EP are inherently straightforward. Indeed they have been found to be very effective aids to communication. Although they do not presuppose the capabilities of an Einstein they do require a certain amount of 'selling' by the analyst to the user and they do require commitment by top management to get the relevant people to make time available. Experience reinforces this view: success stories are usually rooted in this sort of soil.

I have always found that introducing tools to users by familiar example works best. Pick an application the user knows well and talk him or her through your models. Only after the seed has germinated should you start to elaborate on notation. Workshops can then be introduced (as discussed in Section 1.6) as a way of further facilitating communication. This is exactly the approach I have attempted with the restaurant example; no notation has yet been formally introduced. But 'selling the diagram' involves more than explanation, it also involves justification: all too often the developer expects the user somehow to appreciate not only what the modelling rules are but *why* a model is being used in the first place.

This latter point is all too true of ERDs, which can appear extremely academic if their rationale is not explained. This is because they do not relate to what users do but to the data structure required to support what they do. If, however, it is pointed out that part of the reason for the present lengthy response times and long-winded clerical procedures to maintain information in several different places is, in fact, the poor way in which the database is currently structured, then we might expect users to be a little more receptive.

I am suggesting that given a clear explanation of what, why and how models are to be employed, a lot of the problems experienced in using models to communicate with users will be greatly reduced. It is a little akin to our view of someone who does not know how to ride a bicycle. Surely, we would be rather worried about the sanity of the teacher who said, 'No, you will never learn because the structure of the bicycle is too complex, with all those cogs and cables, and it will never stay upright as you do not know how to keep your balance.'

Certainly as Boar (1984) says, 'The user already has a demanding skill and profession. They have a critical business function to perform'. However, it is this very effectiveness of business functions that structured techniques are ultimately designed to improve. Much user 'busy-ness' centres on short-term acute problems: if the end of year accounts do not balance then time is made to ensure they do; if the morning's transactions are lost, then time is made for resubmission. In contrast the pay off with structured techniques is long-term: it is human nature to put chronic problems off until later. The simple fact is that chronic problems do not pose the immediate urgency associated with acute problems. However, this does not justify the assumption that user 'busy-ness' is somehow incompatible with the requirement for the user to review models. If business functions are ineffective then time *should* be made to work at improving them. It is ultimately top management's responsibility to ensure this time is made available.

2.11 Modelling versus prototyping

Although the inherent complexity of the graphical models is often exaggerated, there are three particular deficiencies which are nevertheless very real:

1. They do not bring out the dynamism of the user interface.
2. They make little allowance for changes in system requirements that result from users actually *experiencing* the system.
3. Textual specification ultimately must be used for detailed business logic and business definitions; even where this is well written it is seldom a suitable user communication vehicle.

Even where users have been properly educated in the use of graphical modelling tools these problems remain. Where uncertainty over requirements exists, there is no substitute for *live* models: it is primarily these problems that prototyping seeks to address. Prototyping is viewed here very much as a complementary strategy for assisting in the *verification* of requirements and is discussed in Part Five.

The salient point to note here is that although textual specification will be required for documentation of requirement definition, the decision as to whether to use it (or prototyping) for verification is an open one. Later in the book pointers are given for the most suitable strategies in given general cases.

2.12 Summary

This chapter has sketched out a candidate modelling framework for the development of effective systems and identified an appropriate candidate toolset. Effective CASE support is clearly an important precondition for success. However, it is important to clarify the concept of effective modelling before considering its implementation. Therefore, although the issue of effective CASE support is a critical one, it is one which will be suspended for now but which we will return to. Indeed, the final part of this book is designed to synthesize the central concepts of this book under the umbrella of a suggested CASE blueprint.

The initial requirement for simple and effective modelling techniques was thrown into sharper relief by consideration of three sets of conflicting requirements that are commonly found in systems development:

1. Realism versus abstraction.
2. Pragmatism versus rigour.
3. Creativity versus clarity.

This means managing complexity in terms of the established principle of encapsulation. Clearly, we require more than theoretical lip-service to this principle: it needs to be applied *effectively*. It was suggested that there are two necessary conditions for this, which are all too often lacking:

1. Preservation of an important distinction in the use of models between specification and verification. This requires a toolset which provides flexibility in representation; for example, equivalent high-level and detailed views of the same underlying requirement.
2. Application of the principle not only at system level but also at enterprise level. This requires a toolset which can operate at both levels and provide continuity between the two.

We have already seen that a major premise of this book is that modelling tools cannot be sensibly discussed in isolation from their use: a modelling framework is required. A natural problem solving approach was introduced first by means of a town planning analogy which was then applied in outline to the specific problems of systems development. The modelling toolset of EP was introduced by use of informal example, and the tools related to the framework. No formal notation was introduced. The appeal was to the reader's intuition, through familiarity with a common situation. And this was exactly the approach recommended in guiding users through models. This critical area can be summed up by saying that:

1. The analyst must *sell* the models to the user:
    (a) explaining why models are being used;
    (b) using familiar examples before theoretical notations.
2. The executive sponsor must ensure that user time is made available.

In the final analysis, we are sometimes driven to textual specification as a means of verifying detailed user policy. In many situations this does not work well: live models are needed. It will be vital to ensure a coherent strategy for harnessing prototyping alongside the EP toolset as an alternative means of verification.

The modelling framework used in this book has at its core the toolset of EP. The next part of this book discusses the system perspective; it establishes that toolset with respect to the middle four stages of the modelling framework:

☐ Exploration.
☐ Understanding.
☐ Organization.
☐ Specification.

The first and last activities (determination and verification) have received far less attention in the literature with respect to EP. Parts Three and Four examine problem determination in some detail and Part Five discusses how prototyping can be employed to assist in the verification of requirement definition. Finally Part Six integrates these different *perspectives* in terms of effective CASE support for the modelling framework and toolset.

PART TWO

The System Perspective

This part of the book describes a recommended toolset from the viewpoint of an individual system. We will use the event partitioning toolset (EP).

The system perspective, highlighted in Figure A opposite, entails first establishing the boundary of the system under study. That is, we ask what the system is *for* in some depth before analyzing system requirements in detail. In terms of the our modelling framework we *explore* requirements by first modelling system environment (described in Chapter 3).

Having established system scope we follow our modelling framework in attempting to *understand* and *organize* system requirements by modelling system behaviour (described in Chapter 4).

Part of the essence of modelling is knowing what to diagram and what to specify textually. Equally important is to be aware of the distinction between specification and verification. In Chapter 5 we consider the textual components which serve to rigorously *specify* system requirements, whilst finally considering some alternative approaches to help *verify* system requirements.

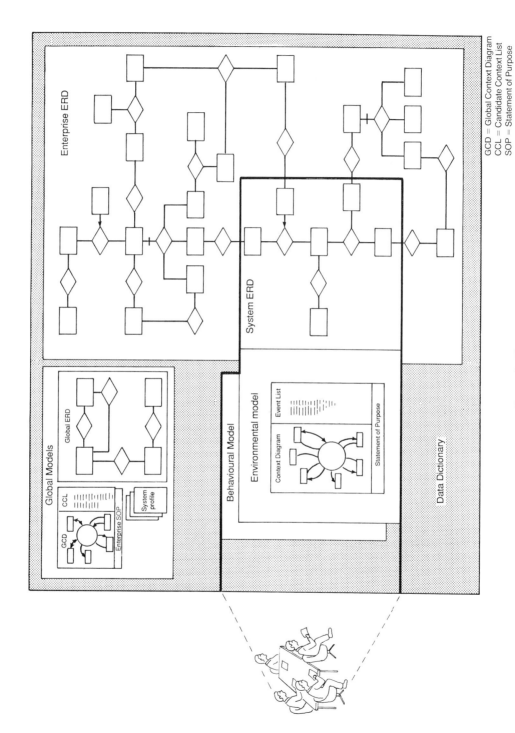

Figure A The System Perspective.

CHAPTER 3

Exploring requirements

At the boundary, life blossoms.

JAMES GLEICK
Chaos

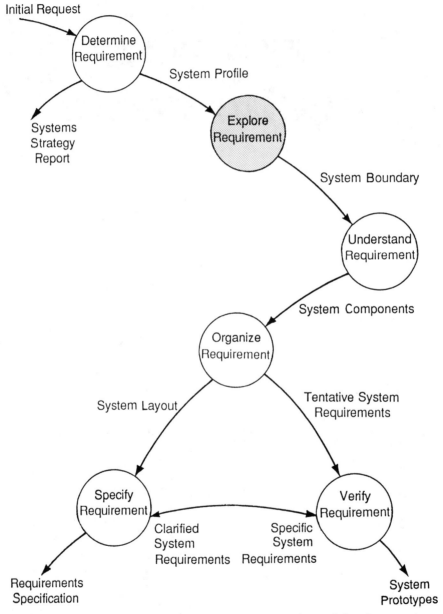

Figure 3.1 Exploring requirements with respect to the modelling framework.

3.1 Introduction

Environmental modelling *explores* the boundary of a system based upon an early profile of business requirements, as shown in Figure 3.1 with respect to our modelling framework. Essentially it is a means of confirming that requirements make sense without incurring the cost of a full-blown specification effort. This chapter begins by examining briefly the outside-in philosophy underlying this statement.

The environmental model consists of the following components:

☐ Statement of purpose.
☐ Context diagram.
☐ Event list.
☐ Data dictionary.

(The system profile which drives this activity will normally consist of several components (as described in Section 6.10.2) including an ERD for development in more detail. For the purposes of explanation, however, the ERD is covered in the next chapter, and the system profile is assumed to be equivalent to the statement of purpose.)

This chapter discusses each of the components of the environmental model, with reference to examples for both information and control systems, drawn from Appendices 2 and 3 respectively. The reader is recommended to read the narrative descriptions in order to understand the examples fully.

3.2 Outside-in philosophy

I recall, soon after moving into systems analysis from programming, making a 'mind's eye translation' of what the user was telling me directly into a system flow chart. The mistake I was making was to avoid considering what the user really wanted in the interest of coming up with a clever solution; needless to say, a clever solution to what turned out to be the wrong problem. Environmental modelling provides a means of counteracting this tendency, by working outside-in, toward the behavioural model covered in Chapter 4, as illustrated in Figure 3.2.

Traditional functional decomposition begins by scoping a system at a high-level and then working top-down toward a specific statement of requirements. Despite the apparent common sense of such an approach its application is often difficult and time consuming. This is firstly because it is difficult to obtain concensus amongst analysts on choosing (from numerous alternatives) exactly how the 'cake should be cut'. Secondly, in deciding *how*, it is difficult for the analyst to concen-

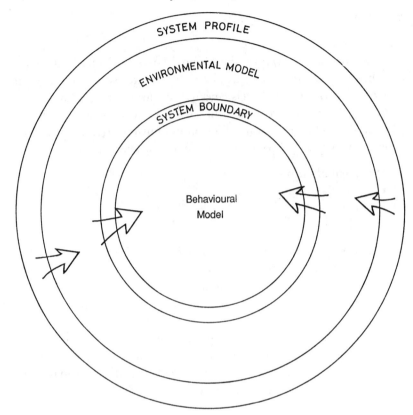

Figure 3.2 Outside-in development.

trate on his or her proper interest in determining *what* user requirements are. Implementation bias inevitably creeps in and we are again creating clever solutions to the wrong problems.

The outside-in approach of event partitioning (EP) was adopted in the mid-1980s by organizations seeking a pathway around the pitfalls of traditional analysis. The approach recognizes the general principle mentioned in Section 2.4, that systems only exist in relation to other systems: before a system can be discussed sensibly you have to establish its interfaces to other systems. In the previous chapter we saw the principle applied to town planning. A context diagram (a high-level DFD with a single bubble) is developed to expose system interfaces.

EP recognizes systems as stimulus-response mechanisms, like a scientist studying organisms as biological systems which respond to stimuli in their environments. The stimuli we are dealing with here are known as *events*: specific happenings outside of our system to which our system must respond.

Events are simply *listed*: we deliberately suspend detailed consideration of system responses until later. This saves time and encourages the analyst to get to grips with a level of detail early in the lifecycle, which is simply not possible with traditional analysis. System complexity, in the form of long event lists, can be exposed and planned for without incurring excessive cost.

The context diagram and event list should be developed together to give a powerful double-edged sword for cutting through to system scoping issues with efficiency and speed. However, we must have good reason for modelling in the first place which takes us on to the statement of purpose covered in the next section.

3.3   Statement of purpose

The statement of purpose is a concise textual statement of rationale of the system and forms the point of departure for building the context diagram and event list. It should answer the question, '*Why* are we building a system?' and is intended primarily for senior management. Indeed, the statement of purpose should emanate from a user manager who has sufficient authority to ensure the required level of user commitment. This user manager is sometimes referred to as the 'Executive Sponsor' as discussed in Section 1.6.

Example statements of purpose, for the Player Administration and Petrol Sale Control Systems are included in Appendices 2 and 3 respectively. Extracts from each are as follows:

☐ *The purpose of the Player Administration System is to support the Well-brian Football Federation and its member clubs in the registration and transfer of players and the recording of all injury details.*
☐ *The purpose of the Petrol Sale Control System is to manage the selling process for an individual pump. This includes calculating cost, maintaining pump registers and ensuring the integrity of each sale.*

Notice, each statement of purpose is kept deliberately short (up to two pages maximum) but that it is possible to extract and distil the essence of the message in a couple of sentences, as shown. To attempt a detailed scenario would be self-defeating as it is the business of the following modelling activity to fill in all the details. Just the relevant facts are stated.

However, it is important to include other relevant facts. An example might be a requirement for generality in that a system might need to be capable of easy extension to cater for slightly different markets. This is often the case for systems which are being sold into the public market place, rather than developed in-house. Another example is compatibility with other systems. Indeed, the reader will find that the full statement of purpose for the Player Administration System contains requirements for both generality and compatibility.

In addition to the above it is not uncommon to find constraints appended to the statement of purpose: for example, 'the purpose of the Player Administration System is to improve turnround time of registrations from five days to eight hours'. Note that such constraints will not play a part in development until the design stage as the analysis is by definition independent of any implementation technology used to try to meet constraints. Therefore, although important, they are not considered here to be part of the statement of purpose. The reader will in fact find that such information forms part of the 'system profile' (see Section 6.10.2) of which the statement of purpose is only part.

However, provisos should be included within the statement of purpose. I recall from my early days as a systems analyst one particularly sagacious project manager who on receipt of a user development request would always telephone the user first. After the initial pleasantries had been exchanged he would ask 'Now what don't you want the system to do?'. As a greenhorn systems analyst this struck me as most strange. It was only after experiencing some project failures that I realized the wisdom of his question. Scoping is the first and most vital step in systems analysis and scoping is all about drawing lines between what a system will do and what *it will not do*. For example, the Player Administration System is not responsible for supporting team selection; the Petrol Sale Control System is not responsible for controlling petrol flow. By stipulating these as provisos we make plain our assumptions for public debate and save ourselves much unnecessary work.

Finally, although the statement of purpose forms the point of departure for the environmental model, it is important not to view it as though it were 'cast in stone'. It may well be that some of the assumptions contained within the statement of purpose are thrown into question as a result of the modelling activity to follow: for example, the scope implied may simply be too big or too small. Such observations should be fed back to the executive sponsor for review of the statement of purpose itself.

3.4   Context diagram

The context diagram is a tool for modelling the boundary between our system and the rest of the world. It is important to note that at this stage our system is viewed simply as a collection of stimulus–response mechanisms. This is a deliberate tactic to counteract the tendency amongst many analysts to 'dive in' and start specifying a system without considering what it is for in the first place. Therefore, our system, concisely named, is just shown as a single circle on the context diagram. Examples are shown in Figures 3.3 and 3.4 for the Player Administration System and the Petrol Sale Control System respectively.

The context diagram is a convenient graphical means of exploring the scope of a system implied by the statement of purpose, and highlights the following important characteristics of the system boundary:

☐ User departments, people, devices and systems that our system interfaces with. These are known as *terminators*, and are shown as boxes on the edge of the context diagram. It is important not to model the 'way things happen to be' in a given current situation (for example, 'Fred Bloggs') but to model the appropriate role (for example, Player in Figure 3.3).

☐ Data which is sent by terminators directly to our system for processing and data which is sent from our system directly to terminators. These are known as *data flows* and are shown as arrowed lines: for example, Transfer Request and Transfer Confirmation in Figure 3.3.

☐ Binary signals sent by terminators directly to our system for processing and binary signals sent from our system directly to terminators are known as *control flows*, which, unlike data flows, do not carry value-bearing data, and are shown as arrowed dashed lines; for example Reset and Gun Lifted in Figure 3.4.

☐ In addition the context diagram may also be used to show stored data which is shared between our system and terminators. These are known as *data stores* (*stores* for short) and are shown as a pair of horizontal parallel lines; for example Player Details in Figure 3.3. (Stored control may also be shown, in the form of a control store, described in Section 4.3)

A data flow between a terminator and a store indicates that the terminator is updating data on that store (where the flow is toward the store) and/or accessing data from that store (where the flow is toward the terminator). Similarly a data flow between our system and a store indicates that our system is updating data on that store (where the flow is toward the store) and/or accessing data from that store (where the flow is toward our system). However, as the main focus of interest here is on data *flow*, it is often expedient not to show stored data on the context diagram, especially where the shared stored data structure is so complex that the context diagram is flooded with detail that detracts from its main purpose. In these cases shared stores are better dealt with separately using a matrix of systems versus stores, the cells of which are filled in to indicate the action (create, read, update or delete) of a particular system on a store.

Notice that in Figure 3.4 some of the terminators are devices and that there is a predominance of control flows. In Figure 3.3 there are no device terminators or control flows. This reflects the distinction between control systems (exemplified in Figure 3.4) and information systems (exemplified in Figure 3.3).

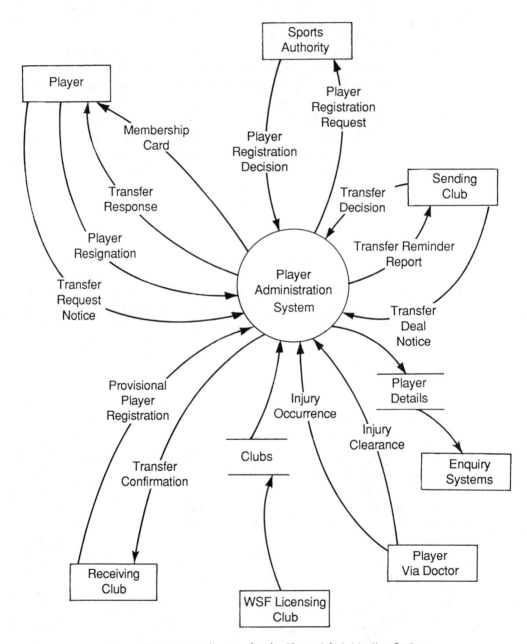

Figure 3.3 Context diagram for the Player Administration System.

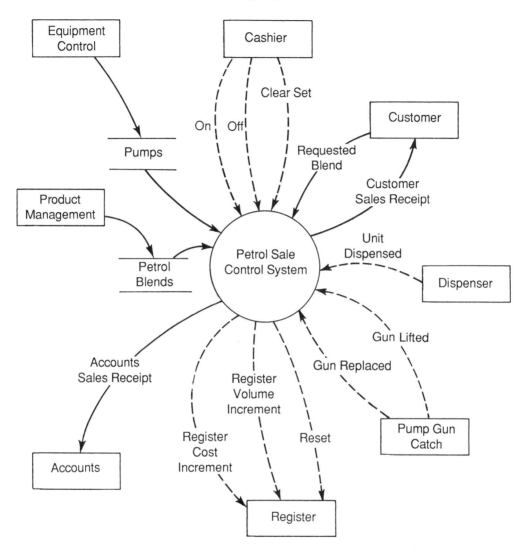

Figure 3.4 Context diagram for the Petrol Sale Control System.

The context diagram is very much a discussion tool to raise often thorny questions about what is part of the system and what is not. Often political issues are raised. Perhaps a user manager disagrees vehemently that he is responsible for supplying certain data to the system when he sees his department named as a terminator on a context diagram. Conversely, perhaps, a user manager who is in charge of a department which is conspicuous by its absence as a terminator feels strongly that his department should be involved. Fine! It is much better that issues such as these are exposed early in the project rather than later, after much time and money have been spent producing detailed specifications.

3.5   Event list

In line with the view of a system as a collection of stimulus–response mechanisms, the event list forms a textual complement to the context diagram, by itemizing each stimulus as an *event*. By definition each event must satisfy the following criteria:

☐ It occurs in the environment.
☐ It occurs at a specific point in time (which may or may not be predetermined.
☐ It requires our system to make a response.

Figure 3.5 shows the event list for the Player Administration System. Notice each event is numbered. Although no particular sequence is implied this is important for identification. Each event must obey the three criteria above; for example, Event 1 'Club registers player provisionally' counts as an event because:

E1. It occurs in the environment; the *club* submits the provisional player registration.
E2. It occurs at a specific point in time; in retrospect, it is possible to say that a given submission actually occurred at a certain time.
E3. It requires our system to make a response; presumably by issuing a new membership card, by producing a player registration request which is sent to the appropriate sports authority and by recording the player and membership details for later reference.

Figure 3.6 shows the event list for the Petrol Sale Control System. Again, each event must obey the three criteria above; for example, Event 7 'Dispenser reports unit dispensed' counts as an event because:

E1. It occurs in the environment; the dispenser reports that a unit has been dispensed.
E2. It occurs at a specific point in time; in retrospect it is possible to say that the dispenser reported a unit was dispensed at a certain time.
E3. It requires our system to make a response; presumably by calculating the cost of the unit, sending control flows to the register to increment volume and price registers, and maintaining the stored totals for that pump (for later analysis).

1. Club registers player provisionally.
2. Sports Authority makes decision on player registration.
3. Player requests transfer.
4. Club makes decision on transfer request.
5. Club transfers player.
6. Player resigns from club.
7. Doctor submits player's injury details.
8. Time to report transfer reminders.
9. Doctor submits clearance of injury.

Figure 3.5 Event list for the Player Administration System.

1. Cashier switches pump on.
2. Cashier switches pump off.
3. Customer lifts petrol gun.
4. Cashier requests to clear register.
5. Customer replaces gun.
6. Customer selects blend.
7. Dispenser reports unit dispensed.

Figure 3.6 Event list for the Petrol Sale Control System.

3.6 Levels of event

What I shall refer to as the *level* of an event is particularly important here. At the one extreme we might have the candidate event, 'Club sends data'. This is very unhelpful as it does not tell us much at all; all systems process data. An event such as this is simply too high-level to be of any use.

At the other extreme we might have the following candidate events:

☐ 'Sports Authority makes a decision to suspend player registration'.
☐ 'Sports Authority makes a decision to refuse player registration'.
☐ 'Sports Authority makes a decision to accept player registration'.
☐ 'Sports Authority makes a decision to defer player registration'.

Clearly such a list is open ended: there might be n different decisions that could be made. The list is too low-level because it has gone down to the level of individual transaction types. These will be catered for within the logic of a *single* resultant response.

What we need is an event list which is *useful*, one which allows the analyst to identify salient features of user policy. Choosing the right level can sometimes lead to endless and rarefied academic debate as distinction between levels can sometimes be a fine one. My advice is to be pragmatic in choosing a consistent level of event, which conforms to our definition. That way you might upset the theorists but you please everyone else. In the above case, 'Club makes decision on transfer request' would represent a much more useful level of event.

3.7   Event classification by response

System responses consist of any combination of the following:

R1. Retrieving and/or updating stored data.
R2. Producing one or more outgoing data and/or control flows.
R3. Sensing for the occurrence of another event.

In Figure 3.5 each event causes a response which entails R1 and/or R2: each one causes the system to respond by transforming data. However, the behaviour of the system does not change over time. Such events are labelled D for 'Data transform'.

In contrast some of the events in Figure 3.6 entail responses which include R3. For example, Event 1 causes the system to sense for Event 6; similarly Event 3 causes the system to sense for Event 4, sometimes for a long time, particularly if you are in a hurry to fill up. Such events cause the behaviour of the system actually to change over time: the system is said to change *state*. Such events are labelled C since they affect the control of the system.

Events may have compound response classifications where they cause both data transformation and state change. For example Event 5 in Figure 3.6 will cause the system to calculate cost and produce a sales receipt; therefore it is a D event. But it will also cause the sale effectively to end which means changing the state of the system so that no more petrol is allowed to flow; therefore it is a C event. Such an event is labelled CD.

'This is all very well', I hear you say 'but what's the point?' The major reason is to gauge an appropriate strategy for detailed development of the system. This is discussed at some length in Section 8.9. However, to give you a preview, I recommend that you have a go at classifying each event in the two example event lists. (The full lists are included in the appendices.) Notice that there is a dynamic dependency between events in the petrol pump example that is not present in the football example. The former contains mainly C events whereas the latter contains exclusively D events. This reflects the distinction between control systems (C dominant) and information systems (D dominant). The event list can thus be used to gain an early indication of system type, and appropriate development strategies planned for accordingly.

3.8 Event classification by time

We have seen that part of the definition of an event is that it must occur at a specific point in time. This leads to a further classification, according to whether that point in time is predetermined or not.

A *flow driven* event is always detected by the arrival of one or more data flows and/or control flows, at an unpredetermined point in time. There is no way of predicting that a flow driven event will occur in advance: the flow(s) just arrives. For example, Customer Submits Order is an event which causes a data flow called Customer Order to arrive, but it is not possible to say *when it will* arrive.

In contrast a *temporal* event is always detected by a predetermined point in time. This can either be an absolute time of day (for example, at 17.00 a report must be produced), or a scheduled time determined from elsewhere within the system (for example, a time has been scheduled for printing statistics). Any data required to be transformed may be accessed from a data store(s) or provided by an incoming data flow(s), or possibly both.

In Figure 3.5 all events are flow driven except Event 8. Clearly Event 1 as discussed above is detected by the arrival of the data flow Provisional Player Registration. Event 8 is temporal as it occurs each Wednesday at 4 p.m. In Figure 3.6 all the events are flow driven and again Event 7 causes a response which entails both R1 and R2.

Again, I hear you ask 'What is the point of all this?'. Once more the answer is that this will be useful information when we come to decide the most appropriate development strategy in Section 8.9. Broadly speaking, temporal events generally involve an emphasis on stored data, which implies a bias toward management information systems. On the other hand, flow driven events generally tend toward transaction processing systems. At this stage this is obviously only meant as a very rough characterization, to provide an initial rationale for what is being suggested.

3.9 Formalizing the event list

Because of its textual nature the event list can be difficult to 'get a handle on' especially when it is being used by project members for the first time. There are two ways of formalizing events to assist comprehension and facilitate development:

1. Adoption of an event grammar.
2. Tabular representation.

Let me explain each in turn.

3.9.1   Event grammar

Adopting a standard grammatical structure for events can introduce discipline and rigour as well as facilitating development (as described in Sections 4.6.3 and 8.6):

☐ Flow driven events should be phrased:
  '*Agent   Action   Subject   (+ qualification)*'.
☐ Temporal events should be phrased:
  '*Time to Action   Subject   (+ qualification)*'.

Agents are always nouns and are normally (though not always) equatable with terminators. In fact all events in the two examples we have seen have agents which are also terminators. If the agent is not a terminator, then it is most likely to be a data flow. An example would be 'Temperature exceeds normal' in a patient monitoring system. Such events often have a response classification of CD and are common in systems which continuously monitor incoming values.

Actions are verbs. Importantly, they should be expressed in the present tense.

Subjects are more complex and fall into three categories. Often they are simple nouns as in 'Player requests *transfer*' or 'Customer selects *blend*'. Most events of the D response classification, which are very common in commercial applications, fall into this category. However, the noun may also be equipment as in 'Customer lifts *petrol gun*' or indeed the system itself as in the common real-time example 'Operator starts *system*'. Such events usually include C as at least part of their response classification.

Subjects may also be adjectives, as in 'Temperature exceeds *normal*' or adjectival expressions as in 'Dispenser reports *unit dispensed*'. Such events effectively indicate the status of something. Finally, subjects can be verbal expressions as in 'Cashier requests *to clear register*'. Often events like this are associated with system house-keeping and are found in a diversity of applications but usually more occasionally than the other two categories.

Qualifications are (as the name implies) optional and their grammatical structure usually falls into one of two categories. Although I hesitate to legislate against other categories I have to say that I have yet to find a qualification which does not fall into one or the other of the following categories.

Prepositions followed by nouns are common; for example, 'Sports Authority makes decision *on player registration*'. These are also found where information arrives via an intermediary which is of significance to the system. In a sales system, examples would be 'Customer submits order *via salesperson*' and 'Customer submits order *via tele-sales*'. Notice in cases like this though the input flow (customer order) is common to both events, we choose to model two events in cases where the business policy is significantly different: perhaps salespersons are allowed to negotiate special deals whereas tele-sales operate to a much tighter policy. Otherwise we would have modelled as single event 'Customer submits order'.

Most other qualifications are of adverbial form. Examples include 'Club registers player *provisionally*' and 'Cashier switches pump *on*'.

3.9.2 Tabular event lists

Tabular representations such as tables and matrices are perhaps one of the most underrated yet underused tools in systems development. Perhaps this is because of the problems of constructing and maintaining them using paper and pencil technology. The modelling toolset of EP provides maximum flexibility in terms of 'views'. It is, in fact, always possible to convert a diagram to a tabular representation using pre-specified parameters. The two 'views' are in effect different ways of looking at the same thing. The key question is therefore not 'What tabular representations would we like?'; this would be rather like an open-ended shopping list. Rather, we should ask 'Does this CASE tool provide sufficient flexibility in generating tabular representations?'. In Chapter 12 we will return to this issue. The reader should understand that in the meantime tabular representations will only be discussed in any detail where they have a special significance: the tabular event list is a case in point.

The event list and context diagram should complement each other. Each event should correspond to one or more flows on the context diagram; conversely each flow on the context diagram should correspond to one or more events. A useful way of ensuring correspondence between the 'two sides of the same coin' is to annotate the event list with a column listing the flows associated with each event and with columns to indicate the event response and time classifications. This is sometimes referred to as a tabular event list.

Also the context diagram may be annotated with the number of each associated event posted against the appropriate flow, on 'working versions' as a useful audit check, although this would probably be inadvisable in a specification document as the diagram would become somewhat cluttered.

The concept of a tabular event list can be extended in several ways:

☐ By grammatical template along the lines discussed above (to enforce rigour).

☐ By user (to act as a check list that all users are catered for).
☐ By frequency (this is an environmental constraint to be used later in system design).

3.10 Partitioning a lengthy event list

How long should the event list be? This is like asking how long is a piece of string. Nevertheless this does seem to be a genuine problem in projects of any complexity. I have found 50 events to be a reasonable maximum, for what this figure is worth. More importantly, there are three useful strategies for managing volume of events:

☐ Ensure the level of event is correct as discussed in Section 3.6.
☐ Use a tabular event list to partition by user, terminator or data flow.
☐ Use a matrix as discussed in Section 8.8.

Partitioning in this way eases comprehension and facilitates parallelism of subsequent work.

3.11 Data dictionary support

Environmental modelling is by nature exploratory and the first versions of context diagram and event list may appear very different from later versions. As they are textual, events may be entered into the data dictionary from the outset. This has the advantage that any teething problems with data dictionary software can be nipped in the bud and simply makes expedient use of the data dictionary as a word processor. However, textual definitions to support the context diagram should wait until the environmental model has stabilized, such that there is broad concensus amongst interested parties. Otherwise much time will be wasted updating continuously changing data dictionary entries. It is important to document textual definitions for the following:

☐ Data flows.
☐ Control flows.
☐ Data stores.
☐ Terminators.

Examples of the above to support the context diagrams shown in Figures 3.3 and 3.4 are included in Appendices 2 and 3 respectively.

3.12 Summary

The reader should understand that there is no implied sequence involved with building a context diagram and an event list. Physically speaking, one or the other has to be drawn first, but *which* is largely academic. The key thing is that they should be developed very much in parallel. One should not linger too long on building one model without developing the other. This is because the two are in essence complementary; like different sides of the same coin.

Moreover, developing the environmental model is the first and most critical task of the EP approach to structured analysis. This task may appear 'easy' from the point of view that the context diagram contains just one 'bubble' and the event list a simple 'shopping list' for the system. However, experience teaches that skill is important here, especially when building the event list as the *level* of event is critical. Also, although interactive techniques (as described in Section 1.6) lend themselves particularly well to forging an initial event list, the definition of event should be applied carefully. Mistakes which are made here are often costly to correct downstream in the lifecycle. Therefore, in the period following such sessions it is wise for an analyst experienced in EP quietly to inspect the event list for adherence to both concept and grammar.

The very essence of the exercise is to raise and explore scoping issues, both political and technical. Effective modelling at this stage will save time and money in the long-term, but remember this will typically involve several iterations; I make no apology therefore for quoting Fred Brooks (1975) again. 'Build one to throw one away, you will anyway' is a particularly appropriate maxim.

CHAPTER 4

Understanding and organizing requirements

☐ ☐ ☐ ☐ ☐ ☐ ☐ ☐ ☐ ☐ ☐ ☐ ☐ ☐ ☐ ☐ ☐

Perfection is spelt P-A-R-A-L-Y-S-I-S.

WINSTON CHURCHILL

4.1 Introduction

Behavioural modelling consists of three major activities with respect to the modelling paradigm:

1. Understanding.
2. Organization.
3. Specification.

This chapter concentrates on diagramming techniques used in building a behavioural model. The focus will therefore be on the heart of event partitioning (EP): understanding and organization of requirements, as shown in Figure 4.1. Chapter 5 deals with textual support for the diagrams with a corresponding focus on specification.

The following diagramming tools are used:

☐ Data Flow Diagrams (DFDs).
☐ State Transition Diagrams (STDs).
☐ Entity Relationship Diagrams (ERDs).

Each diagram type is used to model a different characteristic of system behaviour, as covered in Chapter 2: DFDs model functional behaviour, STDs model time dependent behaviour, and ERDs model the underlying stored data structure. Notice that whereas DFDs and STDs describe aspects of systems, ERDs describe an aspect of the enterprise. Therefore, careful planning will be required for the latter. This is part of the data administration function covered in Chapter 9.

Although the three diagram types provide different abstractions of system behaviour, it is important to remember that each is an abstraction of the *same* system. Therefore integration rules will be required to ensure consistency between diagram types. These are discussed in Chapter 5. Also it is important to understand that in a real life project much specification and integration will happen in parallel with (or even before) the diagramming activities described in this chapter.

The purpose of this chapter is twofold:

☐ To explain the diagramming notations, with some hints and tips on pragmatic application.
☐ To give the reader some flavour of the EP technique itself.

It is my belief that the two objectives are so interdependent that they are best covered within the same chapter. In essence, to understand the diagrams as a coherent toolset, you need to see how they are used. The strategy of this chapter is therefore as follows:

☐ EP is considered in outline.
☐ Diagramming notations are explained.
☐ EP is applied using the diagrams.

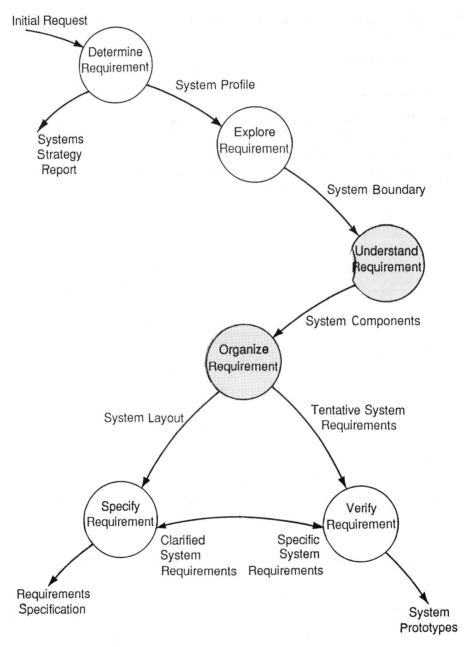

Figure 4.1 Understanding and organizing requirements with respect to the modelling framework.

My intention here is to map out diagramming concepts for use throughout this book. In particular I am most conscious of the wealth of literature that exists on EP and I am anxious not to reinvent any wheels. Indeed the reader should be aware that this is a very brief overview of EP; as mentioned earlier, more detailed accounts of EP itself are contained in McMenamin and Palmer (1984), Ward and Mellor (1985), Kowal (1988) and Yourdon (1989).

4.2 The approach in outline

The scope of the system is used as a basis from which requirement definition is derived. To use EP terminology, the environmental model is used as a platform from which to project the behavioural model. Whereas the former elicits the boundary of the required system with respect to the real world, the latter expresses the definition of the required system with respect to an 'ideal world'.

Ward and Mellor (1985) express the distinction as follows. 'Given that a system must function in a specific environment and given that it has a purpose to accomplish, it is possible to describe what it must do (the *essential activities*) and what data it must store (the *essential memory*) so that the description is true regardless of the technology used to implement the system. Such a description is called an *essential model*.' This implies no technological constraints:

☐ Process memory is infinite.
☐ Process instruction time is zero.
☐ Data storage is infinite.
☐ I–O time is zero.
☐ Any number of processes may run concurrently.
☐ Physical corruption is impossible.

The above features may be summarized by the phrase 'perfect technology'. There are several reasons for this principle, the two most important of which are as follows:

1. The analyst and user are able to concentrate their attentions on clarifying business policy, without being distracted by technological issues which would clutter their thinking.
2. The designer will have full freedom to choose the best possible implementation, focussing his or her attention fully on technological issues.

Hardware and software grows increasingly sophisticated and complex, with a greater potential to cloud business issues and present the designer with a diversity of options. The fast changing face of technology therefore reinforces the attractions of this basic distinction.

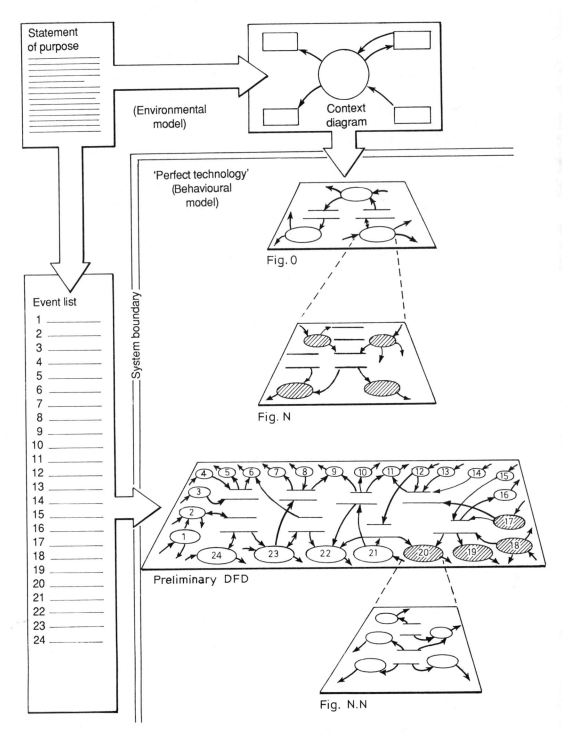

Figure 4.2 'Outside-in' projection of system requirements.

The first step of behavioural modelling is to *understand* the system in terms of processing, dynamics and stored data structure. This involves, respectively building preliminary versions of the DFD, STD and ERD, though there is no implied sequence here. Ideally, in fact, the three preliminary diagrams should be built separately and in parallel to foster maximum insight from different viewpoints before organizing those viewpoints in harmony. However, to concentrate matters on the principle involved I will restrict the explanation to the DFD.

The EP approach is illustrated in Figure 4.2.

The first step of EP is to build a preliminary DFD by drawing a process bubble for each event (type D). Each bubble on the preliminary DFD is a *response* to each event. Flows in and out of the preliminary DFD must correspond with those on the context diagram. The preliminary DFD is a flat picture which is designed to expose system responses in their entirety. It is therefore neutral in that the analyst is free to make rational decisions as to what the best packagings of those processes might be.

We now *organize* the preliminary DFD into process groupings. this is called 'levelling' (because typically there are several levels of such groupings) and follows the principle of encapsulation previously discussed in Section 2.3. Where responses are complex, or where the event list is 'high-level' (see Section 3.6) it will be necessary to break responses down into lower level process groupings.

Notice, that although the objective is to create a top-down structure of DFDs, the approach itself is neither top-down or bottom-up. Clearly it is not top-down in that the event list is designed to expose detailed processing requirements before organizing them. However, it is not bottom-up because in levelling we are constantly aware of the context diagram which 'sits at the top' rather like a reference beacon. The approach is therefore better characterized as 'outside-in'.

The reader should note that the term 'essential model' is used in this book collectively for both environmental and behavioural models.

4.3   Data flow diagrams (DFDs)

The DFD is a tool that has been used for many years and for many different purposes; organizational work flow, domestic plumbing, cooking recipes and so on. This is perhaps because there is something very natural and instinctive about using DFDs. Indeed, they have been used in systems analysis and design for the last twenty years, one of the most readable expositions being DeMarco (1978).

Figure 4.3 shows a DFD for part of the Player Administration System. A brief examination reveals that the symbols used (for process, data flow and data store) are the same as described for the context diagram (Figure 3.3); in fact the context diagram is really a DFD containing just one process. It is fairly easy to get the basic idea of what is going on in the system without going into unnecessary detail: one can simply look at Figure 4.1 and understand it. Therein lies the great strength of DFDs: they facilitate communication between analyst and user as to what a system is *doing* without clouding the basic issues with irrelevant intricacies.

Much has been written in the literature on DFDs and it is not my purpose to repeat what has been said before. However, it is necessary to examine first some of the more pertinent ground rules.

Data flows

The data flow represents a pathway, along which one or more data structures may travel at some unspecified time; there is no implied sequence here, as there is for example on a program flow chart. Data flows may exist as follows:

- ☐ Between processes: in which case the data flow must be named and defined in the data dictionary.
- ☐ Between a process and a terminator: in which case the data flow must be named and defined in the data dictionary. The normal convention is to show the terminators on the context diagram only, to avoid cluttering the DFD. However, it is sometimes expedient to include terminators on the DFD as some people are uncomfortable with data flows coming in from and going out to 'nowhere'.
- ☐ Between a process and a data store: in which case the data flow may sometimes be named (see comments below on data flows to/from data stores).

No implementation medium must be assumed for the data flow. Therefore the data flow name simply describes what data is flowing in noun form (for example, Player Resignation).

Processes

Each process represents work done by the system and must be named. No implementation mechanism must be assumed. Therefore, the process name must describe *what* work is done in noun–verb form (for example, Record Player Resignation). Also notice each process is numbered.

Data stores

The data store represents data which must be held over time for use by the system or by a terminator. It must be named and defined in the data dictionary. Again, no implementation is assumed, for example, in terms of file structure. There must be

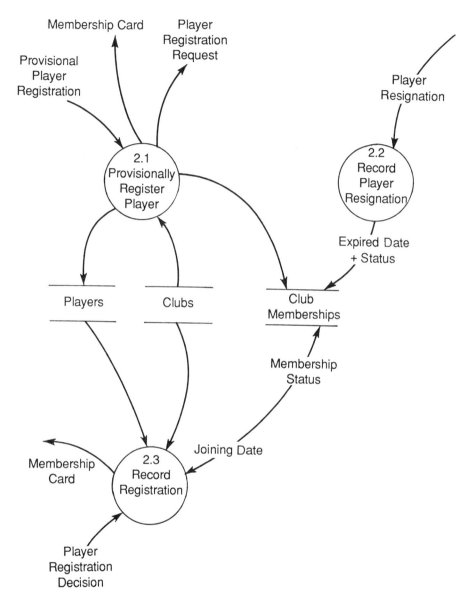

Figure 4.3 DFD Figure 2 for Administrate Registrations.

user policy which dictates the need for a data store, in contrast to implementation constraints which might lead the designer to introduce a data store later on; an example of the latter might be a work file or a back-up file. Finally, note that the data store simply represents a collection of *occurrences* of a particular data structure. The data structure itself is defined in the data dictionary as part of the entity-relationship model (see Section 4.4). The convention is to name the data store as a plural noun describing *what* broad category of data is held (for example Players). An asterisk is used to denote a duplicated data store (for example Pumps in Figure 4.4).

Access flows

Data flows between processes and data stores (or 'access flows') are a special case of data flows in that the data which is flowing here *must* be defined on the data structure for that data store in the data dictionary. Rules are needed for (1) direction and (2) naming:

(1) Direction. An arrow toward a data store means one (or a combination) of the following:

    (a) Occurrence(s) are created.
    (b) Occurrence(s) are deleted.
    (c) One or more data elements on occurrence(s) are amended.

An arrow toward a process means either or both:

    (d) Occurrence(s) are accessed for verification purposes (for example ensuring a match.
    (e) One or more data elements on occurrence(s) are drawn off the store to be processed and transmitted elsewhere by the receiving process.

An arrow at *both* ends of the access flow means (e) and any combination of (a), (b) and (c).

(2) Naming. Leave all such flows unnamed except at the lowest level of DFD where the flow is left unnamed if it represents one or more complete occurrences of the data store. Otherwise name the individual data elements represented. If many data elements are involved then they should be defined under and referenced by a group name, in which case the access flow will require its own definition in the data dictionary.

Although I have found this guideline to work well in practice, one may wish to go a stage further and avoid naming access flows altogether. This would save time and prevent cluttering of the DFD and data dictionary. Indeed, it would be quite safe providing the data elements accessed are declared for each lowest level process within the process descriptions as recommended in Section 5.4.1.

Control flows

In Section 3.4 (Context diagrams) we saw that control flows are used to carry Boolean information. Unlike data flows they do not carry value bearing data and are shown as arrowed dashed lines. Examples from the Petrol Sale Control System were Reset and Gun Lifted. Notice that in line with levelling rules these same two flows which appeared on the context diagram (shown in Figure 3.4) also appear in the lower level DFD (shown in Figure 4.4). Notice also that there are other control flows shown which appear to come in from (or go out to) nowhere. These fall into two categories:

☐ Prompts: which emanate from control processes (see below) as a means of activating/deactivating other processes. Types of prompt are discussed below in the section on state transition diagrams (STDs).

☐ Control signals: which simply report that something is true or false. They may be transmitted or received by any type of process as discussed below in the section on STDs. Control signals, unlike prompts, do not imply activation or deactivation and must be named and defined in the data dictionary.

Continuous flows

Control signals and data flows may be discrete (occur instantaneously) or continuous (persist through time). An example of the latter from Figure 4.4 is the Sale Active control signal. The notation is usefully adapted to denote continuous flows by double headed arrows. Notice all other flows in both our examples are discrete. Prompts are always modelled as discrete control flows.

Control processes

A control process co-ordinates the behaviour of other processes, which may include control processes themselves, in the DFD. It is shown as a dashed circle and deals only in control flows (in contrast to other types of process known as 'data processes'). Most importantly it is responsible for prompts to other processes. The internal behaviour of the control process itself is modelled using a STD; indeed it may be thought of as a short-hand way of *representing* the STD on the DFD. A DFD containing one or more control processes is sometimes referred to as a 'control DFD'.

Continuous processes

Processes, like flows, may also be discrete or continuous; there is no special notation for this. A discrete process executes in zero-time within the perfect

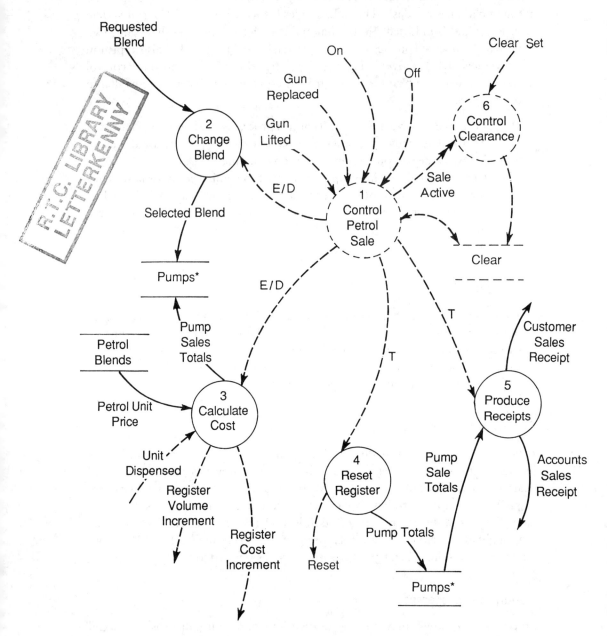

Figure 4.4 DFD Figure 0 for Petrol Sale Control System.

technology of the behavioural model and is therefore unable to wait for its inputs. It must have any required inputs available (as stores or continuous flows) when prompted; for example in Figure 4.4 Produce Receipts may execute discretely as it has its required data available on the Pumps data store. In contrast, a continuous process is available for work over a period of time as required by the environment. For example, Change Blend waits to receive the discrete flow Change Blend.

Control stores

Sometimes control signals, normally indicating the occurrence of an event, may occur which do not necessarily require an immediate response but nevertheless need to be remembered by the system for later use. The control store is a mechanism for handling such situations and is shown as a dashed store; it is analogous to the concept of semaphores first introduced by Dijkstra (1968). The control store must be named and defined in the data dictionary; for example, Clear in Figure 4.4. It represents a simple count but is different from a data store in that:

☐ A control process is always responsible for incrementing the count (initially zero) by one upon valid receipt of a control signal. Where the logic of such a control process is trivial it may be omitted from the DFD, by convention. In this case the control signal, indicating the event, may be drawn as incoming direct to the control store.

☐ One or more different control processes are permitted to sense continuously ('wait on') for the count to be set (greater than zero).

☐ As soon as the count is sensed as set the receiving process is issued a 'pass' and the count is automatically decremented by one. By definition only one receiving process can be issued a 'pass' at a time.

By permitting only one process to consume each occurrence of an event, the control store is also a useful means of handling contention for devices; for example, in an elevator system where there are four cars it is important that all four do not arrive together on request.

The full meaning of the control DFD will become apparent once the reader has read the closely related section which follows on STDs.

A cautionary word. Finally, ground rules are needed but they must be practical. Because there is considerable latitude in the way in which the DFD is interpreted one finds a variety of rule-sets applied. I have listed one set that I have found works well but I am not claiming there is anything sacrosanct in this. This leads to a second point: one must have consistency; it is clearly not good to have one team working in one way and another team in another. The important thing is to choose the rule-set that works best for a particular organization and standardize on that. Increasingly, such rule-sets are enforced by CASE tools used to support the development effort.

4.4   State transition diagrams (STDs)

The STD is a tool that emerged alongside the control DFD, in the mid-1980s (Ward and Mellor, 1985) as a means of modelling time-dependent characteristics of system behaviour. If the DFD is a tool for modelling *what* happens, the STD is a tool for modelling what happens *when*. It provides a mechanism for modelling the essentials of control systems that was simply not available with traditional DFDs.

Figure 4.5 shows the STD for the Control Petrol Sale control process depicted in Figure 4.4. As with a DFD it is reasonably easy to get a feel for what is going on by a fairly brief examination of a STD:

☐ *When* the operator switches the pump on, the system changes state from Idle to Pump Live by activating the Change Blend process. The pump works in the normal way in that a customer is not allowed to take any petrol until the previous sale has been cleared.

☐ Therefore *when* the gun is lifted the state changes to Waiting on Clear. The STD is now sensing to see if the count in the event store, Clear has been set (by the Control Clearance control process).

☐ If and *when* clear is set the STD receives a Clear Passed which will Start Sale: this means deactivating Change Blend, activating Reset Register and Calculate Cost, and setting up a continuous control flow, Sale Active to prevent erroneous clearance in the middle of a sale. The customer is now filling his or her car with petrol.

☐ Finally *when* the gun is replaced this will End Sale (this means deactivating Calculate Cost, activating Produce Receipts and Change Blend, and cancelling the Sale Active flow to permit clearance) and causes the state to change back to Pump Live.

☐ The new customer is allowed to change blends and the cycle is repeated until the pump is switched off *when* Change Blend is deactivated, Reset Register is activated and the STD is back in the Idle state.

The STD comprises four basic symbols (states, transitions, conditions and actions) as follows.

States

Shown as rectangles, states represent constant system behaviour which persists

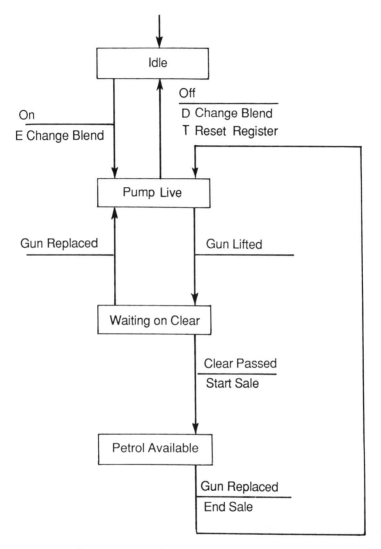

Figure 4.5 STD for Figure 1 Control Petrol Sale.

over time, according to the requirements of the environment. For example, the system stays in the Petrol Available state until something happens to change that situation. There must always be one initial state or state in which the STD is always assumed to start; this is often an Idle state, as in the example. In contrast, final states from which there is no exit are rare in the behavioural model as these are reserved for critical situations, like system aborts.

Importantly the same processes must be active and the same continuous flows produced when in any particular occurrence of a state, irrespective of the route taken to reach that state. This rule ensures consistency of system behaviour and is known as 'behavioural equivalence'. Finally a system can only be in one state within the same STD, although a system can be described by several STDs.

Transitions

A transition represents a change from one state to another state and is shown as an arrowed line. For example, there is a transition from Idle to Pump Live. Transitions occur in zero-time within the perfect technology of the behavioural model.

Conditions

A condition describes what must happen to cause the system to change state. It is shown above a horizontal line which is appended to the appropriate transition. Conditions are typically identified with events. Each transition except the one going into the initial state must have an associated condition. For example, the condition On causes the system to change state from Idle to Pump Live.

Conditions may be simple (a single statement) or complex (a series of statements) as described below.

Actions

An action describes what happens to effect a change of state. It is always the result of a condition, and is shown below the corresponding horizontal line. Actions are typically identified with the activation and deactivation of processes (shown on the control DFD). Transitions may or may not have an associated action. For example, the transition from Idle to Pump Live is effected by an action to enable (see below) the Change Blend process, but the transition from Pump Live to Waiting on Clear requires no action.

Actions may be simple (a single command) or complex (a series of commands) as described below, and will involve the issuing of prompts and/or control signals as follows.

Prompts

Notice that prompts are always effected through actions. It is useful to distinguish three types of prompt (short-hand notation shown in brackets). Each is a discrete control flow which importantly implies activation of some sort and may only be issued by a control process (the examples described in this section all refer to Figure 4.4).

Trigger (T). To activate a discrete process. The salient points here are that the activated process is assumed (in line with the principles of *essential* modelling) to execute instantaneously and also has any required information available in the form of stored data or continuous flow. For example, Produce Sales Receipt can be triggered because the information required is readily available on the data store Pumps. Normally the triggered process is a data process but it is possible to trigger another control process.

Enable (E). To activate a continuous process. The activated process will stay 'live' until the controlling STD chooses to deactivate it (using disable, coming up). Some or all of the information required by the activated process will not be readily available. That is, there is a time constraint imposed by the environment which necessitates an enable (rather than a trigger). For example, Calculate Cost has been enabled because it has to sense continuously for occurrences of the incoming control flow Unit Dispensed. The enabled process may be either a data or a control process.

Disable (D). This is the converse of enable. It is used to deactivate a previously enabled process. The two are usually combined as E/D for short.

Control signals

Control flows not implying activation are transmitted through actions and received by conditions. They may be issued or received by control processes or data processes, and must be named.

Signal (S). A signal represents the issuing of a discrete control flow to either a data or a control process. The discrete control flow occurs at the instant it was signalled and dies immediately. This may be:

- ☐ Transmitted and received by processes within the system (there are not actually any in the example).
- ☐ Transmitted by the system to a terminator (for example, Reset)
- ☐ Received by the system from a terminator (for example, Gun Lifted)

Raise (R). A raise represents the issuing of a continuous control flow to either a data or a control process and follows the same three rules as above for a signal. It is akin to setting a flag, in that the value of the continuous control flow is set to '1'. The continuous control flow occurs as 'raised' following the issue of the raise command until either it is lowered (value = '0') or the process issuing the command is deactivated (value = 'null'). In the latter case the control flow ceases to occur altogether. In the example Sale Active is raised by Control Petrol Sale.

Lower (L). This is the converse of raise and is used to reset the value of a continuous control flow (from 1 to 0), which must be lowered by the same control process that raised it.

Complex conditions and actions

Complex conditions and actions should be defined in the data dictionary, as described in Chapter 5. The definitions for Start Sale and End Sale are as follows:

$$
\begin{array}{lll}
\text{Start Sale} & = \text{Do in order:} & \text{T} \quad \text{Reset register} \\
& & \text{D} \quad \text{Change blend} \\
& & \text{E} \quad \text{Calculate cost} \\
& & \text{R} \quad \text{Sale active}
\end{array}
$$

$$
\begin{array}{lll}
\text{End Sale} & = \text{Do in order:} & \text{D} \quad \text{Calculate cost} \\
& & \text{T} \quad \text{Produce receipts} \\
& & \text{E} \quad \text{Change blend} \\
& & \text{L} \quad \text{Sale active}
\end{array}
$$

(Note, it is also possible to specify 'do concurrently' against component actions).

The emphasis with the STD has been on control systems, because there is an essential requirement with such systems to monitor and/or control devices. That is, the time constraints are imposed by the system environment, not its behaviour (which operates as perfect technology). However, it should be emphasized that the STD may also be applied extensively with information systems when moving into design. In particular it is very useful for modelling interface control, for example, in handling the control of dialogues in online systems.

4.5 Entity relationship diagrams (ERDs)

The DFD is a useful tool for modelling the flow of data around a system and for exposing the processing required to operate on that data. However, *it does not tell us very much about stored data itself*: simply that there are repositories called data stores for holding data over time. This might be satisfactory in a system where the stored data structure is very simple, but in reality this is rarely the case. The ERD allows us to examine the structure of this stored data in its own right, aside from processing or control considerations.

There are, of course, many good reasons for modelling data structure and countless textbooks have been written on the subject; Howe (1989) gives a particularly lucid account. The ERD is now an established part of structured analysis having emerged first through the work of Chen (1976) and Flavin (1981) amongst others. Despite this, experience shows that it is not easy to convince most people of the value of ERDs prior to their actually having used ERDs on a project. Certainly, there is a proliferation of competing notations and we will therefore be concentrating on just one (adapted from Chen). However, I am sure that the underlying reason for this reluctance is that whereas DFDs and STDs are very much procedural descriptions of what a system does, and thus easy to identify with, ERDs are more abstract: they do not actually describe activities that can be identified with. The need to 'sell' diagrams to *users*, covered in Section 2.10, is therefore particularly poignant with ERDs.

Figure 4.6 shows an ERD for the Petrol Sale Control system. There are two basic symbols (entities and relationships) as follows.

Entities

An entity is a conceptual grouping of essential stored data which must:

- ☐ Have business relevance.
- ☐ Be described by one or more attributes (see below).
- ☐ Have a unique identifier.

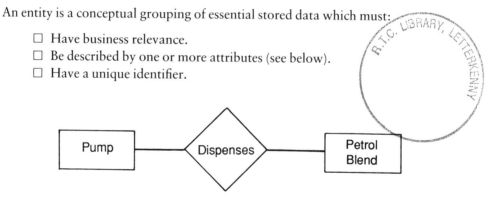

Figure 4.6 ERD for Petrol Sale Control System.

Each entity must be defined in the data dictionary. It is shown as a box and is named using a singular noun or noun phrase which describes the role played; for example, Pump:

- ☐ Clearly has business relevance within this particular system.
- ☐ Is described by the following attributes:
  Pump Number,
  Date Installed,
  Date of Last Maintenance.
- ☐ Has a unique identifier: if Pump Number is known, then an individual Pump can be distinguished.

Entities are very roughly equivalent to data stores: if you cannot imagine the name of an entity as the (singular) name of a data store on a DFD then it is probably not worth defining as one: for example, both Pumps and Petrol Blends are data stores on the DFD (Figure 4.4).

Relationships

A relationship is an association between any number of entities which is of business relevance. Each relationship must be defined in the data dictionary. It is shown as a diamond and named using a verb or verbal expression; for example, Dispenses in Figure 4.6. Relationships are the connections, lacking on the DFD, between categories of data storage.

Before progressing further we need to address two more concepts.

Attributes

An attribute a property of an entity; for example, Player Name. Each attribute must belong to one and only one entity to avoid redundancy. Attributes are not normally shown on the diagram but documented under the containing entity name in the data dictionary, thus forming an entity-relationship model (E-R model for short).

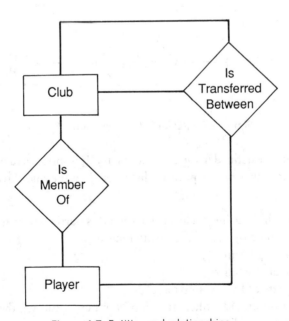

Figure 4.7 Entities and relationships.

Occurrences

It is important not to make the mistake of equating entities with 'things'. Notice that the diagram operates at an abstract level. It is concepts that are being described as opposed to *occurrences* of those concepts. For example, John Brown might be a player about whom data is held in the Player Administration System. John Brown himself is neither an entity nor an entity occurrence: he is a human being. Specific items of data about John Brown (like '1st February 1965') are attribute occurrences (or *values*) of attributes (like Date of Birth). Attributes collectively form conceptual groupings called entities (like Player in Figure 4.7). An occurrence of the entity Player would be the grouping of all of the attribute values of, say, John Brown. Single occurrence entities are actually quite rare, except in control systems which interface with singular equipment, about which information needs to be kept; for example, Camera in a picture taking control system for a satellite.

Relationships (like Is Member Of) should be contrasted with relationship occurrences (like 'John Brown is member of Tooting Athletic') which associate specific entity occurrences. Relationships are either *binary*, which means that a relationship occurrence always involves two participating entity occurrences (exactly two lines connected to the diamond), or they are *complex* which means that more than two entity occurrences are involved (more than two lines connected to the diamond). In Figure 4.7 Is Member Of is an example of a binary relationship; Is Transferred Between is an example of a complex relationship which is also recursive. An occurrence of the latter will involve an occurrence of Player plus two occurrences of Club (for example Bill Sully is transferred from Crawley to Brixton All Stars).

Two further symbols are required: they are described next.

Associative entities

An associative entity is an entity which is dependent on the existence of a relationship between other entities. Data is said to be 'associated' with the relationship. Again, it must be defined in the data dictionary. It is denoted by a heavy arrow drawn from the associative entity box to the relationship (which is left unnamed) on which that entity is dependent. For example, in Figure 4.8 Club Membership is an associative entity because (a) it is an entity which obeys the three defining criteria:

1. It is clearly of business relevance.
2. It is described by attributes:
   - ☐ Membership Number,
   - ☐ Joining Date,
   - ☐ Membership Status.
3. It has a unique identifier in Membership Number.

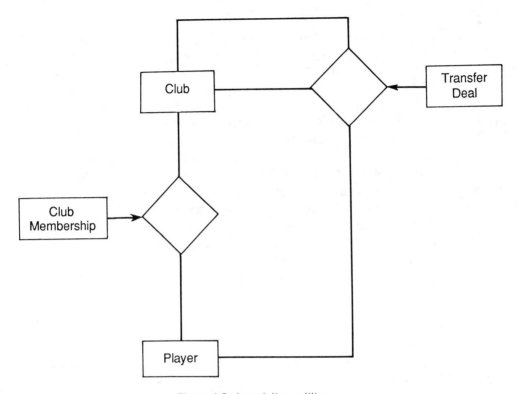

Figure 4.8 Associative entities.

And (b) it depends on the relationship Is Member Of (now left unnamed) between Club and Player. Notice also that Club Membership is the name of a data store on the DFDs (Figure 4.3).

Entity supertypes and subtypes

Entity subtypes (subtypes for short) are sub-classes of an entity to which a narrower definition applies and normally to which certain attributes are exclusive; entity supertypes (supertypes for short) represent attributes which are common to *all* occurrences of that entity. Moreover, for a given occurrence, the subtype *inherits* attributes from the appropriate supertype. The *subtyping* describes the basis upon which division into subtypes is made and is denoted by a bar at right angles between the supertype and a relationship containing the name of the subtyping off which any number of entity subtypes may hang. Note that by definition an entity occurrence is not allowed to belong to more than one entity subtype within the same subtyping. Again, subtyping information must be defined in the data dictionary.

In Figure 4.9 Player is the supertype of the subtyping Nationality of which National Player and Foreign Player are subtypes. Common attributes held in Player would be both Player Name and Date of Birth. An attribute peculiar to National Player would be National Insurance Number. Finally, attributes peculiar to Foreign Player would be Work Permit Number and Nationality.

Although different attributes are usual with subtypes this does not necessarily have to be the case; it may be that certain relationships are exclusive to each subtype. Also there has to be good justification for subtyping otherwise the ERD becomes flooded with them; like swear words they lose their impact if not used sparingly. Usually one would only expect to subtype where there was an important business distinction to be highlighted, and normally this means that exclusive attributes *and* relationships are involved.

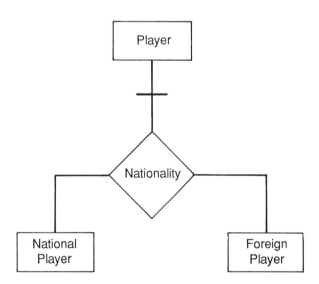

Figure 4.9 Entity supertype and subtypes.

It is possible to create several 'levels' of subtype (for example, Foreign Player could have been further subtyped as Chinese Player and Non-Chinese Player, if indeed there were justification); there is no theoretical limit to this. Note therefore that the same entity can be both a supertype, relative to one subtyping, and a subtype, relative to another.

As noted above there are many variants of ERD notation. Further extensions and refinements to this basic ERD notation are discussed in Chapter 9.

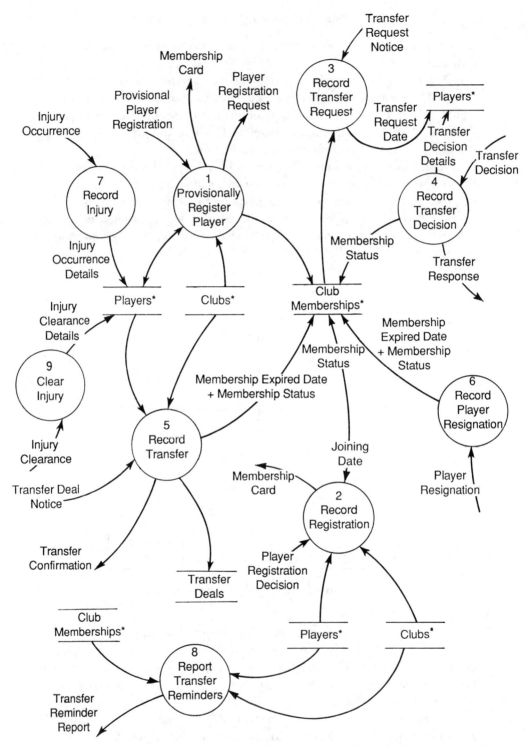

Figure 4.10 Preliminary DFD for Player Administration System.

4.6 **Understanding system requirements**

4.6.1 Building the preliminary DFD

A preliminary DFD is created as follows. A process bubble is drawn to model the response to each event on the event list which requires the system to transform data (that is for class D events). The number of the event is drawn on the appropriate bubble. The data flows from the context diagram are then drawn in against the appropriate bubbles. Finally, supporting data stores are drawn in to complete the first draft preliminary DFD. Figure 4.10 shows an example preliminary DFD for the players administration system based on the event list and context diagram from Chapter 3 (Figures 3.5 and 3.3 respectively). Notice there are nine bubbles corresponding to the nine events and that each flow consumed/produced by each bubble corresponds to a flow on the context diagram.

You will agree that Figure 4.10, based on just nine events, looks quite complex. Therefore, drawn for a system of any size this diagram will appear daunting to the eye at first sight; it will need much revision and involve much discussion *amongst analysts* and its complexity is therefore hidden from the users at this stage. The operative principle is for the analysts to gain an early understanding of the 'nuts and bolts' of a system based upon user requirements identified at the environmental model stage. Once this understanding has been clarified the preliminary DFD can be organized into convenient 'chunks' for user review, using upward levelling, as described in Section 4.7. Because of the problem of complexity it is sometimes useful to partition the event list as mentioned previously in Section 3.10.

4.6.2 Building the preliminary STD

The question remains as to *how* the STD is constructed in the first place. As with the DFD, the event list drives this activity. Class C events are written down and inspected for patterns such as sequences, loops and exclusive groupings. An example based on the event list for the Petrol Sale Control System (which is repeated here as Figure 4.11 for convenience) is shown below in Figure 4.12.

A useful technique is to develop scenarios describing what might happen to a system during the course of a typical period. In the example, Loop (a) reflects the normal loop in that after the pump is switched on there is a discernible cycle of lifting gun, clearing register and replacing gun. Loop (b) is very basic in that it reflects the normal on/off situation. Finally the customer could lift the gun but change his or her mind about the blend of petrol required, which would mean replacing the gun before making the new selection as you are not allowed to switch

1. Cashier switches pump on (C).
2. Cashier switches pump off (C).
3. Customer lifts petrol gun (C).
4. Cashier requests to clear register (C).
5. Customer replaces gun (CD).
6. Customer selects blend (D).
7. Dispenser reports unit dispensed (D).

Figure 4.11 Event list for Petrol Sale Control System.

blends when the gun is raised. This is reflected in Loop (c) which therefore represents a slightly more unusual situation.

Patterns of events are thus developed by looking for normal behaviour patterns first and then establishing less normal patterns gradually progressing toward the

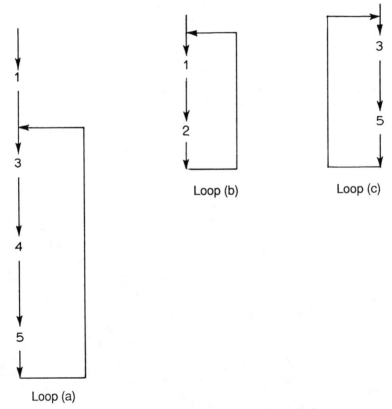

Loop (a)

Figure 4.12 Event patterns for Control Petrol Sale.

abnormal. Such patterns are readily transferrable to what will be the preliminary STD(s):

☐ Event numbers convert to conditions.
☐ The arrowed lines convert to states.
☐ Actions are then added.

The analyst now has a choice to make: whether to model each pattern as a separate STD or to combine diagrams. In the example there is clearly much overlap between patterns as certain events recur on different diagrams; Event 1 is on Loops (a) and (b), and Events 3 and 5 are both on Loops (a) and (c). Therefore there is a good case for combining diagrams. Figure 4.5 represents this. Other situations may reflect less integrated patterns of events best modelled by separate diagrams. On complex systems there is likely to be a combination of the two situations with some patterns best combined and others left separate. Either way, the analyst should not spend long deliberating on these issues at this stage as the main aim is to *understand* the dynamics of the system; organization will be fully considered a little later.

Notice that class C events often have an impact on whether other events are actually detected. For example, Event 6 'Customer selects blend (D)' might occur but would not be detected if the pump were not switched on and the gun was not replaced. The system must be in the right state. Event 6 is dependent upon Events 1 and 5. In cases such as these the event response to the class D event must be enabled when the state is right to sense for the event, and disabled when the state is not right to prevent event detection. Change Blend in Figure 4.4 provides an example of such a response for Event 6.

Each event is also examined to see if an event sensing process is required for the event itself. There are two reasons for these:

1. A value of a flow input to the system needs to be compared with pre-determined values. For example, the event 'Temperature exceeds normal' in a patient monitoring and control system, as shown in Figure 4.13 (a).
2. A stored scheduled time needs to be compared against the current time. For example, the event 'Time to administer dose' where this time is determined by a scheduler according to blood sugar level, as shown in Figure 4.13 (b). Notice that current time is assumed to be available to all processes and is therefore not explicitly shown.

4.6.3 Building the preliminary ERD

Before sketching out a scenario for the development of a preliminary ERD it is important to note two points:

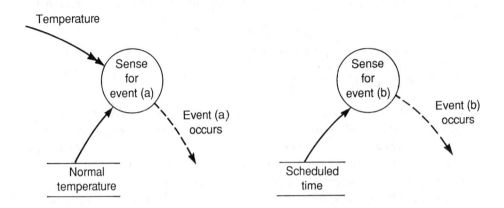

Event (a) : Temperature exceeds normal   Event (b) : Time to administer dose

Figure 4.13 Event sensing processes.

1. We have seen that the ERD is at root an enterprise diagram. Where an ERD is developed for a system this must be consistent with the underlying enterprise ERD as covered in Chapter 9. It may be the case that a scoped version of the enterprise ERD is available as part of the system profile before environmental modelling is even started. Indeed, the approach taken in Part Three of this book is to build a strategic version of the enterprise ERD (known as a global ERD) as a precursor of system level modelling. In such cases the analyst will 'have considerably more to go on' than in the somewhat limited scenario described below.

2. A large part of developing an ERD is bound up with *attribution*: the somewhat unglamorous exercise of searching for attributes and either assigning them to entities or creating new entities to house them. This is not something which suddenly 'occurs' at the end of a project. It is continually going on through all three stages of understanding, organization and specification.

Now look at the ERD shown in Figure 4.7: it is preliminary in the sense that it represents a rough sketch of the stored data requirements that are implied by the event list (Figure 3.5) and context diagram (Figure 3.3) for the Player Administration System. In other words it represents our initial *understanding* of stored data structure required to support the system in its environment.

The event list is first examined for nouns that suggest a requirement for associated stored data and each such noun transposed as an entity: hence Player (Events 1,2,3,5,6,7) and Club (1,4,5,6). Similarly the event list is examined for verbs which suggest a required connection between entities and each such verb transposed as a relationship; hence Is Transferred Between (Event 5) and Is Member Of by translation of Registers (Event 1). Events 8 and 9 suggest a need to maintain data on transfer requests and injury clearances for each player, adding to the argument in favour of Player as an entity. Prior grammatical structuring of the event list as suggested in Section 3.9.1 will greatly facilitate this transposition. Also in parallel, we examine the context diagram and make sure that the ERD seems capable of absorbing data from flows inward and producing data for flows outward.

4.7   Organizing system requirements

Each preliminary diagram represents a different abstraction of system behaviour. Indeed the philosophy itself is to provide as much insight as possible by providing the analyst with different angles on the problem. In organizing the diagrams we will not only be concerned with packaging the different diagrams for presentation and review with users, we will inevitably be seeking to tie the different angles together into a coherent whole. Each diagram type is in essence an abstraction of the *same* system. Although the subject of integration is treated formally in the next chapter it will therefore be necessary to comment on it in this chapter.

4.7.1   Levelling DFDs

The preliminary DFD shown in Figure 4.10 is difficult for the reader to absorb, and remember, this is only a 'small' system with nine events (Figure 3.5). Imagine therefore trying to depict a system with fifty events on one DFD. Even worse imagine trying to read such a DFD after someone else has created it, which is the position the user is going to be in.

Clearly, some means of partitioning complexity is required, such that we can consider manageable portions of the system. This is achieved by organizing the overall DFD into a series of *levels* so that each level provides successively greater detail about a portion of the level above it. The situation is analogous to the way in which maps are organized in an atlas. The top level DFD is the context diagram as already discussed in Chapter 3; this is analogous to a map showing the earth in relation to other planets in the solar system. The DFD immediately beneath the context diagram is known as Figure 0 and represents the major functions of the system and their interfaces; this is analogous to the overview map of the world showing the different continents. Figure 0 inherits the name from

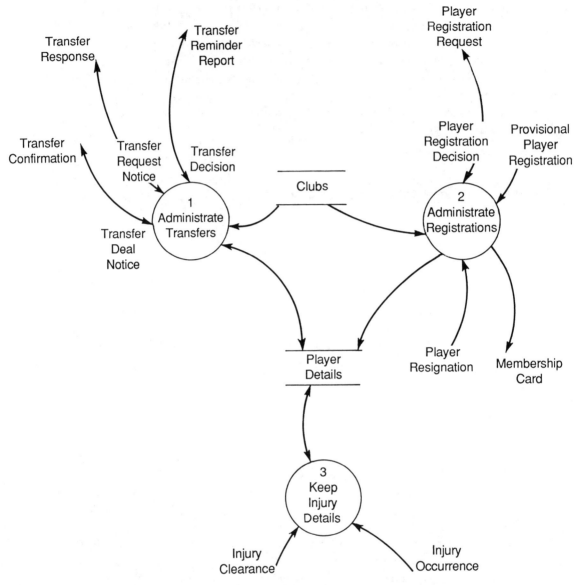

Figure 4.14 DFD Figure 0 for Player Administration System.

the context diagram and each process is numbered (1, 2, 3, . . . and so on). An example Figure 0 for the Player Administration System is shown in Figure 4.14.

This convention is carried through each level. For example, Process 2 is associated with a lower level DFD known as Figure 2 Administrate Registrations (see Figure 4.3); continuing the analogy this is like a map of one of the countries within a continent. If there were a lower level DFD for Process 2.1, this would be called Figure 2.1 Provisionally Register Player; analogous to the map of a particular region of a country. Obviously what we have here is really no more then than a simple conventional indexing system.

However, this hierarchy of DFDs must stop somewhere; we cannot level down forever. Where do we stop? The guideline (DeMarco, 1978) is that we stop when it is possible to write a clearly understandable textual description of a process on a single page; this is known as a process specification. This leads to an important rule: a process has either an associated lower level DFD or a process specification but *never both*.

The name of the game here is to organize DFDs in a way that facilitates communication. Detail must be increasingly limited the higher up the hierarchy we go. This means packaging flows and data stores as well as processes. For example, comparing Figures 4.3 and 4.14:

☐ The flows Player Registration Request and Player Registration Decision are packaged at the higher level as a bi-directional flow (to/from Process 2).
☐ The data stores Players, Transfers, and Memberships have been combined at the higher level to form Player Details.

The operative principle here is the principle of *encapsulation* (discussed in Section 2.3). The ultimate value of applying encapsulation comes strategically and is therefore discussed in Part 3. However, a brief characterization follows.

Bubbles are grouped according to three main criteria:

1. Do they exclusively share the same stored data (entities and relationships)?
2. Are they exclusively shared by the same user (terminators)?
3. Do they require integrated control (where C events are involved)?

As far as possible we try to ensure a 'yes' to all three questions with an ideal encapsulated system as the target in mind as illustrated in Figure 4.15, each quadrant of the diagram representing a potential *object* (as defined in Section 2.3). Because of the realities of everyday life this is an ideal which we often have to compromise. For example, the Player entity in the Player Administration System stretches across different process groupings. The important point is that it is an ideal toward which we approximate.

Thus Processes 1, 2 and 6 have been extracted from the example preliminary DFD shown in Figure 4.10 and grouped on to the separate diagram shown in Figure 4.3 as they appertain to the same terminator (Sports Authority) and the same sort of data (Registrations). This in turn has been levelled under Figure 0 for the system shown in Figure 4.14. Figure 0 would be of more general user interest, particularly to higher managers not interested so much in detail as in general functions covered

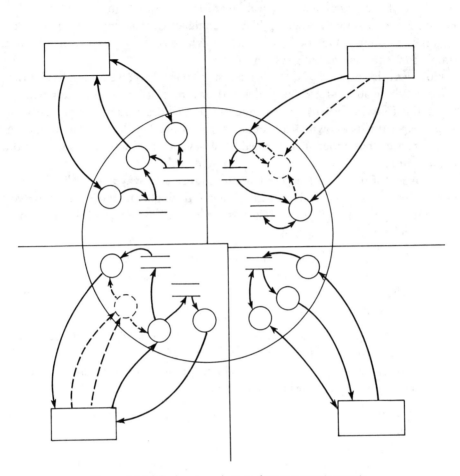

Figure 4.15 Ideal encapsulation of system requirements.

by the system. Finally, this should correspond to the context diagram shown in Figure 3.1.

4.7.2 Levelling STDs

We have already seen that by searching for patterns of events that must occur in sequence or independently or in loops the preliminary STD can be partitioned into multiple STDs. Remember, STDs will effectively be represented on DFDs as control processes. Control processes, control flows and control stores are then added to the DFD prior to organization and levelling. In organizing STDs, DFDs will be examined for common control requirements and STDs integrated to ensure encapsulation.

For example, if control of the petrol sale were part of a much larger system to control the pump itself Figure 4.4 would represent good encapsulation of the sales part of the overall process on each of the above three counts. The STD in Figure 4.5 ensures this. We thus have a DFD and STD which have been organized for review. Events 1 to 4 from the event list shown in Figure 4.11 each correspond to a condition on the STD. Event 5 corresponds to two conditions; the effect of replacing the gun depends on whether any petrol has actually been dispensed. Events 6 and 7 are different in that each results in an input flow to a continuously enabled process which is waiting for the event to occur. All C events are mirrored as control flows on the DFD. (This tie-up between STD and DFD is discussed in some detail in Chapter 5.)

Levelling of DFDs causes STDs to become effectively buried at the lowest level in the control processes. Also note that in control systems of any complexity it is possible to bury control processes within control processes and for the control processes to communicate. This is illustrated in Figure 4.16. Inter-control communication must be added to ensure integrity in the form of control flows issued as actions in one STD and received as conditions in another STD.

4.7.3 Segmenting the ERD

The preliminary ERD now needs *organizing*. There are three issues involved here:

1. Quality.
2. Integration.
3. Presentation.

Quality of the ERD provides a subject for a book in its own right. Indeed, there is a wealth of literature in this area and it is not my wish to regurgitate it. The important thing to be said here is that one should not attempt to formalize the E-R model (ERD plus its textual support) in terms of normalization and so on, before that model is properly understood.

Integration of the ERD involves examining preliminary DFD, (as described, for example, in Figure 4.10) and roughly checking that:

☐ Data stores are mirrored as entities or collections of entities and relationships; for example, associative entities have been created in Figure 4.8 for Club Membership and Transfer Deal.

☐ Each process has access to the appropriate entities and relationships; for example on closer inspection Process 1 (Provisionally Register Player) will

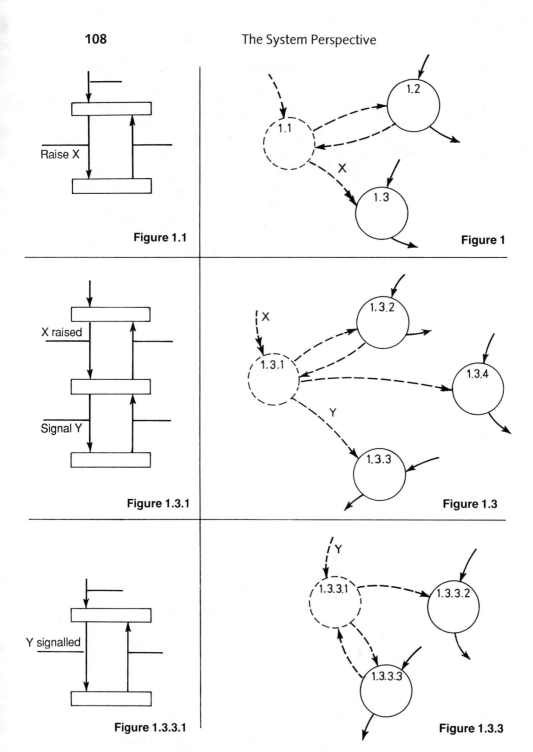

Figure 1.1

Figure 1

Figure 1.3.1

Figure 1.3

Figure 1.3.3.1

Figure 1.3.3

Figure 4.16 Nesting control: abstract DFDs and STDs.

have to distinguish national from foreign players to enable the subsequent formal registration by Process 2 (Record Registration). This suggests splitting the entity Player into appropriate subtypes as in Figure 4.9.

☐ The converse is also applied in that we need to develop the DFD to ensure that the *data stores* fully support the ERD. (The reader is referred to Section 5.5.2 for a full account of the link between DFD and ERD.)

Of course, this scenario is very much a simplification designed to convey the basic principles of EP as applied to the ERD. Figure 4.17 represents the resulting ERD. Normally, some form of matrix (such as entity–process discussed in Chapter 8) showing the tie-up between DFD and ERD would be used to assist in a system of any size.

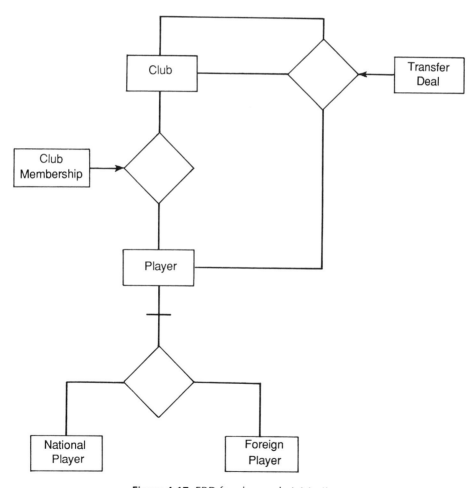

Figure 4.17 ERD for player administration.

Presentation of the ERD can be particularly difficult. One wants to present the necessary details to given users without overwhelming them with lots of detail they are not interested in. Unfortunately, on systems of any size ERDs can grow large, with in excess of twenty entities not uncommon.

The ERD does not lend itself to levelling in the way that a DFD does, although we shall see in Chapter 7 that it is possible to use a form of levelling in distinguishing strategic from system requirements. The ERD can, however, be *segmented* into subsets for review with the relevant interested parties. For example, Figure 4.17 segments into Figures 4.8 and 4.9 with the entity Player overlapping. Although segmentation is virtually indispensable on large systems it must be carefully controlled.

4.8   Summary

In this chapter I have introduced three modelling tools – DFD, STD and ERD – which EP uses for modelling system behaviour, and shown broadly the way in which these 'dimensions' of a system are projected from the environmental model. Collectively they form a strong portfolio of weapons for modelling all types of system from control systems to information systems. The increasing emergence of systems which are sophisticated on *both* control and information fronts is perhaps the most convincing argument for their use.

Up to this point I have talked about each diagram in its own right; I have deliberately avoided, as far as possible, looking at the inter-connections between diagrams. This is because this is a subject important enough to be considered in its own right. Also, I have said little about textual support for the diagrams. Both these subjects are covered in the next chapter.

The major purpose of this chapter has been to introduce the diagramming concepts and notation of the behavioural model. However, as mentioned before, it is impossible to talk intelligibly about the meaning of something without referring to the way in which that thing is used, and *vice-versa*. It has therefore been necessary to give a brief overview of the way EP employs these diagrams.

It is probably fair to say that the bulk of the rest of this book, after the next chapter, is concerned with how we can employ these diagrams with a view to more effective systems development.

CHAPTER 5

Specifying requirements

A picture is worth a thousand words.

ANON

A few words are worth a thousand pictures.

J.K. GALBRAITH

I never read, I just look at pictures.

ANDY WARHOL

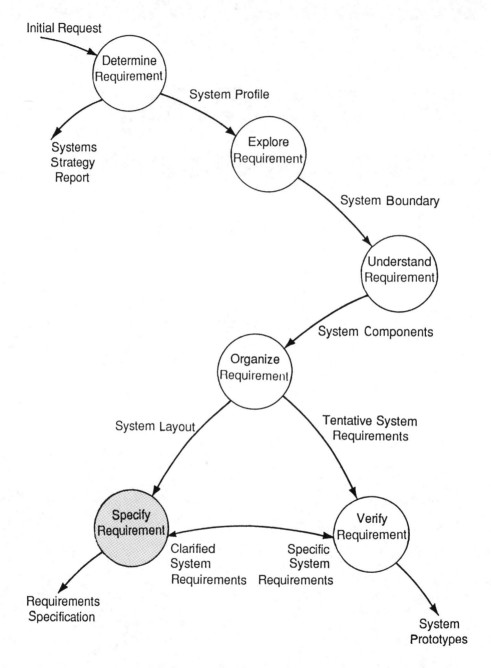

Figure 5.1 Specifying requirements with respect to the modelling framework.

5.1   Introduction

One of the major objectives of specification is to remove all ambiguities from our organized understanding of requirements. Figure 5.1 illustrates the activity with respect to the modelling framework.

Notice the close interdependence between specifying and verifying requirements: if requirements have not been specified then they cannot be verified but if requirements have not been verified then the specification is worthless. This seems to pose something of a dilemma. However, the dilemma is a theoretical one: in practice there is an important distinction to be made here between the requirement specification itself and the way that specification is presented for verification. The former corresponds to the essential model whereas the latter corresponds to the means of presentation or *view* of the essential model. This chapter concentrates mainly on the former, whilst offering some salient practical advice on the latter.

Textual support for the graphic components of the essential model discussed in the previous chapter is first outlined with respect to the framework of the behavioural model. The three textual elements of this framework are then discussed:

1. Data dictionary.
2. Process specification.
3. Integration rules.

Notice that the focus here will be *conceptual*. The most suitable ways of actually supporting the essential model will be discussed in some detail in Chapter 12.

However, because of the intimate relationship between specifying and verifying requirements I have concluded this chapter with a discussion of presentation of requirements specification. One of these involves prototyping which is dealt with at some length in Chapters 10 and 11. In this chapter I focus mainly on the tactic of extending the behavioural model into external design to form a functional specification.

The literature contains numerous accounts of subjects such as data dictionary and process specification, the detail of which lies outside the scope of this chapter. Again, however, whilst my intention here is simply to identify and characterize the various components involved, I have included some more detailed observations which reflect things I have learned whilst applying these concepts 'in anger'.

5.2   Essential model infrastructure

Up to this point DFDs, STDs and ERDs have been presented as tools to understand and organize business requirements with respect to system scope. However, the essential model must ultimately provide the *basis* for a requirements specification: in order to specify a system, textual support is required. Also, although the DFDs, STDs and ERDs have been recognized as different dimensions of system behaviour, thus far, the focus has tended toward each diagram in isolation. Textual support is also required in terms of integration rules to ensure consistency within diagrams of the same type (levelling) and between different diagram types (balancing). Without full textual support it is impossible to verify the behavioural model which should be no less testable than a suite of programs. An analogy helps to illustrate the situation.

The diagrams of the essential model require textual support in the same sense that the components of a building need to be joined securely together upon a firm foundation if the building is not to collapse. This is analagous to providing data dictionary entries to support the diagrams. Secondly, each brick used must be of sound internal structure. This is analagous to writing process specifications for the lowest level processes. Lastly, the components must fit together properly: the bricks must be cemented together (analagous to levelling DFDs), joists must overhang walls by stipulated amounts and be secured in the right way (analagous to integrating different diagram types). The bottom line is that it is impossible to live, with any degree of safety, in a building which is not constructed soundly. Likewise, it is impossible to verify the correctness of an essential model which lacks textual support.

The situation is illustrated more formally in Figure 5.2; the heavy double-ended arrows indicate linkages between components. The data dictionary underpins the whole structure and is discussed in the next section. Process specifications must precisely clarify the business logic of lowest level processes (from the set of DFDs) with reference to terms defined in the data dictionary. Some of the methods that can be used in process specification are identified in Section 5.4. Finally, notice the linkages between diagram types: each control bubble on a DFD effectively represents an STD and each data store on a DFD effectively represents a selection of one or more related entities from the ERD. Integration rules are required to ensure the accurate correspondence of these representations and are discussed in Section 5.5. Although not explicitly shown in Figure 5.2 remember that integration rules are also required for levelling DFDs as discussed in the last chapter.

There are many ways of supporting these components physically in the form of CASE tools; for example, many CASE tools embrace the concept of a system dictionary which contains not only data definitions but also process specifications and integration rules. More importantly perhaps, the means of presenting models for verification is dependent upon the features of the CASE tool itself. Indeed, we will see in Chapter 12 that two of the most desirable features of any CASE tool are:

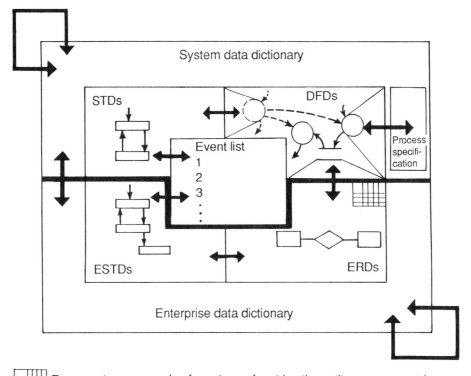

Represents an example of one type of matrix: the entity-process matrix

Figure 5.2 Essential model infrastructure.

1. The ability to *view* portions of the infrastructure in ways appropriate to the particular needs of the audience.
2. The ability to *extend* portions of the infrastructure toward external designs and prototypes.

5.3 Data dictionary

One of the major objectives of specification is to remove all ambiguities from our understanding of requirements. Such ambiguities frequently occur in natural language descriptions. For example, the Morgan Tandoori might offer the following choice of delicacies:

☐ Chicken tikka and green salad or onion bhaji and prawn pathia.

This can obviously be interpreted in different ways:

- ☐ Exclusive choice of combined starters:
  (chicken tikka and green salad) or (onion bhaji and prawn pathia).
- ☐ Three courses with choice of second course:
  chicken tikka and (green salad or onion bhaji) and prawn pathia.
- ☐ Two courses with double starter with choice:
  (chicken tikka and (green salad or onion bhaji)) and prawn pathia.
- ☐ Two courses with double main course with choice:
  chicken tikka and ((green salad or onion bhaji) and prawn pathia).

In a simple case like this the ambiguity has been removed by using simple brackets. In the case of system requirements we will need textual support in terms of expedient notations and rules.

The data dictionary contains definitions for all attributes used by the system and for all of the following diagram items:

- ☐ Data flows.
- ☐ Control flows.
- ☐ Data stores.
- ☐ Control stores.
- ☐ Entities.
- ☐ Relationships.
- ☐ Associative entities.
- ☐ Supertype/subtypes.

Also, definitions may sometimes be required for:

- ☐ Access flows (where specifically named).
- ☐ Conditions.
- ☐ Actions.

In addition the event list is held here. And, optionally, it is possible to include definitions for terminators.

Many of the above diagram items are defined in terms of their component attributes. Therefore, before considering some examples, it is important to understand the handling of attributes and in particular to introduce the term 'elementary attribute'. This is an attribute for which there is no decomposition which has meaning to the user. For example, it may be possible to break down a Player Id into an alpha prefix plus a number, but in this case these components have no separate business relevance and we will therefore stick with Player Id as an elementary attribute. In contrast, a 'composite attribute' is made up of two or more other attributes, each of which may be elementary or composite. An example is Player Address which is made up of Street Line, City and Postcode. The basic principle here is to avoid redundancy by specifying attribute meaning for only the elementary attributes.

The following conceptual notation (adapted from Backus–Naur Form (BNF)) has often been used in the past especially where models have been paper-based.

$\quad$ = $\quad$ means *is equivalent to.*

$\quad$ + $\quad$ means *and.*

$\quad$ [|] $\quad$ means *must choose one* of the components separated within the brackets.

$\quad$ { } $\quad$ means *iterations of* the component enclosed.

$\quad$ ( ) $\quad$ means the enclosed component is *optional.*

$\quad$ ** $\quad$ comment (held between asterisks).

An instructor colleague of mine once told a class, 'You can define anything with this notation'. A delegate, who had been particularly difficult all week, quickly interjected, 'OK then how about "supreme pleasure"?'. Not usually one to be stuck for words, the instructor found himself dumbfounded. After a few moments of embarrassed silence, the delegate took pity on the instructor's plight and offered this suggestion, 'Try wine, woman and song'. This naturally led to some interesting developments:

$\quad$ Supreme Pleasure = Wine + Woman + Song

became

$\quad$ Supreme Pleasure = Wine + Woman + (Song)

which became

$\quad$ Supreme Pleasure = Wine + {Woman} + (Song)

which became

$\quad$ Supreme Pleasure = Wine + {Person} + (Song)
$\quad$ Person = [Man|Woman]

and so on (I will leave the reader to develop his/her own definition).

More seriously, although it is *possible* to use BNF, the advent of CASE tools has seen its decline throughout the 1980s. In cases of any complexity the notation can become unwieldy and ambiguous, and it is expedient to use an adapted form; examples are included in each appendix.

Also, there are many aspects of meaning of elementary attributes (for example values, ranges, defaults, and so on) that are better understood if they are parameterized.

The definition for Song, for example, would include a statement that this attribute is optional.

A good CASE tool should enable the developer to capture and report both the structure and content of the data dictionary even for the most complex systems by the use of templates for each diagram item and attribute. As we will see in Chapter 12 this can be achieved through clear screen design and the expedient use of 'pop-up' panels and windows, to allow the developer to zoom in to certain areas in more detail. For example, the 'entity' diagram item would have certain parameters (definition, identifier, usage and so on) associated with it which were always captured and displayed in the same template. Attributes for the entity would then be popped-up. The developer would then zoom in on a chosen attribute by popping-up a window to expose its properties.

There are two further important practical points to consider here.

Firstly, *each attribute should only be defined once* as a separate entry in the data dictionary. It may be referenced as a component of several different data flows but *it is actually defined as a component of only one entity* (including associative entities). By insisting on this rule we liberate ourselves from redundancy as a matter of good practice.

Secondly, *expedient use should be made of domains*. A domain is the set of possible values that an attribute is allowed to take. For example, the domain Date might be defined as every Gregorian date from 1900 to 1999. By using domains we gain three advantages:

1. Redundancy of definition is minimized; (Date is defined once in the 'domain base').
2. Comparison of attributes in process logic is facilitated.
3. Much attribute validation logic can be readily modularized by the designer.

I have also found the attribute naming convention 'Entity.Descriptor.Domain' to be extremely useful. An attribute that is part of a data flow can be referenced using a preposition within process specifications; for example: 'Read CLUB using CLUB.NAME from PROVISIONAL PLAYER REGISTRATION' in Figure 5.4.

5.4 Process specification

We have seen that requirements specification must ultimately be rigorous. Process specifications will therefore be required for all lowest level processes.

There are two basic methods of textual process specification which will be briefly discussed: procedural and non-procedural. In addition, there are many graphics tools which can be usefully employed; examples are decision tables, decision trees and graphs. As these have received so much attention in the literature I have not found it appropriate to discuss them here. Suffice it to say that very often the most concise and unambiguous statements of business policy are to be found in existing documentation and the analyst is best advised simpy to 'lift' the relevant documents rather than reinvent the wheel. Finally, provision of examples from the user's environment as a glossary to the process specification can be tremendously useful in demonstrating clearly that the problem is properly understood.

The approach recommended here operates on two levels. The first level is 'process description' and serves as a profile of the process in terms of its business objectives and required data. The second level is actually 'process specification' itself and serves as documentation of detailed business logic.

It is the process specifications that define precisely how input is transformed into output by referencing, via the process descriptions, terms defined in the data dictionary with all trace of abstraction finally removed.

5.4.1 Process description

An example process description for Provisionally Register Player is shown as Figure 5.3. Notice that all capitalized terms represent data dictionary entries.

The section 'Process objectives' is vitally important: it is intended for any interested user who needs to know what the process is for without having to examine it in detail. It also serves as an initial sounding board that the analyst is 'on the right track'.

In contrast, 'Process views' acts as an inventory of required data as shown. This section declares all flows, stores, entities, associative relationships, and relationships used by the process. It has to be said that there is redundancy here in that much of this information is derivable via the DFD. However, components of the ERD (entities, associative entities and relationships) used by the process are readily viewable here in a way which they are not from the DFD; they are only derivable via data store definitions from the DFD.

More importantly perhaps, the way in which the process actually uses ERD components is also listed; for example, in Figure 4.3 we see that the process Provisionally Register Player is responsible for creating the associative entity Club Membership. This information will be used later in systems design as a basis upon which to construct primitive database modules.

Finally, the 'Process views' section acts as a bank of declaratives: a base-line from which the process specification itselt can be built.

Process objective: To set up provisional membership and produce a membership card and registration request for a player joining a club.

Process views:

    Flows in : PROVISIONAL PLAYER REGISTRATION REQUEST

    Flows out: PLAYER REGISTRATION REQUEST
                    MEMBERSHIP CARD
                    ERROR MESSAGE

    Entities   : CLUB (*read*)
                 PLAYER (*read, create*)
                 SPORTS AUTHORITY (*read*)

    Associative entities: CLUB MEMBERSHIP (*create*)

    Relationships: SPORTS AUTHORITY *LICENSES* CLUB (*read*)

Algorithms:

    Allocate Player.Id

    Allocate Club.Number

Figure 5.3 Process description for 2.1 Provisionally Register Player.

Similarly, the need for reusable process logic is documented under the 'Algorithms' heading. For example, Allocate Player Id is an algorithm the details of which we may choose to suspend until systems design. By documenting the need for it here we achieve two things. Firstly, we avoid cluttering the process specification with unnecessary detail, and, secondly, the algorithm has been isolated as reusable.

Although not shown in the example, it is also useful to include definitions of items which are local to the specification. Examples are temporary storage items like accumulators and complex logic which is partitioned under a separate name to avoid repetition within the main body of the specification itself.

5.4.2   Procedural process specification

Procedural process specifications are written in some form of structured language, which will provide keywords to structure logic in terms of the following:

☐ *Imperative sentences*; for example, create, read, match, issue.
☐ *Decision constructs*; for example, if, else.
☐ *Control constructs*; for example, next, exit.
☐ *Repetition constructs*; for example, for each, while, until.
☐ *Arithmetic operations*; for example, add, divide.
☐ *Boolean operations*; or, not, greater than.
☐ *Qualifiers*; from, using, referencing, with.

The convention used here is to declare all data dictionary entries used in the process views section of the process description and to capitalize these within the specification itself.

An example procedural process specification is shown in Figure 5.4 for the process previously described in Figure 5.3. There is often a problem in specifications of this type with long-winded attribute names. To avoid this I have used the convention that whenever attributes are used the owning entity name is left blank (it is inherited by virtue of a qualifier; for example 'from'). Relationship navigation can present similar difficulties. Therefore the 'referencing' clause has been used in conjunction with participating entities, instead of naming the relationship itself. Finally, wherever data flows are issued, the attributes contained therein are by definition inherited from their owning entities. This again helps with conciseness.

The great attraction of procedural specifications is best summed up by saying that they can be walked through with rigour. Their limited grammar and vocabulary and 'step by step' nature provide the analyst with a potentially simple yet very exact means of recording requirements, which is *testable*. Secondly, the fact that procedural process specifications have their roots in program structures which appear in block structured languages means that they are easily implementable. Having written a requirements specification in structured language it is a relatively simple step to generate working code, as witnessed by the rapidly growing number of CASE tools with code generators that come as 'part of the package'.

There is, however, a big gap between procedural process specifications which are well written and those that are not. Although the grammar and vocabulary are simple enough, in the wrong hands they can lead to a convoluted and unreadable mess. Any reader who has had the misfortune of debugging a program full of heavily nested 'if' statements will appreciate this. Action diagrams which conveniently bracket logic to provide a neater partitioning can be useful here. An example for the same Provisionally Register Player process is shown in Figure 5.5. The reader is referred to Martin and McClure (1985) for a detailed account.

For each PROVISIONAL PLAYER REGISTRATION

    Read CLUB using CLUB.NAME from PROVISIONAL PLAYER
    REGISTRATION
    If not found
        Issue Error Message = 'Club Not Found'
        Exit

    If matching SPORTS AUTHORITY referencing CLUB
        Next Statement
    Else
        Issue Error Message = 'Licensing Sports Authority Not Found'
        Exit

    If PROVISIONAL PLAYER REGISTRATION has PLAYER.ID present
        Read PLAYER using PLAYER.ID
        If not found
            Issue Error Message = 'Player Not Found'
            Exit
        Else
            Next Statement
    Else
        Create PLAYER with ID set using Allocate Player.Id
            NAME, BIRTH.DATE, address from
            PROVISIONAL PLAYER REGISTRATION

    Create CLUB MEMBERSHIP referencing PLAYER and CLUB with
        NUMBER set using Allocate Club.Number
        JOINING.DATE from PROVISIONAL PLAYER REGISTRATION
        STATUS = 'PROVISIONAL'

    Issue PLAYER REGISTRATION REQUEST

    Issue MEMBERSHIP CARD

Figure 5.4 Procedural specification for 2.1 Provisionally Register Player:
structured language.

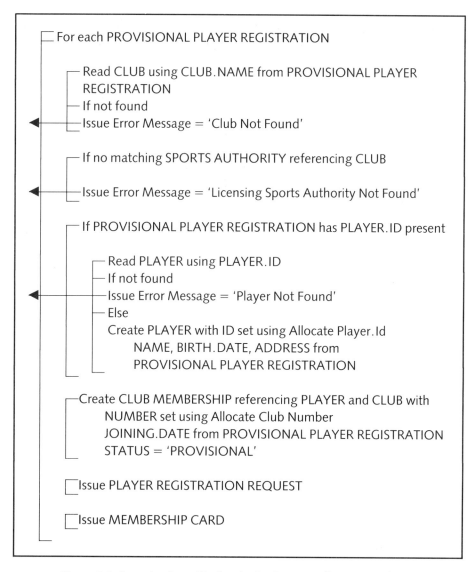

Figure 5.5 Procedural specification for 2.1 Provisionally Register Player:
action diagram.

5.4.3 Non-procedural process specification

Another problem of procedural specification is that because it can look very much like code, there is always the danger that the analyst focusses attention on constructing a clever solution to an assumed business problem, without thinking sufficiently about the problem itself. Analysts can become absorbed in the intricacies of information access (shall I read serially or random?) rather than asking pertinent questions about user requirements. CASE tools can sometimes serve to reinforce this danger.

Pre- and post-conditions are a means of tackling this problem by focussing the analyst's attention on what the process must achieve rather than the means of achieving it. This is very much in the spirit of Ward and Mellor's (1985) earlier definition of an essential model describing what a system must do regardless of the technology used.

Let me illustrate the operative principle by means of an example. If you were asked to write a procedural specification of Calculate Square Root there are several ways in which you could do it: use logarithmic tables, apply mathematical series . . . , and so on. (Actually, you would probably use a calculator.) Notice that what you would in fact be doing would be finding a *means* to the end of Calculate Square Root. This is a very short step from considering how to implement a solution, the calculator being an extreme case in point, before fully understanding the problem. Pre- and post-conditions would cut through this difficulty as follows:

☐ Pre-condition 1: X occurs, where X is not less than zero.
☐ Post-condition 1: The square root of X is produced.

Pre- and post-conditions always come in pairs, and there can be any number of pairs. Usually there are one or two pairs for normal processing with remaining pairs reserved for error and exception situations. To complete the above example, we would add a second pair as follows:

☐ Pre-condition 2: X occurs, where X is less than zero.
☐ Pre-condition 2: An error message is produced.

A pre-condition represents a 'photograph' of input flows and stores before process execution; the post-condition represents a 'photograph' of output flows and stores after the process has executed. Nothing is said regarding the behaviour of the process itself: to do that would require a movie rather than a photograph. Hence this is sometimes referred to as 'external' specification in contrast to procedural or 'internal' specification.

Whereas, in the case of a square root the problem is intuitively understood, we do not have this luxury with the problems of business analysis. We can consider a more complex example of a non-procedural specification as shown in Figure 5.6, for the same process as specified procedurally in Figure 5.4.

Notice that the language used is passive. It is matters of fact that are being described here. That is where the rigour comes from. Again the convention used here is to declare all information used in the process views section of the process description and to capitalize it within the specification itself.

Pre-condition 1: A PROVISIONAL PLAYER REGISTRATION occurs with PLAYER.ID
present for which:
There is a matching PLAYER
There is a matching CLUB
There is a matching SPORTS AUTHORITY with relationship
LICENSES to CLUB

Post-condition 1: There is a CLUB MEMBERSHIP referencing PLAYER and CLUB with
NUMBER calculated using Allocate Club.Number
JOINING.DATE from PROVISIONAL PLAYER REGISTRATION
STATUS = 'PROVISIONAL'
A PLAYER REGISTRATION REQUEST is issued
A MEMBERSHIP CARD is issued

Pre-condition 2: A PROVISIONAL PLAYER REGISTRATION occurs with PLAYER.ID not
present for which
There is no matching PLAYER
There is a matching CLUB
There is a matching SPORTS AUTHORITY with relationship
LICENSES to CLUB

Post-condition 2: There is a PLAYER with ID calculated using Allocate Player.Id
NAME, BIRTH.DATE, ADDRESS from
PROVISIONAL PLAYER REGISTRATION
There is a CLUB MEMBERSHIP referencing PLAYER and CLUB with
NUMBER calculated using Allocate Club.Number
JOINING.DATE from PROVISIONAL PLAYER REGISTRATION
STATUS = 'PROVISIONAL'
A PLAYER REGISTRATION REQUEST is issued
A MEMBERSHIP CARD is issued

Pre-condition 3: A PROVISIONAL PLAYER REGISTRATION occurs with PLAYER.ID present
for which:
There is no matching PLAYER

Post-condition 3: An Error Message is issued stating 'Player Not Found'

Pre-condition 4: A PROVISIONAL PLAYER REGISTRATION occurs for which:
There is no matching club
and Pre-conditon 3 = false

Post-condition 4: An Error Message is issued stating 'Club Not Found'

Pre-condition 5: A PROVISIONAL PLAYER REGISTRATION occurs for which:
There is a matching CLUB and
No matching SPORTS AUTHORITY with relationship LICENSES to CLUB and
Pre-condition 3 = false

Post-condition 5: An Error Message is issued stating 'Sports Authority Not Found'

Figure 5.6 Non-procedural specification for 2.1 Provisionally Register Player.

Another attraction of this approach is that individual pairs of pre- and post-conditions can be studied in their own right; we can focus on certain details without being swamped by irrelevancies. This also lends itself very well later to testing of process logic in that values can be set up corresponding to the pre-conditions and test results then compared against the relevant post-condition.

Perhaps the greatest difficulty with this approach lies in the phraseology. Where there is complex sequencing or matching conditions this can prove extremely unwieldy. Indeed, the example shown in Figure 5.6 stretches use of the technique further than one would practically want to go. However, we can adopt a useful tactic here: package all pre- and post-conditions referring to error processing into a single generic pair. In the example, pairs 3, 4 and 5 could be packaged thus:

☐ Pre-condition 3: Pre-condition 1 and/or Pre-condition 2 fails.
☐ Post-condition 3: An error message is issued stating the problem.

More generally it is often necessary for the systems analyst to deal with error processing in this way where the detail is such as to obscure the mainstream business logic. Moreover, other approaches such as prototyping are often much more suitable to establishing business policy regarding errors.

5.5   Integration rules

For the requirements specification to be totally rigorous it is necessary for the behavioural model to be fully integrated. This requires two basic types of integration rule:

1. *Levelling rules* which concern consistency within diagrams of the *same* type.
2. *Balancing rules* which concern consistency between diagrams of different types.

Integration rules are enforced through the data dictionary. With paper-based structured techniques this often proved so laborious that it rendered their application self-defeating. CASE tools come into their own here. However, integration should not be seen as a final check at the 'end' of the project, rather like compiling a program prior to testing it. A good CASE tool should support the analyst by enforcing integration rules as part of modelling itself, and by providing integration tools (such as matrices). This topic is discussed in Chapter 12.

5.5.1 Levelling rules

The principle of levelling DFDs and STDs was discussed in Chapter 4. The discussion here is confined to the rules used which are simply listed.

- ☐ Each solid bubble on the set of DFDs must be associated with a lower level DFD or with a process specification but not both. (Note that conversely each process specification must refer to a bottom level bubble; inputs and output flows must match between the DFD bubble and its process specification which may only reference attributes defined in the data dictionary within entities contained within stores as referenced by the DFD bubble. This is achieved through the process description described in Section 5.3.1.)
- ☐ Each control bubble must be at the bottom level.
- ☐ Data and control flows input to and output from a bubble must be equivalent to those at the lower level (representing the explosion of the bubble). Where flows have been packaged this is achieved by defining the packaged flow as the optional concatenation of certain flows from the adjacent level. For example, we choose to package the flows Register Volume Increment and Register Cost Increment from Figure 0 for the Petrol Sale Control System shown in Figure 5.7 at context level as follows:

Register Increments = (Register Volume Increment) + (Register Cost Increment)

- ☐ Data stores used by a bubble must be equivalent to those used at the lower level. Where data stores have been packaged this is achieved by defining the packaged data store as a concatenation of lower level data stores; for example, if a combined data store were introduced at a higher level in the same example the definition would be:

Pump Blends = Pumps + Petrol Blends

- ☐ Control stores used by a bubble must be equivalent to those used at the lower level.

We have seen that levelling of DFDs causes STDs to become effectively buried at the lowest level in the control processes. In effect therefore the STD is levelled via the DFD: no separate rules are required.

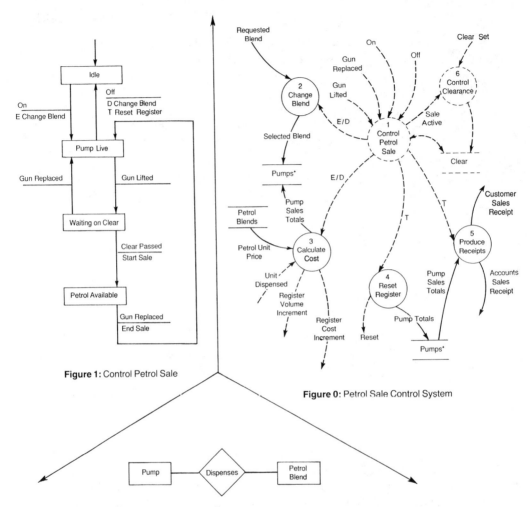

Figure 1: Control Petrol Sale

Figure 0: Petrol Sale Control System

Figure 5.7 Petrol Sale Control System: DFD/STD/ERD.

5.5.2 Balancing rules

Just as levelling rules are required to ensure consistency between different levels of DFD, so rules are also needed for balancing different *types* of diagram. In this section we will discuss these rules with reference to Figure 5.7 which collectively shows the three dimensions of the Petrol Control System.

The STD is embodied by the control bubble of the DFD; indeed, the figure number and name of the STD are inherited from those on the corresponding control bubble. Consistency must be ensured between the two as follows:

☐ Each control flow consumed by the control bubble must correspond to at least one condition (or part of a complex condition) on the STD; conversely each condition (or part of a complex condition) on the STD must correspond to a control flow consumed by the control bubble on the DFD. For example, 'On' is both a condition on the STD and a control flow consumed by control Bubble 1.

☐ Each control flow produced by the control bubble must correspond to at least one action (or part of a complex action) on the STD; conversely each action (or part of a complex action) on the STD must correspond to a control flow produced by the control bubble on the DFD. For example, Trigger Reset Register is a part of an action on the STD which corresponds to a control flow produced by control Bubble 1.

Complex conditions and actions should be defined in the data dictionary. The definitions for Start Sale and End Sale are shown again below:

Start Sale = Do in order: T Reset register
          D Change blend
          E Calculate cost
          R Sale active

End Sale = Do in order: D Calculate cost
          T Produce receipts
          E Change blend
          L Sale active

(Note, it is also possible to specify 'do concurrrently' against component actions).

☐ Each control store is associated with:
 (a) a waiting state and a pass condition on a receiving STD, and
 (b) a 'set' action on a transmitting STD, or an incoming control flow associated with an event, in which case we would choose not to model the transmitting STD as it would be trivial.

Conversely each waiting state and subsequent 'pass' condition on an STD and each 'set' action on an STD is associated with a control store on the DFD.

Similarly, the ERD is embodied in the data stores of the DFD; indeed, as a general rule data store names are the plural of the corresponding entity names. The reason for this is that a data store represents sets of entity *occurrences*. However, the situation here is a little more tricky, and sometimes misunderstood. Therefore, without wishing to labour the point, we shall spend a little longer on this.

Consistency must be ensured as follows (the term 'entity' here includes associative entities and entity super/subtypes):

☐ At the lowest level of DFDs each data store must correspond to either:
  (a) occurrences of a single entity; for example Pumps = {Pump}, or
  (b) occurrences of a group of entities; for example, we might replace the two data stores with a combined data store, Pump Blends = {Pump} + {Petrol Blend}.
☐ Conversely each entity must correspond to either:
  (a) a single data store, or
  (b) a component entity defined as grouped within a data store.

The quest for absolute rigour sometimes tempts developers into imposing a much tighter version of these rules: 'there should be a *one-to-one* correspondence between each data store at the lowest level DFD and each entity *and relationship* on the ERD'. From a 'textbook' viewpoint this might seem reasonable. Despite the laudability of this aim, I would caution against it because in practical project work it leads to confusing and unwelcome results. For example, if we make this rule, the relationship Dispenses will correspond to a data store Dispensations; this is confusing in that nothing is actually *stored* there and is unwelcome in that it introduces a somewhat bizarre irrelevance into the DFD: 'What on earth is a *dispensation?*' you can imagine the puzzled user asking.

A practical way around this problem is to introduce the following rule, again at the lowest level of DFD:

☐ Each data store inherits all relationship occurrences connected between occurrences of entities defined as grouped within that data store. For example, if the data stores were replaced with a combined data store as above, Pump Blends = {Pump} + {Petrol Blend} then all occurrences of the Dispenses relationship are inherited by Pump Blends by definition.
☐ Where more than one data store is accessed by the same process that process has access to all relationship occurrences obtaining between any occurrences of entities defined as grouped within any of those data stores, providing the relationship is declared in the process description. For example, Calculate Cost has access to all occurrences of the Dispenses relationship but Change Blend does not.

Thus, in effect, data stores are convenient 'windows' into portions of the ERD, and the DFD retains its true purpose of modelling data *flow*, leaving the ERD to the business of modelling essential data *structure*.

Although there are intimate connections between STD and DFD and between ERD and DFD there is really no counterpart between STD and ERD. We shall see later, however, that the STD can be usefully adapted to model entity state changes.

5.6   Verifying system requirements

Process specifications are a necessary basis upon which to launch software design: they provide the 'nuts and bolts' from which eventual working code must be constructed. However, although they form a large part of the documentation of user requirements they are often not the best medium for *verifying* system requirements. There are three basic media, shown in Figure 5.8, through which verification may take place:

1. The essential model itself.
2. Prototyping.
3. External design.

We will look at each in turn.

In Chapter 2 we saw that building effective systems requires an organic approach. That means emancipating ourselves from the waterfall lifecycle in order to cope with the demands of iteration. Verification and review should not therefore be seen as 'once-off' activities which are applied to a tome-like specification. They are on-going activities which will require perhaps working on portions of a system which may be at varying degrees of completion. Thus, for example, it may be that there are three different groups of users each reviewing a different portion of a system, with respect to the three media:

1. Essential model for portion A.
2. Prototypes of portion B.
3. External design for portion C.

Without going into the logistics of managing different sub-projects, it is important to make one salient point here: we must liberate ourselves from the notion that before proceeding any further we must complete the essential model in its entirety, rather like compiling a program before testing it. Real-life, I suggest, is much more mercurial. However, for convenience of expression I shall use the term 'essential model' to include a portion of, as well as a whole essential model, throughout the rest of this chapter.

5.6.1   Verifying requirements through the essential model

In some environments, where it is possible for users to verify the essential model directly, a specification deliverable can be formed for review using appropriate components of the underlying essential model plus a few supporting explanatory paragraphs. The following is a typical organization:

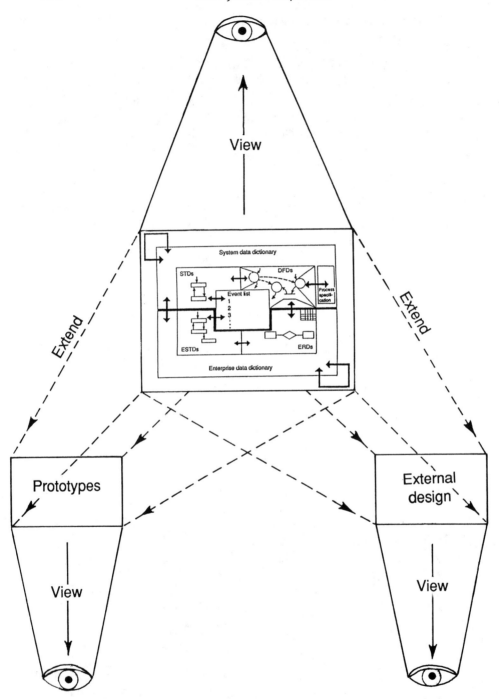

Figure 5.8 Verifying system requirements.

☐ Section 1: Introduction and statement of purpose.
☐ Section 2: Context diagram and event list.
☐ Section 3: DFDs with STDs presented opposite the appropriate control DFDs; ERD.
☐ Section 4: Process specifications.
☐ Section 5: Data dictionary.

An example of such a requirements specification for the Petrol Sale Control System is included in Appendix 3.

Sometimes one simply has no choice but to use a requirements specification for verification as for example in the case of a software house which has been requested by a client to build a fully detailed essential specification of requirements. However, there should be 'no surprises', in that users should have gained familiarity and been heavily involved at the exploration and organization stages of model building. More usually there is a choice: criteria to guide in the making of this decision are included in Chapter 8.

5.6.2   Verifying requirements through prototyping

I have stressed the importance of well-written process specifications. However, even where the specification has been written well and is clearly understood by the users there remains one very real danger irrespective of whether a procedural or non-procedural approach has been taken: *we do not adequately anticipate the evolution of requirements that occurs as users gain experience with a system.* In Chapter 8 I will outline some of the conditions under which prototyping can be appropriate and in Chapters 10 and 11 a prototyping strategy is discussed. For now, let me just consider a particularly common example where prototyping is useful.

It is especially difficult to minimize uncertainty about requirements where a system centres heavily on error and exception processing: the 'What if so and so happens?' types of consideration. For example, in the case of Provisionally Register Player, should there be some sort of check to prevent the same player being inserted twice by searching all occurrences of the Player entity to see if one exists with the name and date of birth input issuing a warning 'Player may already be on file' if this is the case? If we start addressing such issues in the process specification it can become 'top-heavy' with details which detract from the essential business logic. If we ignore them we run the risk of a re-work later on.

It is perhaps ironic in that where a process specification is well written it can sometimes appear a lot more straightforward than it really is. Even though a user may appear to agree it does not encourage him or her to think or flush out potential changes. This can encourage a false optimism that brings the project down with a bump when full implications are realized later on, say, in the testing phase.

5.6.3   Verifying requirements through external design

Often it is necessary at least to sketch an external design of the system in order to verify requirements. Roughly speaking that means a high-level view of architecture plus examples of what the system will look like in terms of screen and report layouts; I will explain exactly what I mean by 'external design' in the next section.

There are two further reasons for constructing an external design earlier rather than later:

☐ Firstly, we shall see that distributed solutions can present particular difficulties in that sections of process logic can change dramatically according
to mapping not only of processes but also of entities. This involves considering the proposed external design of the system.

☐ Secondly, processes that appeared 'essential' when discussing process
specifications may sometimes be dropped when the user becomes aware of
the cost of actually developing and running software to run those processes. Again such cost-benefit decisions can only sensibly be made once we
have a clear idea of the proposed solution in terms of external design. In
these cases the behavioural model would need to be modified and perhaps
the statement of purpose adjusted to remove the superfluous processes.

5.7   External design: functional specification

External design involves applying implementation constraints to the behavioural model with the objective of establishing the following:

☐ Overall system architecture.
☐ System 'appearance' in terms of screen and report layouts.
☐ Cost-benefit analysis

Candidate architectures are considered in terms of *processors* and modelled using a DFD; at the highest level a processor may be a computer or it may be manual. At a lower level it may be classed according to its role, as shown in Figure 5.9 for the Player Administration System; this is known as a 'Processor DFD'.

We have to decide which processors are going to be responsible for executing which processes and for storing which data. The following components of the behavioural model are therefore mapped to each candidate architecture:

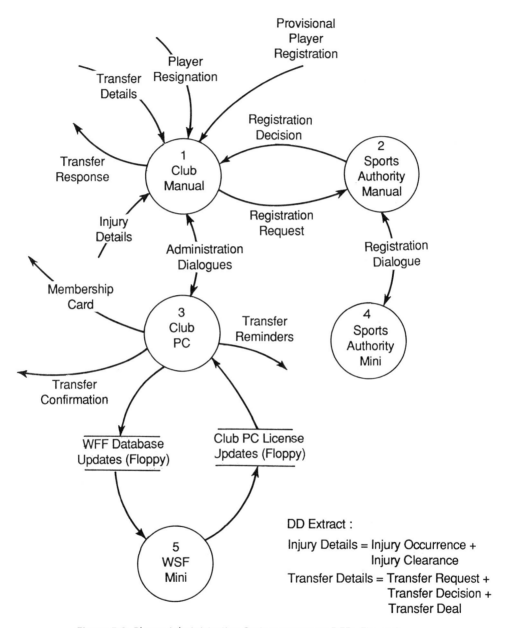

Figure 5.9 Player Administration System processor DFD: Figure 0.

☐ All lowest level processes (including control processes; and therefore by definition STDs); indication should be provided of mode of running (for example, batch or online).

☐ All entities, associative entities and relationships; indication should be provided of mode of storage (for example, flat file or DBMS). An account of how the ERD is actually mapped to a target DBMS is included in Chapter 9.

The mapping to processors can be shown in one of two ways: either by a simple list or by 'cut and paste' of the appropriate DFD and ERD, the latter forming a 'processor ERD' for each processor. Note that it is possible for components to be fragmented and/or duplicated across different processors.

The need for supporting software (for example, DBMS, TP monitors and operating systems) and hardware (for example, message switchers) must also be identified, and documented along with other constraints and the above mapping details as it will be necessary to quantify costs.

For each candidate architecture, screen and report layouts are drawn up to give the user an idea of what the system is actually going to look like from his or her point of view. The level of detail here can vary from rough outlines to detailed specification of key fields. Cost-benefit analyses are finally made for each candidate architecture, the objective being for the user to choose the best value for money.

As mentioned above, distributed solutions can present particular difficulties in that sections of process logic can change dramatically according to mapping not only of processes but also of entities. For example, different portions of the ERD for the Player Administration System have been mapped to different processors which will cause a corresponding fragmentation of process logic. The reader is again referred to Appendix 2 where Record Registration is duplicated across Club PC and Sports Authority Mini; notice, for example, that there is no longer a need to access the Club entity on the processor ERD for the Club PC.

Again, I suggest that processes that appeared 'essential' when discussing process specifications may sometimes be dropped when the user becomes aware of the cost of actually developing and running software to run those processes. Recording of player injury details might be a case in point. The question 'Is there a more cost-effective way of doing this process?' should always be asked.

A functional specification would typically include appropriate elements of the behavioural model plus the following details of the chosen architecture:

☐ Processor DFD.
☐ Mappings for each processor.
☐ Screen and report layouts.
☐ Cost-benefit analysis.
☐ Constraints.

An example of a functional specification is included for the Player Administration System in Appendix 2.

5.8 Summary

We have seen that one of the major objectives of specification is to remove all ambiguities from our organized understanding of requirements. However, the close interdependence between specifying and verifying requirements requires a distinction between specification as a base for documentation and eventual system building and specification as a means of verifying requirements.

Project failures often seem to be caused by a neglect of this basic distinction. Too often the essential model is used blindly as *the* means of verification, without thinking of other approaches. One of two things occurs in these cases: either we find users unable or unwilling to verify requirements; or users appear to concur on requirements only to back-track later on.

Therefore whilst the main objective of this chapter has been to explain the textual components of the essential model in conceptual terms, I have made an effort to offer some salient pointers on the topic of verification. This necessitated a final, brief excursion into external design.

PART THREE

The
Strategic
Perspective

This part of the book looks at applying the recommended toolset, within the organic lifecycle, from the viewpoint of the business objectives of an enterprise. The strategic perspective, highlighted in Figure B opposite, is presented as an imperative for effective systems development. From the viewpoint of our modelling framework this means rationally *determining* which systems are to be developed before embarking on detailed requirement definition.

We shall see in Chapter 6 that this involves developing systems which are corporately cohesive in a way which is both flexible and responsive. Architectural approaches are therefore not suitable. We need to keep to short timescales and maintain senior management interest. A two-pronged approach is recommended.

First, we need to create a broad platform on which requirement definition work can be effectively scoped, planned and budgetted for with respect to the needs of the organization as a whole. This is known as global modelling and is discussed in Chapter 7.

Second, we need to provide advanced information on those areas, drawn from the global model, about which we are least certain. Such research work aims to lift the cover off a proposed system and data, or it may provide more detailed enterprise wide information. This is known as systems reconaissance and is discussed in Chapter 8.

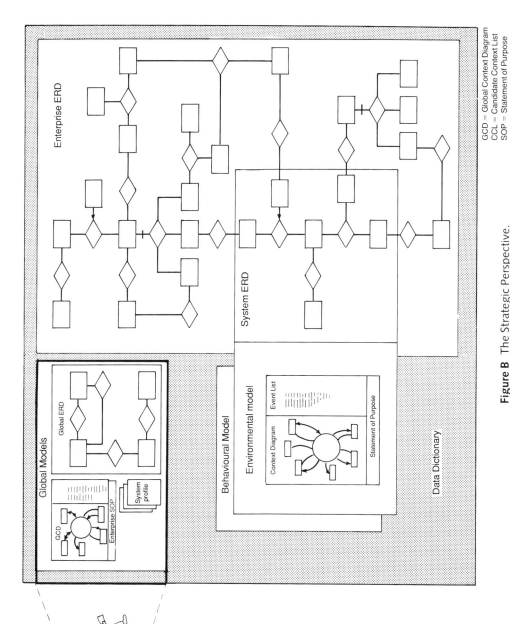

Figure B The Strategic Perspective.

GCD = Global Context Diagram
CCL = Candidate Context List
SOP = Statement of Purpose

CHAPTER 6

The strategic approach

As I see it, a healthy flow of information separates winning organizations from losers.

ARNO PENZIAS
Ideas and Information

6.1 Introduction

We read increasingly today of the importance of developing systems strategically. Structured techniques, it is often argued, are lacking in this respect. What exactly do we mean by 'strategy'? First and foremost this often means different things to different people; various terms are bandied about: business strategy, systems strategy, strategy planning, technical strategy, strategic methods, strategic requirements, corporate strategy . . . , and so on. On the one hand there are organizations which regard a hardware and software selection exercise followed up by a CASE front-end to systems development as constituting a strategy study. This type of approach concentrates on technology at the expense of business requirements. At the other extreme studies into potential business markets using the latest market analysis techniques often ignore the computing side. The term seems open to a number of interpretations and yet has assumed larger and larger importance.

Whilst part of the purpose of this chapter is to untangle some of this terminology, the major objective is to clarify the underlying requirement by developing the concept of the *strategic perspective*. This is more an attitude or disposition toward systems development which is influenced by three dominant needs, each of which will be explained more fully in the next section:

1. To develop information as a corporate asset.
2. To develop systems which support business objectives.
3. To develop systems which are corporately cohesive.

The alleged failures of structured techniques are highlighted as essentially failures of application with respect to the strategic perspective.

After clarifying the important related concept of business strategy, architectural application of structured techniques is explained and considered as a popularized alternative. Such approaches have become attractive because they promise to serve the three dominant needs of the strategic perspective whilst cementing management commitment to a well organized and planned approach to system development. However, it is argued that architectural approaches fail firstly because they are not responsive enough to cope with the management demand to deliver on time and within budget. Secondly, they lack the flexibility necessary to cater for an increasing diversity of user requirements. Indeed, the importance of these two demands will cause us to revise our earlier characterization of the strategic perspective itself.

Structured techniques are reconsidered with respect to the requirements of the strategic perspective. In short an *organic* approach is recommended, as opposed to the architectural or inorganic approach. We shall see that this recognizes both the value of applying structured techniques at strategic level and the value of strategic application of structured techniques at system level. Structured techniques should not be seen as ends in themselves. They are a means to an end: to serve as tools with the overall objective of producing more effective systems.

6.2   The strategic perspective: a first look

What do we mean by 'strategy'? A first look at Webster's New International Dictionary (1966) yields the following definition:

> 'A careful plan or method or a clever stratagem. The art of devising or employing plans or stratagems towards a goal.'
> OK, so what's a stratagem?
> 'A cleverly contrived trick or scheme for gaining an end.'

Military connotations abound in dictionaries. In fact, closer inspection reveals that the word στρατηγά means office or command of a general; it breaks into two roots: στρατυς meaning army and ἄγειν meaning to lead, and as στρατηγυς came to mean either a commander in chief or a chief magistrate in Athens. Although in the present context at least this may not be very helpful, we will see later that the original definitions manifest themselves in the contemporary need to create blueprints of corporate policy from which systems development can be directed like a military campaign. Indeed, we shall see that this is just what the architectural approach discussed later actually seeks to do. However, this rather misses the point. It describes *how* rather than *what*. To find the essential requirements (borrowing an important earlier term) we need to pick up each of the three dominant requirements identified in the introduction to this chapter and examine each in turn.

Develop information as a corporate asset

Historically, the first areas of enterprises in which applications were developed were operational areas, corresponding to the lower layer of the traditional management pyramid (Anthony, 1965) shown in Figure 6.1. Problem definitions in these areas were not too difficult to elicit. There were definite, repetitive tasks to be done, the steps of which could be specified using some form of structured techniques. The tasks were also voluminous. Therefore, the payback of automating them was clear.

As computers have become cheaper and more powerful, applications have moved 'upward' through the levels of the pyramid to aid management at increasingly high levels. This entails providing better quality information faster. For

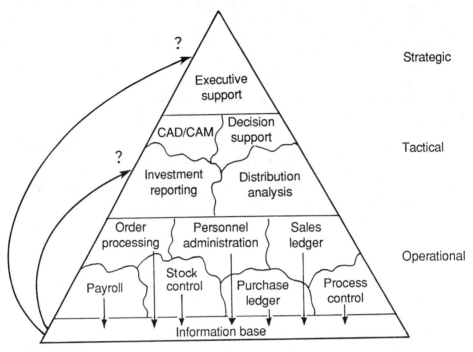

Figure 6.1 The management pyramid.

example, 'Tell me the effects of reducing the price of this product by this much for this customer on expected quarterly profits for this region by this afternoon's meeting'. The data required to service such *ad hoc* enquiries has always been collected at operational level. However, only if this information is well organized across the enterprise is it also immediately accessible. Otherwise, by the time it is produced the business opportunity which prompted its requisition may well have disappeared.

We read increasingly, therefore, of the importance of information as an asset. This involves a certain cultural change which is slow, and well-illustrated in the following observations from Ed Yourdon (1986b): 'The real problem is that the organization has never gotten control over its data; it has not yet recognized that data, or information is an asset . . . If you had never heard of gold before, you probably wouldn't be impressed if someone told you that you had a gold mine in your backyard.' Yourdon points out that standard formats for company balance sheets in the USA are regulated by a number of professional bodies according to Generally Accepted Accounting Principles (GAAP): 'And here is the point of all this: the GAAP policies do not allow information to be shown as an asset on the balance sheet. Nor is software shown as an asset. That's the rule. Information is regarded as an intangible asset; only tangible assets are shown on the balance sheet.'

It is perhaps the integral nature of information to the structure of business that makes it difficult to bring the usual measurements to the task of assessing return on investment. However, as Tom DeMarco (1982) wrote, 'You can't control what you can't measure'. As the importance of information grows, and as general expenditure on computing grows within overall budgets, the need to measure and control this asset becomes critical.

Develop systems which support business objectives

Business environments which are becoming increasingly complex and subject to fluctuation reinforce this trend toward 'strategic information'. Information systems are emerging as powerful weapons for creating competitive advantage. A classical example is the development of airline reservation systems. Once they were perceived as operational vehicles for efficient administration of the seat reservation process. Now they are also sales tools. Airlines leasing their systems to travel agents can and do program the systems with a bias – reflected on the major and minor screens seen by users – toward their own flights. Two of the first to do this, in the late 1970s, in the USA were American and United Airlines with the Sabre and Apollo systems respectively. With these systems the two airlines virtually forced out the competition: by the early 1980s American held 41 per cent and United held 39 per cent of the market.

In short, sellers' markets have become buyers' markets: computing decisions have now become business decisions. In the old days computers lived in back rooms crunching on numbers. Today they sit at the interface of enterprise and marketplace. Systems must respond to business objectives: providing quality, superior service, responsiveness to market forces, differentiation and innovation.

Develop systems which are corporately cohesive

Survey after survey demonstrates that enterprises spend around 75 per cent of their computing budgets on maintenance. A high proportion of this figure is normally spent patching interfaces between systems originally built to exploit the technology of the day, developed in a haphazard fashion for individual users under pressure to produce fast results. As emphasized in Chapter 2 there is a need to develop cohesive systems with minimal interfaces and maximum reusability. It was also suggested that to be applied effectively, however, the principle of encapsulation (discussed in Section 2.3) must be applied to the requirements of the enterprise as a whole, and not only at application level, as has often been the case.

It is now realized that systems must reflect an ever increasing strategic perspective. In short, the strategic perspective dictated by the enterprise requires that systems both provide timely information and respond to business objectives. This requires systems which are *holistic*: an integral part of the enterprise servicing corporate business objectives, instead of isolated applications built to service individual users needs. Therefore, we might simplify the initial characterization of the strategic perspective as follows:

☐ An attitude or disposition toward systems development which is influenced by the dominant need for systems which are holistic.

The strategic perspective dictates that in today's intensely competitive marketplace companies are faced with two strongly related challenges:

1. To exploit the rapidly accelerating technological progress which has made the power of computers available to virtually everybody.
2. To support a widening spectrum of commercial activities and to create new business opportunities.

This is fine in theory. However, what about the practicalities? Clearly such an approach involves a huge investment of money and resources. Are we willing to commit the time and money that the strategic perspective requires? Is it not anathema to management's desire to produce fast, cost-effective solutions?

One company's response to these questions was to divide user requirements into two categories. On the one hand there were *strategic* requirements which were considered as having long-term value with respect to a framework of models which had been created for the whole enterprise. They therefore took their place in the queue to build systems in an orderly way within this framework. On the other hand there were *interim* requirements which were perceived as short-term needs for individual users for which throwaway solutions were acceptable. These could therefore be dealt with very much more quickly without the need to ensure integration to the general scheme of things. If you have worked in systems development for any length of time you can probably guess what happened: *all* requirements except the least urgent soon became interim, under pressure from users to get results fast.

Such 'solutions' to the problem are merely cosmetic. They pay lip-service to the need for a strategic approach without really providing one. Clearly, without a sympathetic political environment any attempt at strategy will struggle. However, the problem goes deeper than this. An effective systems strategy implies a revolution in corporate culture. If information is to be developed as an asset we must reinforce the message that it must be quantified as such. Management cannot have their cake and eat it: like any other investment of comparable size careful planning is a necessity.

We might draw an historical parallel by pointing out that during the Industrial Revolution, the companies that made the best job of organizing and planning their resources prospered and grew; the others vanished. Throughout what we might term the Information Revolution the companies that do the best job of organizing and planning their information resources will likewise have the best chance of prospering and growing. Certainly, the strategic perspective demands top management commitment towards systems development in a sense which is all too often lacking, especially in determining what the holistic needs of the organization actually are. This means that top management commit time and money to an effective approach to system building.

We must therefore underwrite the Characterization of the strategic perspective as follows:

> ☐ An attitude or disposition toward systems development which is influenced by the dominant need for systems which are *holistic* and which is *politically sound* in that it is underwritten by top management.

6.3   'Structured techniques are not strategic'

Our devil's advocate will argue that structured techniques fail on both the above counts. Firstly, they do not produce systems which are holistic. Success may occur when they are applied to the development of stand-alone systems, particularly where an existing system needs to be replaced by a more technically efficient system but with similar functionality. In such cases it is relatively straightforward to build a context diagram and event list given a statement of purpose which mirrors existing functionality.

However, even those systems, which at first sight seem stand-alone, often require integrating within a portfolio of systems which does not emerge until the analyst has scratched a little beneath the surface. For example, a real-time system for monitoring performance of domestic water production and continuously feeding results to a man–machine interface, may appear autonomous until it is realized that results must be captured for eventual feedback for analysis by management information systems.

Secondly, despite appearing to be 'structured' many projects are still initiated on the basis of vague objectives, causing a political failure. Because of pressure to 'produce results on time and within budget' projects are again initiated at an operational level. The tight deadlines compromise the analysis which becomes too localized and overlooks shared data structure. The result is a system with too many interface files to other systems, resulting in heavier rather than lighter maintenance, which leads to more user dissatisfaction, which leads to more pressure to build better systems . . . and so on. Use of a CASE tool incorporating the latest techniques may give the developers the comfort of the illusion of truly structured development. In truth, they are caught in a vicious circle. Due to what is sometimes referred to as WISCY syndrome ('Why Isn't Simon/Sally Coding Yet?' Answer: 'Because of the disaster that happened last time!'), there was a failure to look widely enough across the enterprise or deeply enough at all user levels.

Structured techniques, our devil's advocate will conclude, must be applied architecturally. Before considering what this means let us step back for a moment and focus on the concepts of business strategy and systems strategy.

6.4 The concept of business strategy

It is a prerequisite of the strategic perspective that systems development is rooted in business objectives. It is therefore a prerequisite that business objectives are discoverable. A business strategy is a formal means of making this discovery. It can be characterized as an investigation carried out at board level, but involving a senior member or members of the systems department, which steps back and examines the nature and purpose of the enterprise as a whole. An 'enterprise' may be a whole business or a part of that business which could be sold as a unit. A formal deliverable will certainly *include* the following:

- ☐ Mission: *why* the enterprise is in business.
- ☐ Long-term objectives: *where* the enterprise proposes 'to go'.
- ☐ Directions: *how* broadly are the objectives to be achieved.
- ☐ Critical success factors: *what* it is that *must* happen for objectives to be achieved.
- ☐ Performance measures: *what* the progess is in achieving objectives.
- ☐ Inhibitors: *what* it is that could prevent objectives from being achieved.

This is not an exhaustive list. An example will, however, serve to characterize rather than define what is meant:

- ☐ Mission: to fulfil market need for stationery with high quality goods at a reasonable price.
- ☐ Long-term objectives: (a) dividends to be greater than 5 per cent agreed value of shares, and (b) to be in the top three market leaders.

☐ Directions: (a) reorganize the sales office into regional profit centres, and (b) to open up mail order channels for bulk orders.

☐ Critical success factors: (a) management of product distribution, (b) selection of reliable suppliers, and (c) efficient settlement of customer accounts.

☐ Performance measures: (a) expenditure against budget, (b) cost of defects by product type, and (c) sales against quota.

☐ Inhibitors: (a) lack of information support, and (b) increase on stationery duty.

A business strategy will formalize such parameters into a blueprint of corporate policy. Much research continues to be done to investigate the bridgehead between the parameters of business strategy and definition of system requirements. For example, Henderson *et al.* (1984) have stated that:

'Given the magnitude of the investment and the potential for strategic impact, there is a need for a strategic planning methodology that can achieve the following goals:

1. Provide a linkage between the strategic business plan and strategic information systems plan.

2. Provide a means to coordinate the investment in a range of management support systems that are responsive to management needs.

3. Provide a basis for understanding data as a corporate resource through the construct of a strategic data model.'

The paper then extends the concept of critical success factors as a means toward achieving these goals.

In many organizations the business strategy is not explicit. However, there will certainly have been management communication about these matters in some form or other which implies a business strategy. As long as enterprise requirements are tangible we have a source. Either way it is the business strategy which provides the source information which ultimately drives all other activities, including systems development.

6.5 The concept of systems strategy

The essence of a systems strategy is to determine at a high level what requirements exist for the enterprise as a whole. This can be viewed in terms of the original modelling framework as shown in Figure 6.2.

There should therefore be nothing mystical about this, as is sometimes unfortunately implied in the literature. What we are talking about here is nothing

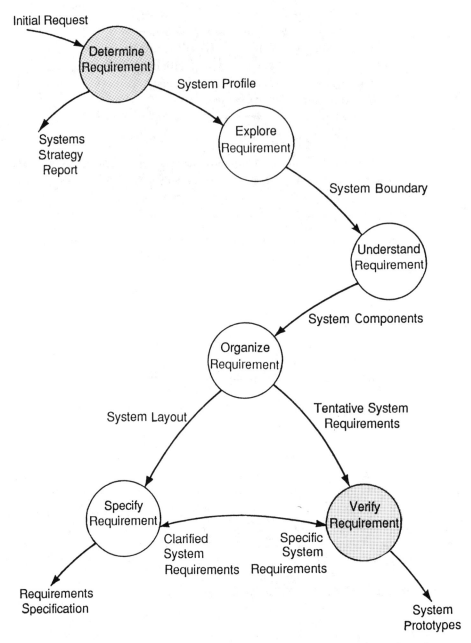

Initial Request

Determine Requirement

Systems Strategy Report

System Profile

Explore Requirement

System Boundary

Understand Requirement

System Components

Organize Requirement

System Layout

Tentative System Requirements

Specify Requirement

Verify Requirement

Clarified System Requirements

Specific System Requirements

Requirements Specification

System Prototypes

Figure 6.2 Determining requirements with respect to the modelling framework.

more than rationalized common sense. Looking at Figure 6.2 the flows in and out of 'Determine requirements' should be understood as follows:

☐ 'Initial request' emanates from the business strategy, described above.
☐ 'Systems strategy report' is a deliverable which is described in this section.
☐ 'System profile' forms the point of departure for individual systems development work. It is described in Section 6.10.2.

First and foremost a systems strategy must meet the requirements of the strategic perspective in that:

(a) It must generate systems which are holistic.
(b) It must provide a firm political foundation.

What then are the deliverables housed within the systems strategy report? Certainly the following would be included:

☐ Strategic models: modelling the data and functions required to support business objectives and grouping data and functions into proposed systems, each of which is outlined within a system profile. Each system profile (see Section 6.10.2) includes a statement of purpose with recommendations as to suitable development techniques.
☐ Technical strategy: a broad statement of resource requirements in terms of proposed hardware, software, and employees. It will figure centrally in design, though less so in analysis where there is a suspension of technical considerations.
☐ Migration strategy: proposals outlining the move from existing systems and databases to the future. Importantly, this will include proposals not only for moving to new technical environments but also to any implied new human organizational structures.
☐ Strategic development plan: a long range plan (typically five years) for the development of systems, normally in the form of Program Evaluation and Review Technique (PERT) and/or bar charts, identifying priorities, establishing resource commitments over time and planning for transition to the new systems, technical environments and organization. Cost-benefit analyses and project profiles (see below Section 6.10.1), would also be provided.

6.6   The architectural approach

The strategic models are commonly referred to by various strategic methodologies as the 'information architecture'. The basic principle of the architectural approach is to develop data and function architectures top-down based upon the business strategy. The data architecture normally consists of E-R models of the corporate data resource; the function architecture normally consists of some form or other of hierarchy diagram, which models different levels of functionality without going into the detail of data flow and storage which would be shown on a DFD.

The technique used here is first to get a 'hazy' picture of the whole and then bring the parts into sharper focus using data analysis techniques based upon normalization for the data architecture and functional decomposition for the function architecture. Various tools, particularly data-function matrices are then used to ensure correlation between the two architectures. At the end of each stage of development deliverables are reviewed before partitioning the problem domain into smaller cohesive subsets, each to be developed through the next phase in its own right and so on.

This approach is apparently very attractive with respect to the strategic perspective. It seems to be holistic: based upon total business objectives, resulting in cohesive systems. It seems to be politically sound: top management commitment can be secured with respect to a blueprint for the enterprise as a whole, and then reinforced at each stage along the road to system realization.

Yet despite the attractions, as one author pointed out, 'even today, the vast majority of applications being developed are defined by and for specific user departments or corporate divisions and give little consideration to the overall business strategy. Is enterprise engineering as elusive and admirable a goal as "peace on earth"? Or is it just more industry hype?' (Roberts, 1989.)

It must be said that this is an intriguingly phrased question. However, before attempting to search for an underlying answer it is important to summarize some of the difficulties the author has experienced with the architectural approach.

The first problem relates to top-down approaches in general. There are always problems with functional decomposition if it is used as the sole technique for function modelling. Even on relatively small systems it is often difficult to obtain concensus amongst analysts and amongst analysts and users as to what the primary functions actually are. If you have a cake it is possible to divide it any number of ways. Applied at corporate level this problem becomes exacerbated to such an extent that the only court of appeal is the existing organization chart. However, this brings us full circle: it will not do simply to seek to reorganize existing applications because it is the very way in which processes and data were grouped into programs and files within applications which are actually causing the problem. Analysis of these systems, if it took place at all, was very much geared to making optimum use of the, often limited, technology of the day.

Furthermore, in mapping out the hierarchy of business functions one is normally forced to model at least four levels of function because of the problem of scale.

Things start to get complex. Having spent much time developing this architecture, after a while analysts and users alike become reluctant to change it, under the pressure to meet deadlines. This can result in the very real danger that the function architecture is cast in stone before we have had time to delve deeper and to understand it more fully, with a view to minimizing interfaces. To put this another way, if what is to count as a function is determined by how cohesive that function is, we will have to examine the interfaces of that function. This means scouting ahead and doing some detailed investigations. However, the architectural approach makes no allowance for this: what you see is what you get.

This problem also applies to the data architecture. The intention of the data architecture is essentially high-level. However, it is impossible to understand data structure without considering attributes; they are after all the very stuff of the model. In order to determine whether or not an entity is genuine it is necessary by definition to consider its attributes. In mapping out a data architecture, therefore, it is virtually impossible to avoid at least some detailed consideration of attributes. Experience teaches that there is a real danger that, before we know it, we are embarked on a normalization exercise for all corporate data (see Section 9.8). Building a construction of such scale, before considering system requirements in any detail, makes it virtually impossible to keep pace with business change and with developing perceptions of users and analysts. Again, there is the danger of casting the data architecture in stone before it has been fully understood.

One of the major attractions of the architectural approach is that it is aimed at providing tangible evidence of management commitment to a well organized and planned approach to building systems. However, this political soundness can soon be eroded by the failure to meet deadlines and produce results. The architectural nature itself is both a strength and a weakness. It is a strength in that it provides a framework for systems development which is rooted in business strategy and management commitment. It is a weakness in that either we are forced to define a pattern of business policy before we have had a chance to understand that policy sufficiently, or we succumb to analysis paralysis. In the first case, uncohesive systems may evolve which do not service business objectives, resulting in loss of political mandate. In the second case, by the time the systems strategy is produced the assumptions upon which it was based have significantly changed: a failure to produce results will again result in loss of political mandate. In short, the architectural approach is not *responsive* enough.

The architectural approach also tends to foster the view that all systems are ultimately of one type, often database, rather than allowing individual types of system to be developed on their merits. For example, an information modelling bias may be appropriate for a management information system but totally inappropriate for a real-time embedded system. When things start to go wrong it is all too easy to blame the tool rather than criticize the choice of tool as appropriate for the job. In short the architectural approach is not *flexible* enough to cater for an increasing variety of types of system.

Both problems are all too real. Is it perhaps time to surrender and answer Mary Lou Roberts' question with a resounding 'yes'? Perhaps the idea of an effective systems strategy is simply too grand. Lest we are tempted to leap suicidally from this ledge I believe it is worth taking a step back and thinking about alternative approaches to descending these perilous slopes. It is time to return to the strategic perspective itself.

6.7   The strategic perspective revisited

There is a certain irony in that the two difficulties identified as endemic to the architectural approach are themselves strategic. They relate not so much to actual systems as to the systems development approach implied. We must therefore extend the characterization of the strategic perspective as follows.

> ☐ An attitude or disposition toward systems development which is influenced by the dominant need for systems which are *holistic* and which are *politically sound* in that it is underwritten by top management commitment. The systems development approach itself must be *responsive* and *flexible*.

Let us examine these additional requirements in a little more detail.

Systems development must be responsive. The approach to system building must be well planned and yet dynamic. Analogies with most types of strategy are therefore not appropriate. For example, cases where chess or military strategy changed as a result of new developments are the exception rather than the rule. However, this is not true of systems, especially in large organizations where, paradoxically, the need for a strategic approach is greatest. Business environments are subject to continual change under the pressure to exploit new commercial opportunities, diversify into new areas, improve customer service, reduce costs, meet new government regulations, keep ahead of the opposition, and so on. It is not surprising, therefore, that by the time the architectural systems strategy is completed, the assumptions upon which the document was originally based are no longer valid.

I can remember one life assurance company committing a team of half-a-dozen analysts, users and consultants for the best part of a year to a systems strategy, only to find, in the month prior to the issue of the document, the Chancellor of the Exchequer announcing that life assurance premium tax relief was to be abolished.

This announcement turned the industry upside down. Executives had to seek new ways of attracting customers, by providing a range of facilities from low budget family income plans to mortgages. Much, though not all, of the results of the systems strategy had to be thrown away.

Systems development must be flexible. Both system development techniques and tools to support them have proliferated in explosive fashion during the past decade. It is common to find in-house computer departments and software houses sticking to one system development methodology as *the* answer to the problems at hand. There is a tendency to ignore the fact that there are various available options open for tackling these problems, and that rational deliberation in choosing a suitable approach for a particular problem can substantially increase the prospect of success. When projects fail, the blame is all too often placed on the techniques and tools used. However, the cause of failure is often to be found not so much in the techniques and tools themselves, but in the fact that the choice of techniques and tools was unsuitable for the particular problem.

Again, a prototyping approach might, for example, be unsuitable for a real-time embedded system but most appropriate for a management information system. Conversely, rigorous use of EP with an emphasis on state transition diagrams might be inappropriate for a management information system but most appropriate for a real-time embedded system. The strategic perspective must, therefore, be flexible in facilitating sensible decisions with regard to the approach most likely to succeed for specific types of system.

The requirements of the strategic perspective are not intended as isolated dictates; in a sense they represent interdependent driving forces. For example, a responsive approach depends upon flexibility in having the facility to choose the best tool for a particular job. Similarly, an approach will only remain politically sound whilst it is responsive. Most significantly perhaps, holistic systems depend on a politically sound basis for their development.

6.8   Applying structured techniques strategically

The assertion of the 'devil's advocate' in Section 6.3 was that 'structured techniques are not strategic', on the grounds that they were neither holistic nor politically sound. Certainly, I have seen structured techniques fail for these reasons. However, a closer look at EP reveals that these are failures of application rather than intrinsic problems.

Structured techniques must be applied holistically. EP is one structured technique which actively encourages a questioning of system scope at the outset of a project. However, constraints often dictate that the statement of purpose is usually such that the scope is localized by application. What is actually needed is a more holistic look at enterprise requirements before making rationally justified decisions as to what statements of purpose should actually be. For the development of holistic systems, systems which integrate rather than interface, we need to apply the principle of encapsulation not only within a system but more significantly across the enterprise itself.

Structured techniques must be applied in a politically sound way. Where structured techniques are applied without political mandate, failure to produce results should not surprise us. Justification for systems development projects is commonly not discussed at director or executive level, resulting in the absence of a political mandate. Sometimes, therefore, 'the plug is pulled', perhaps after several months of hard work by all concerned, the project is simply written off before it has actually had a chance to produce anything. Without underwriting, an insurance policy is worthless. Similarly, without political underwriting, in the form of top management commitment to a well-planned and structured approach to systems development, an effort at system building will always be subject to abandonment. This is because without political underwriting, projects will always be seen more as short-term exercises or one-off solutions to immediate problems rather than as long-term, well-planned development strategies. Great emphasis has already been placed on providing the right political climate for effective systems development. What exactly does this mean?

A politically sound approach must be *proactive* rather than reactive. This means moving away from short-term response to user demands, requiring each system to be developed by considering its immediate business priorities and cost-justified without considering its impact on other systems. It means moving toward a long-term response to user demands which requires each system to be developed by considering its benefits in an open-minded way in relation to the needs of the organization as a whole.

However, this must not be seen as an open cheque-book. We have seen that there must be a balance between the need for a proactive approach on the one hand and the need for responsive systems development on the other. Part of the problem with strategic methodologies was that the time taken and the money spent in building their architectures tipped the balance heavily toward lack of response.

Structured techniques must be applied responsively. Our devil's advocate will present lack of responsiveness as another reason for the failure of structured techniques. We will be exhorted to realize that users want systems and not models.

However, it is important to make three further particular points with respect to responsiveness in a proactive environment:

1. Strategic models must be constructed quickly (weeks rather than months) to maintain the commitment and interest of senior management.
2. The approach needs to be iterative; regular reviews should take place to allow for adjustment in *response to change*.
3. Timescales for all projects must be short (six months absolute maximum), well-planned and interactive communication techniques used (as described in Section 1.6).

In short, a more dynamic approach is required which enables early exposure of specific systems, in the form of prototypes where appropriate, whilst ensuring their fit to the larger whole.

Structured techniques must be applied flexibly. Our devil's advocate will finally present lack of flexibility as another reason for the failure of structured techniques. We will be told that there is a tendency with many structured techniques to focus one particular aspect of a system to the detriment of another. For example, techniques are commonly perceived as data-driven versus function-driven, real-time versus commercial and so on.

In particular, we will be told that EP works well for real-time and transaction processing systems but results in loss of flexibility in that it restricts interest to operational systems, ignoring the groundswell of demand for decision support systems to service the strategic and tactical layers of the pyramid shown in Figure 6.1.

Again, this is a criticism of application rather than nature. Whilst it is true that EP often is applied to operational systems, this does not mean that it cannot be adapted to deal with other types of system. We have already seen that EP actually provides a flexible framework in terms of system dimensions. It recognizes that 'if your only tool is a hammer, the whole world looks like a nail'. EP gives a potential of recognizing the existence of different types of system and applying appropriate tools and techniques. This is particularly important for software houses, manufacturing organizations and other companies whose system portfolio is diverse. This potential should therefore be exploited and not ignored as it often seems to be. Suitable development strategies may then be elicited for each business requirement, rather than blindly pursuing one course of action.

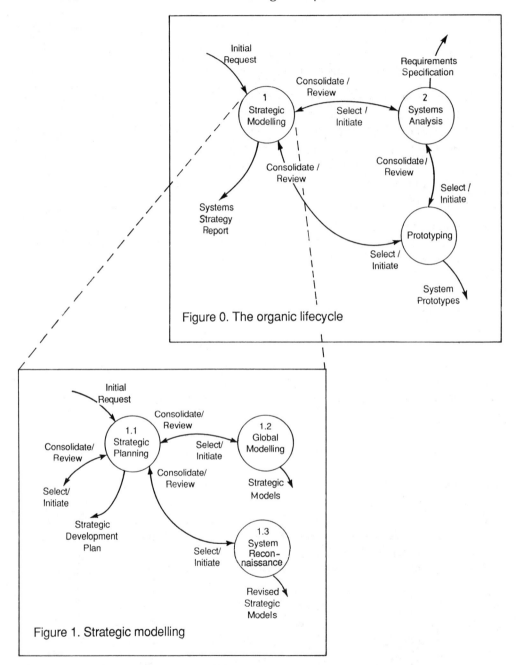

Figure 0. The organic lifecycle

Figure 1. Strategic modelling

Figure 6.3 The strategic perspective with respect to the organic lifecycle.

6.9   An organic approach

The organic approach suggested here shares an important feature of the architectural approach in that it aims to produce a deliverable: the systems strategy report (as described in Section 6.5). It is necessary to have such a deliverable not only as evidence of progress but also as evidence of management commitment. However, the organic approach is inherently different in that it views the systems strategy report as a living document; not something 'that we create once to assuage some feeling of guilt' (Sanders, 1978). Therefore, the systems strategy report must not only be created quickly (weeks rather than months) it must be reviewed and maintained on a regular basis to keep pace with change.

The organic approach also recognizes the need for a framework within which systems development can be co-ordinated and carried out with reference to overall business objectives. Again, it is the systems strategy report that provides this framework. Let us examine Figure 6.3.

Figure 0 represents the organic lifecycle which was introduced initially as Figure 1.3. Again, remember this is a partial picture; it does not, for example, show other activities of systems strategy (migration strategy and technical strategy); neither does it show systems design. Each of the activities is iterative and they may be operating concurrently. The reader should notice that the net input and output data flows correspond with the modelling framework. This is therefore another view of the same thing: effective modelling. (For clarity some input data flows and all data stores have been suppressed.)

Figure 1 shows the pertinent activities of strategic modelling:

☐ Strategic Planning plans and co-ordinates all other activities (including Global Modelling and Systems Reconnaissance projects themselves) which are commissioned on a short-term project basis, thus reducing difficulties in measuring progress, endemic to architectural approaches. It concentrates on initiating projects and in assessing feedback from projects. This involves identifying both technical and human resources and prioritizing systems.

☐ Global Modelling (discussed in Chapter 7) seeks to build an initial (hazy) view of the enterprise in terms of models rooted in EP, and maps out system scopes in terms of system profiles, which form the basis for project initiation. Whereas the architectural approach seeks to use data analysis and function decomposition to build strategic models in some depth, before initiating systems development projects, the organic approach described here deliberately avoids this, seeking first to sketch out *global models*. The basic mistake of the architectural approach is to identify the global model-ling with enterprise modelling. The architectural representation will be provided by the underlying enterprise models (discussed in Chapter 9) which evolve gradually as a result of feedback from later ensuing systems development work. In a sense the global models are disposable: they represent a launching pad from which to develop systems within the strategic perspective.

☐ Systems Reconnaissance (discussed in Chapter 8) applies the tools of EP to provide advance information by scouting ahead to glean more informa-tion about those areas about which we are most uncertain. A systems reconnaissance project is a deliberately short-term intensive affair which may operate at either system or enterprise level. At system level the most appropriate development approaches for particular systems are identified. This might range from EP with the accent on STD modelling for bespoke real-time embedded systems to the purchasing of packages for familiar commercial applications like payroll. The results of system reconnaissance are saved for consolidation within the system profile and initiating systems development projects on a much more confident basis than is the case with architectural strategies where uncertainty with regard to system scope can cause time-consuming inertia.

The organic approach provides flexibility in that all three of the activities in 'Figure 1' can operate concurrently and in that any one can be initiated on a short-term project basis as required. For example, regular strategy planning reviews will be necessary as will the requirement to assimilate and review results from systems analysis and design projects.

The tools of EP form a simple and flexible cornerstone for strategic modelling. The reader will find that there is really nothing new to learn about modelling expertise. This also provides a continuity, so often lacking, between strategic and system level modelling.

The organic lifecycle presented reflects the need for an effective lifecycle which was outlined in Section 1.5. Two other conditions for the development of effective systems were also identified:

1. Effective working methods.
2. Effective mind-set.

Both global modelling and systems reconnaissance are very much interactive in that they rely heavily on group dynamics to produce results. They depend very much on the effective working methods discussed in Section 1.6.

The introduction of systems reconnaissance involves the acceptance of research as a respectable and productive activity. This depends on liberating ourselves from the traditional mind-set described in Section 1.7.

(Strategic planning is a complex process and we do not deal with it in detail in this book. In essence it is a trade-off between various organizational constraints with respect to the business strategy. Ideally, we would want system building to start today with dedicated resources. Resource constraints are the major factor precluding this ideal. Available funds for system building are usually limited. Therefore there are limits to the hardware and software that we can purchase and the people we can hire. Existing systems must be maintained in the face of change. Priorities must be set and risks assessed with the objective of achieving maximum return on investment. Systems development must compete for resources: a balance must be maintained between the pressures of the business environment and utilization of resources to meet those pressures. It is the business strategy which must determine the proportion of the total resources of the enterprise allocated to systems development. It is the systems strategy that must indicate how those resources are to be deployed.

In particular, the reader should note that developing the technical strategy, migration strategy and strategic development plan are important parts of system strategy. However, they are not treated specifically in this book, firstly, as they form subjects in their own right outside the scope of this book and, secondly, as they have been comprehensively covered in a profuse literature. The reader is referred to Connor (1988) for a useful analysis of high level systems development planning and to Blanchard and Fabrycky (1981) who define a set of criteria for the use of models for technical evaluation of proposed systems.)

6.10 Project initiation and consolidation

All activities within the organic lifecycle, including strategic planning, must be initiated as projects. Notice in Figure 6.3 all activities are selected and initiated from Strategic Planning except Prototyping which may also be initiated from Systems Analysis. Feedback from each activity is reviewed and consolidated often for use by another activity. The vehicles through which this is achieved are the *project profile* and *system profile* which are outlined below.

Early system analysis and prototyping projects should ideally have a reasonably small scope, but also high priority ranking. For the first projects, there will be considerable iteration between systems analysis and strategy; not only will our initial strategic view be somewhat hazy but there is always a learning curve involved with any new technique. This is where systems reconnaissance work can come into its own as a means of removing the potential dangers of such iteration. The iteration must of course be controlled, in particular there must be regular feedback meetings in which problems can be resolved. At strategic level there may well be political problems; for example, implied changes in future departmental responsibilities. It is important, however, that these are defused early rather than surfacing later, typically at implementation, causing untold disruption.

For later projects the amount of iteration between analysis and strategy will diminish, since as more and more parts of the business are analyzed so perception of the whole becomes clearer. The need for reconnaissance projects should correspondingly diminish.

6.10.1 The project profile

The recommendation is that each project have a project profile which will include the following:

- ☐ Project name.
- ☐ Project type (Strategic Planning/Global Modelling/Systems Reconnaissance/Systems Analysis/Prototyping).
- ☐ Executive sponsor.
- ☐ Project Plan:
    (a) Project organization, reporting structure, team members, roles etc.
    (b) Schedule, budget.
    (c) Priority.
    (d) Risk assessment.
- ☐ System profile.

This is not meant to be an exhaustive list: it is rather meant as a check list of necessary pre-conditions for project initiation. Typically organizational needs will vary according to circumstances. For example, it is often useful to include a short description of objectives, which may include a cost-benefit analysis for the project (as opposed to the system described below).

6.10.2 The system profile

Let us look at the system profile in a little more detail. Five components are included:

- ☐ Statement of purpose.
- ☐ Systems development strategy.

☐ Constraints.
☐ Models.
☐ Cost-benefit analysis.

The very minimum we would expect here would be a statement of purpose as described in Chapter 3. Also, it is normal to include constraints, reflecting performance requirements and environmental limitations, which would be used in systems design as intimated in Chapter 5.

The systems development strategy describes the means by which realization of the proposed system is to be achieved. This may range from recommendation of a specific software package to a description of modelling tools and methods to be used, including CASE. Guidelines for making these decisions are included in Chapter 8.

Most importantly, however, from the point of view of this book, any models developed from previous work will be consolidated within the system profile. The type and number of models included will vary according to the project being initiated.

6.11 Summary

This chapter has presented the strategic perspective as an imperative for contemporary systems development. To recap, the strategic perspective can be summarized as follows:

☐ An attitude or disposition toward systems development which is influenced by the dominant need for systems, which are holistic, and which is politically sound in that it is underwritten by top management commitment. The systems development approach itself must be responsive and flexible.

The assertion that 'structured techniques are not strategic' was clarified. Architectural approaches were examined as an alternative response to the demand for politically sound development resulting in holistic systems. Despite their laudability it was argued that their very nature is at odds with what remain the overriding concerns of systems development: meeting project deadlines. They are not responsive enough. At root the architectural approach, no less than other types of strategy, such as chess or military strategy, seeks to build structures which are as resilient to change as possible in order to give direction and foundation. This results in an attendant lack of flexibility. Lack of results causes loss of political foundation, and so on.

Structured techniques were revisited. It was argued that their failures were often

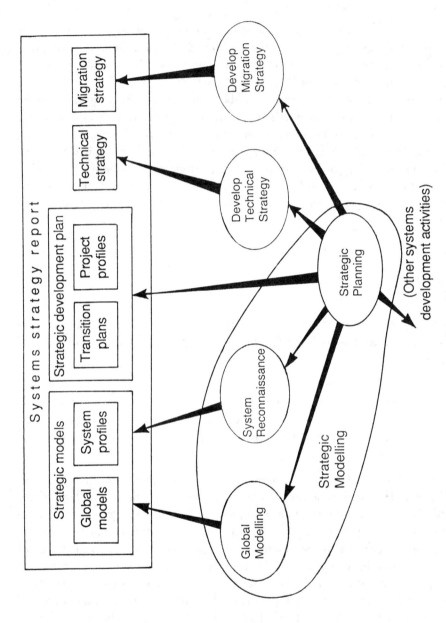

Figure 6.4 Systems strategy deliverables in relation to activities.

failures of application rather than intrinsic failures (as with architectural strategies), and that they could be adapted to cater for the requirements of the strategic perspective. An alternative framework for making structured techniques work strategically was briefly described. Figure 6.4 gives a graphic summary of deliverables in relation to activities. Note, it is most useful within the document itself to include a short section on *why* structured techniques are proposed, with justification for user involvement as described in Section 2.10. It is now time to explore global modelling and systems reconnaissance in some detail.

CHAPTER 7

Global modelling

□ □ □ □ □ □ □ □ □ □ □ □ □ □ □ □ □

The existence of the whole is worth more than the sum of the existences of the parts.

W.V.O. QUINE
From a Logical Point of View

7.1 Introduction

This chapter begins by clarifying the concept of global modelling with respect to strategic modelling as shown in Figure 7.1.

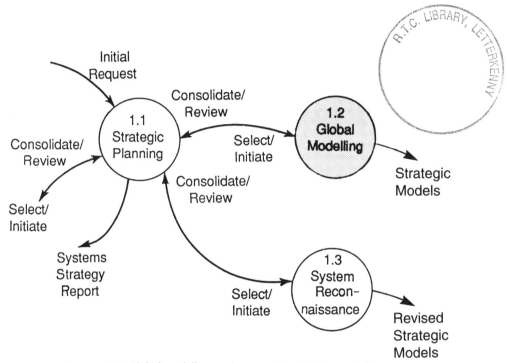

Figure 7.1 Global modelling with respect to strategic modelling.

Clearly there is a need to create strategic models (global models plus system profiles) of the enterprise in a way which meets the requirements of the strategic perspective whilst avoiding the pitfalls of the architectural approach. The components of the global model are identified and explained, and the associated terminology introduced, before embarking on the two main topics of this chapter: strategic data modelling and strategic function modelling.

Initial scoping of systems for further development is discussed before finally examining the relationship between global modelling and systems reconnaissance and subsequent development.

7.2 The concept of global modelling

Global modelling needs to identify the enterprise itself and to model the enterprise at a high level. It is differentiated by its scope: the whole business. This might be a company (for example, a manufacturer), firm (for example, a partnership of solicitors) or organization (for example, a governing body). In the case of especially diverse concerns the term can also be used more locally to mean a division of a company or a department within a firm or organization, providing the division or department can at least be conceived as runnable in its own right. For example, both the Superdeal Petrol Company (see Appendix 3) and a filling station operated by the company could be thought of as enterprises. However, the effort expended in constructing global models for the former is obviously going to be much greater than that for the latter. Clearly it is important that ambiguities are ironed out early to prevent wasted effort: we must understand exactly *what* we are being asked to model.

Therefore, the definition of the enterprise must be formally drawn up and agreed before commencing the remainder of the strategic modelling actitives. We require something akin to the statement of purpose (see Section 3.2) at global level:

☐ The Enterprise Statement of Purpose (ESP) is an agreement between analysts and user executives which outlines the area of the business to be addressed. This will include a broad description of business functions and definition of the audience for whom the models are being built.

The global models included are as follows:

☐ The Global Entity Relationship Diagram (GERD) which is, in fact, the strategic tool for modelling data.
☐ The Global Context Diagram (GCD) and a list of high level corporate functions known as a Candidate Context List (CCL), which are the strategic tools for modelling functions.

Notice that although the scope of these models stretches across the whole enterprise, global modelling does not seek to construct models of any detail or depth. These are very much high-level models as opposed to the underlying deeper view of the enterprise known as the enterprise data model, which is discussed in Chapter 9.

The enterprise data model underpins the whole system lifecycle. However, building a comprehensive and detailed enterprise data model, and using this as the cornerstone for systems development work at project level, involves a major commitment of resources. It aims at long-term benefits tying up resources unproductively over large timescales. If undertaken as a preliminary exercise this is vulnerable to the problems of architectural systems strategy, described in the previous chapter. An enterprise data model of any size can contain hundreds of entities and relationships. Building a construction of such scale, before considering system requirements in any detail, it is virtually impossible to keep pace with business change and with developing perceptions of users and analysts. Analysis of specific systems initiated on the basis of the enterprise data model will lead to a deeper understanding of data structure requiring re-work of parts of the supporting enterprise data model.

The situation is analagous to a tailor making a completely finished suit on first sight of a customer. The customer then tries on the suit which is unpicked and resewn, comes back to the shop for refitting, the suit is unpicked and resewn and so on. In this situation three problems start to emerge:

1. The suit starts to get crumpled and tattered; it loses its crisp newness.
2. Costs start to escalate.
3. The customer grows increasingly frustrated and probably walks out.

The approach of developing a comprehensive and detailed enterprise data model and using this as a platform for systems development is subject to three parallel problems:

1. The essence of systems strategy is destroyed in that there is an unhealthy focusing in on detail before it is understood in context.
2. The budget blows.
3. The interest of top management is lost and the whole exercise abandoned.

Indeed many enterprise modelling efforts have foundered on these rocks. The tailor is of course in the fortunate position of being able to take the customer's measurements and construct the suit on an exact basis (barring a silly mistake). Clearly in systems development we are not in such a fortunate position. Therefore, despite the importance and value of the enterprise ERD (EERD), it is not a good vehicle for effective systems strategy.

Incidentally, it would indeed be good if users could pick and choose systems in the same way that a customer selects a suit. We shall see in Part Five of this book that prototyping can be an excellent vehicle for achieving this. However, we have also seen, in the previous chapter, the anarchy that results from ignoring the need for effective systems strategy.

7.3   User view ERDs

One response to the problem of scale presented by the enterprise data model is to build a separate ERD for each prime user of enterprise data, and to then synthesize these 'user views' to form the enterprise ERD. This has been widely used and described in the literature and therefore warrants attention.

The concept of user views was formally endorsed in the recommendations for data modelling of the ANSI/SPARC committee (American National Standards Institute/Standards Planning and Requirements Committee) (ANSI, 1978). The committee defined a three-schema architecture as a standard for data modelling, as shown in Figure 7.2.

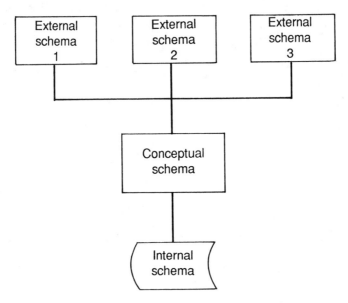

Figure 7.2 The ANSI/SPARC three-schema data architecture.

An external schema is a sub-schema of the overall conceptual schema being modelled, from the point of view of a particular user. Such a user view may be a report, screen or any set of data required for a particular purpose. In effect, the user view describes the presentation of a subset of the underlying business data to a particular user. The conceptual schema is the overall view of the underlying business data in terms which are independent of the way that data is stored and accessed or allocated to particular machine devices. Finally, the internal schema is the physical representation of the conceptual schema in the form of physical files or databases.

The conceptual schema can be synthesized from the user views either bottom-up or top-down. The bottom-up approach was described and popularized by James Martin (1975) under the name 'canonical synthesis'. The principle followed is as follows. Take the first user view and normalize it producing a data model. Then superimpose the second user view over the first and normalize it into a consolidated data model. Repeat until all user views have been normalized and consolidated into the data model. Done manually, this is time consuming and tedious. In response to this problem the first CASE tools to assist in automating canonical synthesis appeared in the mid-1980s. The same principles can be applied to existing file structures to reverse engineer an essential data structure. This has resulted in the increasing emergence of 'normalization engines'.

Despite the proliferation of CASE tools to assist in canonical synthesis and more generally in the reverse engineering of data, considerable manual effort remains: for example, the analyst has to tell the CASE tool what the dependencies are. Without considerable human intervention, some very important aspects of normalization cannot be done. There are other practical problems in that the same data element on existing files or user reports may be called multiple names. Conversely, the same data element name may actually refer to different things. Other data elements may simply be there to support the existing implementation; for example transaction codes. Or they may reflect the inadequacies of the existing implementation; for example, initials which have been included because there was not enough disk space to store a person's first names. Yet another problem is that there is no distinction between primitive and derived data; for example, birthdate may be derived from age and current date, but would nevertheless remain in the model.

However, I do not wish to dwell on the practical difficulties here. The more fundamental problem is that it is assumed at the outset that data elements are given. Therefore, the data model that is produced reflects the adequacy of data as currently used or stored in its various implementations. The data that is actually required by users is assumed to be what the users already have, which seems to be begging the question. Often this data is of *in*adequate quality: obsolete, inaccurate, or poorly defined. Also, any future data needs are simply not to be found within current designs, whether they be master files or screen layouts. This is why this approach will not be used in this book.

This is not to say that the bottom-up approach does not have any value. It may well have application where the agreed goal is to reverse engineer an existing set of files, the structure of which is causing problems, but the content of which is satisfactory. It may also be usefully employed as an aid to evaluating the file structure of a proposed software package by deriving a data model for the package and comparing this to the required data model. Similarly it is sometimes useful as an additional technique, the results of which can be used for comparative purposes. The argument here is that it does not work well as a strategic tool.

The weaknesses of the bottom-up approach have led some authors to advocate a top-down approach to user view modelling (Inmon, 1984 and 1988, and Veryard, 1984). This may be generally characterized as follows. Each user is interviewed with the objective of producing a list of nouns that reflect the data requirements which apply to the user's job. This will usually involve examination of existing system outputs but significantly will also include any future requirements. Nouns on each user view list are then classified into entities, attributes, entity occurrences and attribute occurrences. Relationships are exposed by considering each possible combination of entities in interaction, and a first-cut user view data model is built. This is then refined with the user, and mapped into the underlying enterprise data model. Any derivable entities, relationships and attributes are excluded from the enterprise data model as redundant.

The procedure is eloquently summarized as follows by Veryard (1984):

'The procedure for the data analyst is therefore as follows:

1. Talk to users, conduct fact finding.
2. Build a data model of each user view (UVDM), in the form of an entity-relationship diagram with supporting documentation.
3. Build a data model from which each UVDM can be derived – this is the global view data model (GVDM).
4. Revise each UVDM where necessary and make the derivation from the GVDM explicit.'

Although it avoids many of the problems associated with the bottom-up approach to user view modelling, the top-down approach suffers from two major problems. Firstly, users will typically be wedded to the systems that they currently use: our starting point is, from a psychological viewpoint, going to be very much the current implementation; therefore we may be in danger of reinventing the same wheel with the same problems. In particular, I am suggesting that we want to emancipate ourselves from existing functionality. Secondly, in building user view lists, we are inevitably going to become immersed in a detail of data, which is likely to be out of balance with our much more limited view of function. We are thus back with the problems of creating a complete enterprise data model, which were described in the last section.

Because of these problems a rather different approach is proposed here. Firstly, the requirement is for an approach which does not rest on the assumptions about the existing systems and functional organization, but which minimizes interfaces. Secondly, the need is for an iterative approach that copes with change, and which maintains a balance between data and process modelling.

7.4 The global ERD

The scope of the global ERD is the enterprise itself. The notation is similar to that employed at system level in Chapter 4, but associative entity and supertype-subtype symbols are not recommended here as the pitch is now at a much higher level. Double-edged boxes represent *global entities*: broad data areas of prime strategic importance. Double-edged diamonds represent *global relationships*: associations of prime strategic importance between global entities. It is important that both global entities and global relationships are perceived, independently from existing application areas, as supporting the essential business objectives of the enterprise. We shall see on more detailed analysis global entities represent aggregations of one or more actual entities and (often) one or more actual relationships. Similarly global relationships represent aggregations of one or more actual relationships and (often) one or more actual entities. The relationship between the GERD and EERD is depicted in Figure 7.3. As a rough guide the GERD should contain between five and fifteen each of global entities and global relationships. An example for the Wellbrian Soccer Federation is shown as Figure 7.4.

The purpose is to provide a basis upon which actual entities and relationships can be determined. Therefore, although textual support for the global ERD will be minimal it is important to provide a definition for each global entity and global relationship. For example:

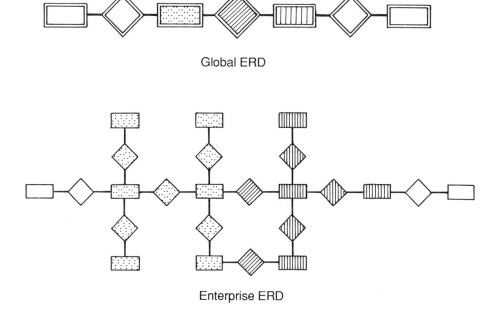

Global ERD

Enterprise ERD

Figure 7.3 Global ERD and enterprise ERD compared.

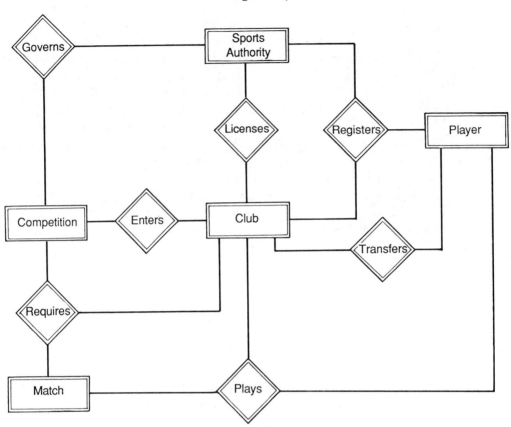

Figure 7.4 Global ERD for WSF.

Club   = Organization whose purpose is to run teams participating in sports governed by the WSF

Licenses = A sports authority's decision to grant a license to a club under regulation 5.23

It might be tempting to omit this textual support under the knowledge that the global ERD is, in effect, only a means to the more important end of determining actual entities and relationships. But there are two good reasons for this.

Firstly, to record the business policy which actually led us to create the global entity or global relationship. The global ERD highlights strategic information requirements. As such it is tangible evidence of top management's commitment to a strategic approach to system building. Therefore, despite the obvious overhead it is sometimes useful to maintain the global ERD to reflect developments at the more detailed level. It can then be reviewed at regular intervals to reaffirm the commitment of top management.

Secondly, textual definitions for global entities and global relationships can provide useful clues in determining actual entities and relationships at the analysis stage. For example, in the definition for Club, 'team' and 'sport' may well emerge as entities; 'governs' may well emerge as a relationship. In Chapter 8 we will examine this technique more closely.

Despite the limits on numbers of symbols and despite the emphasis on high-level categories of business information, we sometimes find the resulting GERD is somewhat complex. This is due, in part, to the fact that global relationships can typically join not just two but three or four global entities: the very nature of the exercise is in a sense to highlight potential complexity for subsequent analysis. It may therefore be expedient not to diagram at all here but to represent the information in a simple list format, showing for each global entity its involvement in global relationships. The entry for 'Club' in the above example would read as follows:

☐ Club: Transfers Player
Registers Player with Sports Authority
Licensed by Sports Authority
Enters Competition
Plays Match involving Player
Required for Match in Competition

Indeed, it may be that both the diagram and its textual equivalent are required for different purposes or audiences. Again, a flexible CASE tool should supply leverage in making such alternative views (as we have previously called them) readily available.

7.5 Constructing the global ERD

The objective of the global ERD is to provide an enterprise-wide representation of data which can be used as a foundation for system development without suffering the problems encountered in building an enterprise ERD. The essence of systems strategy must be maintained by focusing at a high level on only those broad data areas, and the associations between them, that are of prime strategic interest. The key question to ask is 'does this gobal entity highlight a broad category of data which is critical in supporting business objectives?' Where a business strategy has been undertaken, elements from this can be very useful as a guide to selecting global entities. In particular, work has been done to use critical success factors in this connection (Henderson *et al.*, 1984).

Global entities can be found by thinking of the information that the enterprise requires to achieve its business objectives, independently of any existing application areas, systems or databases. Sometimes this is fairly obvious with certain global entities recurring in similar types of enterprise. For example, Supplier, Purchase, Sale, Product in retail environments; Proposal, Policy, Client in insurance environments. Indeed some research is being done into reference models, paradigms for different enterprise types, which can be adapted to the needs of a specific enterprise of that particular type. However, it is possible to cite some more general guidelines in terms of the following requirements of the enterprise, with reference to examples from each case study:

Enterprise requirement	Sports case study	Petrol case study
Resource	Player	Station Facility
	Club	Supplier
		Purchase
		Supplier
		Employee
		In Payment
Event	Match	Delivery
Product		Product
		Sale
		Out Payment
Reference structure	Sports Authority	Customer Account
	Competition	

Global entities can be tangible, like Player or Product; or intangible like Competition or Customer Account. The important criteria is that each represents information which is perceived as critical in supporting business objectives.

The general categories are not intended as rigid dichotomies; for example, it might be a matter of debate as to whether a Customer Account is a product or a reference structure. However, this is academic: the categories are intended as thinking aids and not for formal classification. They can be usefully further subdivided (with examples) as follows:

☐ Resource: personnel (Employee), finance (In Payment), suppliers (Hirer), materials (Chemical), equipment (Station Facility).
☐ Event: scheduled events (Match), unscheduled events (Machine Fault).
☐ Product: goods (Product), contracts (Policy), services (Advertising Campaign), finance (Out Payment).
☐ Reference structure: internal structures (Department), external structure (Government Office), product structure (Customer Account, Competition).

In order to address enterprise requirements it is important to think of future as well as present requirements. A financial services company I was working with some years ago had no effective means of marketing using demographic targetting. This became increasingly necessary as competitors started to exploit new marketing tools. Therefore, they came up with the idea of using 'ACORN' (ACORN stands for 'A Classification of Residential Neighbourhoods' and is a trademark of CACI, 26–28 The Quadrant, Richmond, Surrey, TW9 1DL, UK) as a means of achieving this objective. ACORN gave them the ability to target certain types of financial contract to certain classifications of socio-economic areas identified with UK postcodes. The business criticality of this concept gave rise to a global entity called 'Area'.

Global relationships can be found by considering different global entities in combination and thinking of the interactions and associations that might be of interest. One way of doing this is to create a table with the entities listed as row and column headings and tick off each cell representing each combination considered. This works well for two-way relationships. For three-way (and upward) relationships, consider each cell relative to each of the other entities or simply list them longhand. Many global relationships will, in fact, be three- or four-way. As such, they will appear complex and not fully understood. The global ERD provides a means of highlighting these areas of complexity. Therefore, we should leave the business of actually breaking them down to the subsequent analysis projects which will follow this strategic exercise.

Logically there could be numerous different ways of drawing a global ERD for the same underlying data structure, depending in effect on how entities and relationships have been aggregated. However, once concensus has been reached on what the diagram is modelling it is pointless to keep tinkering around with it. We must be pragmatic and use it with its true purpose in mind: to provide a good feel at strategic level for what the broad data areas are and to use this as a basis for determining actual entities and relationships. Systems can then be developed with the sharing of data effectively planned.

7.6   The concept of global function modelling

The purpose of global function modelling is to survey and map out at a high level the functions required to support the enterprise in its environment. A function may be broadly understood as a group of processes which collectively support one part of the mission of the enterprise. Functions identified therefore must be geared to business strategy. Where this has been formally expressed, parameters such as critical success factors can be particularly useful as a source of identifying functions, as mentioned below. One of the most critical aspects of function modelling is to avoid the mistake of modelling in a way that merely reflects current functional structure. After all it is most likely that it is the very ineffectiveness of existing functional structure that is at the root of many of the current problems. This tends to be the mistake made by architectural approaches which we have seen concentrate on identifying the functions and then breaking them down through several hierarchical layers before embarking on systems analysis of lower level functions.

The point, however, is that at the outset functions are not necessarily obvious. The question of what is to count as a function must not be assumed. We will in fact see in Chapter 9 that system reconnaissance is a useful, iterative way of helping to identify functions.

7.7   **The global context diagram and candidate context list**

It is advisable first to picture the enterprise in relation to its environment. Just as we first picture a system as a set of processes which are responses to events occurring in the environment of that system, so we picture the enterprise as a set of functions which are responses to strategic requirements with respect to the environment of that enterprise. This can be achieved by drawing a context diagram at enterprise level, known as a Global Context Diagram (GCD). The notation is the same as for a context diagram, with the proviso that stores are not shown. An example of GCD for the sports administration enterprise is shown in Figure 7.5.

The GCD forces us to concentrate on the business environment implied by the business strategy, and to address interfaces over which we have no real choice rather than becoming bogged down in unpicking existing organizational structures. It will help to confirm or question the enterprise statement of purpose and to provide a basis for roughing out a tentative list of those functions (or *candidate contexts*) which would seem to be necessary to support the enterprise in its environment, known as a 'Candidate context list', a partial example of which for the sports administration enterprise follows:

> *Partial candidate context list for sports administration enterprise.*
>   Competition control
>   Fixture scheduling
>   Club licensing
>   Match administration
>   Player administration
>   Team selection and control

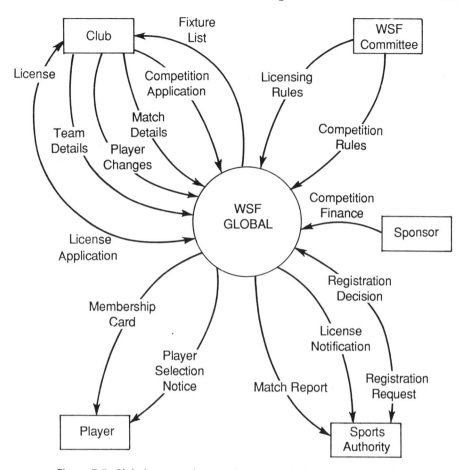

Figure 7.5 Global context diagram for sports administration enterprise.

Later on it will be important to prioritize each candidate context, but early efforts will, by definition, be tentative and open to revision in the light of further analysis. Each candidate context will also require a statement of purpose to be defined as the take-off point for environmental modelling at system level.

7.8 Constructing the global context diagram and candidate context list

Candidate contexts can be found by thinking of those activities that the enterprise needs to perform in order to achieve its business objectives, independently of any existing application areas, systems or databases. As with global entities, sometimes this is fairly obvious with certain functions recurring in similar types of enterprise. Again, reference models of paradigms can be useful. For example, Purchasing, Purchase accounting, Order processing in retail environments; Underwriting, Marketing, Client servicing in insurance environments.

Each candidate context should represent aspects of enterprise behaviour which are perceived as necessary to achieve strategic requirements. If business strategy has been formally documented this can be a particularly useful source in searching for candidate contexts. For example, the above list for sports administration might be derived from consideration of corresponding Critical Success Factors (CSFs):

CSF	*Corresponding candidate context*
Control of competitions	Competition control
Scheduling of fixtures	Fixture scheduling
Licensing of clubs	Club licensing
Administration of matches	Match administration
Administration of players	Player administration
Support for team selection	Team selection and control

Each CSF should be documented within the appropriate system profile under the cost-benefit section; meeting a CSF is an important system benefit and it is important to recognize this.

Indeed some CSFs tend to be characteristic of certain enterprise types. Rockart (1979), for example, quotes four CSFs of the supermarket industry:

1. Product mix.
2. Inventory.
3. Sales promotion.
4. Pricing.

Another strategic source of candidate contexts is exemplified in the concept of a value chain as decribed by Porter (1985).

Each candidate context should be of around the same scale of size and complexity. Typically one can expect the number of candidate contexts to be roughly double the number of global entities.

Candidate contexts may or may not reflect the existing organization, for example, in terms of departments. The important thing is not to assume this, and to emancipate oneself from existing organizational structures. Also, we need to think of possible future requirements implied by the business strategy. For example, a company making a strategic decision to change existing purchasing policy from conventional stock control to materials requirement planning might typically require a candidate context called 'Material management' rather than (or as well as) 'Purchasing'.

The GCD provides a means of identifying the environment with which our functions will have to interact. It is important therefore that we determine the terminators with some accuracy; those organizations, other systems, competitors and so on with which our enterprise interacts may be ascertained by reference to business objectives. Note that the example in Figure 7.5 actually implies a very narrow scope as both Sports Authority and WSF committee are depicted as terminators. Policy making about competitions is clearly outside of the scope of the enterprise depicted; it is carried out by the WSF committee. Also, the actual decisions about registration are made outside of the scope by the Sports Authority. These may actually be questionable assumptions. Perhaps 'Competition policy making' and 'Registration' should be added to the CCL? The important point to note is that the diagram forces us to address fundamental issues like these early in development and to adjust the enterprise statement of purpose accordingly.

Candidate contexts must be *cohesive* with a view to two major criteria:

1. Importance in supporting business objectives.
2. Minimization of interfaces.

However, to aim for too much detail on the GCD in terms of data flow is rather self defeating. We just require a broad grasp of the main categories of data that are coming in and going out of the enterprise. The detailed data flows will be identified by subsequent analysis projects.

7.9 **The event list as a global modelling tool**

Sometimes much fact finding activity may have already preceded strategic work. This may have resulted in detailed interview notes and minutes of meetings. I have found a useful approach in such cases is to translate this information into a global event list: an event list for the whole enterprise. For example, I worked with one firm who extracted 360 events from detailed fact finding information over a period of just two weeks. The global event list was then used to assist in identifying potential system scopes (see Section 7.11) and formed part of the documentation within the system strategy.

Generally, however, such background information is either not to hand or of questionable worth, and it would take far too long to build a global event list as part of global modelling. In that case it would be better to set up a global reconnaissance project to identify events as described in Section 8.2.

7.10 Developing the global models

Timescales for building global models need to be short, for all of the reasons already discussed in the last chapter. A target of between two and six weeks for developing the GERD, GCD and CCL is reasonable. Remember that what we are aiming at here is an initial, albeit hazy, concensus view as to what the enterprise is all about, which will provide the springboard for analysis projects to bring the components of that view into sharper focus. Importantly, the GERD, GCD and CCL represent tangible evidence of top management's commitment to a well-planned approach to building systems that support the business needs of the enterprise.

The organic lifecycle recognizes enterprise models as living models, changes to which will reflect changes in systems strategy. Therefore, we must be prepared to hold regular reviews of the systems strategy. It is important that the strategic and administrative views of data structure exemplified in the GERD and EERD in Figure 7.3 are consistent. What I have described in this chapter is the strategic dimension. Very little has yet been said about the administrative side. This is described in Chapter 9.

Group interaction techniques, described in Section 1.6, are particularly useful especially here. The executive sponsor should be at least a senior executive or board member. Those charged with the responsibility of actually delivering the global models should form a tight, cohesive team, of ideally between four and six people; although experience suggests it is sometimes necessary to go a little higher. The importance of the composition of the team cannot be stressed strongly enough. There should be a good skill mix which reflects both knowledge of all angles of the business on the one hand and experience in the use of structured techniques on the other. The former will be provided by senior user managers, preferably at board level to carry the necessary authority; the latter by business analysts drawn from either the ranks of in-house staff or from external consultancies. For further information regarding the management of such a group the reader is referred to Page-Jones (1985) (Chapter 4) for a particularly lucid account of running a 'business understanding and strategy group' (Bus group).

7.11 Initial scoping of systems

Proposed systems are mapped out in terms of candidate contexts on the one hand and global entities and global relationships on the other. Often a system may include just one candidate context and the task then is to identify which global entities and global relationships fall within the domain of that appropriate candidate context. One way of doing this for an individual candidate context is simply to draw a line around the area of the GERD which represents the scope relative to this particular system, or to cut and paste to form a scoped GERD. Figure 7.6 shows the scoped GERD for Player Administration. Notice that where a global relationship falls within a proposed scope it should not be left 'unconnected': *all* global entities connected to that global relationship must also be included within the proposed scope.

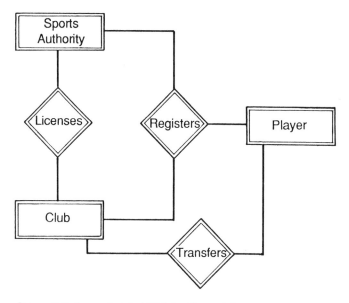

Figure 7.6 Scoped global ERD for Player Administration System.

This simple technique is effective at individual system level. However, to obtain a broad enterprise-wide view, a matrix representation such as that shown in Figure 7.7 is useful. Also, it may be that we choose to group several candidate contexts into one system. We have seen the importance of applying the principle of encapsulation at enterprise (as well as system) level. The matrix forms a useful starting point for system reconnaissance which can be used to encapsulate entities and candidate contexts. Cells of the matrix are filled in to indicate how the candidate context supports the entity: R stands for read and M stands for maintain

Candidate contexts	Global entities → Sports Authority	Player	Club	Competition	Match
Sports policy	M				
Fixture scheduling	R		R	R	M
Club licensing	R		M		
Player administration	R	M	R		
Team selection/control		R	M		R
Match administration			R		M
Competition control				M	

Figure 7.7 Partial global entity–candidate context matrix for WSF.

which covers create, update or delete, not indicated separately as the focus here is high-level. (Note that it is also useful to apply the same tool with global relationships.)

Construction of the matrix will often lead to, sometimes heated, discussion over the merits of the GERD and CCL, which are altered and then re-tested until, after several iterations they become reasonably stable and concensus is reached. It is important that the time allowed here is fixed, say to four one-hour review sessions between the members of the systems strategy team, in order to prevent ceaseless debate.

7.12 Ownership

A distinction is made here between global entities/relationships which are only read by the candidate context(s) and those which are updated by the candidate context(s). The former are said to be 'minor' relative to the system under study whereas the latter are said to be 'major' relative to the system under study. This distinction will also be applied to the actual entities and relationships underlying the GERD, minor entities often appearing as read only data stores on the context diagram; for example Clubs in Figure 3.1.

Thus in Figure 7.6 the global entities Sports Authority and Club are minor whereas Player is major relative to the Player Administration System. Similarly, the global relationship Licenses is minor, in contrast to both Transfers and Registers which are major, relative to that system. Notice also that an entity or relationship which is major relative to one system, may well be minor relative to another system. For example, Player is minor relative to Team Selection and Control.

This is all very well, but what is the point of this distinction? It was emphasized earlier that data must be viewed as a resource which is owned like any other. Since data is typically shared across different systems it is important to establish exactly who *owns* that data, that is, who is responsible for that data. This responsibility can be divided into two types.

Firstly there is development responsibility: who is responsible for analyzing the data? Where several development teams are referencing the same entity it is vital to avoid confusion and to establish who is responsible for analyzing that entity down to attribute level. The guideline here is that a project team assumes this responsibility where an entity is major relative to the system that team is analyzing, the onus is on *that* team to do a thorough job.

The second type of responsibility involves ownership of the data itself: who is responsible for the accuracy and upkeep of that data? The final court of appeal here lies with the user who is responsible for *deleting* occurrences of the entity in question; with authority to delete goes the greatest responsibility. This will normally be the user executive sponsor of the deleting system. If this responsibility cannot be established at this stage, I suggest there are serious problems: perhaps it is time to think again.

Where an entity is major relative to different systems, it is recommended that different teams do not work concurrently on that entity. In practice, the team that is first in the queue will do the detailed analysis. However, if concurrent working really is necessary, the team working on the system with authority to *delete* occurrences of the entity should be deemed 'owners'.

An indication of each type of responsibility should be included in the appropriate data dictionary entry and also within the system profile of any project using that entity or relationship.

7.13 Subsequent project initiation

In modelling at global level it is natural for analysts to have a mind's eye view of the next level of data and function. Indeed, we would not expect the transition to system development work to take place before the analysts had at least some anticipation of what might be encountered next.

7.13.1 Initiating systems analysis projects

Where analysts have a clear mind's eye view and there is little uncertainty about the nature of the proposed system and about its interfaces, a development strategy for the system may be directly determined as described in Chapter 8, before initiating systems analysis project work with respect to the strategic development plan. The scoped GERD and candidate context(s) will be filtered to the system profile for such a project. This is very much in addition to the statement of purpose which is used to drive systems analysis as described previously in Chapters 3 to 5.

7.13.2 Initiating systems reconnaissance projects

Where there is uncertainty a systems reconnaissance project should be initiated. This may occur in two ways. Firstly, where there is uncertainty about the global models themselves, as is normally the case in large corporations with diverse business interests, it will be prudent to initiate a global reconnaissance project to explore system interfaces in some depth using modelling tools described in Chapter 8. Feedback from global reconnaissance will then be used to refresh the global models. In this case the complete set of global models will be filtered through to the system profile for that project.

Secondly, where there is uncertainty about individual systems, as is often the case for a software house developing a system in response to client request, it is advisable to initiate an individual system reconnaissance project to explore the nature of that system using fast-track environmental modelling as described in Chapter 8. In this case the scoped GERD and candidate context(s) will be filtered into the system profile for that project. Later feedback may cause revision of global models, but the main aim will be to provide more detailed information on which a systems development strategy can be determined before initiating further project work for that system. The importance of regular review of the global models therefore becomes particularly important with respect to handling feedback from systems reconnaissance.

7.13.3 Initiating prototyping projects

Often prototyping is only appropriate following systems analysis work. Sometimes, however, it is worth initiating prototyping projects without performing systems analysis first. This is particularly useful for so called 'independent entities' (see Section 9.3): entities whose existence is not dependent upon participation in any relationship. Independent entities are usually mirrored as central global entities on the GERD. Examples might be Player in the WSF enterprise and Patient in a hospital enterprise.

Such direct initiation of prototyping from strategic planning applies to both primitive and decision support prototyping which are described in Chapters 10 and 11. Typically, this occurs where there is a need to establish the underlying enterprise E-R model in more detail or where there are decision support requirements. In such cases it is the task of data administration to develop the selected portion of the underlying enterprise E-R model and to map this into an appropriate database structure, which is filtered to the system profile for the prototyping project.

7.14 Summary

The three salient features of the approach described are as follows:

1. The essence of systems strategy is maintained by focusing at a high level on:
   - ☐ Those broad data areas, and the associations between them, that are required for the enterprise to meet business objectives. The GERD is used for this.
   - ☐ Those functions that are required to support the enterprise in meeting its business objectives. The GCD and CCL are used for this.
2. The timescale for building these models must be fixed; between two and six weeks is sufficient. To aim for too much detail will waste time and probably produce false results. The detail will be addressed in subsequent systems analysis studies which will analyze a coherent portion of the enterprise rather than the whole enterprise.
3. The interest of top management is maintained by concentrating on strategic issues, avoiding 'technical' detail and by developing the GERD, GCD and CCL using a combination of intensive group dynamics and more conventional rational investigation and thought. Ideally, a team of four to six consisting of two senior analysts (one acting as project manager) and two to four senior user managers (one acting as the user executive) should be *responsible* for the actual development of the initial model. Group reviews including much wider sections of top management should be held to confirm the initial model. Also, regular reviews should be scheduled subsequently to review progress, to handle feedback from system reconnaissance and to underwrite top management commitment.

Systems reconnaissance

8.1 Introduction

Systems reconnaissance is work which provides advanced information on the next level of detail of the global models. It centres on those areas of the global models about which we are most uncertain, as illustrated in Figure 8.1. In military terms it is akin to scouting ahead to see what sort of terrain awaits us and what the strengths and weaknesses of the enemy are. If global modelling provides a hazy view of enterprise requirements, then systems reconnaissance focuses in on those areas which are haziest to provide a sharper picture. One of the major common benefits of this is to provide advanced information on the resources required to undertake development work and on underlying enterprise entities and relationships.

There are two main types of system reconnaissance – local and global – and the benefits of each are rather different. Local systems reconnaissance seeks to 'lift the cover' off a proposed system (as identified by global modelling) along the lines discussed above. The major benefit of this is to provide advanced information on which to base a decision as to the most suitable development strategy to be pursued for this system. In contrast, global system reconnaissance operates at a much higher level exploring the interfaces between proposed systems. The major benefit of this

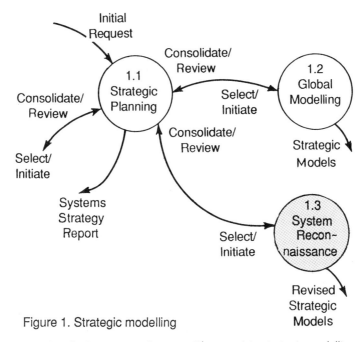

Figure 1. Strategic modelling

Figure 8.1 System reconnaissance with respect to strategic modelling.

is to provide advanced information as to the validity of the partitioning into proposed systems.

In medical terms we might make the following analogy. First, the doctor makes an initial assessment of the patient's health based upon interview and basic examination (global modelling). Based on tentative diagnosis of the problem the doctor commissions an X-ray of an individual organ (local reconnaissance). Blood and urine tests are used to bring the patient's overall profile into sharper focus (global reconnaissance). Obviously these are not isolated unco-ordinated activities: all contribute to the overall goal of making the patient well. Similarly global modelling and systems reconnaissance are intimately related toward the overall goal of 'making the enterprise well'.

Such activity has an unfortunate image of 'dabbling around'. Perhaps this is because there appear to be very few deliverables associated with it, very little visible evidence of productivity, and management are justifiably reluctant to release funds for non-productive activity. We will see the same 'mind-set' appearing later on with respect to prototyping. However, it should be stressed that this is project work which must be planned for and controlled like anything else. Again, timescales should be short. The view here is that it is a vital part of system development which is all too often glossed over or missed out altogether. The advantage here comes with thinking the problem through, in either confirming or questioning assumptions made in global modelling. The real pay off comes with the savings in time which might otherwise be spent much more expensively, later in the lifecycle, undoing earlier mistakes. In effect we are making a small investment to glean information to maximize return later on.

A significant advantage of this approach will be that essentially, there are no new additional tools that we need to spend time and money learning. In summary, we will be using the environmental modelling tools of Chapter 3 in 'fast track' mode, and adapting the DFDs and STDs on a wider basis. Interactive communication techniques (described in Section 1.6) are highly recommended for much of this work.

8.2   Global systems reconnaissance

The principle of environmental modelling discussed in Chapter 3 is a critical theme of systems reconnaissance. Just as systems were first considered in relation to their environment, we are now making the same step with respect to the enterprise itself. Continuing the medical analogy, the anatomy of this situation is pictured in Figure 8.2. The outer layer of Figure 8.2 represents the business environment. Terminators here are dictated by the marketplace itself. Therefore they will have their roots

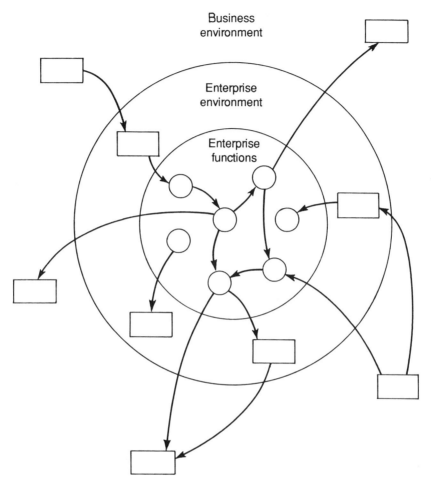

Figure 8.2 Anatomy of the enterprise.

in the business strategy. Examples of 'external terminators' as I shall call them, are customer, stockholder, supplier, distributor, government departments, competitors and external machinery.

The inner two layers represent the enterprise itself, the 'core' of which represents functions (candidate contexts shown as bubbles) to be analyzed and the skin of which represents terminators internal to the enterprise but external to the functions to be analyzed. Examples of 'internal terminators' are user departments, systems (computerized or manual), user roles, and internal equipment.

The important point to note here is that we have really virtually no control over what is to count as an external terminator. If a weekly report is required by the

Inland Revenue or a Customer submits an order then so be it. However, the situation with internal terminators can often be much less restricting. Although a report may have to be produced for management, whether it is the responsibility of one department or another to provide or receive information from the system can sometimes be a matter of some debate.

An illustration of this last point occurred in one financial concern who were organized to deal with their clients on a 'product basis'. Different departments were sectioned to deal with different aspects of different products: pensions, trusts, life assurance, annuities, and so on. However, whilst the need for specialist knowledge necessitated separate sections to administer the details, it was also recognized that a major cause of customer dissatisfaction, where different types of contract were held, was in having to deal with so many different departments. A more personalized service was required. This necessitated the setting up of a Customer Servicing Department, composed of good all-rounders, to deal with queries on a friendlier and more comprehensive basis.

The point is that we do sometimes have a choice over what is to count as an 'internal terminator'. Rather than making dangerous assumptions this choice needs ventilating.

The functions at the core of Figure 8.2 are the area over which we have most choice. Complex interfaces with external terminators are something we are stuck with, and interfaces with internal terminators are something we should attempt to control where possible. In contrast, interfaces between business functions reflect our own choice of partitioning. They therefore represent the area over which we have the greatest influence. An important part of the task of systems strategy is to partition into candidate contexts in such a way that these interfaces are minimized.

Having 'completed' a systems strategy in terms of global modelling it is often tempting to think 'right, we've analyzed enterprise requirements and got the big picture, now we'll press on and deliver the system that the marketing director has been shouting so loud for'. However, we must realize that initial system scopes and their statements of purpose will often be tentative. Building a full-scale environmental model (as described in Chapter 3) on the basis of a vague statement of purpose will waste time and introduce unnecessary interfaces. The full value of the environmental model comes with determining the boundary of a system with respect to established terminators. With external terminators this does not usually present too much of a problem. With internal terminators we have seen that this is not the case. For example, are we justified in accepting, say Sales Administration as a terminator, when the whole function of this department may be open to question, review and restructuring? During systems development, although we *can* raise such thorny issues, we are not generally encouraged to do so because of the limitations of our brief, and because we are normally working to tight timescales. One of the main objectives of system reconnaissance is to raise such issues early, when they have the least potential of causing damage.

The situation is a little akin to jigsaw building. Using the picture on the front of the box will make life a lot easier, if less challenging. However, life will be made yet more easier if we then sort the pieces into categories based on straight edges and colour. Different parts of the jigsaw can then be assembled before bringing it all together. Similarly, the picture presented to us by system strategy is by definition a hazy one. If we jump in and focus too sharply on one area without due regard to the surrounding areas we run a high risk of getting certain things wrong. Far better if we can scout ahead and anticipate potential problems, especially with interfacing.

Hence the need to apply the concept of system reconnaissance globally. The system profile for a global reconnaissance project will be the GERD plus the CCL, or it may be a subset of these. Our task will be essentially to achieve a broad brush feel for system scopes as they relate to one another across the enterprise, rather than to get a rigorous definition of any single system scope. This is done to investigate the overall partitioning at global level into potential systems with the emphasis on Global DFDs (as discussed in Section 8.4). However, any of the tools described in this chapter may also be applied, bearing in mind that the scope of the exercise is enterprise wide. In particular, we shall see that results from local systems reconnaissance can be a useful aid in tackling enterprise scoping problems.

8.3   Local systems reconnaissance

The system profile for a local systems reconnaissance project will be either:

☐ A potential system: one (or more) candidate contexts plus the supporting global entities and global relationships shown on the scoped GERD.

or:

☐ A selection of global entities and global relationships.

I will refer to systems reconnaissance as 'function oriented' in the first case and 'data oriented' in the second.

8.3.1   Function oriented systems reconnaissance

Function oriented systems reconnaissance is driven by the statement of purpose(s) for the candidate context(s). The objective is to throw more light on those candidate contexts about which we are least confident. The task is to construct a 'preliminary' environmental model very quickly, and to recommend an appropriate development strategy for the system. The 'preliminary event list' and 'preliminary context diagram' created will be added to the system profile (as described in Section 6.10.2). Also, events are used to break down the scoped global ERD as described in Section 8.6. The resulting 'preliminary ERD' will be a useful precursor to E-R modelling proper and again be added to the system profile.

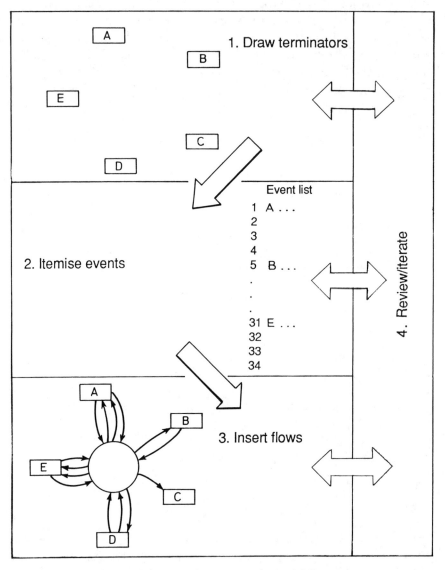

Figure 8.3 'Fast track' environmental modelling.

Since the main features of the tools and techniques used have already been described in Chapter 3, I will restrict the discussion here to salient points with regard to system reconnaissance.

Experience suggests that a good approach, when faced with a short timescale, is to rough out an environmental model as follows:

1. Draw the terminators.
2. Construct events for each terminator.
3. Draw in flows and construct a context diagram.
4. Iterate.

The procedure is shown graphically in Figure 8.3.

Each event should be classified (as described in Section 3.6). This will be important information used when deciding upon system development strategies (as described in Section 8.8).

8.3.2   Data oriented systems reconnaissance

In the second case above systems reconnaissance centres upon analyzing certain global entities and global relationships. The objective is to expose the underlying Enterprise E-R model; often the focus of attention is a single independent global entity (see Section 9.3).

The depth to which data is analyzed can vary. Where prototyping is envisaged it will be necessary to develop the underlying Enterprise E-R model such that it is mature enough for mapping to an appropriate database structure (this is discussed in Section 9.8).

There are several strategies that can be employed:

☐ Again, event lists can be constructed to break down the GERD as described in Section 8.6.

☐ Global ESTDs as described in Section 8.5.

☐ Conventional E-R modelling and associated normalization as described for example in Howe (1989).

Finally, whatever the system profile might be, the activity here is iterative with global reconnaissance: results of systems reconnaissance may well have an impact on global models which will need adjusting. Events gleaned here will be used to assist in global reconnaissance work as will become apparent from reading the subsequent sections. Conversely, a global DFD will be seen to translate easily into separate context diagrams which can form a take-off point for local reconnaissance.

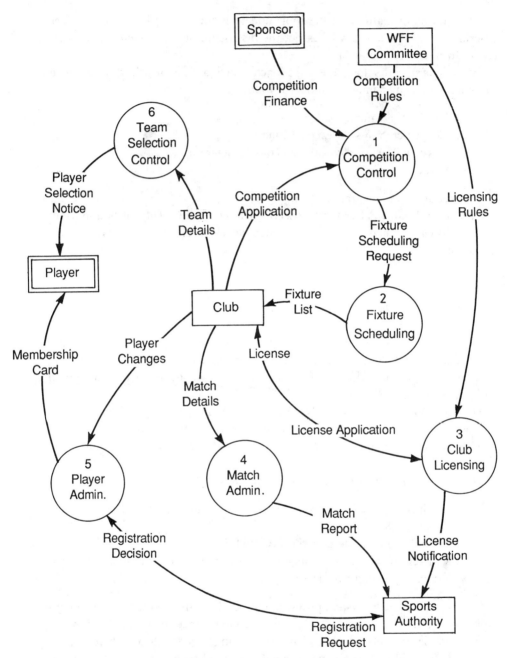

Figure 8.4 Global DFD for sports enterprise.

8.4   The global DFD

The global data flow diagram (GDFD) is a useful way of roughing out the interfaces implied by the CCL. An example for the sports administration enterprise is shown in Figure 8.4. Notice that the diagram follows the same notation as for a DFD with the exception that stores are not shown, whereas terminators are. Moreover, external terminators are shown as double-edged. It is suggested that stored data, at this stage, is much more appropriately understood using a GERD. For reasons discussed below the GDFD is not used for formal documentation or presentation.

Sketching out the GDFD will supply us with a fairly broad indication of the degree of interfacing implied by our choice of candidate contexts. The idea is to get a GDFD which minimizes internal interfaces, whilst maintaining those interfaces with the environment which are imposed by the business strategy. However, like its system level cousin, the preliminary DFD, this model will be complex involving typically 20 to 30 bubbles. It should therefore be used very much as an analyst's thinking tool, as a means of exploring interfaces and not as a tool for formal presentation.

Notice, each bubble on the GDFD can be modelled as a context diagram bubble with communicating bubbles shown as terminators. For example, the GDFD in Figure 8.4 generates a context diagram for Competition Control, with an interface to the terminator Fixture Scheduling, as shown below in Figure 8.5.

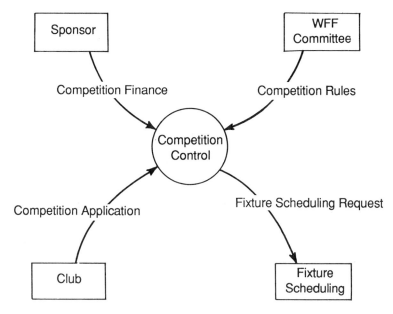

Figure 8.5 Context diagram for competition control.

Where appropriate, such systems can be analyzed further using local reconnaissance.

8.5   The global event list

Events which impact interfaces between functions need to be considered, and can be documented on a global event list; indeed in appropriate circumstances this may be readily available as we saw in Section 7.9. Where local reconnaissance work has taken place we can use resultant event lists from there. Each event must be a necessary condition of the business environment. Only events such as these are deemed to be genuine or external to the system. Where an event is the result of something happening in another system within the enterprise we must scrutinize the event carefully to ensure its validity.

Consider a typical company trading in goods over the 'phone. The strategic team have, somewhat unwisely we shall see, extracted four of the functions from the company organization chart as follows:

- ☐ Sales.
- ☐ Credit control.
- ☐ Inventory control.
- ☐ Invoicing.

Figure 8.6 shows a partial context diagram and event list for each function. Event modelling may be applied to yield the following analysis:

Event	Response
Customer submits order	Sales call Credit Control with Order Credit Request.
Sales request credit check	Check credit. If good, call Inventory Control with Order Inventory Request. If not good reply to Sales with Order Credit Refusal.
Credit Control refuses order	Reply to customer with negative Order Response.
Credit Control requests order inventory request	Check inventory and reduce if available. Report Verified Order to Sales
Inventory Control reports verified order	If sufficient stock on Verified Order reply to customer with positive Order Response and send Invoice Request to Invoicing. Otherwise reply to customer with negative Order Response
Sales request invoice	Raise Invoice and send to customer

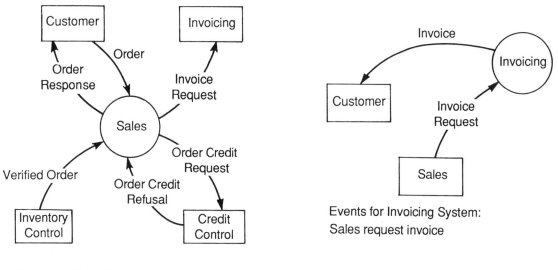

Events for Sales System:

Customer submits order
Credit Control refuses order
Inventory control reports verified order

Events for Invoicing System:
Sales request invoice

Events for Credit Control System:
Sales request credit check

Events for Inventory Control System:
Credit Control requests order inventory check

Figure 8.6 Partial context diagrams and event lists for tele-sales enterprise.

Less formally, imagine a typical scenario. A customer rings in with an order. The salesperson asks the customer to hang on while things are checked out. A telephone call is made to credit control and there is a wait while the customer's credit is checked out. All being well a further call is then made from credit control to inventory control to check the goods are available. While this is going on the salesperson apologizes to the customer for the delay in between the 'courtesy music'. Eventually, all being well, a call is received by the salesperson from inventory control to say that the goods are available. Finally, the salesperson gets back on the telephone with the good news only to find that the customer has hung up in frustration.

The inadequacies of this situation may be exposed by considering the systems in relation to each other by drawing a GDFD as in Figure 8.7. Notice the proliferation of internal interfaces between the different systems. Five out of the six events are in fact only there to support the existing infrastructure.

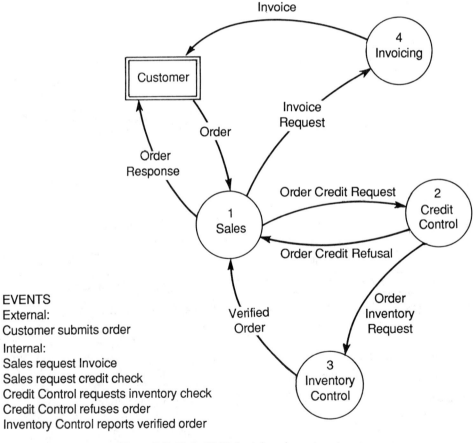

Figure 8.7 Global DFD for tele-sales enterprise.

In reality, if interfaces are to be minimized, we must consider the total requirement in relation to the environment of the enterprise in line with the principle of encapsulation. The example scenario can, in fact, be reduced to just one event and a simple context diagram with three flows, as shown in Figure 8.8. The true business function is Order Processing which will need access to customer and inventory stored data to make an immediate response to the event 'Customer submits order'. In this way customer orders can be processed with a promptness which was previously not possible.

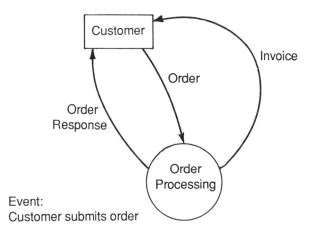

Figure 8.8 Partial context diagram and event list for Order Processing System.

8.6 The global entity state transition diagram (GESTD)

The GESTD employs the same notation as the ESTD. ESTDs themselves are simple adaptations of STDs and are described in Chapter 9, to which the reader is referred for a detailed account of the notation. The only difference is that whereas an ESTD models changes of state of an entity, a GESTD models changes of state of a global entity. GESTDs will therefore be explained here by example, rather than by definition.

We have seen that a state on an STD can be pictured as a timeframe, during which certain things are and certain things are not allowed to happen to a system. Similarly, a state on a GESTD represents a timeframe during which certain things are and certain things are not allowed to happen to global entity. The common currency here is the concept of event: it is the event which causes changes of state, be they states of a system, entity or global entity. Just as events appear as conditions on STDs so they appear in the same way on GESTDs. Actions are left blank.

The GESTD is essentially a high-level scoping tool to be used in conjunction with event modelling with two prime purposes:

1. Ensuring a cohesive packaging of events within potential systems.
2. Breaking down global entities into actual entities and relationships as a precursor to detailed E-R modelling.

Again, the principle which will be applied here is actually the same as that of object oriented analysis which seeks to encapsulate data with its associated processing and control into objects. What we will be attempting here is to localize state changes within candidate contexts.

We can put this another way: if retaining an event within a system's scope means increasing interfaces with other systems then there must be very good reasons for this; otherwise the offender must be allocated to a different system which will involve less interfaces. Similarly, if retaining a global entity as an actual entity involves associated events spread across different systems, the global entity may have to be broken down into entities each with associated events packaged within separate systems. The strategic perspective requires systems which *integrate*, not systems which *interface*. Let us look at an example to see how this actually works in practice.

Consider again the telephone sales company. This time, however, the situation is a little more complex in that what is being sold are contracts to develop computer systems. A simplified scenario for this might be as follows.

We start with the event 'Customer expresses interest' which leads to a *Tentative* contract. This can be pictured as a state of the global entity Contract, as shown in Figure 8.9, during which negotiations are taking place with a view to constructing a proposal. Next comes the event 'Salesperson submits proposal' which causes the entity state to change to *Proposed*. Next, all being well, the event 'Salesperson closes deal' causes a change of state to *Closed*. Once work is commenced, progress will have to be monitored. Therefore, the event 'Consultants commence work' causes a further change of state to *In Progress*. Finally, the event 'Consultants complete work' results in the state *Completed*.

The principle of localizing state changes within candidate contexts leads to a single sales system, responding to each of the above five events, maintaining the Contract entity. However some of the information will clearly be sales related (for example the closure and contract documents) whereas other information will be more project management related (for example, progress reports). That is, the system does not appear to be very cohesive from a business viewpoint.

Closer inspection of the GESTD reveals that the Contract entity goes through two discernible life cycles *in sequence*. Therefore one response to the lack of

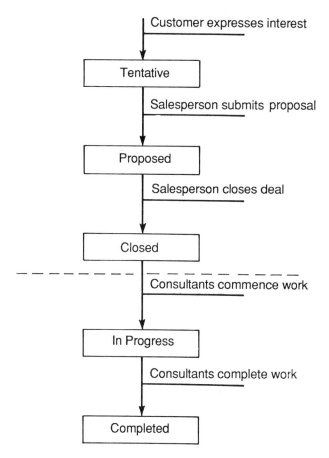

Figure 8.9 Global ESTD for progress status of Contract.

cohesion problem would be to divide the GESTD into two separate ESTDs: one for the sales related events/states (shown above the dashed line in Figure 8.9) and another for the management related events/states (shown below the dashed line). This might result in two separate systems: a sales system and a management system.

Each system may also be concerned with different attributes: proposal and closure dates and terms in the case of the sales system; contract progress status, hours spent and so on in the case of the management system. A better alternative, which should always be considered in cases like this, is therefore to split the Contract global entity into two entities Proposal and Contract with a relationship from the former to the latter of Results In as shown in Figure 8.10. Each entity then has its own encapsulated ESTD, as indicated in Figure 8.11 relative to the requirements of each system.

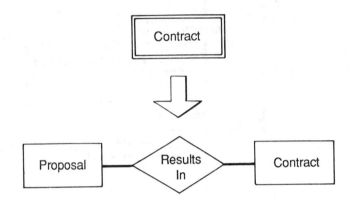

Figure 8.10 Explosion of a global entity.

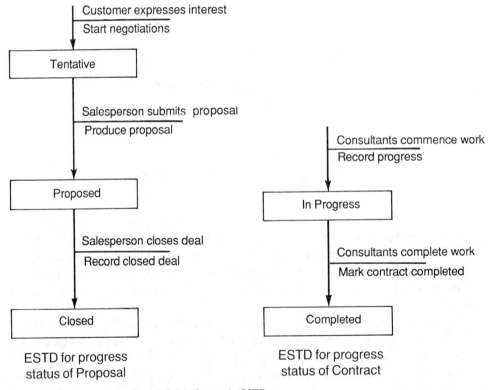

Figure 8.11 Separate ESTDs.

8.7   **Exposing the enterprise E-R model**

Each scoped global ERD constitutes a high-level view of enterprise data relative to a given system. The results of system reconnaissance, especially at local level, can be used to break down each scoped global ERD to expose the entities and relationships forming the underlying data structure (enterprise E-R model).

A global entity may be exploded into actual entities and/or relationships; normally there will be a mix of both. A global relationship may also be exploded into entities and/or relationships; normally there will be at least one associative entity.

System reconnaissance needs to be done quickly. Therefore although an inherent part of E-R modelling is the identification of attributes and the posting (or 'attribution') of those attributes to entities we try to restrict the exercise here to the bare essential that each entity created has an identifier. Where attribution does occur it is very much tentative and secondary. It is tentative in the sense that it is subject to revision and review during later more detailed systems development work. It is secondary in that the main point of the presently discussed exercise is to get a rough, preliminary view of the underlying data structure, prior to more detailed E-R modelling or prototyping.

The operative principle here is the 'outside-in principle': consider what it is that the user actually needs before determining the structure required to support that need. That is, consider what data the system will need to absorb and produce to satisfy user requirements, without becoming bogged down in structural concepts best applied after the basic requirements have been roughed out.

The technique, described in Chapter 3, of examining the event list and transposing nouns to entities and verbs to relationships can be most useful. This can be applied by considering each event and applying it to the scoped global ERD to create entities and relationships to support the data flows associated with it. To illustrate the principle consider the event list for the Player Administration System developed in Chapter 3. This can be presented in terms of events and their associated data flows thus:

Event	*Data flows*
1. Club registers player provisionally	*In*: Provisional Player Registration
	Out: New Membership Card, Player Registration Request
2. Sports Authority makes decision on player registration	*In*: Player Registration Decision
	Out: Confirmed Membership Card

3. Player requests transfer   *In*: Transfer Request

4. Club makes decision on transfer request   *In*: Transfer Decision

     Out: Transfer Response

5. Club transfers player   *In*: Transfer Deal
     Out: Transfer Confirmation

6. Player resigns from club   *In*: Player Resignation

7. Doctor submits player's injury details   *In*: Injury Occurrence

8. Time to report transfer reminders   *Out*: Transfer Reminders

9. Doctor submits clearance of injury   *In*: Injury Clearance

Now let us consider each event and its associated data flows with a view to exploding the scoped global ERD shown in Figure 8.12.

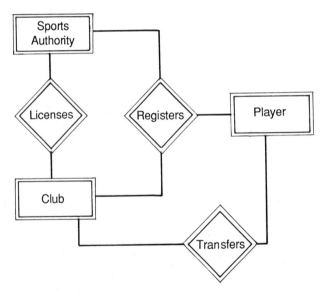

Figure 8.12 Scoped global ERD for Player Administration System.

EVENT 1
- ☐ Creates the global relationship Registers, which like all other global relationships falling within the system scope will be treated as an actual relationship on the ERD we are creating.
- ☐ Accesses the global relationship Licenses in order to find out which Sports Authority to send the Player Registration Request.

☐ Existing global entities Player and Club seem to support storage of the incoming data. Like all other global entities these will be treated as actual entities on the ERD we are creating.

EVENT 2

☐ The requirement to store details of both membership and registration causes Registers to be factored into two corresponding associative entities: Club Membership and Registration as shown in Figure 8.13. This reflects the realization that it is a player's membership that is registered, not the actual player.

☐ Accesses the Licenses relationship (see Figure 8.12) to verify the correct Sports Authority to which to associate the Registration.

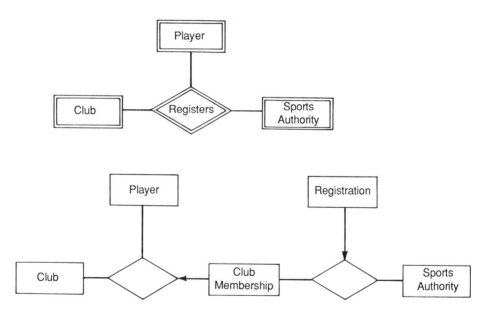

Figure 8.13 Explosion of a global relationship into component associative entities.

EVENT 3

☐ A player may make numerous transfer requests, the date of each of which needs to be stored. This information could, at this early stage, be left as a repeating attribute of Player. However, we will see later, certainly before database design, that in the interests of non-redundancy there will be a need to remove indeterminate repeating groups, and treat them as new entities related to the original entities. Therefore we anticipate this and introduce an entity Transfer Request to house the attribute

Transfer Request Date, and a relationship Makes from Player to the new entity.

EVENT 4

☐ The attributes Transfer Decision (yes/no) and Transfer Decision Date can be held in the Player entity.

EVENT 5

☐ The requirement to store the attribute Transfer Fee creates a need to factor the global relationship Transfers into an associative entity Transfer Deal, which will be associative to Player and both involved Clubs. Figure 8.14 shows this complex associative entity. Note that it is also recursive.

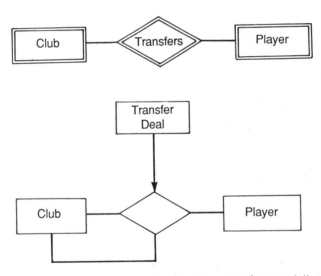

Figure 8.14 Explosion of a global relationship into a complex associative entity.

EVENT 6

☐ This can be dealt with simply by storing Resignation Date as an attribute of Player.

EVENT 7

☐ A player can be injured many times, resulting in a repeating group within Player to house the following incoming attributes: Injury Type, Injury Occurrence Date, and Injury Doctor's Comment. To deal with this, on similar grounds to those for Event 3, we introduce a new entity Injury and a new relationship Incurs between Player and Injury.

EVENT 8

☐ Reinforces Events 3 and 4.

EVENT 9

☐ Reinforces Event 7; attributes Injury Treatment and Injury Cleared Date to be held in Injury.

The ERD resulting from this event-walking exercise is shown in Figure 8.15. This

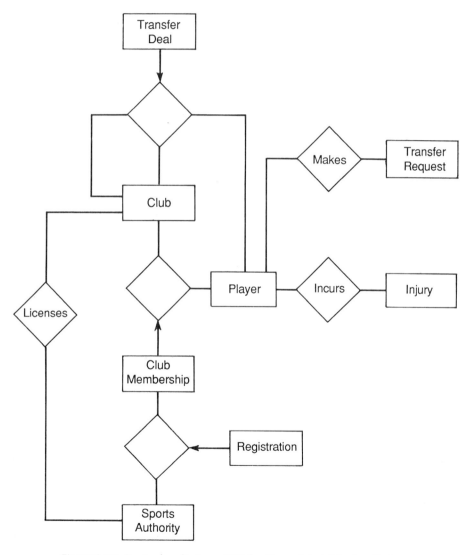

Figure 8.15 Revised preliminary ERD for Player Administration System.

is, in effect, a preliminary ERD (a term introduced in Chapter 4) for the Player Administration System. Compare this with our original ERD for this system (shown in Figure 4.17). Notice that we now have a much more integrated picture with respect to enterprise wide requirements. In particular we have highlighted the need to relate information to the entity Sports Authority which was missing from our earlier diagram.

This raises an important point regarding single occurrence entities. As we saw in Section 4.5, these are rarely modelled as entities because the data is actually of no interest and there is no need to distinguish occurrences; typical examples are Management and Company. Notice, this is not a hard and fast rule, particularly with embedded systems. Also we sometimes need to be aware of possible business expansion; for example, a business may only have a single sales office at present but future plans may involve consideration of a distributed network of sales offices. More importantly for the present discussion we have to be heedful of scope. If we are modelling from the point of view of a single sports authority, in the above example, then the Sports Authority entity would be a single occurrence and therefore probably omitted from the diagram. However, if our brief stretches across sports authorities with the result that we need to distinguish one sports authority from another then Sports Authority may well be an entity. And, in the example, this is indeed the case.

To recap, what we have done is to apply environmental modelling to the global ERD, using event list and context diagram as a stimuli for asking questions, exposing assumptions and exploring potential system scope. The objective of gaining early understanding of the underlying data structure is achieved in terms of a preliminary ERD. This will form part of the system profile for a subsequent systems analysis project. Before making this step, however, we would normally need to consolidate within the enterprise ERD. This subject will be discussed in Chapter 9.

8.8 The use of matrices

In Section 4.7.1 event responses in the Player Administration System were grouped in the way they were largely on the grounds of commonality of business purpose and relevance to particular users. This would make it relatively easy to 'lift' relevant material for customized presentation to those users. However, we saw that there are other factors that will influence our decision. To recap, bubbles may be grouped according to three main criteria:

1. Do they exclusively share the same stored data (entities and relationships)?

2. Are they exclusively shared by the same user (terminators)?
3. Do they require integrated control (where C events are involved)?

It was suggested that 'yes' answers to all three questions tend toward an ideal encapsulation of requirements as illustrated in Figure 4.15. Effectively, this means *shaping* the system itself into sub-systems which are as insulated as possible from one another, thus reducing the threat of inevitable future change in requirements by localizing it. Clearly this is not simply a presentation issue.

An entity–event matrix can assist immensely in shaping a system according to the first of the above questions. Event responses are plotted against entities and cells filled in to indicate whether the response creates (C), reads (R), updates (U) or deletes (D) the entity in question; Figure 8.16 shows an example for the Player Administration System. The matrix can be used to explore different ways

Event number	Event response	Player	Club	Transfer Deal	Club Membership	Registration	Transfer Request	Injury	Sports Authority
1	Provisionally Register Player	C/U	R		C				R
2	Record Registration	R	R		U	C			R
3	Record Transfer Request	R			R		C		
4	Record Transfer Decision	R			U		U		
5	Record Transfer	R	R	C	C/U				
6	Record Player Resignation				U				
7	Record Injury	R						C	
8	Report Transfer Reminders	R	R		R				
9	Clear Injury	R						U	

Figure 8.16 Entity–event matrix for Player Administration System.

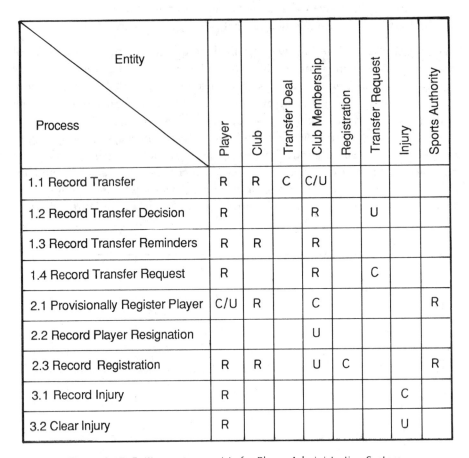

Process \ Entity	Player	Club	Transfer Deal	Club Membership	Registration	Transfer Request	Injury	Sports Authority
1.1 Record Transfer	R	R	C	C/U				
1.2 Record Transfer Decision	R			R		U		
1.3 Record Transfer Reminders	R	R		R				
1.4 Record Transfer Request	R			R		C		
2.1 Provisionally Register Player	C/U	R		C				R
2.2 Record Player Resignation				U				
2.3 Record Registration	R	R		U	C			R
3.1 Record Injury	R						C	
3.2 Clear Injury	R						U	

Figure 8.17 Entity–process matrix for Player Administration System.

of shaping the system into groupings of processes and entities, and reordering processes and entities into clusters. Ideally entities and processes should fall out as neat encapsulated clusters. In practice, however, this is rare; often there are several different alternatives, none of which is perfect, and a choice must be made as to the most suitable.

The result is an entity–process matrix with processes renumbered to indicate clusters. Figure 8.17 shows an example for the Player Administration System based upon the choice made previously in Section 4.7.1.

The matrix is also a useful means of ensuring completeness. We need to ask the question 'Are all entities supported in terms of C, R, U and D?'. If not, why not? A couple of hypothetical examples follow:

☐ *Question*: Why are there no processes to delete any entity?

- □ *Answer*: In the case of Club Membership, Transfer Request and Injury our system might be responsible for deletion. Therefore we would need to introduce events to cater for this. These might well be temporal events such as Time To Delete Transfer Requests. However, in the case of all other entities we might find that other systems are responsible for deletion.
- □ *Question*: Why are Transfer Deals, Registrations, Transfer Requests and Injuries not read by any processes?
- □ *Answer*: Actually this is all right as the system only captures this information for use by other systems.

Had we conducted a local systems reconnaissance project as a forerunner to mainstream development to explore scoping and completeness issues we might well have chosen a different partitioning to that indicated in Figure 8.17. For example, we might have chosen to cluster into sub-systems based more heavily on stored data usage, resulting in the following partitioning:

- □ Injury administration: to include responses to Events 7 and 9 which exclusively maintain Injury.
- □ Transfer request handling: to include responses to Events 3 and 8 which exclusively maintain Transfer Request.
- □ Membership administration: to include remaining responses which exclusively maintain Club Membership.

Shaping systems of any complexity will involve a certain compromise between what are sometimes conflicting criteria. The entity–event and entity–process matrices help visualize the consequences of these choices in a rational manner. Also, they are a convenient means of assisting project planning by clustering complex systems into sub-systems, each of which can be developed in its own right. Indeed, this is a useful strategy for dealing with the problem of lengthy event lists, discussion in Section 3.10. Finally, this technique can be applied globally in which case the 'complex system' is the enterprise itself. In this case a global event list, described in Section 8.5, can be used alongside the GERD to identify potential system scopes.

8.9 Alternatives to systems development

The cost-effectiveness of systems development is in large part a measure of the effectiveness of the system delivered. Efforts to improve knowledge in this area are developing only slowly. Difficulty in estimating the costs of systems development, particularly early in the lifecycle, remains at the root of the software crisis. Boehm (1981) describes a model using 15 factors which together contribute toward the cost of systems development; more latterly (Jones, 1986) describes 45 such factors. Research commonly reinforces the view that despite all the new tools and techniques there is no substitute for talented and dedicated people applying them.

Whilst acknowledging both the complexity of the situation and the importance of good people I wish to focus here on one particular aspect of the problem that often seems to be somewhat glossed over, with the objective of providing some tentative guidelines on suitable development strategies. It has already been pointed out that when projects fail the blame is all too often placed on the techniques and tools used. However, the cause of failure is often to be found not so much in the techniques and tools themselves, but in the fact that the choice of techniques and tools was unsuitable for the particular problem. In general, we stick to what we know best; however, what we know best is not always appropriate to the demands of a specific job.

We need a rational basis for choosing a systems development strategy. We shall see that there is no single answer: each system must be judged on its merits. Firstly, the results of system reconnaissance work are used to gauge the type of system we are faced with. A spectrum of different development techniques is then broadly described. Recommendations are made as to which techniques are most suitable for which system types.

Before this, however, we should take a critical look at whether a *development* strategy as such is, in fact, appropriate. Two alternatives that we shall briefly explore are end-user computing and software packages.

8.9.1 End-user computing

In certain situations end-users may be able to develop their own applications (Martin, 1982) using an appropriate software tool; hence the term 'end-user computing'. Professional support is often necessary to provide both expertise and co-ordination and is increasingly found in the 'Information Centre'; for example see Wetherbe and Leitheiser (1985). The advantage with end-user computing is that it cuts right across the problem of developer-user communication as the two are one and the same, and that it can considerably lighten the load on systems development departments. Indeed, it seemed to me, as a programmer in the early 1970s, I was forever writing, enhancing, and eventually rewriting reporting programs running off existing files. Had an Information Centre existed then it would obviously have freed me for much more creative and rewarding tasks.

Despite the attractions of end-user computing its application is more limited than is sometimes appreciated. The requirement must feed off existing databases in a way that does not affect the integrity of those databases. Enquiry and reporting systems, and distributed systems where updating is carried out autonomously from the main database are two particular cases in point.

8.9.2   Software packages

A package solution is sometimes appropriate where the requirement is for a system common to many organizations (Gremillion and Pyburn, 1983). Examples are payroll, general ledger and personnel systems. The increasing sophistication and decreasing price of software packages render them an attractive alternative to bespoke development. The latter is usually more costly and will certainly take longer to deliver.

EP can be extremely useful in evaluating the suitability of a package, as follows. Firstly, build a behavioural model of user requirements. Secondly, reverse engineer the package by abstracting a context diagram, event list and ERD and then developing a behavioural model. The two behavioural models are then compared to assess the compatibility of the package with the requirements in terms of essential content and interfaces. Packages will generally be most suitable where there is a good match of essential content and where interface requirements to other systems are low.

Mismatches of essential content affect cost-effectiveness on either or both of two counts. Firstly, that the package lacks required functionality and/or data structure in which case money must be spent on providing them. Secondly, that the package contains superfluous functionality and/or data structure in which case money will effectively be wasted on purchasing it.

Where there are complex interfaces to other systems it will usually be necessary to spend money on developing customized routines to support them. Even where standard downloading and uploading facilities are provided as part of the package it is rarely the case that these can be used without modification.

The package should also be evaluated in terms of the reliability of the supplier and of flexibility. Situations occur where initially acceptable packages come after a few years to call for considerable modification requiring alteration of the source code. Such alterations normally cancel the suppliers' contractual responsibilities for maintaining those packages, although the advent of open-ended packages written partly in fourth generation languages (4GLs) has gone some way to removing this problem. We must therefore be confident that requirements are clearly understood. Again EP is a useful precursor to achieving this.

To summarize, a package solution may well be appropriate for requirements which:

> ☐ Are common to many organizations.
> ☐ Closely match the essentials of the package.

☐ Are low on interfacing.
☐ Are well understood.

Package selection and system modelling should not be seen as separate: I have suggested that often it is necessary to build system models using EP as a means of ascertaining these four factors.

8.10 Determining systems development strategy

Given that end-user computing or a package solution is not appropriate we are faced with choosing a development strategy. At one extreme, we might choose to use EP to build a fully detailed requirement specification as described in Chapters 3 to 5. At the other extreme lie prototyping approaches described in Chapters 10 and 11. In the middle lie various mix and matches of the two. The purpose of this section is to give the reader some insight as to the most appropriate strategy for certain system types as identified below.

It is important to emphasize again the complexity of the situation. Systems type is one, albeit crucial, factor amongst many. The importance of factors such as company culture, politics and user mentality has already been intimated in the opening chapter of this book. Three particularly pertinent further questions to ask are as follows:

1. Is the requirement new (i.e. no existing system)?
2. Are there few (if any) interfaces to other systems?
3. Is the system particularly specialized?

A 'no' answer to the first question suggests reverse engineering using EP to produce a behavioural model might well be appropriate. In addition, where existing processes are well established with users following set routines, procedural process specifications are often a useful way of confirming the analyst's understanding.

'Yes' answers to all three questions tend toward a prototyping strategy.

8.10.1 Determining system type

Determining system type involves weighing up a complexity of factors with the objective of choosing an appropriate development strategy. It is possible to distinguish two basic species of system, the development strategy for each of which will be rather different: *event driven systems* and *information systems*. Broadly speaking, information systems are 'about the business' whereas event driven systems are 'the business'; in that sense the former tend to service the upper levels of the pyramid shown in Figure 6.1, whereas the latter tend to service the lower levels. Between the two species lie various hybrids such as expert and real-time data capture systems. Clearly exact definition of system type is a complex and perhaps impossible business. What I am aiming at here is the much more limited objective of providing some practical guidelines on determining development strategy by using an event list which has been constructed in 'fast-track' mode as part of a systems reconnaissance project.

Event driven systems are characterized by a predominance of reflex actions in response to predicted events. Even for a medium to small size system we can expect an event list of some import, with 50 events not uncommon. Event driven systems can be classed according to the predominance of certain event classifications (as described in Sections 3.7 and 3.8) within the event list as follows:

C:	Digital control	Domestic appliances
CD:	Embedded communications	Process control Transmission control
TC:	Time-dependent control systems	Alarms
D:	Transaction processing Scientific	Online financial Linear programming
TD:	Batch processing	Contractual processing
CDT:	Embedded schedulers Communications schedulers	Medical control Space transmission

Event driven systems can also be classed according to the proportion of events which represent errors and exceptions to which the system must respond. Such events are labelled E.

Information systems are characterized by a predominance of discretionary actions where it is not possible to predict events with any precision. Typically, they are decision support systems serving middle and upper management. The environmental model for a decision support system will either contain very few events or be dominated by flow driven data events expressing a need for *ad hoc* information to be produced. In these cases, even where the requirement appears complex, it is difficult to find many genuine events. If the generalized *ad hoc* queries are probed in any depth they may give rise to hundreds of events which fail to throw much light on the problem. For example, the generally expressed event 'Marketing request product details' might under interview generate a whole stream of possible events:

☐ Marketing requests number of XYZ contracts sold in Europe last year.
☐ Marketing requests number of XYZ contracts sold to pensioners ever.
☐ Marketing requests proportion of XYZ proposals to fail this year.
☐ Marketing requests value of XYZ business conducted with this customer.
☐ Marketing requests number of bad debtors for XYZ.
☐ Marketing requests total commission earnt for XYZ contracts.
☐ Marketing requests value of XYZ business sold by this salesperson.
☐ Marketing requests projected profit margins on XYZ business in Asia next year.
☐ Etc.

Clearly, although an event list like this has some value I am suggesting that it has a very limited value. We are faced fairly quickly with the law of diminishing returns in that we seem to be putting a lot of effort into fact finding without getting very much useful information out. This is because in these cases the users seldom can anticipate what they want before they are put in the position of actually requiring the information. It is a little like asking someone to construct an open ended shopping list. We could spend all day writing a list of everything we would like to buy, go to the shop, buy it and still find there were certain essentials we had forgotten, as well, of course, lots of things for which we have little use after all. In essence therefore information systems are characterized by a lack of genuine events.

8.10.2 Guidelines by system type

Event driven systems

Systems analysis should be initiated along the lines discussed in Part 2 in order to explore, understand and organize requirements:

☐ Explore by building environmental model.
☐ Understand by building preliminary models. Ideally different diagram types should be built *in parallel* depending on event classification as follows:
STD for C and TC events,
DFD for D and TD events,
STD and DFD for CD and CDT events,
ERD for D, CD and CDT events requiring usage of stored data.
☐ Organize the preliminary models.

We must now select the most appropriate strategy for specifying and verifying requirements. Two approaches to specification – procedural and non-procedural – were discussed in Section 5.4 and three broad means of verifying requirements were earlier intimated in Section 5.6; they are illustrated in Figure 8.18 (which is a repeat of Figure 5.8).

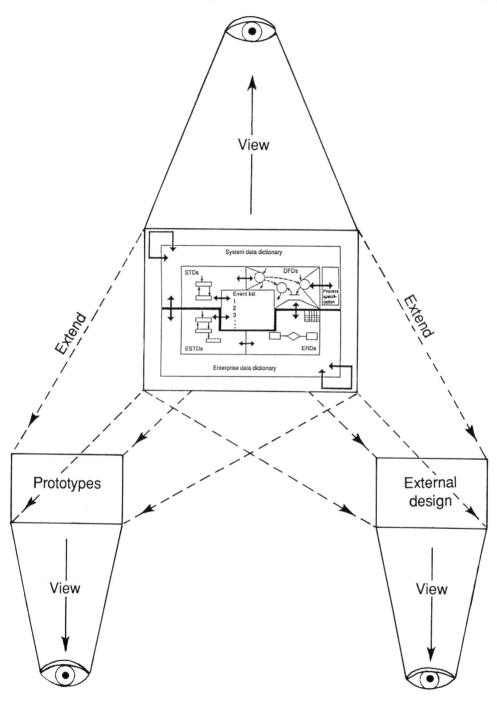

Figure 8.18 Verifying system requirements.

Let us examine various approaches, which may be 'mixed and matched', with respect to each event classification as follows.

1. *C (Digital control) and TC (Time dependent control systems).* A detailed behavioural model with the accent on STDs is recommended. Non-procedural process specifications (see Section 5.4.3) and decision tables are particularly appropriate as control processes for such systems will be driven by Boolean logic. Extending ahead into early external design is unlikely to be appropriate as user interfaces are not normally an issue. However, technical prototyping or simulation may well be appropriate; this is briefly discussed in Section 10.4.2.

2. *CD (Embedded) and CDT (Embedded schedulers).* A detailed behavioural model with the accent on both STDs and DFDs is recommended. ERDs will play a lesser role unless interfaces to other systems indicate complex data capture in which case developers will need to ensure compatibility with the underlying enterprise E-R model. Non-procedural process specifications are unlikely to be appropriate as they do not highlight the behaviour over time of the *continuous* processes that are likely to dominate such a system. Procedural specifications with the accent on equations (Hatley and Pirbhai, 1987) are normally most suitable. Early extension into external design can be appropriate where there is user interfacing. Also technical prototyping or simulation (which is briefly discussed in Section 10.4.2) may well be appropriate.

3. *CD (Communications) and CDT (Communications schedulers).* A detailed behavioural model with the accent on both STDs and DFDs is recommended. ERDs will almost certainly play a lesser role as even where interfaces to other systems indicate complex data capture, the system under development is unlikely to be influenced by the structure itself of this data. Non-procedural process specifications (see Section 5.4.3) may well be appropriate as they are good at highlighting the behaviour of discrete proceeses that tend to dominate such a system under the control of Boolean logic. External design is likely to be appropriate as user interfacing is often an important part of such systems. Although simulation may well be appropriate there is the further problem that once the software has been developed on a particular machine it may well require porting to different hardware.

4. *D (Transaction processing).* A detailed behavioural model alone is not the best vehicle for verifying requirements here. Where prototyping tools are unavailable some attempt should be made at external design to involve users in verifying outline requirements, before using process specifications to verify the detailed logic. Normally procedural specifications work best where there is complexity of matching of stored data and where sequence of activities are crucial. In simpler situations

a non-procedural approach also works well. However, given that the tools are available, prototyping is most appropriate alongside process specifications for such systems. The accent should actually be on *event prototyping* where a database structure is in place. Where the database structure is not in place *primitive proto-typing* should be carried out first to establish it. Once prototypes have been agreed the underlying logic can be filtered back to form process specifications to complete documentation of the behavioural model. These concepts are described in Chapters 10 and 11.

5. *D (Scientific).* The emphasis here is likely to be on detailed verification of complex algorithms to which prototyping and external design do not lend them-selves well but for which mathematical modelling tools may well, however, be appropriate (although this area is outside the scope of this book). Emphasis is likely to be on the DFD in tandem with procedural process specifications referencing equations. Where the supporting stored data structure is complex ERDs should also be employed.

6. *TD (Batch processing).* A detailed behavioural model with the accent on both DFDs and ERDs is recommended. ERDs will almost certainly play a major role as stored data structure is usually an important aspect of such systems. Procedural, rather than non-procedural process specifications are likely to be more appropriate as there is normally a need to verify complex matching logic. External design is also likely to be appropriate as a means of highlighting the heavy report content normally associated with such systems. Although prototyping, is almost certain to be unsuitable, report generation facilities may be most useful.

7. *E plus any of the above (Error and exception handling).* A small number of E type events are normal with most systems. Where there is a dominance of these however it is likely that the very statement of purpose of the system centres upon error or exception handling. One of the problems with such events is that it is always possible to think of more; in that sense they are similar to the bogus 'events' uncovered for information systems. In thinking of possible errors and exceptions the user is usually stimulated to ask yet more 'What happens if?' questions. There-fore the time spent on using environmental modelling to explore such system requirements needs to be limited. Understanding and organization of requirements should then take place with a view to either simulating or prototyping as appro-priate for other event classifications. If suitable tools are not available then it is advisable to extend an early external design. Only once the user has had a chance to 'experience' the system in this way should a fully detailed behavioural model be completed.

Information systems

With information systems we require a good stored information structure which is flexible enough to meet the demands of decision support. Development will therefore focus heavily on the scoped global ERD or the underlying E-R model (where data oriented systems reconnaissance has occurred).

The underlying strategy with information systems is firstly to build simple prototype screens to verify information captured by event driven systems and to confirm independent entities (this is known as primitive prototyping); and secondly to build sets of prototype screens to verify decision support requirements (this is known as decision support prototyping). Both species of prototyping are discussed in detail in Chapters 10 and 11. The development strategy will, in fact, depend to a large extent upon how many of the entities and relationships in question are reflected in existing database structures as follows:

1. *Existing database structure.* Where most of the entities and relationships are 'in place', and given that prototyping tools are available, decision support prototyping is the most effective approach.

2. *No existing database structure.* Where most of the entities and relationships are not 'in place' it is important first to establish them before attempting decision support prototyping. This can be done in complementary ways:

□ By conventional E-R modelling as previously described.
□ By primitive prototyping.

Whichever route is taken it is vital that once components of the underlying enterprise E-R model are exposed they should at least be filtered through data administration for formal documentation. Indeed, it is often appropriate for data administration to be actively involved in development work itself as described in Chapter 9.

Hybrid systems

Many systems obviously fall somewhere between the two ends of the spectrum presented here and require a combination of approaches. Nevertheless, such systems can be regarded as comprised of sub-systems which can then be compartmentalized as suggested. Mix and match methods using the above guidelines can then be selected on a fairly flexible basis.

Certain organizations will have portfolios of widely varying system types; for example a manufacturer with shopfloor robotics systems and factory information systems. Therefore, one word of caution: where complex stored data structures are involved and especially where those structures are shared across systems the recommendation is to investigate those structures first. In such cases data oriented systems reconnaissance followed by primitve prototyping should be carried out to establish the independent entities before proceeding further.

8.11 Summary

We have seen that there are two main types of system reconnaissance – local and global – and the benefits of each are rather different. Global system reconnaissance operates at a high level exploring the interfaces between proposed systems. The guiding force here is the principle of encapsulation applied at enterprise level. The major benefit of this is to provide advanced information as to the validity of the partitioning into proposed systems. Local systems reconnaissance seeks to 'lift the cover' from a proposed system. Again the guiding force is the principle of encapsulation, but this time applied at system or entity level, depending upon whether the reconnaissance is function or data oriented. The major benefit of this is to provide advanced information on which to base a decision as to the most suitable development strategy to be pursued for this system.

The reader will notice that although the mode and focus of working is rather different to systems analysis projects using EP, the modelling tools and the guiding principle of encapsulation are essentially the same. Also, what is being done is very much in line with our original modelling framework. Therefore there is really very little overhead in terms of learning new notations. Common modelling coinage also lends a consistency between systems reconnaissance work and more conventional analysis projects.

The main barrier to systems reconnaissance is liable to be management culture as expressed in the traditional mind-set described in Chapter 1. That is why I have been at pains to stress that systems reconnaissance is important project work. A systems reconnaissance project, no less than any other project, must have a *project profile* if it is to assume serious status. The results of systems reconnaissance must be channelled to the appropriate system profile as visible evidence of productivity, if it is not to be dismissed as mere dabbling around. In short, such projects must be seen to be cost-effective.

The general objective of this chapter was to give the reader some sort of flavour of which development strategies were appropriate for which types of system, and to show how EP lends itself toward that requirement. In Chapters 10 and 11 prototyping will be explained as a useful strategy for the development of effective systems. However, it must not be viewed as a panacea for all ills. The particular objective of this chapter was to outline the types of system for which it both is and *is not* appropriate.

PART FOUR

The Enterprise Perspective

This part of the book looks at applying the recommended toolset from the viewpoint of effective administration enterprise-wide. The enterprise perspective is highlighted in Figure C opposite.

Underpinning all development work, from strategy to prototyping, is the Enterprise Data Model, for which extensions to the modelling toolset are introduced and explained.

The organic lifecycle implies an upward change of gear for the data administration function. We therefore explore this area in some detail viewing it from perspectives of different systems development activities.

Finally, database mapping rules are explained. This is an important but often neglected area which is covered partly for the reader's reference, but also necessary to give a foundation for the prototyping work discussed in the next part.

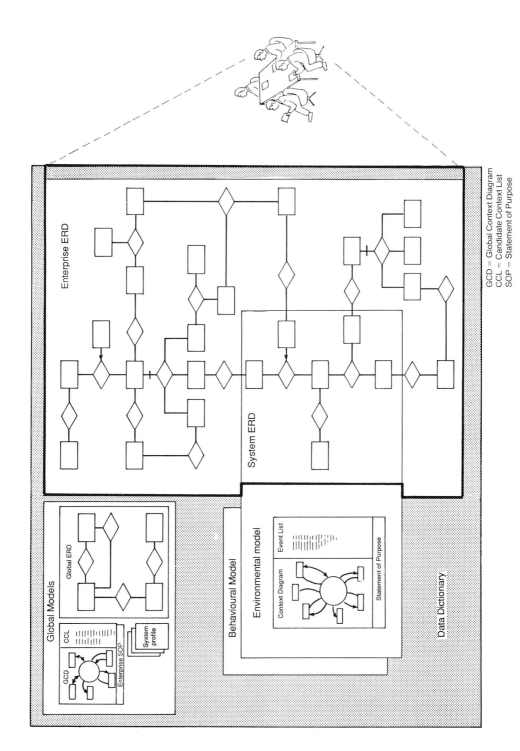

Enterprise ERD

System ERD

Global Models

Global ERD

CCL

GCD

Enterprise SOP

System profile

Behavioural Model

Environmental model

Context Diagram

Event List

Statement of Purpose

Data Dictionary

GCD = Global Context Diagram
CCL = Candidate Context List
SOP = Statement of Purpose

Figure C The Enterprise Perspective.

CHAPTER 9

The enterprise data model

□ □ □ □ □ □ □ □ □ □ □ □ □ □ □ □ □

Where is the information we have lost in data?

HIROSHI INOSE and J.R. PIERCE
Information, Technology and Civilisation

9.1 Introduction

This chapter describes the enterprise data model and discusses its relationship with strategic and system models, and with protoyping. The basic ERD notation discussed in Chapter 4 is extended and the entity state transition diagram introduced. We have seen that enterprise modelling is differentiated by its scope: the whole business. Because of its centrality, and importance to system development, guidelines are included for data administration.

We will be focussing here primarily on essential models. However, if verifying essential policy through extensions into external design or prototyping as suggested in Chapter 5 (see Figure 5.8) it will be necessary to map the required portion of the enterprise E-R model to the proposed database structure. Therefore an outline sketch of database design modelling will be provided to put the mapping work into context, before discussing mapping rules for relational architectures in some detail. This should give some direction as to 'what happens next' as well as providing the necessary foundation for prototyping work which is discussed in the next part of this book.

9.2 The enterprise entity relationship model (EERM)

The enterprise data model consists of the following components:

☐ The enterprise entity relationship model (EERM) consisting of an enterprise ERD (EERD) plus supporting data dictionary definitions.
☐ Entity state transition diagrams (ESTDs).
☐ The enterprise database model (EDBM) consisting of database structure diagrams plus schema definitions and database transaction validation tables.

The EERM reflects *what* data is required to support the business of the enterprise as opposed to the EDBM which reflects *how* that data is to be implemented in terms of database structure.

Different systems are able to share data, which is documented only once, on the EERM. As such it provides the foundation for all E-R models, included within system profiles for all projects, as shown in Figure 9.1, which gives diagramatic views of this model. Notice the term 'system ERD' is introduced to describe the diagrammatic view of the EERM from the point of view of an individual system.

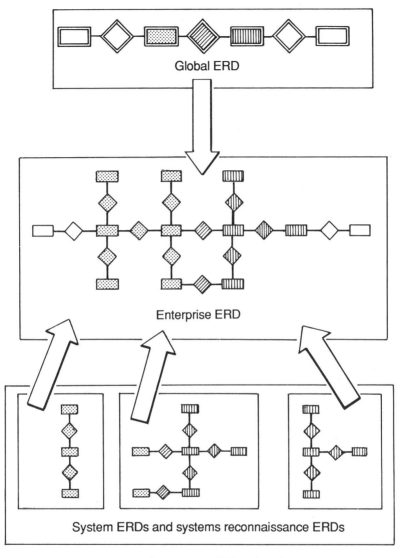

Figure 9.1 The enterprise ERD as foundation.

The EERM provides the architecture on which all development is based. However, it is important again to distinguish *what* is being built, which is an architecture, from *how* it is actually built, which is not architectural, at least in the traditional sense of the term. In Chapter 7 we saw the pitfalls of such an approach and suggested that the strategic perspective calls for an organic approach. One of the major advantages of an organic approach is that system development can get off the ground quickly and with the added boost of systems reconnaissance information to minimize uncertainty and increase confidence. Results of both global and systems E-R modelling must, however, be channelled to the underpinning architecture. This requires an investment in efficient and knowledgeable data administration which is discussed in its own right in Section 9.7.

9.3   Extending the ERD notation

The basic ERD notation is extended in two ways. Firstly, cardinality and optionality of relationships is introduced. Secondly, further subtyping concepts are catered for.

Cardinality.   Cardinality of a relationship is a rule regarding the potential numbers of entity occurrences that are permitted to participate as members, from the point of view of each entity concerned. Looking from the point of view of an occurrence of one entity the number of potential occurrences of the other entity is denoted on the diagram by one of the following symbols:

- ☐ '1': zero or one occurrence only.
- ☐ 'N'/'M': zero, one or more occurrences.
- ☐ 'X': a fixed number of occurrences denoted by the value of X.

We can thus talk of 1–1, 1–N and N–M relationships, examples of which are shown in Figure 9.2. An explanation of each example follows:

- ☐ A single Customer Holds at most one Account; therefore a '1' is placed on the relationship line adjacent to account. Conversely, a single Account is Held By at most one Customer; therefore a '1' is placed on the relationship line adjacent to Customer.
- ☐ A single Petrol Blend Is Contained In any number of Storage Tanks; an 'N' is placed next to Storage Tank. A single Storage Tank contains at most one Petrol Blend; a '1' is placed next to Petrol Blend.
- ☐ A single Team Enters any number of Competitions; an 'M' is placed next to Competition. A single Competition Is Entered By any number of Teams; an 'N' is placed next to Team.

On most diagrams that I have seen 1–N relationships tend to be the most common, N–M much less common, and 1–1 unusual. Relationships of fixed cardinality are rare in most practical situations, although it is easy enough to think of examples, as shown in Figure 9.3: here a Match is always played by exactly Two Teams. For example, if Manchester play a match against Birmingham on 20

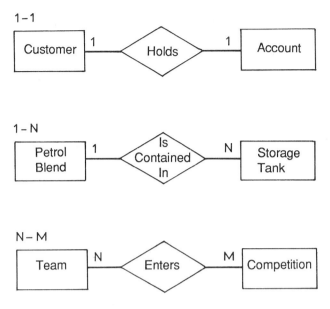

Figure 9.2 Examples showing cardinality.

November 1990, the example diagrammed in Figure 9.3 would represent this fact as *two* separate relationship occurrences. Note this relationship is subtly different from a recursive relationship between Teams, also joined to Match. This would represent the same fact as a single relationship occurrence joining all three entity occurrences: Manchester and Birmingham from Team and 20 November 1990 from Match.

Figure 9.3 Example showing fixed cardinality.

Cardinality can also be applied to associative entities and complex relationships by asking how many occurrences of an entity can occur for exactly one of each of the others as shown in Figure 9.4, although the value of this is perhaps more open to question.

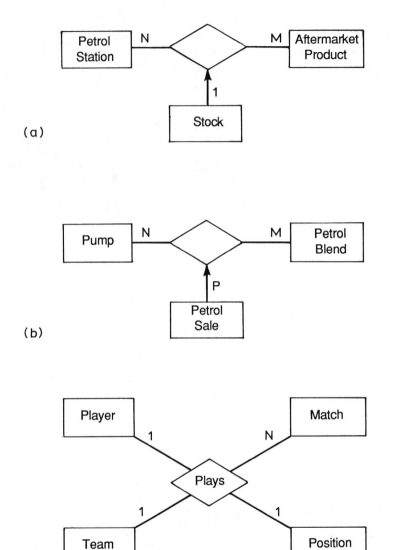

Figure 9.4 Examples showing cardinality for associative entities and complex relationships.

Cardinality of associative entities is dealt with separately from cardinality of the relationship itself. For example, Figure 9.4 (a) should be read in two parts:

   1. Statement 1 says: a single Petrol Station is associated with any number of

Aftermarket Products; a single Aftermarket Product is associated with any number of Petrol Stations.

2. Statement 2 says: for a single Petrol Station and a single Aftermarket Product there is at most one Stock.

Another way of expressing this is to describe the relationship embodied in the associative entity Stock as single occurrence between the same two entities. This example should be contrasted with the one below it, in Figure 9.4 (b), which states that any number of Petrol Sales may be associated with exactly the same Pump and Petrol Blend. The relationship embodied within Petrol Sale is therefore said to be multiple occurrence.

Complex relationships (see Section 4.5) present more difficulty. It is possible to specify cardinality here as follows. Again, cardinality indicates the potential number of entity occurrences of one entity given a single occurrence of each of the other entities. Thus in Figure 9.4 (c), any number of Matches can be associated with exactly the same Player, Team and Position. Therefore the cardinality of Match is 'N'; for example, Tom Wilson plays at centre-half for Shadwell Rovers in ten matches. However, it only makes sense for a single player to be associated with the same position for the same team in a single match. Therefore the cardinality of Player is '1'; for example, Tom Wilson cannot be chosen to play at centre-half and goalkeeper for Shadwell Rovers' New Years Day Fixture against Sullys Old Boys.

Because complex relationships are awkward to comprehend it is usually best to split them into several relationships, each involving fewer entities. Factoring is one possible way of achieving this which we will consider in Section 9.8.

Optionality. Optionality of a relationship is paradoxically a rule governing the existence of an entity occurrence: it signifies whether or not a given entity occurrence is permitted to exist without participating as a member of a relationship. If the answer is 'yes' an 'O' is placed on the line joining the relationship diamond to the entity in question, signifying optional membership. If the answer is 'no' the line is left as it is, signifying mandatory membership.

Thus in Figure 9.5 (a), Customer is optionally related to Account but Account is mandatorily related to Customer. A full translation of each example relationship, in Figures 9.5 (a)–(c) respectively, follows:

☐ A single Customer may Hold at most one Account.
A single Account must be Held By at most one Customer.

☐ A single Petrol Station may Stock any number of Aftermarket Products.
A single Aftermarket Product may Be Stocked By any number of Petrol Stations.
One Stock is always associated with a single Petrol Station and a single Aftermarket Product.

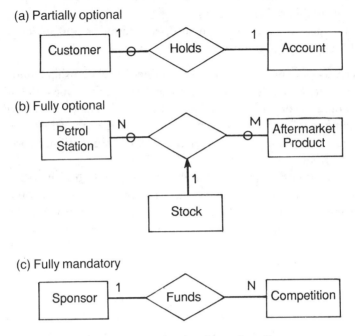

(a) Partially optional

(b) Fully optional

(c) Fully mandatory

Figure 9.5 Examples showing optionality.

(Note that associated entities are always mandatorily related to the entities they effectively join).

☐ A single Competition must be Funded By exactly one Sponsor.
   A single sponsor must Fund one or more Competitions.

Those entities which only participate in optional relationships are termed '*independent entities*', for which it is sometimes expedient to set up separate data oriented local reconnaissance projects as described in the previous chapter (Section 8.3.2). 'Petrol Station' is an example of an independent entity (see Appendix 2).

The issue of whether or not to diagram cardinality and optionality sometimes seems to be something of a hot topic in the modelling fraternity. My own view is that they should be diagrammed, they are then publically visible. This facilitates questioning of assumptions: important statements regarding business policy are being made here and by diagramming we put them up for discussion. Some cases may be relatively obvious:

☐ Clearly, a Petrol Station may Stock any number of Aftermarket Products.

However, other cases are less obvious: by diagramming optionality and cardinality important issues are raised that otherwise might have lain dormant. For example:

☐ Do we really wish to insist that a single Customer Holds at most one Account: isn't this somewhat constricting? Might we want to say the same Customer can at least Hold different types of Account? Conversely is it really necessary that a single Account is Held By only one Customer? What about joint accounts?

The counter argument is that they clutter the diagram. However, whether or not you choose to diagram these features is a somewhat unrewarding argument. Eventually we must make a decision, the really important thing being that we remain consistent. What is critical is that if they are not diagrammed they should be documented in the data dictionary under the appropriate relationship entry. Indeed, a good CASE tool should allow windowing of data dictionary entries on diagram screens, as described in Chapter 12.

'This is all very well', I can hear you say. 'But what is the point of cardinality and optionality?'. We have already seen they mirror important statements on business policy about data, which facilitates early verification of that policy. Also, cardinality and optionality will have a most significant bearing on process logic. For example, Petrol Station can exist independently. That means that the process which sets the Petrol Station data up in the first place is not subjected to any existence constraints. In contrast, Account is mandatorily related to Customer. Therefore the process that creates Accounts needs to verify the existence of a Customer. Once linked to a Customer the E-R model also says you cannot by definition link an Account to any more. Again this is a constraint on processing.

A second rather different but equally important reason for including cardinality

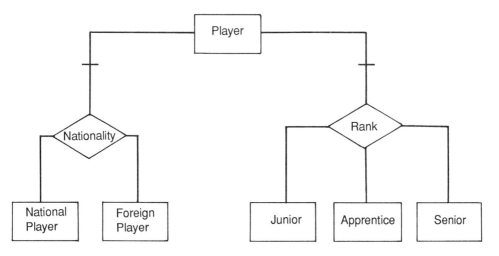

Figure 9.6 Example of multiple subtypings.

and optionality is that it is necessary information to enable mapping of the EERM into a first-cut database design. This is described in Section 9.9.

Subtyping extensions.   There may be several ways of subtyping the same entity. The supertype–subtype notation can be extended to allow for *multiple subtypings*. For example, in Figure 4.10, the entity Player was earlier subtyped by nationality. Suppose, however, we are also interested in specific data relating to juniors, apprentices and seniors. This might result in a further subtyping by status as indicated in Figure 9.6.

The rule that the same occurrence of an entity can be described by different subtypes provided they are not within the same subtyping also applies here. Thus a player can be an apprentice national player, apprentice foreign player and so on. Again, the subtype is said to '*inherit*' data from its supertypes and there is no limit to the number of levels.

Finally, subtypings can be specified as optional by placing an 'O' over the line linking the supertype to the subtype diamond. If, for example, we wanted to alter the nationality subtyping such that we kept specific data about nationals and Australians only whilst still retaining an interest in players of all nationalities this would be diagrammed as shown in Figure 9.7.

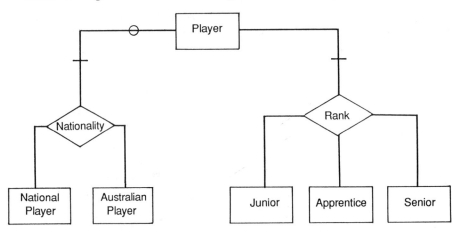

Figure 9.7 Example of optional subtyping.

9.4   Extending the data dictionary

There are many other features of data that can and should be catered for on the data dictionary. The following is a list with a brief description of some of the more important ones:

☐ Exclusivity: whether participation in one relationship excludes participation in another relationship(s). For example suppose a petrol station could be run in one of two exclusive ways: either under lease or direct control. The relationships Leased To (entity Leaseholder) and Controlled By (entity Area Manager) would be said to be *exclusive* relative to the entity Petrol Station.

☐ Quantitative data: for example, numbers of expected entity occurrences and relationship occurrences.

☐ Ownership: both user and developer (see Section 7.11).

☐ Privacy: whether access is restricted to specific users and who these users are.

☐ Integrity conditions: rules governing the existence of relationships and attributes in terms of dependencies.

☐ Domain: domains, which were discussed in Section 5.3, should be defined centrally in a 'domain base'.

9.5 Entity state transition diagrams (ESTDs)

Roughly speaking the ESTD is often said to model changes of state of an entity, and therefore to be very similar to an STD. On both diagrams states are periods of specific duration and transitions are changes of state dictated by events. Closer inspection reveals that an entity state represents a time window in the life of an entity occurrence which is of interest to the business and which governs operations which may take place with respect to that entity occurrence. Thus, to be more accurate, whereas an STD models changes of state of *system* the ESTD represents the dependency between permitted states of an *entity occurrence*. States are mutually exclusive on both diagrams: an STD can only be in one state at any given time, but in the case of an ESTD we must qualify this by saying that an ESTD describing a particular entity occurrence can only be in one state at a particular time. Each diagram ultimately seeks out rules: but those governing system behaviour in the case of an STD in contrast to rules governing information processing in the case of an ESTD. Therefore although the notation is basically the same for the two diagrams we should be aware that their intent is very different. This is reflected in that, unlike an STD, an ESTD may actually have more than one initial state. This is because the ESTD operates at micro level and not like its dynamic cousin at macro level. For example, an employee joining a company might be in any of the following initial states:

☐ Single.
☐ Married.

☐ Divorced.
☐ Widowed.

Also, whereas final states are rare with STDs, they are the expected norm in ESTDs. Sooner or later data ceases to be of interest and is either archived or deleted. This raises one of those little anomalies of modelling: the convention is to show Deleted as a state; nevertheless (as students have often pointed out to me) it would

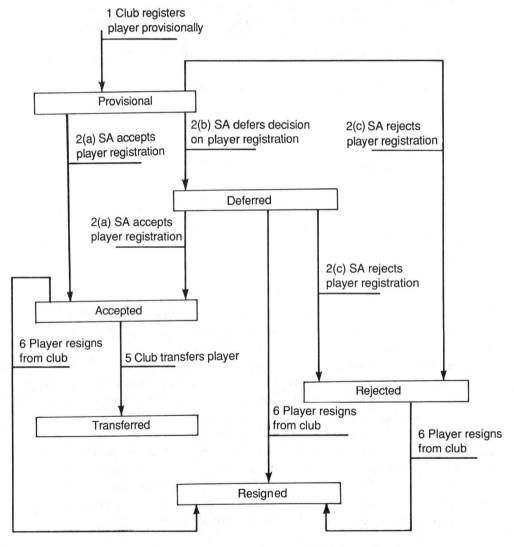

Figure 9.8 ESTD for Club Membership Status of Club Membership.

be more cogent to show a transition going 'to nowhere' as it does not really make sense to speak of a state of an entity occurrence which is no longer present.

Having amplified this crucial distinction of intent, the STD notation can now be applied to modelling changes of entity state. Again, events will be equatable with conditions on the ESTD: it is events that cause changes of entity state. Similarly, where there are different event patterns which effect the same entity separate ESTDs can be constructed; there is no theoretical limit to the number of ESTDs that can be drawn for the same entity although more than two is rare in practice. Therefore it is important to name the diagram accurately with respect to the event pattern modelled; for example, in the case above, Marital Status of Employee.

Initial diagrams should leave actions blank as shown in Figure 9.8. Actions can be filled in later on once we have understood patterns of events impacting the entity in question.

Notice that Event 2 (Sports Authority makes decision on player registration) has been factored into three sub-events to clarify the transitions from the Provisional state to Accepted, Deferred and Rejected.

Again the reader might ask 'OK the diagram's simple enough but what's the point?'. Really, the benefits of ESTDs are two-fold. Firstly, to assist in scoping decisions in the early stages of a project or in systems reconnaissance work as described in Section 8.6. What we would like to do is to 'package' events with their associated entities to form coherent system scopes, in line with the principle of encapsulation. Incidentally, we see the increasing appearance of this same idea dressed in new clothes as object oriented analysis.

Secondly, the ESTD will form useful reference information for the designer of database functions in that it can easily be converted into database transaction validation tables, states becoming table status values and events becoming transaction codes.

However, despite their advantages ESTDs should only be used to illuminate the darker corners that have not succumbed to our other modelling efforts; like swear words they lose their impact if overemployed. If we are not careful we could end up with 200 diagrams, one for each entity, each with the states Inserted, Amended, Deleted. We should restrict ourselves to those entities with associated event patterns which are interesting, complex or problematic.

9.6　The enterprise database model (EDBM)

The main purpose of this short section is to clarify some of the terminology used with respect to the EDBM and to prepare the ground for database mapping in Section 9.9.

The EDBM reflects integration of database requirements across the enterprise and is traditionally divided into two models which have their roots in the ANSI/ SPARC three-schema data architecture shown in Figure 7.2. The *logical database model* corresponds to the top two layers of this architecture: the external schema and conceptual schema; the *physical database model* corresponds to the internal schema.

The logical database model describes the organization of data into record types (or tables) according to DBMS architectural constraints but independently of physical characteristics. This would normally be expressed in Data Description Language (DDL). The physical database model describes the blocks of consecutive storage locations and exact access methods which are actually to be used to support the logical database model. This would normally be expressed in a Data Storage Description Language (DSDL).

One of the main advantages of this distinction is that if we change the way the data is physically stored, accessed or laid out on physical devices (that is change the physical database model) then we should not have to change the logical database model. Also, database design can take place in a graduated manner in classical *what* followed by *how* fashion.

The external schemas of the logical database model are important in that they allow the database administrator to control access of information by defining those portions of the database that a user is permitted to access. However, the under-lying foundation of the logical database model corresponds to the conceptual schema: it is this that is primarily described in DDL. And it is the conceptual schema that is diagrammed in terms of a Logical Data Structure Diagram (LDSD). The logical database model can thus be considered as LDSDs plus their supporting DDL.

The LDSD is used to represent a first-cut view of database design. It is based upon the generic type of the target database architecture; for example, 'relational', 'network' or 'hierarchy'. No matter whether say Oracle, DB2 or Ingres is the target DBMS the LDSD will look the same, because they are all relational architectures. The notation which is illustrated in Figure 9.9 is very simple.

For relational architectures, boxes represent tables and dotted arrows represent embedded (or 'foreign') keys. The latter are keys which are posted from one table to another to implement relationships. In Figure 9.9 (a) Table B has an embedded key pointing back to its owner Table A.

For network and hierarchy architectures, boxes represent record types and solid arrows represent sets. A set is a collection of pointers which is created to implement a relationship between an owner record and member records. A pointer sits in each record in a set containing the address of the next record in a set. In Figure 9.9 (b) there is a set C linking the owner record type A to its members B.

The LDSD can also be adapted to deal with features of the particular DBMS

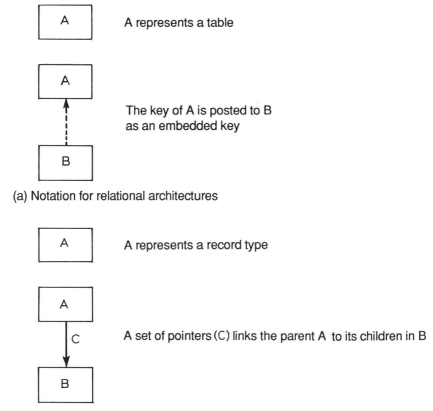

(a) Notation for relational architectures

(b) Notation for network and hierarchical architectures

Figure 9.9 Logical data structure diagram notation.

product; for example, in terms of alternative access paths and indices. Also, it can be partitioned by user corresponding to the appropriate external schema.

Included within the EDBM are database transaction validation tables.

Clearly, the topic of database design has received prolific attention in the literature and my intention here is not to repeat what has already been said eloquently by so many others. It has been to provide a rough sketch of the EDBM so we can better understand the bridge between the EERM and database design, which is important from the point of view of this book. It is this bridge that provides the focus for the remainder of this chapter.

9.7   Data administration

Whenever resources are shared it is imperative that they are managed effectively. This is especially so in the case of 'data' which presents a variety of complex problems. On the one hand the need for centralized co-ordination of the design, implementation and maintenance of databases requires a technical bent, on the other, the balance of conflicting interests requires a managerial perspective and the need to record business policy accurately requires a good knowledge of the business. This gives rise to the distinction between the *database* administrator, who is responsible for administration of the EDBM, and the *data* administrator, who is responsible for administration of the EERM and ESTDs. (I will use the terms here to refer to different roles; whether or not they are performed by individuals or teams is an open question depending on the size and complexity of the particular enterprise).

The distinction between database administrator and data administrator, once found in a few enlightened pockets, is now common in enterprises with large databases. It is reflected in different positions within the organizational hierarchy: the database administrator is normally a member of management services whereas the data administrator is placed at corporate management level.

Although detailed consideration of these topics is outside of the scope of this book it is necessary here to make some salient observations with regard to the *modelling* process itself.

Database administration responsibilities begin with the mapping of selected portions of the EERM to the LDSDs of first-cut database design. Those 'selected portions' would be included within system profiles and must be guaranteed 'mature' by the data administrator before they can be mapped. They continue with development and refinement of the database design itself. The 'routing' of various E-R models produced at project level via the EERM through to the EDBM, is shown in Figure 9.10 with respect to the roles of the data administrator (upward and downward arrows) and the database administrator (left to right arrow). Again it is important to note that the diagrams illustrated here form only part of a much larger picture.

The reader should also note that Figure 9.10 is an oversimplification in that it is assumed that the selected portion of the EERM is mapped to a single processor. However, as intimated in Section 5.7, it may well be that several processors (including manual ones) may be involved. In these cases the selected portion of the EERM must first be allocated to appropriate processors before it is mapped to an appropriate LDSD for each processor. Again where relationships are mapped it is important to include all connected entities in the mapping; this may result in duplication of data. The reader is referred to Appendix 2, where the entity 'Player' is mapped to three processors.

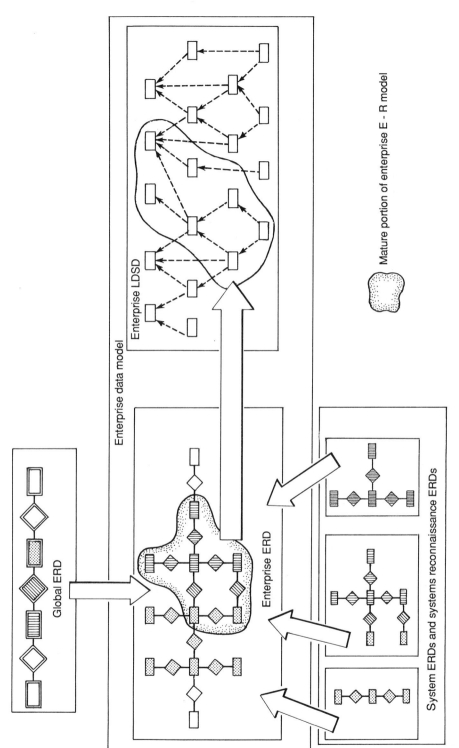

Figure 9.10 The routing of E-R models toward implementation.

Despite its apparently increasing position of significance within the oganizational hierarchy, data administration often seems to operate in a way which is ancillary to the mainstream tasks of systems development. Certainly, the data administrator fulfills the important role of custodian of the data dictionary. However, development and co-ordination of the policies and procedures regarding the enterprise data resource involves more than recording those policies.

We have seen that the EERM is the structure upon which both the global ERD and system ERD views are ultimately based: therefore data administration will involve an intimate relationship with systems strategy and active participation in the systems development process itself. Let us look at each of these points in a little more detail.

9.7.1   Data administration and systems strategy

The role of the data administrator with respect to system strategy is three-fold:

   □ Custodian.
   □ Politician.
   □ Expert.

Let us look at each in turn.

In the interests of traceability it is necessary to correlate global entities and global relationships with their component entities and relationships on the EERM. At inception, the global ERD will, in fact, be equivalent to the EERM. However, correlations must be adjusted as systems are developed and business needs change. This responsibility falls to the data administrator as *custodian*.

More significantly, the data administrator may also be expected to act in a consultative role as *politician* during the systems strategy itself. We have seen that the systems strategy cuts across the company organization chart and therefore across departmental 'empires'. In doing this it may well raise management resistance. This may well be fuelled by exposure of duplication of work in user departments, giving result to dissent from lower in the chain of command. In such cases the consultative role becomes one of political arbitration. The respected neutrality of the data administrators places him or her in a unique position to fulfil this role.

We have also seen that the systems strategy requires a good mix of technical and business skills. The requirements of the job dictate that the data administrator is often the very personification of this mix. The consultative role now becomes one of *expert*. Let me illustrate the point with regard to a situation I once experienced.

A large systems department were once having particular difficulties with a particularly bright and experienced user manager who had developed a fondness for developing his own PC-based applications, often in contradiction to the needs of the organization as a whole. This was especially galling from the systems department's point of view as he would not hesitate to draw on their programming expertise if ever a bug occurred. When the position of data administrator became free here was the ideal candidate. In one stroke the organization would benefit from his unique 'techno-business' experience whilst removing a prickly thorn from the side of the systems department. Needless to say, the successful candidate's views on PC development in the user community changed somewhat after his promotion.

9.7.2   Data administration and systems analysis

The role of the data administrator with respect to system modelling is again three-fold. It is *custodial* in that we need to ensure consistency of the 'smaller picture' with regard to the integrated 'larger picture'. It is *expert* in that we need to ensure correctness of the 'smaller picture' itself. The fact that the system developer no longer makes the final modelling decisions may well lead to resistance. In an extreme case we may have to face the possibility that E-R modelling carried out at project level is either of poor quality or does not fit well to the overall need. This requires a certain *political* skill on the part of the data administrator in being both objective, tactful and sometimes thick-skinned.

All E-R models are preliminary until they have passed through the data administrator. This not only applies to system reconnaissance models it also applies to system E-R models. In 'early' system developments analysts will use global ERDs and system reconnaissance models to construct system ERDs probably in conjunction with the data administrator. After the EERM has 'matured' sufficiently (as described in Section 9.8) analysts will most likely develop copies of subsets of this model and then feed them back to the data administrator for verification. Finally in 'later' systems developments very little E-R modelling may be required at all; the analysts can work from an already established subset of the EERM.

9.7.3   Data administration and system reconnaissance

Again the same three-fold role applies. However, where data oriented local reconnaissance projects are initiated, for example, to analyze independent entities in their own right, it is normally appropriate for this work to be carried out in close harmony with data administration; indeed sometimes by members of the data administration team itself in large organizations.

Where prototyping (see Section 9.7.4) is to be initiated directly from strategic modelling, mapping to the required database structure would normally be included as part of the reconnaissance project.

9.7.4   Data/database administration and prototyping

We shall see in the next part of this book that the foundation of prototyping is the database structure. Where prototyping projects are initiated as a means of discovering information requirements (usually from or as part of strategic modelling) the data administrator must confirm that the required portion of the EERM to be mapped looks a reasonable candidate, and that results from prototyping are carefully integrated.

On the other hand where prototyping projects are initiated as a means of determining required functionality (usually from or as part of systems analysis), the data administrator is acting very much more as expert. He or she must ensure that the supporting portion of the EERM is sufficiently mature (as described in Section 9.8).

Whatever the subject of prototyping, the database administrator must guarantee that the database mapping is technically correct and compatible with any existing database structure (as described in Section 9.9). The reader is referred back to Figure 9.10 for a graphic illustration of the situation.

9.7.5   Data/database administration and external design

If we are dealing with external design, not so much as a means of verification, but as the next step along the road to implementation, then clearly requirements specification must be rigorously defined. The data administrator will be acting in the role of expert to ensure that the supporting portion of the EERM is sufficiently mature (as described in Section 9.8).

However, if we are dealing with an *early* design, as a means of verification as described in Section 5.7, the requirement may be less rigorous in that detailed mapping would be inappropriate. The onus would then be on the database administrator to ensure technical feasibility of a proposed database architecture without having to carry out the mapping itself.

9.8   Preparing for mapping: the concept of maturity

Before a required portion of the EERM can be mapped to a LDSD it must be 'mature', that is, it must be:

- ☐ Free from undesired redundancy.
- ☐ Factored into binary relationships.

Both tasks are properly performed by the data administrator. Before explaining each in turn there is an important rule to address:

☐ If a relationship is included within the required portion of the EERM, then all entities participating in that relationship must also be included within that portion.

This rule is necessary to ensure compatibility not only with existing database structures but also possible future ones.

'Free from undesired redundancy'

The required portion of EERM must be both normalized and free from undesired derived data. Normalization has received prolific attention in the literature since its inception by E.F. Codd (1970, 1972). To argue the merits of normalization as a method or technique for E-R modelling is not my aim here. Whether we choose to model 'top-down' or 'bottom-up', or adopt the route suggested in this book of 'outside-in' modelling we are always going to be faced with a common requirement for non-redundancy. This is sometimes expressed in what has become something of a catch phrase of third normal form:

☐ Each attribute must be functionally dependent on the identifier, the whole identifier, and nothing but the identifier.

Just as evidence in a courtroom must be tested and true, so the 'testimony' embodied in the EERM must be non-redundant if we are to achieve a sound mapping.

The reader will find that good E-R modelling practice should actually yield an E-R model which is well-normalized. Contrary to the (sometimes expressed) view of 'E-R modelling' and 'normalization' as exclusive approaches in some black art, the two are seen here as complementary. Application in practical situations is, I believe, the real issue. And application of normalization generally becomes an inspection task to be performed at the end of the assembly line rather than the assembly line itself.

The major limitation of normalization is that it does not raise questions as to the *meaning* of the data. It is a syntactic as opposed to a semantic approach. An area of particular concern is derived data. A derived attribute is one whose value can be calculated from the values of other attributes and/or the occurrence of relationships. For example, totals, averages and certain dates (like date of birth). Often such attributes can be of vital interest to the user. A bank manager, for example, is likely to be far more interested in your current balance rather than the individual transactions from which it is derived. Therefore, it is necessary to treat derived data on its merits and not blindly cut it out. Indeed, if we are not careful the concept can

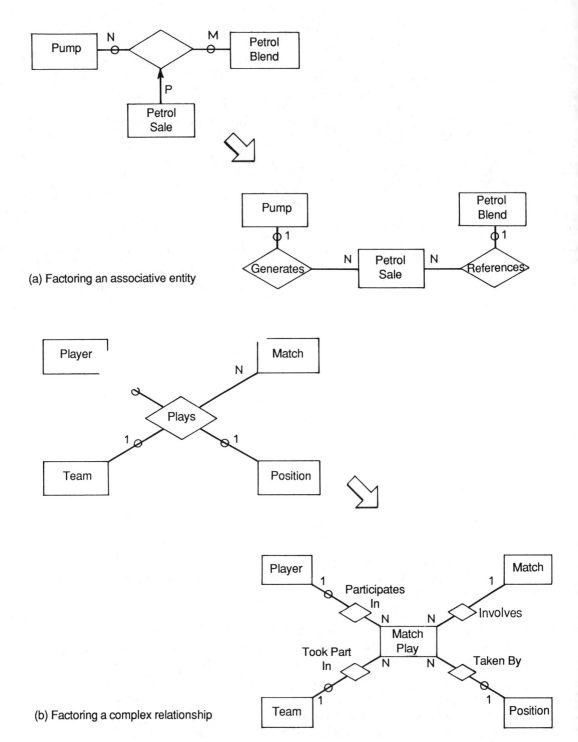

(a) Factoring an associative entity

(b) Factoring a complex relationship

Figure 9.11 Examples of factoring.

sometimes be applied with such gusto that we are left with an EERM which contains only 'atomic' attributes and actually says very little. Where an attribute is derived we actually have to make a choice between the following:

☐ Leave it in and document its derivation in the form of an algorithm for use by any process that needs to update that attribute.
☐ Leave it out and document its derivation in the form of an algorithm for use by any process wishing to access or report that attribute.

Either way we cannot escape documenting the derivation. The price paid for the first way is to include a data dictionary entry for the attribute (under the appropriate entity) with a reference to the algorithm. In my view this is actually a small overhead for what is often useful information.

Factored into binary relationships

For the purposes of mapping the required portion of the EERM to the LDSD it is most convenient to factor complex relationships into binary relationships. Complex relationships include associative entities and any relationships involving more than two associations. The former are dealt with by replacing the associative entity with an entity of the same name and inserting a 1–N relationship from each of the participating entities to the new entity. The latter are dealt with by replacing the complex relationship with an entity and inserting a 1–N relationship from each of the participating entities to the new entity. Examples are shown in Figure 9.11.

The results of factoring should not be documented on the EERM as the relationships obtained are usually somewhat artificial. The intention here is rather to expedite the mapping process.

Once the required portion of the EERM has been checked for undesired redundancy and factored into binary relationships, simple mapping rules are applied to yield a first-cut LDSD. This is discussed in the next section.

9.9 Mapping to a first-cut logical data structure

The rules described here are for relational architectures. Rules for network, hierarchical and other architectures are not included here as they can be derived from the ones described. Also, my main intention is to illustrate application of the principle, rather than specific variants.

Firstly, a table is created for each entity with key = identifier and fields =

attributes. The rules themselves actually govern whether to implement relationships as tables or as embedded keys, and are driven by both cardinality and
optionality. Let me illustrate each in turn.

Supertype–subtypes

There are two possibilities illustrated here in Figure 9.12. Either (a) create a single
table for both supertype and subtypes, which will have some attributes (from the
subtypes) which may take null values. Or (b) create a table for each subtype and a
table for the supertype. In addition, post the identifier from the supertype into each
subtype table, thus creating embedded keys. Generally speaking, the more special
attributes in the subtypes, the more attractive mapping (b) becomes.

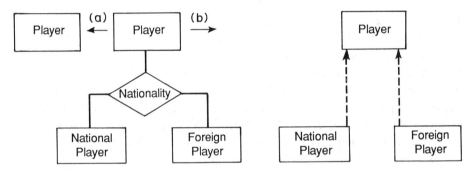

Figure 9.12 Alternative examples of relational mappings for super-subtypes.

1–1 relationships

These are treated as illustrated in Figure 9.13. The possibilities are as follows:

(i) *Fully mandatory.* Create a single combined table with key = identifier of either
entity.

(ii) *Partially optional.* There are two possibilities here. Either (a) create a single
combined table which will have some attributes (from the mandatorily related
entity) which may take null values. The key will be the identifier of the optionally
related entity. Or (b) create a table for each entity with the identifier of the optionally related entity posted the mandatorily related entity's table as embedded key.
(In the example, the identifier of Customer is posted to Account as an embedded
key).

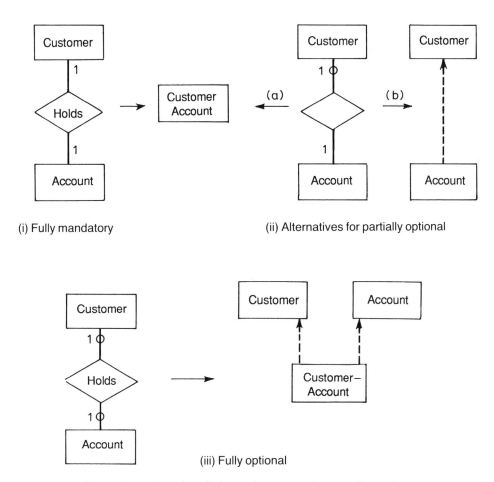

Figure 9.13 Examples of relational mappings for 1–1 relationships.

(iii) *Fully optional.* Create a table for each entity. Also create a new table with identifiers of both entities posted as embedded keys. Note: the key of the new table may be either embedded key.

1–N relationships

There are two possibilities here, as illustrated in Figure 9.14. Note the optionality of the 'one' entity is insignificant.

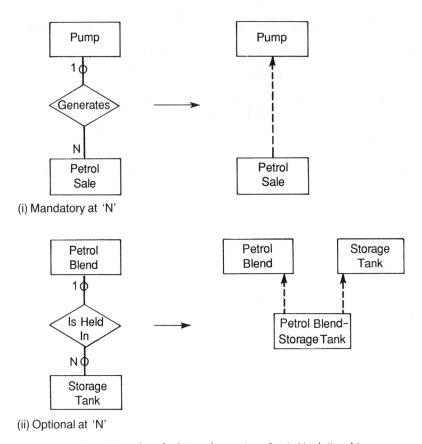

Figure 9.14 Examples of relational mappings for 1–N relationships.

(i) *'Many' entity mandatorily related.* Create a separate table for each entity. Post the identifier of the 'one' entity's table into the 'many' entity's table as an embedded key. (In the example, the identifier of Pump is posted to the Petrol Sale table).

(ii) *'Many' entity optionally related.* Create a separate table for each entity. Also create a new table with identifiers of both entities posted as embedded keys. Note: the key of the new table will be the embedded key posted from the 'many' entity (in the example Petrol Blend – Storage Tank has key = identifier of Storage Tank).

N–M relationships

Although N–M relationships are usually among the most difficult to understand

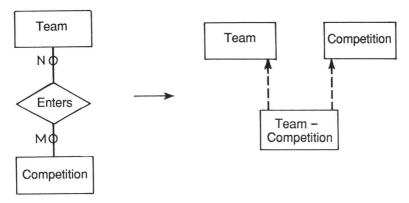

Figure 9.15 Example of relational mappings for N–M relationships.

there is a single mapping rule as illustrated in Figure 9.15. Irrespective of optionality, create a separate table for each entity and a new table with identifiers of both entities posted as embedded keys. Note: the key of the new table will consist of the concatenation of embedded keys.

A full example of mapping a selected portion of the EERM to a LDSD is included in Appendix 2.

9.10 Summary

The purpose of this chapter has been to map out the anatomy of the Enterprise Data Model and to make some salient comments on its administration. This has been done very much from the point of view of attempting to place it in perspective with strategic modelling, system modelling and prototyping.

In particular, the concept of the organic lifecycle entails something of an upward change of gear for the vehicle of data administration, with certain organizational implications.

Mapping rules were introduced for creating a first-cut LDSD. Good preparation of the selected portion of the EERM was stressed in terms of normalization and factoring. The LDSD and its textual support will form an important foundation for prototyping which is the subject of the next part of this book.

PART FIVE

The
User
Perspective

We have already stressed the importance of applying structured techniques in a way which encourages user involvement in defining and verifying requirements. This requires an integrated user perspective. In this part of the book we seek to develop this perspective with reference to prototyping tools.

Prototyping sometimes acquires a rather unfortunate image of 'dabbling around' and of being in disharmony with structured techniques. It is important then to clarify exactly what is meant by the term. To this end, certain species of prototyping are identified and a basic framework laid down in Chapter 10.

Chapter 11 amplifies the basic concepts by illustrating how they can actually be galvanized with the tools and techniques previously described in this book, to form a coherent approach to system building within the organic lifecycle.

The principles of prototyping

□ □ □ □ □ □ □ □ □ □ □ □ □ □ □ □ □

If a picture is worth a thousand words, an animated model is worth a thousand pictures.

BERNARD BOAR
Application Prototyping

10.1 Introduction

The ultimate objective of effective systems is to raise the degree of user satisfaction with respect to delivered software and to make that software easy to modify in place. This requires effective communication techniques to establish requirements during the development of that software. Again we see the goals of effective systems and effective techniques for development of systems are fast converging. It is here that prototyping comes into its own both as a tool for establishing requirements and as a tool for facilitating development: as a *communication tool*. To be cost-effective, however, communications tools have to be controlled and to be controlled assumes that they are understood. Unfortunately this is often not the case with prototyping.

The term 'prototyping' has become part and parcel of everyday parlance amongst software developers to such an extent that its meaning is assumed without the need for explanation. Closer examination, reflected in questions I am continually faced with in my role as consultant and instructor, reveals that interpretations vary:

- ☐ A tuning tool for enhancing system performance.
- ☐ A means of establishing the human-machine interface.
- ☐ A quick and dirty approach to system building.
- ☐ A fast-track strategy for circumventing requirement definition.
- ☐ And so on.

Actually the 'prototyping' I am interested in is none of these. In order to consider it as a way toward development of more effective systems it will be necessary to begin by clarifying the concept of prototyping itself. That will mean exploding some misconceptions which I believe are founded in stereotype images, before clarifying the subject of interest: *essential prototyping*. This is contrasted with other classes of prototyping: *user-interface prototyping* and *technical prototyping*.

We will see that essential prototyping seeks to verify requirements. In that sense it is no more than an element in our common or garden modelling framework which we have followed throughout this book. Similarly, we will see that it integrates with strategic and system modelling activity through the common currency of the organic lifecycle. Prototyping and structured techniques will emerge as complementary approaches with a common aim: the building of effective systems.

The universal principles of all forms of prototyping are articulated in terms of the *prototyping skeleton* (Section 10.7) before explaining in outline (in Section 10.8) the four sub-classes of essential prototyping with respect to the appropriate modelling tools outlined earlier in the book. Each sub-class of essential prototyping applies the prototyping skeleton in a rather different way.

Cost-effective development requires also that the right software tools are available. A summary of desirable features is offered to reinforce this point, which will be treated in some detail in Chapter 12.

The benefits of essential prototyping are clarified before considering some of the hazards typically associated with prototyping and measures for avoiding them, with respect to good project management practice.

10.2 Prototyping versus structured techniques

Senior managers often seem to harbour misconceptions about prototyping which they view from the perspective of the traditional mind-set discussed in Chapter 1. To recap briefly, systems development is seen as a production line which produces systems mechanically. Within the traditional mind-set, prototyping provides an opportunity to explore various design alternatives *after* requirements have been rigorously defined. It is not a tool for helping to establish requirements in the first place. This view is unfortunate not least because the individuals holding it are responsible for initiating and controlling many types of activity within the organization, including software development. In the next section I shall try to reveal a little more about this myth. Firstly, let me consider a piece of popular folklore which does much to sustain it.

Structured techniques and prototyping are commonly perceived as competing approaches, each with their own sets of supporters, to the problems of systems development. Supporters of structured techniques decry prototyping as an uncontrollable cottage industry approach in contrast to their own engineering discipline. On the other hand, adherents of prototyping view structured techniques as too purist and theoretical compared with their chief aim of obtaining practical results quickly.

Fostering this conflict we find stereotypical images. The structured techniques camp hold a misconception of prototyping embodied in the stereotype image of developer and user producing systems which are quickly knocked together over a few sessions at a terminal. This is seen as an uncontrolled activity, with no organization. Such an image is particularly anathema to both user and systems development management: when you are working to deadlines within tight budgets, there is no room for the 'toys for the boys' mentality.

On the other hand, the prototyping camp view the models of structured techniques as a poor user communication vehicle: too abstract to capture the reality of user requirements. Users are not able to communicate what they want until they have had some chance to *experience* what they can have. This results in another stereotypical image: that of developers closeted over their impressive looking graphics, in isolated debate, free from the everyday problems of users. Schooled in the esoterics of structured techniques, they will employ this mysterious discipline somehow to engineer systems for users. Again, this is anathema to both user and systems development management: when you are working to deadlines within tight budgets, there is no room for requirement definition: it takes too long and produces few useful results.

Although both views are founded on stereotypes their common strength in fuelling management anxiety, means that we must take them seriously. In order to expose them as *mis*conceptions we must clarify the concept of prototyping and examine its relationship with structured techniques, in particular EP.

10.3 The concept of prototyping

The concept of prototyping is certainly not new. It has been prevalent in many branches of engineering throughout history, from aeroplane design to bridge building. The basic idea is to spend a limited amount of money in building and developing a *working* model before committing resources to producing the real thing. The prime objective is to get it right 'in the small' before creating it 'in the large' thus preventing unnecessary costs in making changes to the real thing. If we can minimize uncertainty about how the real thing is going to behave under various conditions we achieve that goal. In most branches of engineering this uncertainty centres on *how* the product will behave in a test environment. Thus, for example, prototypes of aeroplanes are subjected to various tests involving speed and pressure; prototypes of bridges are subjected to various stresses. Results from the tests are then noted and changes made to the prototype which is then retested and so on. Prototyping is therefore characteristically iterative.

Prototyping in systems development can similarly mean creating part of a system on a small scale, subjecting it to various tests, modifying the prototype where necessary and iterating. Screens can be created for prototyping by a user to make sure they are ergonomically acceptable. This is an example of what is sometimes called 'user-interface prototyping'. The prototype can also be run alongside existing systems to measure the effects on response times, plus any degradation in performance of those systems. This is an example of what is sometimes called 'technical prototyping'.

Notice, however, that in other branches of engineering it is normally the case that *what* the product is required to do is not a matter of great debate. An aeroplane must be designed to carry around 300 passengers in reasonable comfort for, say, 1500 miles; a bridge must be capable of conveying 200 vehicles an hour over a 150 foot span, and so forth. This is not true in systems development: before we can tackle uncertainty about either the user-interface or the system performance, we have to address the more basic uncertainty about what the system is required to do in the first place. This is what makes so-called software engineering especially challenging and unique compared to other branches of engineering.

Addressing uncertainty about what a system is required to do is, of course, just what structured techniques are designed to do. This is also what 'essential prototyping' as it is sometimes called is designed to do. Essential prototyping, far from being in conflict with structured techniques, is actually *akin to* structured techniques in that it involves building models to reduce uncertainty about essential requirements. The thing that distinguishes essential prototyping is that its models are *working models* as opposed to the abstract models of structured techniques. Another way of expressing this is to say that the models of the former are 'active' as opposed to the 'passive' models of the latter.

In the practical world controllability is vital: if we are to avoid anarchy, prototyping only makes sense after structured techniques have been used to gain sufficient insight into business requirements. This means employing graphical modelling tools, as recommended in previous parts of this book, to grasp the problem at hand before using prototyping as a means of flushing out user requirements. Essential prototyping is at heart a means of *verifying* requirements with respect to the original modelling framework, depicted in Figure 10.1. Verification involves establishing the following:

1. The correctness of what we have specified.
2. That what we have specified is necessary from a business viewpoint.
3. That what we have specified is sufficient from a business viewpoint.

Textual methods of specification tend to be equally adept as tools for verification on the first count. It is possible to write a structured language specification (as in Figure 5.4) and verify its correctness simply by carefully 'walking through it' with a user. On the second and third counts, however, textual methods tend to be much less useful. They are not particularly good at encouraging questions as to whether (on the second count) a process is really needed or is merely superfluous to requirements. Neither are they at all good at encouraging questions as to whether (on the third count) the specification is complete. How often do we see developers throw their hands up in amazement at the moans of users who, though apparently in complete agreement with structured language specifications, express dissatisfaction at lack of functionality when confronted with the working systems?

Essential prototyping lends itself especially well to the second and third points, especially the third. If a feature is missing then it stands out like a sore thumb when we come to *use* that part of the system. Similarly, superfluous functionality is often only recognized as such when we come to *use* it. Indeed, we saw in Chapter 5 that even where the process specifications have been well written

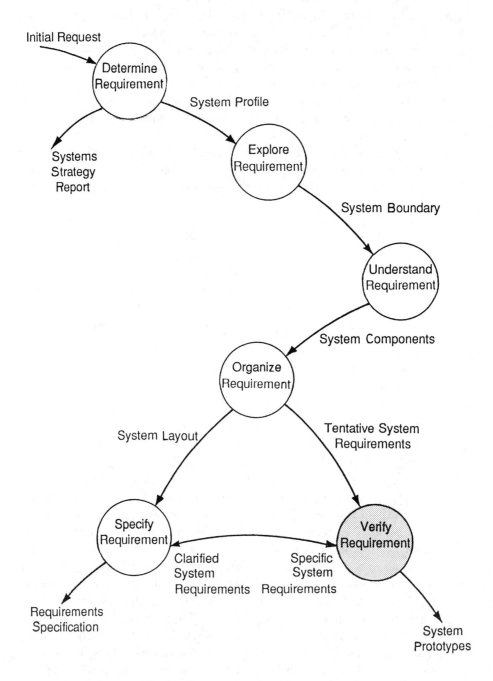

Figure 10.1 Prototyping with respect to the modelling framework.

and are clearly understood by the users there remained one very real danger: we do not adequately anticipate the evolution of requirements that occurs as users gain experience with a system. Essential prototyping seeks to anticipate such changes in verifying requirements by putting them to actual use.

Three further points need to be made for clarification.

1. The close interdependence between specifying and verifying requirements (see Section 5.1) entails that essential prototyping will, in fact, involve elements of specification itself. We shall see that in creating a prototype we are in effect specifying business requirements: the 'working code' of the prototype is the incarnation of requirement specification.

2. Essential prototyping extends the concept of verification to embrace the earlier aspects of EP – organization, understanding and exploration of requirements – in a way which is not possible with textual specification. Indeed, early prototypes will tend to highlight areas of concern (for example, simply by menus of candidate functions) without containing very much in the way of detailed business logic.

3. Essential prototyping is *one* means of verification among many (see Figure 5.8). It is vital that we establish the system as a suitable candidate for prototyping (see Section 8.10).

We will be concentrating here on essential prototyping, as complementary to structured techniques, but not to the approach sometimes labelled 'pre-specification' which advocates building a detailed and rigorous essential model prior to embarking on any kind of design activity. Boar (1984) states 'This distinction between pre-specification and prototyping is important. They represent divergent philosophies on how to approach optimally the requirements definition problem.' As already suggested, we shall find that far from being a totally separate and independent activity essential prototyping actually *involves* elements of EP. Before explaining how this actually works let me throw the concept into sharper relief by contrasting it with other classes of prototyping.

10.4 Design prototyping

If essential prototyping seeks to establish *what* business requirements are, design prototyping seeks to determine *how* best to support those requirements. Two classes of design prototyping may be distinguished:

1. User interface prototyping.
2. Technical prototyping.

10.4.1 User interface prototyping

The purpose of user interface prototyping is to establish how the interface between user and computer system will look and behave. The focus is upon such matters as screen layout, dialogue style and ergonomics. Although the subject is only treated most briefly here, as a means of highlighting the concept of essential prototyping, we should not underestimate its importance. Indeed, experience suggests the criticality of the user interface is too often disregarded with disastrous results. Let me give you an example.

A financial services company had just implemented a sales enquiry and quotations system, the objective of which was to enable salespersons to display information held on the corporate mainframe, using dial-up facilities, on television sets in the customers' homes. The system was a great success.

The next project was to develop a new enquiry system to support servicing clerks. The information to be displayed was remarkably similar in content to that used in the sales enquiry system. The essentials were pretty much the same. Someone then recognized that screen widths for television display are 40 characters, which is exactly half the character width of the VDU screens to be used by servicing clerks. This led to the decision to 'cut and paste' screens for the users which were divided into left and right halves of 40 characters; in effect, two television screens into one VDU. The proposal was heralded as a brilliant idea on the grounds that it not only dramatically cut costs but also enforced standardization.

There was only one problem: the users were barely consulted. The result was a catastrophe, on implementation of the new system. There were two main reasons for this. Firstly, information was too densely packed on to a screen. There was simply too much for a user to handle. Secondly, the screen format and dialogue style ran counter to existing modes of working. Enquiries in the customers' homes tended to focus on one or two key items, for example, the price of a contract. In contrast, enquiries in the users' offices were usually both much more diverse and to a greater level of detail. The users simply could not make effective use of the new system, which was abandoned within a few months of inception. And all this, despite getting their requirement definition right.

It is important to appreciate classes of prototyping as abstractions: they are not meant as mutually exclusive classes. Indeed, it is possible for exactly the same prototype to be used in all three ways. Furthermore there is something of a paradox here in that for all practical purposes it is impossible to build a prototype of essential requirements without building a user-interface prototype to support those requirements. There will always be a certain amount of overlap between the two, which is indeed reflected in the overlap which we would normally expect between analysis and design models. The question here, however, is one of degree of use to which the prototype is put.

In essential prototyping the emphasis is upon data content and function as opposed to matters of dialogue style such as screen layout, presentation standards, sequencing, scroll-over facilities and so on. If something were seriously amiss regarding dialogue style we might reasonably be expected to correct it. However, the main purpose is to remove uncertainty over essential requirements.

In contrast, by the time we get to user-interface prototyping it is expected that most (if not all) essential requirements will have been established. This enables the focus of interest to switch to matters of dialogue style, without, of course, precluding unforeseen changes in essential requirements. We would however expect any such changes to be relatively minor.

Again, passive models can be used alongside user interface prototypes. In particular, state transition diagrams lend themselves particularly well. For example, we can model as follows:

- ☐ Screens as states.
- ☐ User commands (such as pressing a PF key) as conditions.
- ☐ System processes as actions.

10.4.2 Technical prototyping

Technical prototyping or 'simulation' is performed in detailed systems design in order to determine the adequacy of a proposed solution from a performance viewpoint. The key question raised is 'Can the system handle the anticipated workload?' In order to help answer this question a technical prototype should provide a simulation: a working model of the environment to which the software system must interact.

A queueing model provides an example of simulation where we can view the effect of varying message arrival rates and service rates on system performance, with the objective of tuning the system for optimum performance.

This is particularly relevant for real-time systems where response to events in the environment and control of devices in the environment is time sensitive. For example, simulation makes practical verification of the real-time design by allowing fine measurement of response times under variable conditions. In effect we are getting a preview of how a system based upon the proposed design will perform in its target environment, although with embedded systems there is the further problem that once the software has been developed on a particular machine it may well require porting to different hardware. The reader is referred to Houtchens and Pollock (1987) for a detailed account.

Again, it is important to appreciate classes of prototyping as abstractions. Particularly with real-time embedded systems where there is little user interface, it may be impossible to build a prototype of essential requirements without building a technical prototype to support those requirements. There will always be a certain amount of common ground, reflected in the overlap which we would normally expect between analysis and design models. Once again, the question here, however, is one of degree of use to which the prototype is put. Finally, diagrams used in structured design (such as state transition diagrams, as in Section 10.4.1) can usefully be employed alongside, rather than replaced by, technical prototypes.

10.5 Evolutionary prototyping

Before progressing further it is important to clear up one further source of potential confusion over the concept of prototyping. The term 'essential prototyping' is used here primarily to refer to an approach to obtaining requirements and not as *the* strategy for developing systems, which is sometimes referred to as 'evolutionary prototyping' (Floyd, 1984) and more latterly 'rapid prototyping' (Connell and Shafer, 1989). That particular strategy recognizes that as soon as you implement a system you change the working environment. Therefore there will always be *some* changes which cause the prototype to evolve. There is a deliberate policy to implement with as few changes as possible the prototype itself.

In this connection, it is also worth bearing in mind some observations from Roland Vonk (1990): 'Prototyping assumes that "real" requirements exist. To establish just what the user actually needs it may be necessary to go through a number of iterations, but ultimately the requirements definition will stabilize. The basic assumption of evolutionary development, on the other hand, is that the requirements will be subject to continual change. In such a situation there is no point in prototyping, because the iterative process will never end . . . such an environment demands a flexible end product – in other words an evolutionary development approach.'

Experience suggests that the realities of the commercial world often dictate that such an evolutionary approach is something of a luxury in practice. John L. Connell and Linda Brice Shafer (1989) cite the desirable features of such an environment: 'an architecture that allows very easy replacement of functional modules, transparent interfaces to other development environments, ultimate flexibility in creating and modifying data storage structures, and very little operating overhead associated with basic application structures. If any of these characteristics are not present, then the tool is only suitable for producing disposable prototypes.' We will return to the subject of the ideal environment in Chapter 12 where the galvanizing of EP with prototyping is seen as the critical issue. The transition to such environments is, however, a slow one; in the commercial world they remain very much in their infancy. I have therefore chosen to err on the side of caution and to not assume that all features of such an environment are always present. Whether or not the prototype itself is retained for gradual evolution or whether it is simply thrown away will not be the issue here. I leave this question open.

What is recommended here is that essential prototypes should where possible be used within the actual working environment. Terminals sited in user departments can, for example, be used to parallel run prototypes alongside production systems. Such simulation will help to reduce uncertainty about how the system will actually fare in the workplace.

10.6 Essential prototyping within the organic lifecycle

Essential prototyping can take various forms with respect to the organic lifecycle. It can be initiated as project work in its own right from either strategic modelling or systems analysis, to clarify requirements for subsequent consolidation and

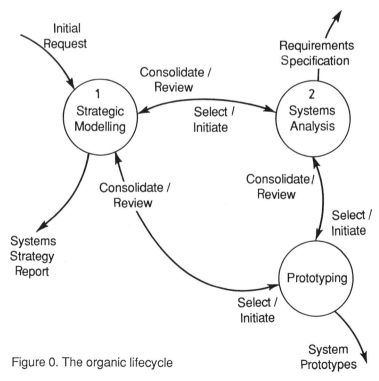

Figure 0. The organic lifecycle

Figure 10.2 Prototyping with respect to the organic lifecycle.

review as illustrated in Figure 10.2. On the other hand, it can be employed as one verification technique amongst others as part of strategic modelling or systems analysis. One area of particular application that we have not considered is the use of prototyping tools to assist in systems reconnaissance work. Remember as well that the activities of the organic lifecycle typically operate concurrently.

Also, we saw in Chapter 5 that it might, for example, be the case that there are three different groups of users each reviewing a different portion of a system, with respect to the three mediums illustrated in Figure 5.8.

1. Essential model for portion A.
2. Prototypes of portion B.
3. External design for portion C.

Again, for convenience of expression I shall use the term 'essential model' to include a portion of, as well as a whole, essential model throughout the rest of this part of the book. Also, I shall refer to 'prototyping projects' to include the case where prototyping is but one aspect of a project.

Clearly one has to start somewhere: it does not make sense to begin constructing prototypes out of thin air. A system profile will be required. The system profile of a prototyping project will depend upon whether it is being initiated from strategic modelling or systems analysis. Typically, in the former case it will contain a portion of the enterprise E-R model whereas in the latter case it will additionally contain a portion of the essential model for a system. The objective of the iterations of essential prototyping is to enhance the model described in the system profile by experiencing working portions of it; not to build it from scratch.

Ultimately, it is recognized here that there is no substitute for rigorous requirements specification and thorough systems design. Rigorous requirement definition will form the basis from which we develop systems and databases in the target production environment. This means going through the normal steps of systems and program design to both tune and document the eventual programs. Therefore, having used essential prototyping to establish user requirements, those requirements still have to be documented. In effect, we are buying information about user requirements. Once that information has been obtained, the prototype that revealed it may be thrown away or shelved for later use. However, the essentials of the prototype must be filtered back to the essential model or the enterprise E-R model as appropriate.

The activities of the organic lifecycle operate in a spiral fashion, as depicted in Figure 1.2. As discoveries are made from essential prototyping, the working model and the essential model will evolve. Early iterations will involve issues of scope, understanding and organization of requirements. For example, a function identified during prototyping as superfluous to requirements may well cause restriction of the statement of purpose with consequent lowering of projected costs. Conversely identification of additional functions may well cause expansion of the statement of purpose with a consequent increase in projected costs. It is important that such cost-benefit issues are made explicit in the early iterations. In later iterations attention will switch much more toward issues of detailed specification.

We have seen that such an organic approach requires liberation from the rigid sequential phasing of traditional waterfall lifecycles. However, the imperative for iteration demands effective project planning and control. To this end the familiar milestones and deliverables of traditional waterfall lifecycles are practically necessary and often contractually required. In order to facilitate planning and control it is necessary to identify:

☐ A lifecycle for the prototyping concept itself, known as 'the prototyping skeleton'.
☐ Further classification of essential prototyping.

These topics are discussed in the next two sections.

10.7 The prototyping skeleton

The basic principle of prototyping is illustrated in Figure 10.3. Because it lies at the core of all forms of prototyping I refer to this as the prototyping skeleton.

Before considering the prototyping skeleton it is important to understand what is meant by the driving data flow 'system requirements', that will form the system profile for a prototyping project. There are two important points to be made here. Firstly, it must have been established that the system requirements are a good candidate for prototyping as mentioned above. Secondly, the required system might do either or both of the following:

☐ Display and/or maintain selected portions of the enterprise E-R model mapped to the enterprise database model (see Figure 9.10).
☐ Respond to certain chosen events.

Whatever the case the source for creating the prototype will be in the data dictionary entries that support the chosen entities/relationships and event responses. The fact that the creation process in effect has its roots in requirement definition models underlines a basic premise of this book: that prototyping is in no sense in conflict with structured techniques, but actually augments structured techniques. Let me briefly explain each of the bubbles in the prototyping skeleton.

Creation. Creation involves building a working model to support system requirements. The level of detail to which this working model is built depends very much

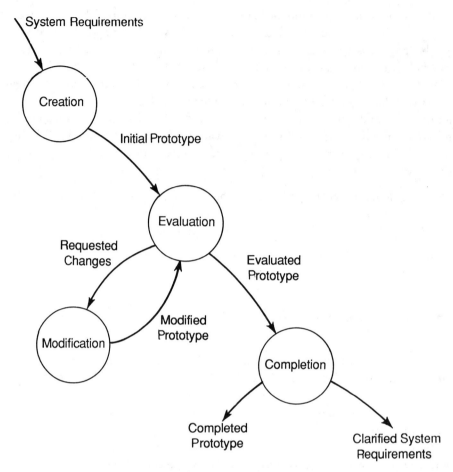

Figure 10.3 The prototyping skeleton.

on the sub-class of prototyping as described in the next section. At one extreme we may be creating a shell consisting simply of a menu of functions reflecting organisation modelled on a high level DFD; at the other extreme we may be translating detailed process specifications in structured language more or less directly into working code.

Normally pre-existing software building blocks are used to create and initially test a prototype in rapid fashion. Alternatively, specialized prototyping tools may facilitate construction and execution of prototypes. Continuity between the essential model and essential prototypes lends particular leverage as we shall see in Chapter 12.

However, it should be emphasized that even where automated implementation of a prototype is not feasible, the prototyping skeleton can still be applied. For example, it is often possible to create a 'paper prototype' that mimics the user interface using a series of 'story board sheets'. A screen image is represented on each story board sheet with a short series of bulleted points describing the interaction. The user then reviews the story board sheets as part of the following evaluation phase.

Evaluation. Evaluation involves three steps. Firstly, a formal demonstration to users not only to introduce users to the prototype and invite initial comments, but also to explain the objectives of the activity. Secondly, the user 'test drives' the prototype and compiles a list of required modifications. This step is really the heart of the prototyping skeleton. It is here that the user has real influence in shaping the application. There may be various users compiling lists, and some requested changes may be more justifiable than others. Hence the need for the third step of actually reviewing the required changes.

Modification. Modification consists of making agreed changes to the prototype as a result of the evaluation stage. Decisions have to be made as to when and how often to modify: iteration must be controlled to prevent the prototype being in a continual state of flux and developers running around like headless chickens.

Completion. Completion only takes place providing there is formal agreement that the prototype is satisfactory to all parties. Changes to the original prototype must now be reflected as appropriate in the essential model and in the relevant portion of the enterprise E-R model. In the case of more far reaching changes it may also be that adjustments have to be made to strategic models.

10.8 Sub-classes of essential prototyping

There are three ways in which the prototyping skeleton is embodied. These are known as 'primitive prototyping', 'event prototyping' and 'decision support prototyping'. These may be considered as converging toward a fourth form known as 'object oriented prototyping'.

There follows a simple characterization of each sub-class of essential prototyping. There are important guidelines which concern both preparing for prototyping and with the techniques themselves which are covered in detail in the next chapter. For now the reader should appreciate that the ordering of the these processes is in fact much more subtle than the apparently simple sequence implied here.

Primitive prototyping

Primitive prototyping is normally initiated directly from strategic modelling as a means of verifying portions of the enterprise data model produced as a result of data oriented systems reconnaissance. In Chapter 9 we saw that those entities which are mature enough are mapped to the appropriate database structure. Primitive database modules are developed in conjunction with screens to create/read/ update/delete the tables thus mapped. Each screen is roughly equatable with one entity. We thus start to address two important objectives:

1. Determine the validity of the data structure.
2. Prepare reusable modules for use by systems.

We shall see in the next chapter that E-R model maturity may be achieved through prototyping as a means of discovering information requirements as well as through E-R modelling itself. The degree of emphasis depends very much on cultural factors which we will discuss in the next chapter.

The ultimate objective here is to build a library of reusable packages that can be mixed and matched by various applications wishing to use or manipulate the database.

Event prototyping

Event prototyping is usually initiated from a systems analysis project employing EP, although it can also be initiated from strategic modelling as a means of verifying the results of function oriented systems reconnaissance. It seeks to test responses to events determined in (part of) the essential model for a specific system. Routines are created to implement the required functionality in harness with the previously created primitive routines. Screens are created to mimic the organization of the essential model, and to navigate the user around the application. This process is iterative with primitive prototyping in that there may be a need to revise the previously created data structure. We thus start to address four further objectives:

1. Determine the validity of the event list itself.
2. Verify organization of requirements.
3. Determine the correctness of responses to the events.
4. Further determine the validity of the supporting data structure.

The level of detail to which the prototype is constructed depends directly upon the level of detail to which event responses have been specified. Initial event prototyping may be done simply on the basis of a high level DFD by building menu shells hooked in to event response groupings. This provides a framework on which to 'hang the details'. Far from being a totally radical approach this is actually very much akin to traditional top-down design of program structures. In adding in more detailed processing it is not necessary to have complete process specifications as this would be self defeating. However, it is recommended that at least a process description (see Section 5.4.1) has been prepared for each response to be prototyped. Again, this serves to ensure control through common data definitions in DDL.

Decision support prototyping

Decision support prototyping is normally initiated directly from strategic modelling, probably after systems reconnaissance has revealed the need for a decision support system. It subjects the database structure created to various *ad hoc* enquiries provided by different levels of management. Typically this will result in the need for further relationships but will also result in new entities and attributes on the first iterations of this activity. The objective here is to enhance the data structure.

Object oriented prototyping

Object oriented prototyping represents the natural convergence of primitive and event prototyping. One of the major aims of the principle of encapsulation which we first met in Section 2.3 and have followed throughout this book, is to localize functions around their required entities. Ideally a single entity should be created, read, updated, and deleted as a result of a clustering of events which should fall within the same sub-system. In practice, data is often shared across different systems, and therefore events will be drawn from different systems. However, this does not affect the validity of the principle. What object oriented prototyping seeks to do therefore is to utilize primitive prototypes with respect to all events affecting that entity. The emergence of 'object oriented knowledge bases' lends practical witness to the theory.

10.9 The benefits of essential prototyping

The underlying benefit of essential prototyping has already been mentioned: reduction of uncertainty. Where there is little or no uncertainty the benefits will be negligible. Other strategies may be employed such as conventional EP, packages, end-user computing etc.

Prototyping provides a vehicle of communication which:

☐ Is powerful because it is tangible and real.
☐ Lends itself to iteration required in channelling the learning process in the right direction.

A common misconception is that one of the main benefits of prototyping is reduction in development costs. Whether or not the prototype is to serve as the basis for the production system has a large effect on costs. However, regardless of this there will be a new cost pattern which should reflect slightly higher costs in the early stages of the lifecycle more than offset by savings in maintenance.

Despite the likelihood of increased costs it should be appreciated that systems will in the long-term be delivered faster, although costs may even be higher due to the increased amount of user effort required. The real benefit, however, comes when it becomes clear that the delivered system actually does meet the user's requirements and that expensive post implementation 'enhancements' are unnecessary.

Finally, another benefit is in the positive psychological effect on users that is often reported. Some years back I was working on managing development projects to produce financial systems for a company in which users had become very disenchanted with the efforts of the systems department. System specifications would be 'signed off' after very little real user participation reflected in poor attendance at review meetings and a certain cynicism toward computers in general. In response to this malaise, and having just invested a large amount of money in a new DBMS it was decided to adopt a prototyping approach to develop the new systems for maintaining that database. The first of these systems was a 'Client system' which stretched across many departmental boundaries involving a variety of users. The effects on previously apathetic users were quite striking when they first came into contact with the prototype screens. Here was something they could actually get their hands on. Requested changes could often be dealt with on the spot, thus giving users a positive feeling of contribution. A feeling of involvement was generated that was simply not present with the more conventional systems developments that had taken place before.

10.10 The dangers of prototyping

Enumerated below is a list of some of the different dangers of prototyping:

1. The prototype becomes the finished system (unless this is a conscious decision as in evolutionary prototyping; for example, build pilot system, throw it away, build another system and so on).

2. Inflated user expectations: users do not always appreciate the limitations of prototypes with a result that the prototype becomes the finished system (as above) because of pressure for early delivery. Users could walk off with the prototype under the impression that it will evolve into the real thing via a magical metamorphosis. However, the magic will be no more than the on-going maintenance that the principle was supposed to help overcome in the first place.

3. Insufficient preparatory analysis resulting in poor initial understanding of the problem.
4. Too much attention to cosmetic details by developers and especially users in evaluating screens, etc. This is often the result of confusing essential prototyping with user interface prototyping.
5. Prototyping is employed indiscriminately as a panacea for all ills.
6. The toys for boys image becomes reality.
7. There is too much iteration.

10.11 Counteracting the dangers of prototyping

Most of the dangers discussed above arise not from the concept of prototyping but from management based upon a poor understanding of that concept. As with any development effort from building a house to writing a book, disaster will occur if we do not understand what we are being asked to do and the limitations within which we are asked to do it.

A project plan should be presented to all involved parties that emphasizes the following general points about prototyping:

☐ It is part of a well planned strategic approach to building effective systems.
☐ It is not 'quick and dirty'.
☐ It does not replace, but complements existing structured techniques.
☐ It is a user friendly way of enhancing the accuracy of documented structured specifications.
☐ There are different classes of prototying (essential/user-interface/technical).
☐ There are different sub-classes of essential prototyping (primitive/event/decision support/object oriented).

The project profile should clarify certain specific points:

☐ System profile.
☐ Class and sub-class of prototyping.
☐ Specific user responsibilities.
☐ Schedule of prototyping activities, showing specific resource requirements and allowing for a specified number of iterations.
☐ Milestones with respect to the overall project lifecycle.
☐ Projected cost-benefit statement.

There follow specific counter measures to the dangers enumerated in the previous section.

1. Make the development strategy explicit within the project profile.
2. Manage expectations by making limitations clear to all concerned.
3. It is recommended here that the relevant portion of the enterprise E-R model be sufficiently mature and that process descriptions are available as a minimum for each event response. A more radical approach may be adopted with prototyping, for example, used as a deliberate strategy for capturing information requirements. If this is done the risks should be made explicit.
4. Establish the different classes of prototyping outlined above, preferably as 'standards'. Make it clear that what is being done here is essential prototyping. It is important to spell out exactly what the purpose is as part of the project profile.
5. Establish prototyping as a viable approach firstly by building reconnaissance models and then inspecting for suitability, as explained in Chapter 8. Remember, we do not have to prototype the whole system. Often it is expedient to focus on one part of the system. Secondly, having established suitability, start to prototype where user needs are greatest.
6. Prototyping is not game playing. Management commitment must be made to prototyping as a serious approach, which needs to be planned and properly controlled like any other. Roles of participants and specific task objectives need to be clarified.
7. The number of iterations must be minimized and controlled. Users must not see prototyping as a license to change their minds repeatedly. Developers must not see it as a license to tinker. Agree in advance the timescales and numbers of iterations and make them explicit in the project profile.

10.12 Summary

The main thrust of this chapter is that far from being incompatible, prototyping and structured techniques actually complement one another very well in many situations. Indeed, the major objective of essential prototyping is to produce a requirements specification. The closer the requirements specification is to actual user needs, the greater the chance of producing an effective system. Experience demonstrates that the largest number of requirements errors are found when the user has the opportunity to get to grips with the working system.

We have seen, however, that there are dangers. And here perhaps we come to the very nub of the issue: *prototyping is project work*: it has a project profile including a system profile like any other project. This chapter has helped lay the ground for identifying classes and sub-classes of prototyping which would typically become tasks within a project. We now need practical guidelines on how to make this work. That will be the subject of the next chapter. We need, also, the right support environment in terms of integrated CASE and prototyping tools. These will be the subject of Chapter 12.

Finally, at the risk of repetition, the appropriateness of the system type as a candidate for prototyping cannot be stressed strongly enough. Indeed, a major reason for the system reconnaissance work described in Chapter 8 was to lay the ground for making rational decisions regarding systems development strategy: prototyping should not be viewed as a panacea for all ills. Before proceeding further the reader is recommended to consider the Player Administration and Petrol Sale Control Systems (described in Appendices 2 and 3 respectively) with respect to the criteria of Section 8.10. For each system ask yourself the question 'Is this a good candidate?'.

CHAPTER 11

The practice of essential prototyping

Nothing ever becomes real till it is experienced — even a proverb is no proverb to you till your life has illustrated it.

JOHN KEATS
Letter to George and Georgina Keats, 19 March 1819

11.1 Introduction

We have seen that prototyping, no less than any other systems development activity, needs to be effectively controlled. The purpose of this chapter is to provide practical guidelines for carrying out the four sub-classes of essential prototyping:

- ☐ Primitive.
- ☐ Event.
- ☐ Decision support.
- ☐ Object oriented.

Each is explained according to the principles outlined in Chapter 10 and with reference to the basic prototyping skeleton, before exploring their collective control.

Before getting down to details it is important to appreciate that what is being suggested here, is recommended with respect to the strategic perspective as a whole. It is important to take a view as to the degree of emphasis we are going to place upon prototyping compared with EP modelling techniques. This will depend upon many factors from deadline pressure to perceived risk. Overall guidelines will be suggested for achieving a balanced approach by first invoking a distinction between radical and conservative approaches to development.

Although, clearly, the approach depends above all on the right software tools, complete identification of desirable features of those tools is left until the next chapter in order to place in the context of full support for the organic lifecycle. In this chapter we restrict attention to fourth generation languages (4GLs) which will therefore be briefly characterized.

11.2 Radical and conservative approaches

A useful distinction is made by Ed Yourdon (1988) with respect to approaches to a lifecycle based upon top-down implementation: 'A radical approach to the structured project lifecycle is one in which activities 1 through 9 take place in parallel from the very beginning of the project – that is, coding begins on the first day of the project, and the survey and analysis continue until the last day of the project. By contrast, in a conservative approach to the structured project lifecycle all of activity N is completed before activity N + 1 begins. Obviously, no manager in his right mind would adopt either one of these two extremes. The key is to recognize that the radical and conservative extremes defined above are the two end points in a range of choices.'

Yourdon suggests certain factors as paramount in ascertaining the right approach, which I believe are equally pertinent in today's environment. I have summarized these under the following headings:

User temperament. Are you dealing with 'a fickle user – one whose personality is such that he delays final decisions until he sees how the system is going to work'?

Deadline pressures. Are you under great pressure 'to produce immediate, tangible results'?

Planning stringency. Is it important to produce an 'accurate schedule, budget and estimate of manpower and other resources'?

Risk. Is there considerable danger 'of making a major technical blunder'?

Broadly speaking fickle user temperament, tight deadline pressure, lack of planning stringency and low risk tend toward a radical approach. Conversely, reliable user temperament, lack of deadline pressure, high planning stringency and high risk tend toward a conservative approach. Most projects, of course, tend toward somewhere in between. The real skill of the manager comes into play in actually making a balanced choice somewhere between these extremes.

Prototyping is often mistakenly identified as a 'radical' approach in the above sense; certainly it will help diffuse the unpredictability of the fickle user. Regarding the final three points, however, we must proceed with caution.

Firstly, do not expect any great cuts in overall development timescales, especially in the first projects to embark on the new approach where there will be a learning curve to be taken into account. However, the fact that we can deliver to the user *something tangible quickly* will help to cut through the 'Why isn't Sally coding yet?' syndrome. This is not the finished system though and that fact needs to be made transparently plain.

Secondly, I have already intimated that prototyping should not be seen as an excuse to avoid project planning. Indeed, we shall see that contrary to this assumption thorough planning and control is an absolute necessity.

Finally, and perhaps most importantly, we come to the issue of risk. The subject of risk analysis is a large one which for reasons of scope I will only touch upon here, but which is important enough to at least place in context. It is my experience that much of the danger of risk comes from insufficient preparatory analysis with respect to the needs of the organization as a whole. If we prototype 'on the fly' at individual application level, we run the risk of mismatching with wider needs. If, however, we adopt a strategic perspective, as described in Part 3 of this book, we considerably lessen that risk. To recap, the strategic perspective can be summarized as follows:

- ☐ An attitude or disposition toward systems development which is influenced by the dominant need for systems which are *holistic* and which is *politically sound* in that it is underwritten by top management commitment. The systems development approach itself must be *responsive* and *flexible*.

Reduction of risk is further enhanced if we have conducted systems reconnaissance to establish the system as a good candidate for prototyping. By adopting the organic lifecycle we help to diffuse such risk.

It is a mistake then to think of prototyping as simply 'radical'. The situation is much more subtle than that. Indeed, we can usefully characterize essential prototyping with respect to the conservative–radical spectrum as follows. At the conservative extreme EP is used to develop a complete rigorous essential model prior to constructing prototypes; prototyping is then used for pure verification. At the radical extreme, a bare prototype shell reflecting intentionally incomplete requirements is constructed; prototyping is then used as a means of capturing the complete rigorous requirements definition.

So how do conservative and radical approaches fare with reference to the four factors cited above? Both approaches are designed to remove uncertainty over requirements and must therefore help with the problem of fickle users. I have also stressed that there is no escape, whatever the approach, from thorough planning. However, the two approaches differ as follows. A conservative approach involves lower risk but is likely to take longer to produce tangible results. It depends upon good prototyping tools, but the need to integrate with EP diagramming techniques is much less than with the radical approach. A radical approach involves higher risk but is more likely to produce fast results. It depends above all on the right supporting software tools to integrate EP diagramming techniques with prototyping. In the discussions which follow I have indicated where one would *tend* toward one extreme or the other. Remember though that in practice of course it will be expedient to achieve a balance between the two extremes. Let me explain how this works in general terms.

Firstly, initial requirements models are built for data and functions. These initial models may be quite sketchy but there are certain minimum requirements. We must at least know what the events are and have made an attempt at specifying incoming and outgoing flows from the context diagram. Supporting this will be the relevant portion of the enterprise E-R model (EERM). These models will form a provisional specification within a system profile for which an intentionally incomplete prototype can be constructed. (Note that, first projects will concentrate on establishing the database structure, in which case there may actually not be any essential model at all). The prototype is used to verify and discover essential data and functions which are fed back to the system profile for review and con-solidation within the essential model and relevant portion of the supporting EERM. Further prototyping is initiated on the basis of a system profile which will contain more specification detail. This iterative process continues until the proto-type accurately mirrors the requirements models to the satisfaction of all concerned.

11.3 Prototyping tools

The term fourth generation language (or 4GL) covers a wide range of techniques implemented using software tools which have one common feature: each provides the developer with the facility to specify some characteristic of software at a high level. Source code is then generated from the developer's specification. Such a cluster of software tools will include all or some of the following:

1. Non-procedural languages for:
   - database query and update,
   - report generation,
   - screen handling,
   - code generation with interfaces to 3GLs.
2. User friendly interface for:
   - screen painting,
   - data definition using standard templates,
   - default application generation,
   - code generation.

The ultimate capability of the above features stems from a common data diction-ary through which the supporting database definitions themselves are maintained. Such a data dictionary is often labelled 'active' as opposed to 'passive' and will contain cross references via which reusable source modules may be maintained. For example, primitive database modules can be generated by the application gener-ator and then reused for more complex processing by the code generator.

Relational databases lend themselves particularly well because, in contrast to network databases, modification of database structure and reorganization of the database are fairly simple and cheap to perform. This is in sharp contrast to a network DBMS where schema changes entail stopping the system, recompiling the schema, dumping and restoring the whole database (Date, 1982).

11.4 Primitive prototyping

Primitive prototyping seeks to build a foundation for later work by serving a dual purpose:

1. To confirm a chosen portion of the enterprise E-R model.
2. To construct reusable primitive database modules to create/read/update/delete tables on the database.

The activity is therefore in a sense preliminary to prototyping proper in that 'Building a prototype without knowing the underlying data structure is as pointless as building a scale model of a bridge without knowing the depth of river and angle of the banks' (Veryard, 1984.)

Primitive prototyping is normally initiated directly from strategic modelling as a means of verifying the results of data oriented systems reconnaissance; that is, portions of the enterprise E-R model. In a conservative environment, those entities which are mature enough (as described in Section 9.8) are mapped to the appropriate database structure and database modules developed in conjunction with screens to create/read/update/delete those entities. Each screen is roughly equatable with one entity.

With a radical approach primitive prototyping may be used as a deliberate experimental strategy for capturing information requirements. In such a case it may be that an E-R model is roughed out with very few attributes and mapped to the appropriate database structure. The principle then becomes to mature the E-R model through prototyping. Clearly flexible and fast database unload and load facilities are required for this as described by Connell and Shafer (1989).

In situations where databases are being constructed afresh a radical approach may well be feasible. In particular, it is best to establish the independent entities first, especially those exposed by data-process matrices as lying at the very heart of the system. Examples of such entities would be Player in the sports enterprise, discussed below, or Station Facility in the petrol company; others might be Patient (hospital), Policy (insurance house), Vehicle (vehicle hire), Product (manufacturer) and so on.

More typically it will be the case that the new database structures have to embed within an existing database. In such situations there is clearly less latitude and a more conservative approach may be expedient: E-R modelling techniques would be used to establish the maturity of the chosen portion of the enterprise E-R model before mapping to the appropriate database architecture in the form of a LDSD as described in the previous chapter.

Finally, remember that systems analysis projects will create system E-R models

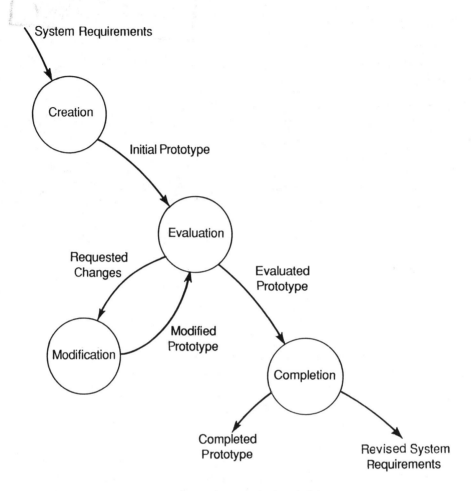

Figure 11.1 The prototyping skeleton.

which require primitive prototypes. The resulting primitive database modules will actually be used by event prototypes (discussed in the next section) developed for the application itself.

Figure 11.1 repeats the prototyping skeleton originally shown in Figure 10.3 and discussed in Section 10.7. Let us look at how this is applied to primitive prototyping step by step.

System requirements. The 'system requirements' of primitive prototyping is a defined portion of the enterprise E-R model, which will have been mapped to a LDSD as described in Chapter 9.

Creation. Creation of primitive prototypes will involve creating and compiling a database schema in data description language (DDL), for the tables of the LDSD. Primitive database modules are then constructed to create/read/update/delete the database tables, with appropriate supporting screens to capture and display data.

An established method is to use a 4GL, embracing a structured query language (SQL) and an application generator (AG). AGs supply leverage in allowing the developer to create default screens for data capture and display from relational database tables in a scale of minutes, rather than in hours as would be the case with a conventional 3GL.

Let us consider how such an approach could be applied to primitive prototyping for the Player table, as shown in Figure 11.2.

Step 1. Create an empty table for Player by setting up appropriate DDL entries, using a language such as SQL.

Step 2. Invoke AG and specify a new application called Admin. A screen appears from which we can choose either a custom or default option. We choose the default option.

Step 3. Specify the table name Player, how many rows are to be shown on one screen (in this case one) and which columns (in this case all). Now select the 'generate' option. The AG now uses embedded rules to create primitive database modules for the Player table and a default screen for the display and maintenance of data in that table. On successful completion the AG responds 'Admin created' and displays its main menu.

Step 4. Select the Admin application and execute it by pressing the appropriate keys. This will cause a default screen to be displayed which will allow us to enter and store data. Further, by pressing appropriate keys we can also display data and also amend or delete data.

Basic test data can now be loaded to the database using the creation screen that we have built, and the primitive database modules tested for basic errors. Report generators are particularly useful here. An area of systems development which is often woefully neglected and underestimated is that of creating good testbeds. It is sometimes overlooked that application generators with good reporting facilities lend particular advantage here.

Evaluation. Evaluation of the primitive prototype consists of the normal three-tier cycle described in Section 10.7 of demonstration, usage and review.

The main invitees will be the *owners* of the data in question. That effectively means the user executive sponsor of systems relative to which the entities/relationships are major. Data administrators should also be actively involved. In my experience it is healthy for the owner to bring along the manager or supervisor who

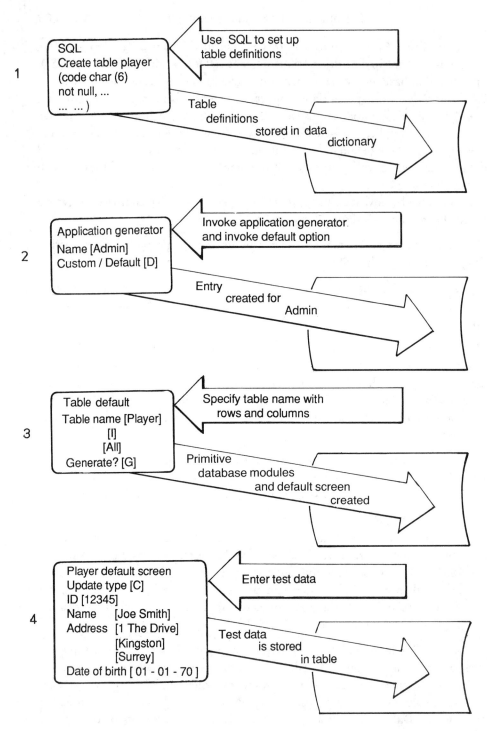

1

SQL
Create table player
(code char (6)
not null, ...
... ...)

Use SQL to set up
table definitions

Table
definitions
stored in data
dictionary

2

Application generator
Name [Admin]
Custom / Default [D]

Invoke application generator
and invoke default option

Entry
created for
Admin

3

Table default
Table name [Player]
[I]
[All]
Generate? [G]

Specify table name with
rows and columns

Primitive
database modules
and default screen
created

4

Player default screen
Update type [C]
ID [12345]
Name [Joe Smith]
Address [1 The Drive]
[Kingston]
[Surrey]
Date of birth [01 - 01 - 70]

Enter test data

Test data
is stored
in table

Figure 11.2 Using an application generator to set up a primitive prototype for Player.

is actually going to be responsible for operational use of the data. The early demonstrations are certainly also going to be high profile in that they should generate widespread interest right to the top of the company. Therefore one should also be prepared to present more, politically, at board level: it is important that things go well. This is particularly true here especially as the initial demonstrations of primitive prototypes will in all likelihood be breaking new ground to important audiences. Demonstrations should be thoroughly rehearsed and the objectives of the session fully and clearly explained to the participants. Questions should be positively encouraged. A large screen VDU projector, as well as being of practical necessity for large audiences, can give an extra dimension to the credibility of the demonstration.

Printed documentation of the screens can be issued at this stage but is not particularly recommended as it will foster the tendency to evaluate screen layouts when it is the *content* of those layouts, the data, that is of primary interest here. A timetable should be issued showing agreed prototyping time slots, a review date(s) and completion date. A check list should be provided to those who are actually going to use the prototype. Normally this will be the owner or the delegated owners, but experience suggests that it can be difficult to dissuade a particularly insistent managing director or president. The check list should include the following:

- ☐ A list of all attributes within each table for ticking, with spaces for filling in any missing attributes.
- ☐ A matrix for ticking create/read/update/delete for each table.

On later iterations, 'join' operations can be introduced and a matrix of tables versus tables can be included to allow indication of whether a 'join' was actually tried with an indication of usefulness.

Modification. Modification at the primitive prototyping stage will almost certainly involve altering the database structure, which means recompiling the DDL schema. Although this is simple enough with RDBMs as opposed to network DBMSs, it is something we would certainly want to limit. It should be restricted following each review, of which there should be, typically, two per user, culminating in an all party review. If there is a need for more iteration than this it is normally an indication that input is required from other users who, although they may not own the data, actually have a greater knowledge of it.

An example of this latter point sometimes occurs over independent entities which are shared across many different user departments. 'Customer' is a typical case in point. Marketing department are often the owners as they choose when to delete. However, Customer Servicing often have a greater knowledge of the data itself. In such a case it is clearly vital to involve all parties who have a contribution to make.

Completion.   Completion of primitive prototyping takes place following full agreement at the final evaluation review. This would involve documentation of both essential data and essential function. The former means ensuring that the enterprise E-R model maps to the revised database structure. The latter means reverse engineering the source code generated by the application generator to reusable process algorithms, for use by process specifications within the behavioural model. The source code takes the shape of primitive database modules and will normally reference the data dictionary for its attribute validation rules in a fourth generation environment. Clearly then, although this might seem superficially easy (just adjusting a few diagrams) – there is the potential for an adminstrative nightmare (changing hundreds of data dictionary entries) if this is attempted manually. Again this is where good supporting software lends special leverage. I therefore return to this topic in Chapter 12.

Primitive prototypes will form a useful starting point for later work, but should be viewed at this stage for what they are: useful vehicles that have enabled us to develop primitive database modules, to confirm the E-R model and develop its supporting database structure.

11.5 Event prototyping

Event prototyping seeks to resolve uncertainty over event responses from the essential model. Three criteria must be satisfied before an event response can be prototyped:

1. The responses must be suitable candidates, as discussed in Section 8.10; for example, *transactions*.
2. Primitive prototypes must have been completed for all entities and relationships required by the event response.
3. A process description (see Section 5.4.1) must be available for the event response.

Let us look at how the prototyping skeleton, shown in Figure 11.1, is applied here.

System requirements.   The system requirements which drive the process of event prototyping are known as provisional specifications. Before describing event prototyping therefore it is important to explain the concept of a provisional specification.

All provisional specifications must contain the following:

☐ Data dictionary definitions for all data flows consumed by and produced by the event responses to be prototyped. It is the data flows that describe the content of the user interface and without initially agreed definitions for these there is no sensible basis on which to construct prototype screens.

☐ Process descriptions for all event responses to be prototyped (primitive prototypes must exist for all entities/relationships listed within the process descriptions for the responses).

The scope of a provisional specification can vary from a single event response which needs to be examined in its own right, to an organized collection of event responses in the form of a set of levelled DFDs from the behavioural model as described in Chapter 4. More typically it will lie between these extremes in the form of an encapsulated packaging of responses from within that levelled set.

This fits well with incorporating functions into menus, which is a standard feature of most 4GLs, as suggested in Figure 11.3. Menu structures are also flexible in that it is relatively simple to use a 4GL to add in a new function here or remove one there. This is particularly important in essential prototyping where the very nature of the exercise demands fast responses to changing requirements.

If adopting a radical approach then the provisional specification will consist of a process description for each event response, plus data flow definitions which contain bare details and will typically be only partially completed. It is these that must be initially agreed with the user: the inherent business of essential prototyping becomes the establishment of basic system duties and organization via a menu shell before filling in the details. Functions are hung off the menu shell for elicitation of exact essential logic and data flow.

At the conservative extreme, a provisional specification for a single event response should also additionally contain a process specification in the form of structured language and/or pre- and post-conditions, not for communicating with the user but to aid the developer in the mechanics of creating the prototype as discussed below.

In between these extremes a specification for an encapsulated packaging will contain an intermediate level of detail: some processes may have logic which has been rigorously defined, others may simply have a process description.

Creation. Creation of event prototypes involves two basic activities:

☐ Constructing screens to capture and display data flows specified within the provisional specification.

☐ Mapping the essential logic of the responses into source code, which will employ primitive database modules previously created in primitive prototyping.

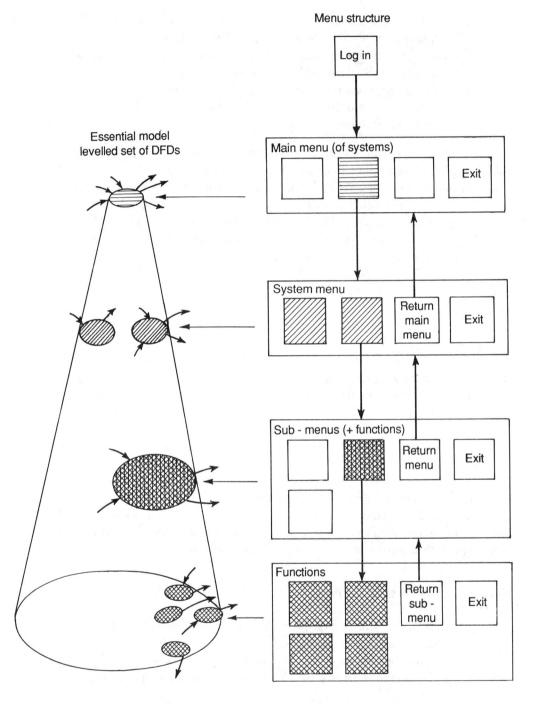

Figure 11.3 Levelled DFDs and menu structure compared.

In the Player Administration System we first construct a menu shell as depicted in Figure 11.4: this reflects the required structure of the system without involving us in the intricacies of updating logic. Certain PF keys would be specified as standard options (for example, PF8 to return to previous screen and PF9 to return to main menu).

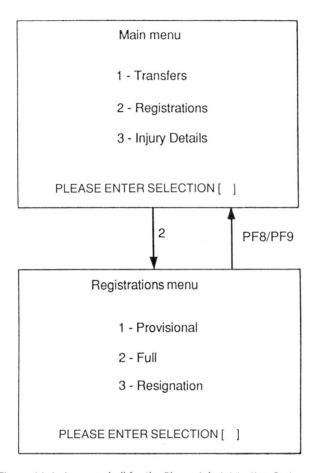

Figure 11.4 A menu shell for the Player Administration System.

Let us consider developing an event prototype for the event response Provisionally Register Player; process description and process specification (action diagram) for this response are repeated here as Figures 11.5 and 11.6 respectively.

If taking a radical approach we have a process description only. This will tell us which tables (corresponding to entities, associative entities and relationships as per the mapping rules discussed in Section 9.9) are to be used and the type of access

Process objective: To set up provisional membership and produce a
                    membership card and registration request for a
                    player joining a club.

Process views:

    Flows in   :   PROVISIONAL PLAYER REGISTRATION REQUEST

    Flows out :   PLAYER REGISTRATION REQUEST
                  MEMBERSHIP CARD
                  ERROR MESSAGE

    Entities   :   CLUB (*read*)
                PLAYER (*read, create*)
                SPORTS AUTHORITY (*read*)

    Associative entities: CLUB MEMBERSHIP (*create*)

    Relationships: SPORTS AUTHORITY *LICENSES* CLUB (*read*)

Algorithms:

    Allocate Player.Id

    Allocate Club.Number

Figure 11.5 Process description for 2.1 Provisionally Register Player.

required. From this we know which primitive prototypes are required. For example, we will require the application to read and create Players.

The next step is to examine the input and output flows and decide exactly which data items are to be captured, which used as keys to access tables and which displayed from tables. The input flow Provisional Player Registration contains the following:

☐ Player.Id: used to access Player table. We note it can be null in which case we will have to create a row in Player.
☐ Player.Name, Player.Address and Player.Birth.Date: all captured as corresponding column entries (if Player Id is null). Otherwise all displayed from Player table.
☐ Club.Name: used to access Club table.
☐ Club.Membership.Joining.Date: captured as a column entry of a newly created row of Club Membership.

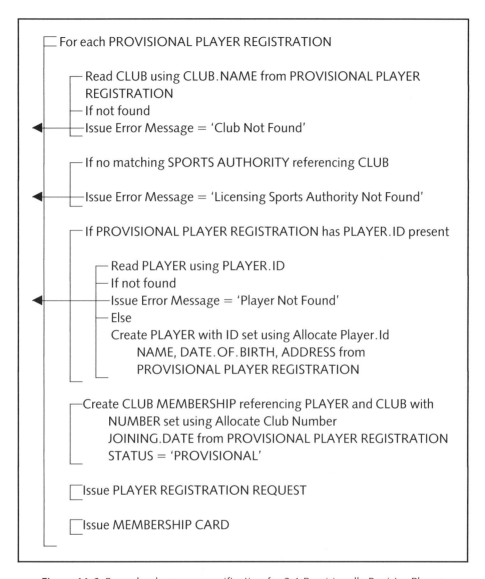

For each PROVISIONAL PLAYER REGISTRATION

    Read CLUB using CLUB.NAME from PROVISIONAL PLAYER
    REGISTRATION
    If not found
    Issue Error Message = 'Club Not Found'

    If no matching SPORTS AUTHORITY referencing CLUB

    Issue Error Message = 'Licensing Sports Authority Not Found'

    If PROVISIONAL PLAYER REGISTRATION has PLAYER.ID present

        Read PLAYER using PLAYER.ID
        If not found
        Issue Error Message = 'Player Not Found'
        Else
          Create PLAYER with ID set using Allocate Player.Id
              NAME, DATE.OF.BIRTH, ADDRESS from
              PROVISIONAL PLAYER REGISTRATION

    Create CLUB MEMBERSHIP referencing PLAYER and CLUB with
        NUMBER set using Allocate Club Number
        JOINING.DATE from PROVISIONAL PLAYER REGISTRATION
        STATUS = 'PROVISIONAL'

    Issue PLAYER REGISTRATION REQUEST

    Issue MEMBERSHIP CARD

Figure 11.6 Procedural process specification for 2.1 Provisionally Register Player:
action diagram.

Similarly we examine the output flows and notice in particular:

☐ Club.Membership.Status (on Club Membership Card) is set to Provisional; a column entry that will have to be set up in the new Club
Membership table row.

☐ Sports.Authority.Name (on Player Registration Request) is accessed from the appropriate row of Sports Authority.

If adopting a radical approach it is likely that the list of algorithms in the process description will be incomplete. We would typically expect to simply leave 'hooks' to these, for example, substituting literals for calculated numbers, for the time being.

We can now start to assemble an event prototype by invoking a screen painter to specify the data capture screen layout and field definitions, making implicit use of the primitive database modules set up during primitive prototyping. Field definition would normally include the following:

☐ Table field: corresponding column name.
☐ Key field: whether this key is used to access the table.
☐ Data type: the domain of the field.
☐ Displayed: whether the field *appears* on the screen; it is possible to have invisible work fields.
☐ Input: whether data entry allowed.
☐ Mandatory: whether data entry must take place.
☐ Update: whether you can change data accessed into this field by a query.
☐ Error messages: reference to the messages to be displayed by specific failure type.
☐ Validation: specific validation rules such as ranges, defaults and dependencies (for example Player Id must be entered if Player Name is null). This facility is normally provided as an overlay window or different screen.
☐ SQL use: the name of any SQL statements used in changing values; for example algorithms used. This facility allows windowing into SQL to create complex and conditional logic.

In the example we could combine input flow items and output flow items on a single screen as shown in Figure 11.7. The menu structure as a whole is shown in Figure 11.8.

If adopting a radical approach we can expect initially to have little information under the last three headings above: error messages, validation, and SQL use. This is a deliberate strategy as the very nature of the exercise is to uncover them as we go, and then build the process specifications.

On the other hand if a process specification is available, then we can fill in a lot of these details in advance. For example, we might be able to use SQL statements to reference algorithms (written as modules in a 3GL) and to specify conditional logic, and to specify detailed validation and error messages. This would be a conservative approach.

Two further points should be noted:

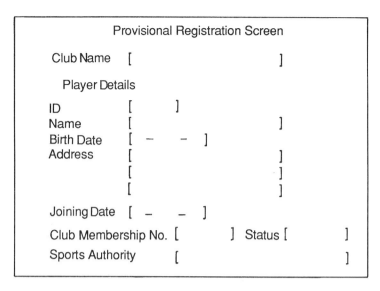

Figure 11.7 The Provisional Registration screen.

1. Firstly, there are often parts of a system which though they lend themselves well to prototyping, will not, in fact, be implemented as parts of dialogues. For example, the Membership Card and Player Registration Request, discussed above, would need to be printed. Questions such as whether to print 'online' or to spool for later printing in 'batch' will need to be addressed as part of the subsequent system design phase. Again we see the danger of equating prototypes with finished systems.

2. Secondly, although the above discussion has focussed on menu based structures, the reader should not feel constrained by this. For example, command driven facilities can be extremely useful if wishing to focus on one particularly complex event response in its own right. In a case like this, repeated passage through the menu structure can become a source of great irritation and frustration. Indeed, as users accumulate more and more experience with the system this can become more generally true, making command driven facilities a virtual necessity.

Evaluation. Evaluation of event prototypes consists of the normal three-tier cycle of demonstration, usage and review. Demonstration of event prototypes is very much along lines previously discussed for primitive prototypes. Again the importance of preparation and professional presentation cannot be overstressed.

There is more of an argument for issuing printed documentation of the screens

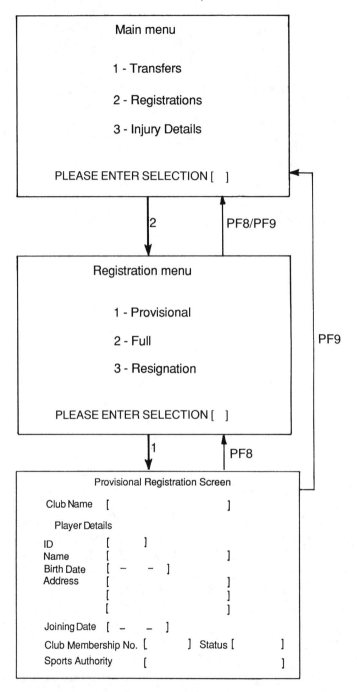

Figure 11.8 Provisional Registration in relation to menu structure.

at this stage but it should be made clear that it is not so much the design of the evaluated screen layouts as the *content* of those layouts and the sequence and structuring of those layouts in relation to one another, that is of primary interest here. A timetable should be issued showing agreed prototyping time slots, with review and completion dates. A check list should be provided to those who are actually going to use the prototype. The check list should include the following:

☐ A list of menu screens and a diagram showing their overall structure as suggested on the right hand side of Figure 11.3.
☐ A list of event responses to be prototyped individually.

Despite the importance of good demonstration, the emphasis with event prototyping shifts toward actual system use. This should not be surprising as here we are actually mimicking an operational system in which users will have immediate and personal interests. Event prototypes will typically be carried out by operational users reporting to the appropriate executive sponsor. It is useful therefore if event prototyping can take place in the work environment itself using realistic test data supplied by the user.

Typically, a menu shell of proposed event responses is prototyped to evaluate the structure of the system; to ensure that the correct responses had been identified and that the sequencing and control of these responses was correct. Individual responses may be prototyped in command driven form for evaluation of their logic content and these introduced in stages for evaluation within the menu structure.

Different levels of the menu structure can be worked on in parallel. I recollect a life assurance system development in which the claims manager concentrated on the menu structure of the claims function, whilst a clerk with an intricate knowledge of death benefits for one particular type of policy worked on that particular element of the system in some depth.

Finally, in the more advanced stages, the event prototypes can be used for simulation of actual business practices, with results compared against those of existing production systems.

Modification. Modification at the event prototyping stage comes in two different forms. Firstly, there are modifications to system structure. They largely involve changes to menus and screen linkages, and should be easily implemented through the 4GL. Secondly, there are changes to source code itself. For obvious reasons, we would hope to minimize alterations to the database structure. Following the approach suggested we should expect a mix of the two types of change, with an emphasis on the former in the early iterations and on the latter in the later iterations. In contrast to primitive prototyping many of these can be dealt with on an on-going basis, rather than necessitating formal review, because of the following:

- ☐ Although the processing done in event prototyping is going to be more complex than in primitive prototyping, the number of users involved will normally be a lot less; two or three working in the same department is very common.
- ☐ Most changes should involve detail that can easily be achieved through the 4GL and not impact the database itself.

However, a target date for formal agreement will have been set and therefore at least one review will need to be planned for.

Finally it is worth mentioning that there may be some event responses within the menu structure which are too complex to benefit from prototyping or not suitable for prototyping. In these cases the system simply provides a 'hook' from which the complex response, developed using conventional techniques, can eventually be supported.

Completion. Completion of event prototyping takes place following full agreement at the final evaluation review. The provisional specifications of the essential model are updated to reflect the business logic of individual responses in the form of rigorous definition, for example, by using structured language. The levelled set of DFDs may also need to be adjusted where response groupings have been changed. Again such reworking can be a burdensome overhead: the ability of supporting software to assist in this reverse engineering becomes critical and is an issue we will return to in the next chapter.

Also, the prototype screens themselves and any STDs that have been constructed to help better understand the structure of the user interface should be saved but not formally documented. They will form a useful starting point for later work. Indeed, they may well be used as part of the design specification. However, for now, they should be viewed for what they are: useful vehicles that have enabled us to develop event responses and to confirm processing structure as mirrored in the set of levelled DFDs.

11.6 Decision support prototyping

The objective of decision support prototyping is to verify underlying data structure as flexible enough to meet a wide range of *ad hoc* enquiries. It is akin to primitive prototyping in that system requirements of the prototyping skeleton will also consist of a chosen portion of the enterprise E-R model.

However, there are two important differences between decision support prototyping and primitive prototyping:

☐ Primitive prototyping concentrates on building the foundation stones of the database: on verifying attribution and confirming entities. In contrast decision support prototyping focusses on developing suitable structures upon those foundation stones: it therefore tends toward exploring and creating relationships and dependent entities.
☐ Primitive prototyping seeks to build primitive database modules. Decision support prototyping does not build code. It will make extensive use of 4GL query and reporting facilities.

Let us look at how the prototyping skeleton shown in Figure 11.1 is applied here.

System requirements. System requirements for decision support prototyping consist of a chosen portion of the enterprise E-R model mapped to a LDSD, usually already prototyped at primitive and event level.

Creation. Creation of decision support prototypes will involve creating and compiling a database schema in data description language (DDL), for the tables of the LDSD. In most cases the majority of tables will be readily available as a result of previous primitive and event prototyping.

Although the building of custom built enquiry screens and menus, using screen painting facilities should not be ruled out, decision support prototyping will generally restrict itself to making extensive use of available structured query and reporting facilities, which are normally powerful features of 4GLs. There are two good reasons for this. Firstly, it is obviously more economical than spending time setting up custom built screens. Secondly, it is more desirable as the intention here is to focus upon the adequacy of the database structure rather than screen formats and the design of the user interface.

Evaluation. Evaluation of decision support prototypes involves the by now familiar cycle of demonstration, use and review. Demonstrations will again be critical, particularly in view of the seniority of the audience, and the previous recommendations should be followed. The executive sponsor will typically be a senior manager. It is important that the users understand how to use the query facilities of the 4GL so there may be an extra element of training involved.

The nature of the exercise here is by definition flexible: users are being asked to anticipate the types of enquiry that they might conceivably wish to make. This can be difficult for users working in isolation. It is therefore useful to encourage group sessions (along lines suggested in Section 1.6) for the interested parties with the objective of generating lists of potential enquiries.

In contrast to the pre-defined check lists of primitive and event prototyping, users should in effect therefore be generating their own check lists of enquiries in the form of parameters such as the following:

- ☐ All players transferred more than four times.
- ☐ All players of a specific club who have been shown 'red cards'.
- ☐ All clubs finishing in the top six of division 1 since 1977.
- ☐ The number of times two clubs have played each other in a certain competition.

The check list is not intended as a straightjacket. Although all enquiries on that list should be tested it must not be allowed to rule out the more spontaneous enquiries that result from the generation of ideas that take place within the head of an individual user once he or she has got deeply involved at the terminal. These will be added to the list, and each item given an importance weighting according its criticality in meeting business objectives.

Each item on the list should be prototyped interactively using structured query facilities and/or non-interactively using a report generator and given an information rating. This is intended not as a score of system performance in terms of factors such as response times, although that may well be done later in user-interface and/or performance prototyping. The information rating is intended as a measure of how successful the system was in supplying the user with the required data.

Following the prototyping sessions a review takes place at which check lists are compared and weighting and ratings averaged with the objective of providing a single resultant list reflecting overall decision support requirements for each item. The objective is to establish and agree which items necessitate modification.

It is possible to use this application of 'weighted lists' to come up with an overall 'score' for decision support in the area under study. Individual item scores are calculated by multiplying importance weighting by information rating and then totalled to give an overall score. This can be recalculated at each iteration to gauge level of improvement.

Modification. Modification of decision support prototypes should be dealt with in order of business priority as indicated by the importance weighting on the reviewed check list. This will almost certainly involve altering the database structure, which means recompiling the DDL schema. Again although this is simple enough with RDBMs as opposed to network DBMSs, it is something we would certainly want to limit, and not to carry out in an uncontrolled and piecemeal fashion. It should be restricted following each review, of which there should be typically two or three.

The feasibility of the change also has to be determined. For example, addition of a linkage table to implement a new relationship is a simple matter. However, changes in entity structure involving, say, shifting certain attributes from one entity to another, perhaps new, entity will present much more difficulty. This is especially the case where other systems have been prototyped on the basis of the original structure. This leads to the need to control essential prototyping as described in Section 11.8.

Completion. Completion of decision support prototyping takes place following full agreement at the final evaluation review. This means ensuring that the enterprise E-R model maps to the revised database structure. Again, reverse engineering software can assist in this process, although it is usually fairly straightforward to make the necessary adjustments to ERD and supporting data dictionary entries manually.

11.7 Object oriented prototyping

Although object oriented knowledge bases founded in relational technology are fast emerging, the tools required for object oriented prototyping are at the time of writing not yet commercially available. Nevertheless it is of interest to step back for a moment and consider the sort of features such a tool might be expected to possess.

Object oriented prototyping, in fact, represents the natural convergence of primitive and event prototyping. The principle here is to integrate facts and rules to form objects and to then subject the objects to essential prototyping. There are various ways of constructing an object oriented requirements model. In a 'pure' object oriented approach to analysis the analyst begins by identifying objects and developing the object oriented requirements model on this basis. In an 'applied' approach the object oriented model is derived from a more conventional model by clustering of data and processing representations in line with the principle of encapsulation. The approach used here is very much of the second genre:

- ☐ Strategic modelling is used to create the enterprise E-R model.
- ☐ Systems are scoped in line with the principle of encapsulation.
- ☐ EP is used to create a behavioural model clustered into groupings, using this same principle, which include:

(a) stored data (System ERD),
(b) processes (DFDs),
(c) control processes (STDs).

It is possible to think of these groupings as *objects*. We can make this transition to an object oriented representation by applying what we have already learnt. Let me give you an example.

We can consider entities from the point of view of processing. The strategy here focusses on event list(s) with the objective of relating events to entities. Clearly a single event response may impact several entities and conversely a single entity may be impacted by several events. We have seen that the events which impact an entity will often stretch across different systems. Entity–event matrices drawn at enterprise level are a useful device for making this connection. A further source will be ESTDs which track the effects of events across systems upon a single entity. The strategy is to find the area of commonality and to isolate those portions of event responses which impact the single entity in question.

Entity–process matrices can be particularly useful here. Figure 11.9 illustrates how the above strategy can be applied using the entity–process matrix created earlier in Chapter 8 (Figure 8.17) for the Player Administration System. Entities and their associated process portions effectively become objects by taking vertical slices through the matrix. These are shown as clouds in the illustration. Each process portion becomes a 'method' relative to the object in which it is being used. Thus for example the Create Player portion of the process Provisionally Register Player is now a method of the Player object.

Interfaces between objects are easily identified and become 'messages', to use the object oriented term. In creating a Transfer Request entity occurrence the process Record Transfer Request requires to access certain details from both Player and Club Membership. In object oriented terms 'An arrow, together with an arrow head, indicates that a message connection exists: the sender "sends" a message. The receiver "receives" the message. The receiver returns a response to the sender.' (Coad and Yourdon, 1990.) Therefore the object Transfer Request would send messages to Player and Club Membership to request accessing of the appropriate details. Messages are illustrated using arrows between clouds in Figure 11.9. Notice there is a two-way connection between the objects Player and Club Membership as each requires certain processing to be done by the other, in line with the interfaces exposed on the matrix.

A suitable prototyping tool would have to allow primitive prototypes to be set up more or less as already described, but with the primitive database modules actually triggered as methods from entries within the tables themselves. This would give us 'primitive objects'.

The ERD would be used as a blueprint on which to structure objects in relation

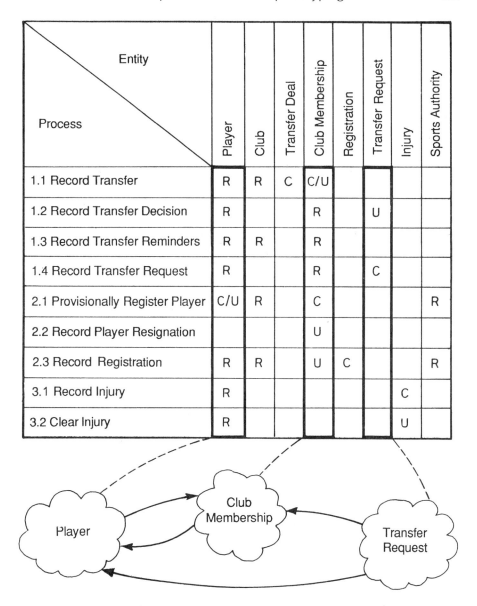

Process \ Entity	Player	Club	Transfer Deal	Club Membership	Registration	Transfer Request	Injury	Sports Authority
1.1 Record Transfer	R	R	C	C/U				
1.2 Record Transfer Decision	R			R		U		
1.3 Record Transfer Reminders	R	R		R				
1.4 Record Transfer Request	R			R		C		
2.1 Provisionally Register Player	C/U	R		C				R
2.2 Record Player Resignation				U				
2.3 Record Registration	R	R		U	C			R
3.1 Record Injury	R						C	
3.2 Clear Injury	R						U	

Figure 11.9 The entity–process matrix as a source for object orientation.

to one another. In particular super-subtypes would be used as a basis for inheritance of attributes.

We would then have to distribute the appropriate pockets of process logic into their appropriate tables to form methods within objects. Interfaces would be implemented as messages between objects specifying which method and which object occurrence was required. Event prototyping would then be performed to develop the objects, with guidelines for evaluation, modification and completion very much a composite of those already described.

The above scenario is an oversimplification in that other relevant aspects of systems have not been touched on for reasons of scope. In particular:

☐ Co-ordinator objects will need to be introduced to ensure control (as for example modelled on STDs).

☐ Actor and sensor objects will be required to ensure interfaces with the environment (for example data flows to and from terminators).

☐ Server objects will need to be constructed to house reusable processing (for example algorithms).

We will return to such an idealized object oriented environment in Chapter 12.

11.8 *Controlling essential prototyping*

Classification of prototyping is intended to facilitate project planning and control. The guiding principle here has been to apply the sub-classes of essential prototyping in a certain sense sequentially. Primitive prototyping seeks to provide a foundation for event prototyping by confirming a core database structure and supplying primitive database modules. These are after all the building blocks from which systems are constructed. Event prototyping in turn provides for functional development upon this sound base and further enhances database structure. Finally, decision support prototyping develops the database structure further in relation to management information requirements.

Despite the obvious attractions of this scenario we should be aware that it represents an idealization of reality. For example, one of the problems of primitive prototyping can be the difficulty users sometimes experience in relating it to what they actually do. By combining event prototyping with primitive prototyping we can supply the latter with a context that the user can readily identify with.

It is important to encourage user confidence. Employment of actual production data with which users are readily familiar will greatly assist in this. As already intimated, users should be encouraged to use primitive prototypes to enter test data. However, if wishing to simulate real working situations, quantity as well as quality of data will be important in essential prototyping. It will be important later on anyhow for comparison of technical prototypes with production systems. Therefore conversion routines should be developed early to migrate production data into the new database structure, thus providing a natural testbed.

However, it is difficult to generalize to a greater degree than this. There can be exceptions to the general rule: For example, it might be expedient to decision support prototype a part of the database, the structure of which is uncertain, using a specially set up testbed *before* event prototyping. That is, we take the view that we need to establish exactly what is to be updated before creating a system to actually do the updating. On the other hand life may simply not be very kind: it may well be for example that decision support prototyping uncovers a need to maintain some new attributes. This might raise the need for some new events to be prototyped. In an extreme case it could give rise to a new data capture system with its own essential model which will require event prototyping. Similarly even where we have been apparently thorough in data analysis and primitive prototyping of independent entities, this does not preclude the exposure by some later project of unforeseen attributes or a need to restructure the underlying enterprise E-R model.

As well as iteration, there will also be overlap between categories of essential prototyping. In the petrol company case study (Appendix 3) we could, for example, have the following scenario:

- ☐ The entity Product undergoing primitive prototyping.
- ☐ The system Station Facility Maintenance undergoing event prototyping.
- ☐ The entity Customer undergoing decision support prototyping.

The same comments also apply to the relationship between essential and user-interface prototyping, and between user-interface and technical prototyping. There will always be a certain degree of iteration and overlap.

What we therefore have is a graduated approach to prototyping which is illustrated in Figure 11.10. (The number of reviews applies to a single user.) The

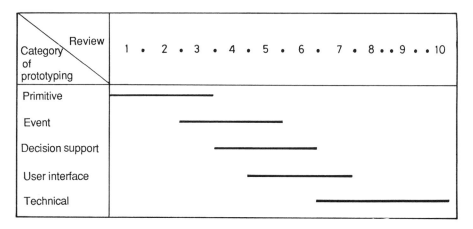

Figure 11.10 Graduation of prototyping.

reader should note that in a sense object oriented prototyping transcends the distinction between primitive, event and decision support prototyping and imagine the lines for each collapsed into a single line for this. The recommendation is to use the diagram as a guideline rather than a blueprint for the control of essential prototyping.

11.9 Summary

The various categories of prototyping are summed up in Figure 11.11. Essential prototyping is designed to reduce uncertainty. It provides a sounding board for the enterprise E-R model in the form of primitive and decision support prototyping, and for the essential model in the form of event prototyping.

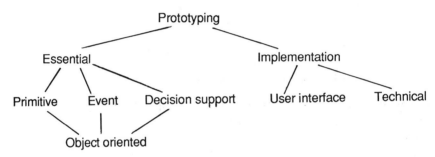

Figure 11.11 The 'prototyping tree'.

Primitive prototyping provides a proof of attribution and a confirmation of basic data structure as modelled on the enterprise E-R model. EP's first pass results in provisional specifications prior to event prototyping which is a means of verifying the correctness and completeness of the essential model. Finally, decision support prototyping is designed to confirm and enhance the more detailed data structure as modelled on the enterprise E-R model.

Object oriented prototyping represents the natural convergence of these subclasses of prototyping. It relies very much on the principle of encapsulation which we have followed throughout this book. However, it is also more heavily dependent on effective software support to facilitate transition to an object oriented representation. We shall see in Chapter 12 that, at the time of writing, this is still some way off. However, the contention will be that its future emergence is inevitable.

Finally, for effective control, one has to take a view on the strength of role that essential prototyping is to play in all this. Is it a conservatively employed tool for plain and simple verification of pre-specified requirements? Or is it a radical tool for actually capturing the requirements specification based upon an initially sketchy requirement definition? We have seen that the degree of emphasis placed in relation to these extremes is important in determining the exact mechanisms to be followed.

PART SIX

The CASE Perspective

In line with the principles followed throughout this book we have sought to clarify the concept of effective modelling before considering its implementation. The time has now come to consider development of effective systems from the latter technical viewpoint. This involves arguably the most exciting perspective of all: computer aided software engineering (CASE). Indeed it is now commonly acknowledged that the potential of any set of structured techniques can only be realized through CASE.

In this part of the book we consider first *what* CASE is by examining the evolution of the term over the past decade. Technical advances have been staggering leading to a far larger and more sophisticated use of the term than originally intended. However, we shall need to cut through some of the industry hype which has come to surround such a huge money winner.

We are then in a position to consider *how* CASE can best be employed toward effective systems development, using the tools and techniques recommended in the previous parts of this book within the context of the organic lifecycle. This will include a futuristic assessment of the related trend toward object orientation.

CHAPTER 12

CASE support for the organic lifecycle

☐ ☐ ☐ ☐ ☐ ☐ ☐ ☐ ☐ ☐ ☐ ☐ ☐ ☐ ☐ ☐

A good workman is known by his tools.

PROVERB

12.1 Introduction

It is now widely accepted that the practical value of any software development methodology comes with computer aided software engineering (CASE). We shall see that this term has not only grown in importance over the last decade; it has also assumed a much wider denotation, the bottom line of which is automatic code generation from requirements specification.

However, code generation really only makes good sense on the basis of sound requirement definition. This reinforces a basic principle which we have followed throughout this book: getting problem definition right before embarking on possible solutions. Indeed, the book itself has sought to clarify the concept of effective modelling before considering its implementation in this chapter. We start with the basic assumption that CASE tools should support methods and techniques rather than *vice-versa* as is sometimes mistakenly assumed.

Study after study has shown that effective CASE entails a redistribution of effort such that a greater percentage of overall development time is spent in the early lifecycle phases. As one author has put it: 'The essence of computer-aided software engineering is providing leverage during the early development phases to save effort and expense in the later phases' (Fisher, 1988). In short, just as a word processor cannot do a writer's thinking, so a CASE tool will not interview your users. It should nevertheless stimulate discussion and exploration of business issues at a level that was undreamt of with manual support. That means more user participation, leading to more effort invested in analysis. Contrary to what is sometimes supposed, the new technology reaffirms the realization of traditional structured techniques that more, and not less time, needs to be invested in establishing user requirements.

This book has so far centred on strategy, analysis and prototyping. However, we shall see that the organic lifecycle requires CASE support not only in terms of automated diagramming and prototyping tools, but also in terms of tools for maintenance, code generation and project management. An organic approach involves *growth*. Tools need to be applied toward building upon what we have learnt. Broadly speaking this will require a move away from stand-alone CASE tools toward integrated CASE environments. In this chapter we consider how such tools might be employed toward effective system building.

Finally, we consider the implications in terms of the trend toward object orientation. It will be argued that developments in CASE tools open the way toward making this a practical alternative which can be based upon established practice rather than as some revolutionary silver bullet.

To avoid broadening scope into the realms of specific CASE evaluation – a subject for a book in its own right – the discussion has been kept as far as possible deliberately product neutral. It is not my purpose to add to the wealth of studies on the CASE 'marketplace'. The pitch is at a more modest level of suggestions as to how the organic lifecycle might be supported given current trends in CASE.

12.2 Three streams of CASE

The multitude of products that sit under the umbrella of CASE can, in fact, be divided according to which stream of software development activity they support as follows:

- ☐ Analysis and design.
- ☐ Coding and maintenance.
- ☐ Project management.

Indeed the historical development of CASE can be viewed in terms of three fast converging corresponding streams of products, as shown in Figure 12.1. The first stream sometimes goes under the banner of 'upper CASE' and consists of products which seek to automate the early stages of the traditional waterfall model of systems development. The second stream products, known euphemistically as 'lower CASE', are aimed very much at the later stages of this lifecycle. Finally, products in the project management stream seek to provide support in the overall planning and control of all lifecycle activities.

We have seen that the 1970s saw a general recognition of software engineering in the form of manually based structured techniques centering around the early phases of the waterfall lifecycle. The CASE acronym first appeared in the early 1980s to describe first attempts to automate these techniques in the form of PC-based computer aided diagramming and documentation tools. By the mid-1980s automatic consistency checking and integrated data dictionaries were fast being incorporated and engineering workstations were emerging as a much more powerful hardware platform.

In parallel the early 1980s saw the emergence of an increasing number of mainframe-based products concerned with increasing the productivity of the coding and maintenance parts of the waterfall lifecycle.

The former fall into two overlapping categories: code generators and application generators. The first code generators created code normally by manipulating templates of existing code which perform standard functions. Early fourth generation languages (4GLs) centred on prototyping the user interface to generate screen dialogue and data entry procedures. The arrival of the first application generators allowed the developer to use 4GL capabilities to construct code to display screens and produce reports and to generate database access routines. Both product ranges

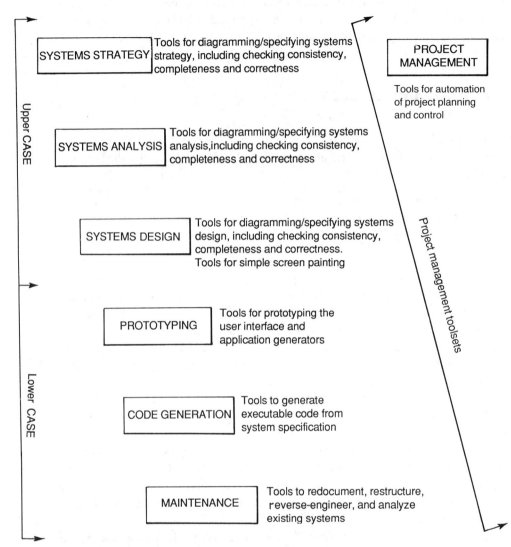

Figure 12.1 The diversity of CASE tools.

have grown in technical sophistication throughout the 1980s, with PC-based code generators now emerging, and code reuse as a major feature.

Maintenance tools cover a yet wider spectrum originating in programming support tools such as performance monitors and program analyzers. The early 1980s saw a growing sophistication of these products in the form of program and file restructuring tools. Structured programs released the potential of reverse engineering of processing: automatically translating an existing program back into its design specification, and more latterly to its requirement specification. Database definition opened the door to the reverse engineering of data, ultimately into E-R models, in the form of today's 'normalization engines'.

The final range of products aim to support the lifecycle itself in the form of project management tools. The early timesheet processing systems, often developed in house as a means of relieving project managers of wearisome administrative tasks, heralded a move toward more generalized products with the inclusion of automated PERT and bar charts, and project status reporting in the early 1980s.

12.3 Upper CASE tools

Perhaps the most impressive feature of upper CASE tools is their graphics capabilities which lend themselves so well to the sort of modelling activities which have been recommended in this book. In this section we examine the minimum desirable graphics dimension for any supporting CASE tool. There are four basic facilities in ascending order of sophistication:

1. Automatic diagramming.
2. Automatic diagram administration.
3. Diagramming views.
4. Textual integration.

12.3.1 Automatic diagramming

Diagramming tools lie at the very heart of the approach recommended in this book. Supporting such an approach manually is fraught with inefficiencies. For example, in terms of:

☐ The time it takes to draw original diagrams.
☐ The time it takes to change diagrams.
☐ The time it takes to navigate between diagrams.

Diagramming tools cut through such problems. The ease with which symbols can be made to appear, disappear and move around the screen with a simple press of a mouse button is in dramatic contrast to the unwieldiness of paper and pencil. The way in which the developer can flip back and forth between different diagrams, by clicking the mouse using simple pop-up panels, is in sharp contrast to the number of fingers needed to navigate the traditional manual specification. Clearly the user-friendliness of the graphics interface is a key issue in facilitating effective systems development. Moreover, the less time spent manipulating diagrams, the more productive the developer can be.

12.3.2 Automatic diagram administration

Other problems with manually based approaches centre on administration and quality assurance; for example:

☐ The difficulty in keeping diagrams consistent with one another in terms of levelling (Section 5.4.1) and balancing (Section 5.4.2).
☐ The difficulty of enforcing standards.
☐ The difficulty of removing all errors.

Interactive diagramming has huge administrative benefits. The impact of changes to one diagram type on another can be automatically generated and viewed. Standards are automatically enforced. Error checking is not only incomparably more efficient but can be dealt with as the developer works, instead of as a separate exercise after a specification has been produced, which leads to excessive re-work. For example, is a data flow already defined? If so, is it being used properly?

Cross referencing improves model administration. Firstly, whenever a change is proposed to one part of the system the repercussions of that change can be quickly evaluated. Secondly, all parts of the system related to the change will be amended during the change, ensuring that no unforeseen errors arise when the change is implemented.

12.3.3 Diagramming views

We have seen (Section 4.7) that diagramming techniques are used to give different views of a system both in terms of levelling and segmentation. Organization of diagrams is thus a key area particularly with regard to review and presentation. Manual support is notoriously weak in this area.

CASE tools offer great leverage in allowing the developer to choose the most appropriate view for the task being performed. We start to move away here from mere automation of paper and pencil techniques. If presenting system strategy to a high-level user executive we might choose, for example, to view the global ERD. If reviewing a system with the user executive, we might, for example, choose to view the context diagram. If we need a more detailed view for an operational user we can use the mouse to click to the appropriate more detailed DFD. If talking to the data administrator we can switch to the system ERD and view it in relation to the enterprise ERD. Facilities to scan across diagrams and to zoom in or out of particular diagram areas offer yet further leverage. The potential of upper CASE to support the diversity of views required is one of their most attractive features.

12.3.4 Textual integration

Necessary though diagramming tools are, particularly for verification by different personnel, they are only part of the story. When it comes to specification of requirements we have also seen the critical nature of textual support in terms of an integrated data dictionary. With manually based methods, the data dictionary is maintained separately from the diagrams, as shown in Figure 12.2.
The consequences are:

☐ The data dictionary assumes only a secondary importance.
☐ It is difficult to keep data dictionary and diagrams consistent.
☐ It is difficult to control redundancy.

Automatic integration of diagramming tools and data dictionary cuts across these problems. Data dictionary entries can be generated directly from diagramming screens at the mere click of a mouse button. The impact of textual changes on different diagrams (and *vice-versa*) can be assessed as the developer works. Windowing facilities provide visual integration; for example, the mouse is clicked on an entity and the definition for that entity showing component attributes appears on a pop-up window in the form of a template. Templates allow the information to be structured, for both data entry and display, in a rigorous yet user friendly way. Further definitions can be called up and entered in this way and windows overlaid. Rigour is ensured through common definition and error checking facilities. Rules embodied within the CASE tool effectively guide the developer through the method.

Imagine the situation with regard to the Petrol Sale Control System. The user has requested that cashiers be 'flashed' with a continuous bleep as soon as a customer lifts a gun. This entails adding an additional control flow Customer Present to the Figure 0 DFD, as shown (enlarged) in Figure 12.3 (a). Certain parts of the definition for this flow (its name and persistence) are automatically stored by clicking the mouse. A template is displayed inviting entry of remaining details as shown in Figure 12.3 (b). The details are entered as indicated in Figure 12.3 (c), and stored upon pressing enter, whereupon the assoiated STD is displayed on an overlay as shown in Figure 12.3 (d). Two actions are added to bring the STD in line with the DFD as depicted (enlarged) in Figure 12.3 (e). Although the illustration stops at this point the scenario would continue with invocation of a template for the action 'Start sale' (to add 'L Customer present') and display of the context diagram on an overlay to add in the 'Customer present' control flow. Three diagrams and two data

Fig.0 Petrol Sale Control System

Figure 12.2 Separation of graphics and text causes administrative headaches.

dictionary entries have been affected by the change, which has been made in a controlled manner guaranteeing consistency. Contrast this with the length of time the change would have taken if done manually and with the attached risk of inconsistency posed by the possibility of human error. Moreover, instead of consulting the rules of the method separately we are now actively prompted to follow them in direct association with what we are doing. We are now a far cry from simple automation of paper and pencil-based techniques. Although CASE tools only serve to support methods we see that this is an oversimplification: technical advances in CASE have served to evolve those methods into previously undreamt dimensions.

We have also seen that full rigour is only achieved through detailed error-free process specification integrated with the data dictionary. At the end of the day the essential model must be no less testable than a suite of programs. Again automated integration of diagramming tools with the data dictionary, together with error checking facilities, allows CASE tools to capture a rigorous specification of requirements. This is the very basis which underlies not only all views of the essential model but also extensions of that model in the form of external design

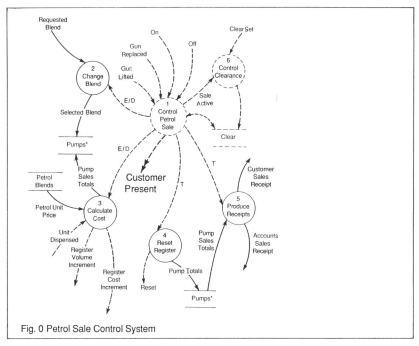

Fig. 0 Petrol Sale Control System

(a) The Customer Present control flow is added to Fig. 0
   Petrol Sale Control System

Figure 12.3 (a–e) A scenario using templates and overlays.

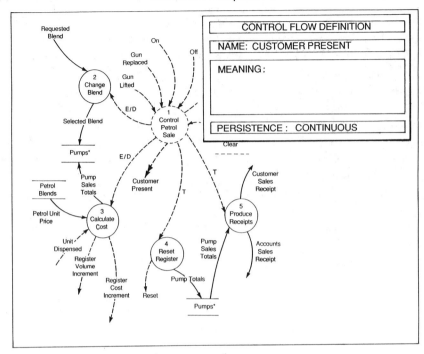

(b) On clicking mouse, pop-up panel appears prompting
definition of Customer Present within template

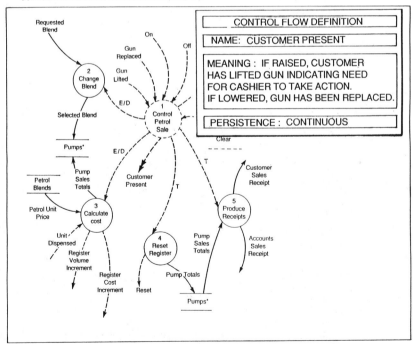

(c) Definition of meaning of Customer Present is entered

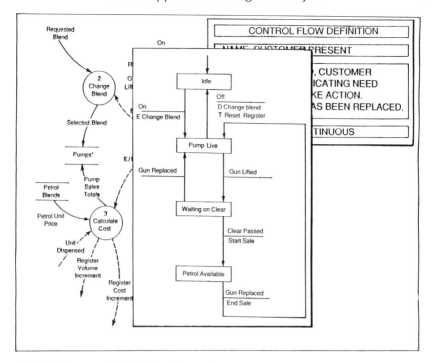

(d) On clicking mouse, STD is displayed on overlay

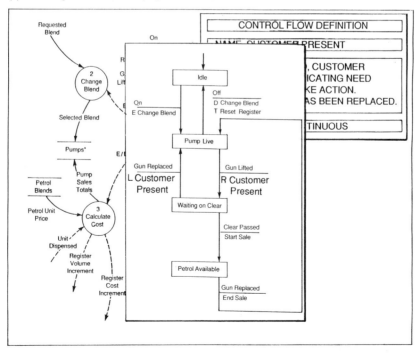

(e) Actions are added

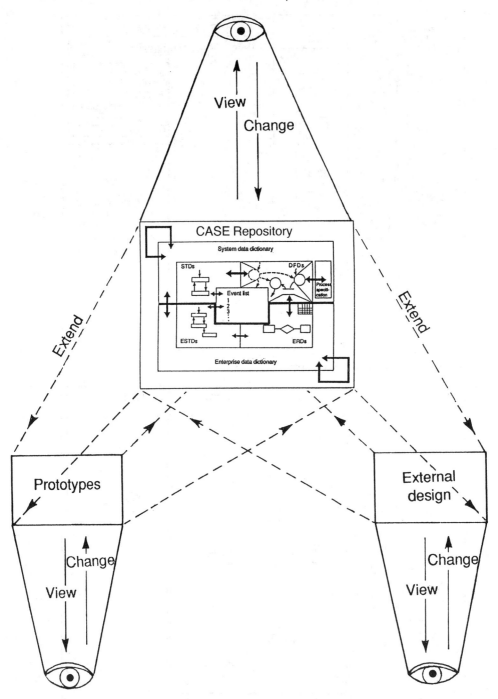

Figure 12.4 Verifying and maintaining requirements.

and prototypes. Indeed many upper CASE tools offer integrated system design modelling and user interface prototyping tools. At this level, however, no code is generated: the system design consists literally of models and the prototypes are little more than screen mock-ups with no facilities for updating or complex data capture.

To add real leverage we would like to go beyond extensions of the essential model to the capability to modify the essential model by consolidating results from prototyping or external design. In other words the CASE tools should be able to capture requirements definition through prototyping or external design models. These further facilities are shown in Figure 12.4 added in to the original infrastructure (from Figure 5.8).

Ultimately, rigorous specification of requirements does open the door to great productivity gains as a basis for code and database generation. How is all this achieved? We have now progressed beyond automatic diagramming. It is the CASE repository that provides the key.

12.3.5 The CASE repository: a first look

To achieve more than the simplistic automatic diagramming features of early CASE tools a CASE repository is required for representing:

☐ Each item (diagram symbol or textual component).
☐ The meaning of each item.
☐ All information associated with each item.
☐ All relationships between items.
☐ Rules governing the use of each item.

In order to maintain such information and to provide powerful facilities for its development and administration the CASE repository clearly needs to be more than a simple data dictionary. Typically, it will be a relational database supported by a full DBMS. It will serve as the single unifying place in which all this information can be entered once, kept consistent, and at the disposal of all who require it. As such it must transcend system boundaries and provide support for both the strategic planning and data administration functions, which we have seen to be key areas. In short it must support our recommended model infrastructure shown in Figure 12.5.

Certain types of cross reference are automatically generated by the CASE tool from diagrams. For example:

☐ Flows and their source and destination.
☐ Processes and stores used by them.
☐ States and associated conditions, and resultant actions.

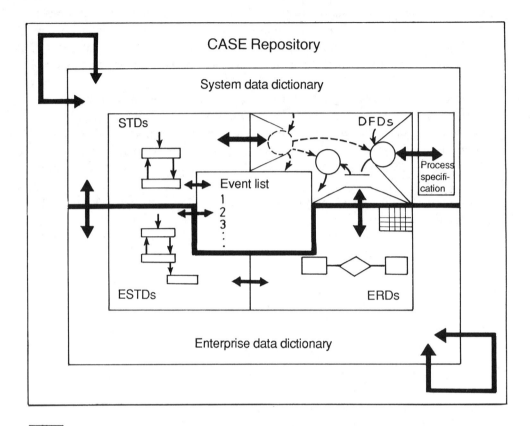

⊞ Represents an example of one type of matrix: the entity-process matrix

Figure 12.5 The CASE repository and modelling infrastructure.

☐ Entities and relationships.

Cross referencing of data structures is via the use of a set of unique names sharing common domains, a requirement first intimated in Section 5.3. For example, there must only be a single entry for Player.Name in the data dictionary. Importantly this is also in line with our requirement for 'once only' definition of attributes. Any data structure that includes Player.Name in its description includes it as a name which provides a cross-reference to the single attribute entry. Examples of the cross referencing of data structures set up by the developer are as follows:

☐ Attributes and the composite attributes that contain them.
☐ Attributes and the data flows that contain them.
☐ Attributes and the entities that contain them.
☐ Data stores and the entities and relationships they contain.

Levelling is also a form of cross-referencing. For example, the developer is able to enter information and subsequently retrieve it as follows:

- ☐ DFD processes exploded to lower level DFD.
- ☐ DFD processes imploded to higher level DFD.
- ☐ Selected global entities/relationships exploded to ERD.
- ☐ Selected entities/relationships imploded to GERD.

However, this is only the beginning. The CASE repository represents the same information in different but equivalent forms when the meaning of a graphics symbol is captured. This permits the developer to capture information in one form, and to generate it in an associated form with automated support. For example:

- ☐ To use event list to generate a skeleton preliminary DFD.
- ☐ To use lowest level DFD to generate process descriptions.
- ☐ To use STD to generate partial control DFD.
- ☐ To use ERD to create fully factored ERD.

By virtue of the meaning embedded into the CASE repository in the form of rules associated with items, further powerful cross-referencing facilities can be generated in the form of matrices. Indeed, we have seen these to be of tremendous value, for example, in scoping systems and impact analysis. Examples of such matrices were global entity–context, entity–event and entity–process. However, we can go much further than this: the CASE repository should facilitate representation in tabular form of *any* associated items; for example, generation of state transition tables (plotting 'from' states against 'to' states with conditions and actions inserted in appropriate cells) from STDs. Such powerful features were a mere dream with manually based methods.

I recall in the late 1970s a huge pencil drawn entity-process matrix, which appeared very impressive on its first appearance outside the DP manager's office but which grew increasingly tattered and smudged as changes were made to it; rather like a map of the London underground that grows increasingly incomprehensible under the continued pressure of commuters' fingers. Eventually the matrix had to be abandoned. However, underground maps can simply be replaced. We did not have that luxury. Information stored on a shared repository makes such luxuries the expected norm in the form of readily reproducible documentation.

Meiler Page-Jones, writing the first edition of the *Practical Guide to Structured Design* over a decade ago on the subject of creating a structure chart from a DFD using transform analysis commented, 'One day, transform analysis may become an algorithm. But if it does, the structure chart will disappear and the DFD will be implemented directly, for a machine can obey an alogorithm much better than can a human being. At the moment, however, arbitrary DFDs cannot be implemented directly, because, in general, languages and operating systems are just not sophisticated enough. By the year 2000 perhaps, we shall see DFDs being executed on a horde of dynamically reconfigurable microprocessors. But until then we must rely on transform analysis.' (Page-Jones, 1988 (2nd edn).) How prophetic these words have turned out to be. Although we are still some way off the year 2000 the vision grows closer. Ultimately the CASE repository provides the platform from which rigorous requirement definition can be generated into working systems. However, before we can find our way to the 'coalface' containing this rich seam it is important to ensure the 'tunnel' does not collapse. That means looking at lower CASE tools and project management toolsets to put matters into a broader and more realistic context.

12.4 Lower CASE tools

Lower CASE tools can be classified into three types.

1. Prototyping tools.
2. Code generators.
3. Maintenance tools.

How can such products assist us in our goal of producing more effective systems?

12.4.1 Prototyping with 4GLs

The term fourth generation language (4GL) covers a wide range of techniques implemented using software tools which have one common feature: each provides the developer with the facility to specify some characteristic of software at a high level. Source code is then generated from the developer's specification. Such a cluster of software tools will include all or some of the features described in Section 11.3. To recap, these were:

1. Non-procedural languages for:
   - □ database query and update,
   - □ report generation,
   - □ screen handling,
   - □ code generation with interfaces to 3GLs.

2. User friendly interface for:
   - □ screen painting,
   - □ data definition using standard templates,
   - □ default application generation,
   - □ code generation.

We have seen (in Section 11.4) that an application generator should allow the developer to create default screens for basic data capture and display from database tables in a matter of minutes. This is in dramatic contrast to programming primitive database modules and associated screen handlers in a conventional 3GL which is normally a somewhat lengthy process taking hours (or days) rather than minutes. Clearly, such tools lend particular leverage in realizing the principles of essential prototyping advocated in this book.

We also saw that once primitive prototypes have been constructed, event prototypes can be constructed and developed using screen painting and code generation facilities. The menu-based features of such tools lend themselves particularly well to modelling the hierarchy of functions modelled by the levelled set of DFDs.

12.4.2 Code generators

Commercial pressure to deliver more effective systems is arguably the most dominant feature of the software industry. Marketing hype often seems to present CASE as a panacea for the software crisis. This is especially so in the area of code generation.

In the mounting pressure to implement state of the art solutions to pressing problems it is easy to ignore the importance of assessing how well software technologies fare in practice. Industry reviews and evaluations bear this out. The 1987 report from Ovum by Hewett and Durham (1987) makes a particularly salient observation:

'If ever there was a requirement looking for a solution, it must be the requirement that Software Engineering and CASE set out to satisfy. Everyone has their own horror stories about software development experiences, but the combined effect is even more horrifying. According to industry experts:

- ☐ Large software projects ('large' meaning those with over 60,000 lines of code) cost twice as much as their initial budgets on average.
- ☐ Typically they are delivered one year late; 25 per cent are never delivered at all.
- ☐ Maintenance activities soak up two thirds of most companies development resources.

So unlike many new technologies which need to create and educate their own markets, here is a clear requirement crying out for the solution that software engineering and CASE may provide. As a result this report identifies a market in the USA worth around $140 million in 1987, growing to over $1 billion by 1991.'

We should tread carefully here. The distinction between a code generator and an application generator is sometimes rather a fine one. The terms tend to be used rather loosely as convenient labels. For example, many products marketed as code generators share many of the features we have already discussed under the label application generator. Unfortunately, there seems to be something of a tendency when talking of code generators to focus questions on the end-product ('does it generate object code in COBOL for an MVS environment?') rather than on the input requirements ('what form does my specification need to be in to make the product work?'). That is, having established the important point of technical feasibility of actually running the code, there is too often a failure to elicit what exactly it is that the developer has to do to provide the code generator with something to work with. Often, this leads to disenchantment, especially where a product requires a particularly constraining and unwieldy input specification which ties up developers' time and compromises the quality of system modelling.

This is unfortunate in that the feature that really earmarks a *code* generator, at least as understood in this book, is translation of elements of a *requirements specification* into code, with minimal developer intervention. In the terms of this book the important question is 'in what form does the essential model have to be to permit code generation?'.

If we are to maintain leverage we do not want to be constrained by having to spend huge amounts of effort in building detailed specifications before we can see some working code. The code generated may be more or it may be less complete, depending on the degree of detail contained within the essential model. For example, full code can be generated where the essential logic of the process specification is expressed in a highly structured and rigorous fashion; action diagrams (as discussed in Section 5.4.2) are a particularly good example. On the other hand, a program shell can be generated from a process description. This might, for example, contain database access and reporting code, leaving the actual logic to be developed.

The situation is shown graphically in Figure 12.6. Again, we must guard against what seems to be a widespread assumption that this is simply a pure transformation from one representation to another. Much design specific information normally needs to be specified by the developer. Even the most focussed of code generators make certain assumptions about the target implementation environment, resulting in default code. However, nuances can almost certainly be guaranteed even in the most apparently uniform of environments. Examples might be terminal interfacing or specific customized database access mechanisms. Therefore, even in the case of 'full' code generation a certain amount of developer intervention is often necessary to tune the code in line with implementation constraints. This means that,

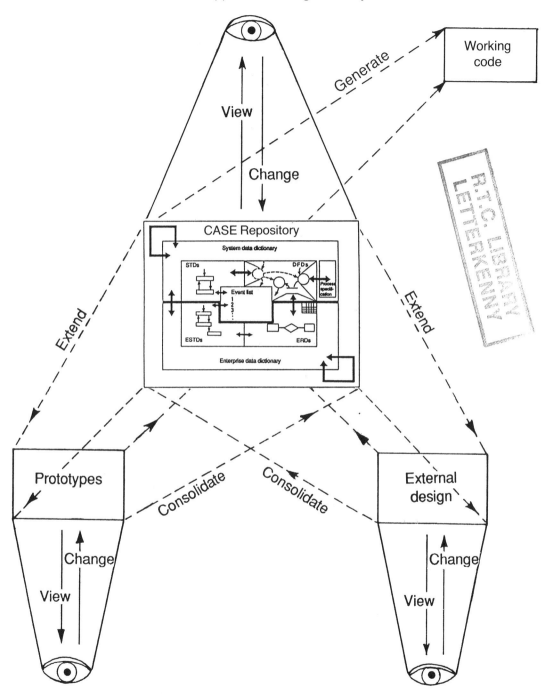

Figure 12.6 The CASE repository as a basis for code generation.

today at least, although generation of object code is desirable, preliminary generation of source code is a provided with many products to provide the developer with the necessary flexibility.

This is a problem the industry needs to solve if the CASE repository is to be kept consistent with working systems. Again, the greatest leverage comes with generation of object code from the CASE repository, all changes being made through the latter.

12.4.3 Maintenance tools

The dominant cost of maintenance relative to systems development activities has been well documented. According to one source over 30 billion dollars per annum is spent on software maintenance world-wide (Parikh, 1986). Effective CASE needs to include maintenance tools alongside development tools in the battle against the software crisis. Indeed it is only by freeing up the developer from the burden of maintenance that we can provide the resources needed to tackle the applications backlog that is a result of our preoccupation with maintenance.

A wide variety of programming support tools exist to assist in the analysis, documentation, and restructuring of code and files. The greatest leverage comes from tools which assist the developer in reverse engineering of programs and databases. By abstracting an essential model from existing system code and supporting enterprise E-R model from file design, we open up the possibility of *re-engineering* and ultimately of maintenance of existing systems by making changes to the essential model and subsequently generating modified code. This cuts right through the maintenance problem as traditionally stated. The situation is illustrated graphically in Figure 12.7.

Although some variety of reverse engineering tools are currently available, the technology is very much in its infancy. Also, just as with code generators a totally developer-independent translation from working system to essential model is simply not possible. For example, software cannot reverse engineer a data structure using normalization principles, unless the developer specifies what the data dependencies are. In the case of code the problem is yet more difficult; the developer has to specify which statements are essential and which program statements are merely there to support the implementation. In badly designed systems it might, for example, be the case that the logic of the same event response is actually distributed over several different programs and part might even be done manually. Therefore we should not underestimate such a task. Considerable human resources need to be made available, even where reverse engineering software exists, if such an exercise

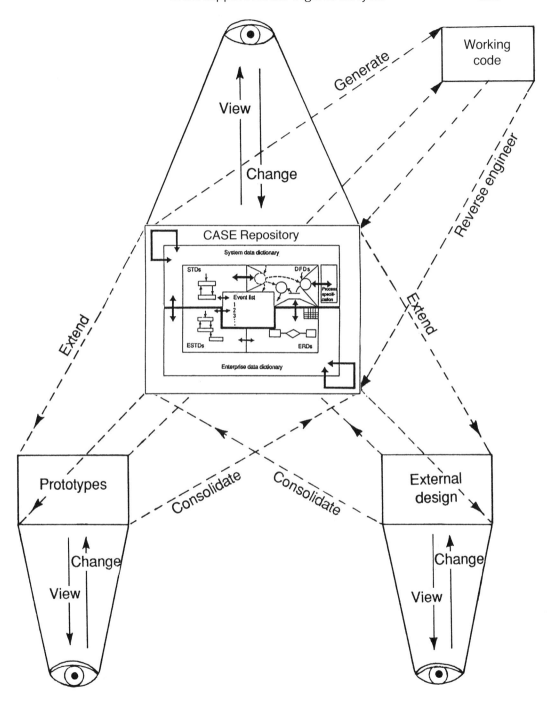

Figure 12.7 The CASE repository as a target for reverse engineering.

is to be conducted for an enterprise. Again, the cost-justification only comes with direct maintenance through the essential model coupled with regeneration of production code. After all that means that the cost of reverse engineering existing systems and databases is incurred as a one-off effort which can be viewed as a long-term investment.

12.5 Project management toolsets

The importance of effective planning and control has been continually stressed throughout this book. This is particularly so in the key areas of systems reconnaissance, prototyping, and effective co-ordination of strategic modelling, enterprise modelling and systems modelling.

Although specific products will supply various facilities from word processing to configuration management, a project management toolset normally consists, at heart, of tools for automated estimation, scheduling and control of software projects.

Automated estimation tools allow the manager to quantify cost and effort of various tasks using automated estimation formulas or models. There is a huge range of both formulae and models that have been developed over the years to address what is perhaps the thorniest of all systems development problems: estimation. Diverse though they are, all are driven by some form or other of *metric*. Perhaps the most common examples of such metrics are lines of code and function points. The Putnam estimation model (Putnam, 1978) is an example of the former, whilst the latter were first proposed by Albrecht (1979). The merits of individual approaches are often arguable and controversial. To be useful an automated estimation tool needs to recognize that estimation depends on a variety of metrics, not just quantitative but also *qualitative*. In his classic book Boehm (1981) presents a hierarchy of estimation models under the generic name COCOMO (COnstructive COst MOdel). This consists of a portfolio of techniques which are driven by a variety of metrics ranging from basic lines of code metrics on the one hand to 'cost drivers' that include subjective estimates of product, hardware, personnel and project properties.

Clearly no one organization is exactly the same as another. To develop accurate estimates therefore we require a *historical baseline*, which consists of accurate information collected from past systems development projects, in the form of an 'empirical database' (DeMarco, 1982). Such an empirical database may consist of a variety of cost drivers from numbers of bubbles on a DFD to the skill level of an analyst. The specific metric value that is attached to a specific cost driver (for example 'a primitive bubble with X incoming data flows, updating

Y entities with Z attributes has a metric of three days to specify') clearly depends on capture of relevant information and upon tools for retrospective analysis.

Automated estimation tools allow a manager to make estimates of cost and effort on the basis of an empirical database plus *system and project specific information* or a 'quantum indication' (DeMarco, 1982) supplied by the manager, and to perform 'what if' analyses using key project variables such as target date or staffing. The quantum indication supplied by the manager is usually in the form of simple quantitative data such as function points but may also include qualitative characteristics, such as required system reliability or staff ability.

Unlike estimating, scheduling of systems development work does not differ greatly from the scheduling of any multitask development effort. Therefore generalized scheduling packages can usually be applied with little customization. For example, Program Evaluation and Review Technique (PERT) and Critical Path Method (CPM) have a widely accepted universal application. Automation of such methods and techniques provides the manager with some powerful tools. For example, given a deadline date and task dependencies and estimates the manager needs to know optimum staff numbers and distribution of effort. Conversely given certain staff with certain skills the manager needs to know the earliest feasible deadline date.

A project management toolset should then, at minimum, integrate automation of both estimation and scheduling and contain facilities for the capture and reporting of all project data. For example, schedules need to be kept up to date, progress reported against time and budget and data collected for refinement of estimates. The advent of networking has seen a trend toward multi-user project control systems, opening up the possibility of better estimating via empirical databases.

However, the greatest leverage must surely come from storing both the empirical database and the quantum indicator within the CASE repository. The way to integrate this information within the organic lifecycle is through the vehicles of project profile and system profile discussed again below in Section 12.8.

12.6 Toward integrated support

Automatic diagramming tools lend leverage to strategic and system modelling, especially where a CASE repository can be shared by developers working at different PCs or workstations. Importantly this houses the necessary underlying enterprise data model. Fourth generation prototyping tools facilitate the application of essential prototyping. Code generators and reverse engineering tools provide useful ultimate pathways respectively to and from working systems; coupled together they provide real leverage in coming to terms with the applications backlog that has plagued the software industry for so long. Last but not least project management toolsets can be used to support effective planning and control of systems within the organic lifecycle.

Unfortunately the leverage supplied by such products is compromised by their stand-alone nature. This problem is often exacerbated by the fact that upper and lower CASE tools normally operate on different hardware platforms. For example, upper CASE tools to support the developer in requirements specification are very largely PC-based. Fourth generation languages are very largely mainframe based. One key to providing an integrated approach is eloquently cited by Carma McClure (1989): 'To join together design automation and program automation will require bridging two hardware environments – PC and mainframe – and two software technologies – CASE and fourth generation. An important part of this bridge will be the addition of a repository to the CASE environment.' Also, user interfaces can vary greatly. More fundamentally, we see that the products are based very much on the waterfall model of systems development. That means a linear series of trans-formations which done *manually* results in administrative overload as shown in Figure 12.8.

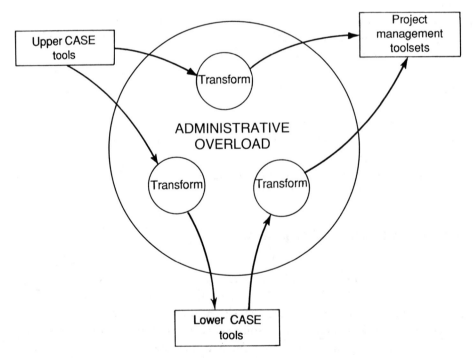

Figure 12.8 The administrative overload of stand-alone CASE tools.

The problem of data exchange is reflected in the different storage representations that are often used to support each product stream:

☐ Data dictionaries for upper CASE.
☐ Design databases for lower CASE.
☐ Project databases for project management toolsets.

Even within the same product stream representations vary; for example, the ANSI/SPARC three schema data achitecture shown in Figure 7.2.

Automatic translation from one means of representation to another goes some way to removing this problem as shown in Figure 12.9; for example, generation of source code from program design specifications. Indeed, the late 1980s has seen many vendors go to some lengths to develop interfaces to ensure compatibility with other products, usually downstream in the lifecycle; for example a PC-based upper CASE tool with well-defined ASCII file formats, allowing interfacing to mainframe facilities.

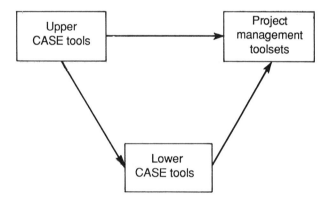

Figure 12.9 Data exchange between stand-alone CASE tools.

The problem with this is that technical difficulties aside (and there are plenty of them) such approaches are rooted firmly in the soil of the waterfall lifecycle. And, although it provides expedient milestones for the measurement of progress, we have already seen that such an approach is unworkable: an organic approach which recognizes iteration is required. We have also seen that an organic approach requires cross-fertilization between tasks which are traditionally seen as belonging to separate parts of the lifecycle. In particular to expedite the organic lifecycle we would like to be able to generate prototypes directly from the requirements specifications. Conversely we would like to view the effects of a change to a prototype on the requirements specifications. Ultimately we would like to be able

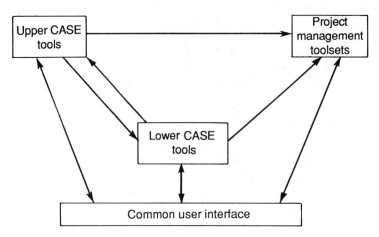

Figure 12.10 Diversity of views via a common user interface.

to maintain systems and databases through the essential model and enterprise E-R model respectively. More generally, the ideal environment requires the following further facilities, as illustrated in Figure 12.10.

1. The ability to map and extend representations downstream; for example:
   ☐ ERDs to LDSDs.
   ☐ Process descriptions to code skeletons.
   ☐ Process specifications to code.
   ☐ Common business logic to reusable code modules.
   ☐ ESTDs to transaction validation tables.
   ☐ DFDs and STDs to structure charts or code skeletons.
2. The ability to reverse engineer representations upstream; for example:
   ☐ Database to enterprise E-R model.
   ☐ Working code to process specifications.
   ☐ Screen linkages to STDs.
3. The ability to view and manipulate different lifecycle products concurrently; for example:
   ☐ Cross-fertilize diagramming tools from EP with prototyping.
   ☐ Assess the impact of changes to a behavioural model on the strategic model.
4. Effective management support; for example:
   ☐ Integrate estimating tools with the system profiles of the organic lifecycle (for example: event lists, context diagrams, DFDs, ERDs, STDs, process specifications) through the common medium of an empirical database.

☐ Integrate scheduling and project control through the project profiles of the organic lifecycle.

☐ Audit trail of system and project profiles through the CASE repository.

The late 1980s and early 1990s have seen a major commitment away from stand-alone tools supporting various lifecycle activities toward fully integrated tools under the banner of ICASE (Integrated CASE). This depends very much on the CASE repository (as discussed above in Section 12.3.5) providing a common mechanism for storing and organizing all information collected at each point in the lifecycle from strategic planning to implementation, and project management information. The author believes this is an imperative for effective systems development using the organic lifecycle. It is akin to an engine which drives and co-ordinates the various CASE components as shown in Figure 12.11.

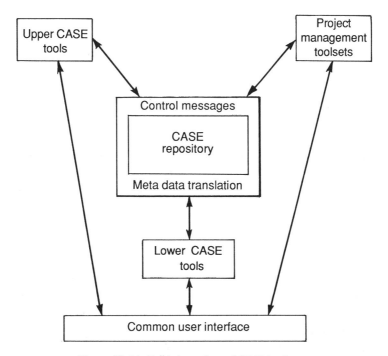

Figure 12.11 Full integration of CASE tools.

Another factor influencing this trend is the need for traceability: the ability to track the correspondence between requirement definition and supporting code and data structure is essential. For example, event to response to processor to task to program to module. A pathway is needed from requirement specification to code to ensure the correctness and completeness of a system. Traceability also means being able to walk this pathway in the opposite direction to pinpoint the effects of changes to code. Indeed, in the USA traceability has become a compulsory requirement in the development of mission critical defense systems under Department of Defense Standard 2167.

IBM's announcement of AD/Cycle in September 1989 has added fuel to the acceleration toward ICASE. However, although a CASE repository is a necessary condition for effective systems development the form which ICASE products take are varied and it must be said very much in their infancy.

12.7 Horizontal and vertical integration

Individual ICASE products tend toward closed architectures in the form of integrated proprietry tools hooking the purchaser into a particular methodology targeted toward a very specific implementation environment. This means there is effectively no room for choice in systems development strategy; an area we have seen to be particularly important.

Rigorous structured specification tools and techniques, such as action diagrams, are embedded within ICASE products thus facilitating code generation. However, we would like some flexibility in methods of actually verifying requirements: we have seen the trap of identifying specification with verification is an easy one to fall into. Therefore we need to be careful in ensuring such tools do not ensnare us in this trap.

Also, the cost of ICASE products is high not only in terms of initial cost but also in terms of changing to such an environment. Therefore, an organization considering purchasing such a product must clearly be totally convinced of its appropriateness for addressing its particular needs.

Another way of viewing the situation is with respect to the concepts of horizontal and vertical integration. Stand-alone products have generally reached a high degree of horizontal integration. ICASE products on the other hand tend to give very narrow vertical integration. Additionally there is a lack of integrated support for project planning and control.

A more cost effective approach based upon the organic lifecycle requires more open architectures allowing the developer the ability to mix and match between various approaches supplied as modules interfacing to the common CASE repository. Most systems managers are indeed justifiably disillusioned at talk of yet another revolution. Realistically we must settle for evolution: the majority of organizations with tight budgets and pressure for results, can perhaps expect a gradual migration to this sort of environment.

12.8 Reusability

Reusability of software components has been well documented as a key to dramatic development productivity increases. The CASE repository, in which software components are stored, clearly facilitates reusability. However, the concept stretches much further than this.

It is a simple fact that we learn from experience: we do this through the reuse of facts. The first time you touched a flame you got burnt. This fact is reused to ensure you do not do it again. Similarly systems development work should involve not starting each project 'from scratch' but building upon what we have already learnt: we have seen that the organic lifecycle centres on growth. Reusability is required not only in terms of software components be they database tables, modules, or in terms of objects, but also in terms of project work experience. The CASE repository can be used to build an encyclopaedia of such experience. In this book such information will include both project profiles and system profiles, which we discussed in Sections 6.10.1 and 6.10.2. The definitions are repeated here for convenience:

PROJECT PROFILE
- ☐ Project name
- ☐ Project type (Strategic planning/Global modelling/Systems reconnaissance/ Systems analysis/Prototyping).
- ☐ Executive sponsor.
- ☐ Project plan:
    - (a) Project organization, reporting structure, team members, roles etc.
    - (b) Schedule, budget.
    - (c) Priority.
    - (d) Risk assessment.
- ☐ System profile.

(Remember, this is not meant to be an exhaustive list: it is rather meant as a check list of necessary pre-conditions for project initiation. Typically, organizational needs will vary according to circumstances. For example it is often useful to include a short description of objectives, which may include a cost-benefit analysis for the project (as opposed to the system)).

SYSTEM PROFILE
- ☐ Statement of purpose.
- ☐ Systems development strategy.
- ☐ Constraints.
- ☐ Models.
- ☐ Cost-benefit analysis.

System profiles will evolve, with information filtering in from each project. The maintenance of such information on an on-going basis makes practical the concept of an empirical database, for project planning and control. This lends crucial leverage to the organic lifecycle. For example, we have seen systems reconnaissance to be a key concept in the development of effective systems. The usefulness of such research work depends on effective planning. The productivity of such work depends on effective control. Too often system reconnaissance has been done in an 'on the fly' manner giving research a bad name. However, an integrated empirical database makes practical the planning and control of systems reconnaissance.

12.9 CASE for people

Despite the imperative trend toward CASE, many organizations have found that implementing it means making huge changes in the way they work which cause friction amongst different staff groups as they adapt. They have also found that anticipated upturns in productivity have yet to appear. Much of this malaise is bound up as much with cultural as with technical change. This subject is large and complex enough to warrant a book in its own right. In this more limited context we will focus on three particularly relevant points.

Firstly, the benefits of CASE are not, as is commonly assumed, in shorter development times. Indeed, we have seen that more and not less time is spent in the early lifecycle stages. The real benefits come in realizing the potential to support the organic lifecycle toward long-term benefits. Certainly in most organizations it is simply too early to measure such benefits.

Secondly, the costs of CASE cannot be equated with the cost of hardware and software. Personnel need to be trained in the new methods and techniques supported by the CASE tool. A small fraction of this learning might be in the classroom. In reality most of it takes place on the job. Therefore there is the cost of pilot projects. A pool of expertise needs to be built. This can cost a great deal of money, far in excess of original estimates.

Thirdly, and most important, too often attempts to introduce CASE into organizations are treated very much as 'technical' projects rather than for what they are: major cultural changes. Unfortunately this is reflected in the names that vendors often give to their products, which are often prefixed by the word 'Analyst' or 'Designer'. There is thus an overt assumption that 'these tools are only for the initiated'.

In reality, however, CASE tools have an influence which stretches across the traditional boundary between analyst and user. Users have the potential to *participate* in development as never before.

There are two basic reasons for this:

1. A revitalized focus on business problems from strategy to operational use of systems.
2. The switch to systems development information as a shared resource via the CASE repository.

History suggests that developments in CASE technology are opening up the possibility of employing structured techniques at a more strategic level: they realize the potential of the organic lifecycle. The ability to view the CASE repository from different perspectives, as first intimated in Figure 1.4, is perhaps the key to this. The ideal CASE environment should foster and not restrict such positive trends, as shown in Figure 12.12.

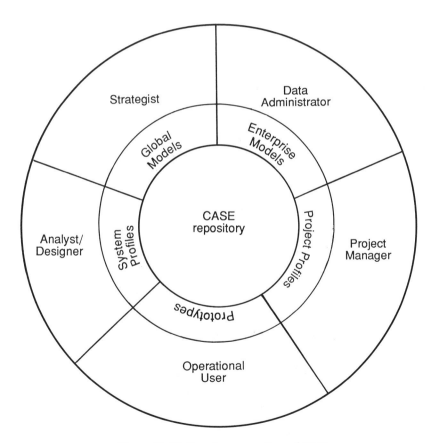

Figure 12.12 People perspectives of CASE.

12.10 Toward object oriented CASE

The increase in popularity of languages such as C++ and Smalltalk has fuelled the acceleration toward object orientation using CASE tools. The scope of this trend has tended thus far toward local applications in engineering environments.

A few DBMSs, notably Ingres, now include object oriented front-ends to their databases. Products with facilities to encapsulate database tables with associated modules for manipulation of data are fast emerging making practical the principle of object oriented prototyping. The Sapiens applications generator has been developed to support object orientation in an IBM mainframe environment. However, at the time of writing such products remain the exception rather than the rule. In short, technology capable of supporting the development of object oriented systems in the wider marketplace is still largely unavailable.

The attractions of object orientation, however, are too irresistible for the software industry to ignore. Indeed, I believe the next decade will see increasing attempts to fill the wider technical void, in the form of more sophisticated and wider ranging object oriented programming languages and operating environments.

Does this mean that existing structured techniques and methods should be thrown out and that we should start afresh in the quest for object orientation? A major argument of this book has been that to do so would be to throw the baby out with the bath water. The following observations serve to reinforce this argument:

☐ Systems management have grown tired at the talk of yet another revolution in software development. Too many 'silver bullets' have failed to live up to promised expectations.

☐ The principles of object orientated development (as opposed to programming) are really nothing new. Indeed encapsulation and hierarchy are well established general systems development principles.

☐ Effective systems require a strategic perspective. This is not a means toward the end of object orientation. This puts the cart before the horse. Rather, object orientation is one means of achieving the strategic perspective.

☐ Pragmatism is required: the organic lifecycle involves building upon what we have learnt as systems are developed. More generally we should build upon what we have learnt regarding good systems development practice.

The key technical issue for CASE is to exploit the rapidly advancing technologies, ultimately by automated generation of object oriented systems. The key methodological issue becomes to facilitate maximum leverage of requirement definition, in terms of an essential model which lends itself toward subsequent object oriented implementation. Some general examples of how CASE can support this by cross-fertilizing different models are as follows:

☐ Matrices to encapsulate processes and entities into 'objects'.
☐ DFDs to expose hierarchies of processes, clustered around stored data to form 'objects'.
☐ DFDs to expose interfaces or messages between 'objects'.
☐ ESTDs to encapsulate events with respect to entities to form 'objects'.
☐ STDs to localize system control with respect to stored data to form 'objects'.
☐ E-R modelling to find classes in terms of super-subtypes thus exposing the inheritance feature of 'objects'.

The reader will notice that the above refers to 'objects' and not objects. This is because there is really nothing new here: we are using established modelling tools. No new notation has been developed for 'objects': this term refers to a representation within the CASE repository in the form of cross-references to other model components. The key issue thus becomes how best to hold this representation for subsequent generation to an object oriented system. This will be a major challenge for the years ahead.

12.11 Summary

In this chapter some suggestions have been made as to how current CASE tools can be applied to the task of creating requirement definition for effective systems. A problem with using such tools is their stand-alone nature. Whilst applying leverage at certain points in the lifecycle, they do not lend the integrated support that is required for real gains in productivity.

On the other hand truly integrated products under the banner of ICASE tend to be highly focussed toward specific implementations and hook the purchaser in to proprietary methods. This can involve great expense and attendant risk, particularly as such products are very much in their infancy. Moreover, it was also intimated that ICASE stands currently at least very much within the traditional mind-set.

A more flexible ICASE with an open architecture capable of supporting the requirements of the organic lifecycle stands some way off. It was suggested that a more cost-effective approach is to mix and match various products within an organic environment centering on a common CASE repository.

Two particularly important features of such an environment were reusability and the 'people dimension'. We saw that reusability is important not only in terms of delivered software components but also in terms of project planning and control.

The 'people dimension' involves a cultural change which is often underestimated. A viable environment therefore should facilitate cultural change via suitable user interfaces.

Finally, we entered into the somewhat controversial area of possible future trends with respect to object orientation. It was contended that the tools and techniques of the organic lifecycle lend themselves particularly well here without the need for new notations. The real benefit will come with eventual generation into an object oriented implementation.

The Morgan Tandoori

□ □ □ □ □ □ □ □ □ □ □ □ □ □ □ □ □

A1.1 Background

The Morgan Tandoori works on the same lines as most of the popular Indian restaurants found throughout Great Britain. In the following pages we will seek to model a system for controlling the behaviour of a waiter. Specifically we will examine the behaviour associated with receiving customers into the restaurant and with taking orders.

In terms of the modelling framework, the requirement has been determined thus; the EP term for this starting point (described in Chapter 3) is the 'statement of purpose'. Our brief will be largely to *explore* and *understand* the requirement but we will also touch on the final three phases of the modelling framework: *organization*, *specification* and *verification*.

Technical modelling terms have been avoided as far as possible; the objective is for the reader to get an intuitive grasp of how modelling tools are applied, as vehicles for raising important questions, before embarking on a more formal treatment in Appendices 2 and 3. (It is assumed here that the reader may not yet have read Part Two of the book which deals with terminology.) The principle is to understand what things mean, first by seeing how they are used, and second by formal definition. However, where necessary, comments have been added to explain technical terms.

The reader will find that the 'initial view' from Chapter 2 has now been developed to introduce the reader to some of these technical terms, albeit in an intentionally informal manner.

A1.2 Modelling the problem

Requirements are first explored by the use of an event list and a context diagram. An event list is a list of things that happen outside our system. These things occur at specific points in time and our system must respond to them. An example is shown in Figure A1.1.

1. Time to open restaurant.
2. Customer enters restaurant.
3. Customer summons waiter.
4. Customer completes order.
5. Time to close restaurant.

Figure A1.1 Accept Customers event list.

A context diagram for our system is shown in Figure A1.2. This names our system, Accept Customers, and shows interfaces to other systems (for example Waiter Control Systems, which includes all other waiter functions) and people (for example Chef); these are shown as boxes and known as terminators. Interfaces come in two flavours, which will be explained with the minimum of technical fuss.

Data stores are shown as horizontal parallel lines, which model data shared over time between our system and terminators.

Flows are shown as arrowed lines. Flows shown between our system and terminators represent data (in the case of a solid line) or control (in the case of dashed lines) which is either sent directly to a terminator or received directly from a terminator. Data flows contain value-bearing data (for example, the number of an item on the menu), whereas control flows are binary (for example, it is true that the waiter is free). Flows may be discrete which means they have only an instantaneous presence or they may be continuous which means they have a presence which obtains through time. The latter are shown with double arrow heads. In Figure A1.2 there is only one continuous flow: Waiter Free. Flows to or from data stores represent accessing of data from those stores, either by our system or by a terminator.

What does this context diagram actually say. Well, we can start with waking the system up! It is Event 1, 'Time to open restaurant' that causes this to happen. We will respond by issuing a control flow Waiter Free to indicate the waiter is available for duties.

Now let us work our way clockwise around the diagram: a prospective customer entering the restaurant is indicated by the control flow Customer Entry coming in from Prospective Customer. Clearly, this is associated with Event 2, 'Customer enters restaurant', the response to which will either be an Apology (the restaurant is full) or a Welcome Greeting (a table is free). If a table is found for the customer it must be updated as 'occupied'. The 'Tables' data store will be needed for this.

When the customer is ready, he or she will summon the waiter (Event 3) as indicated by the incoming control flow Customer Summons. The response of our system will be to wait for the customer to complete the order and turn off the control flow Waiter Free; in other words to wait for Event 4 to happen, as indicated by the incoming flow Order Selection, whilst locking out all other systems from employing the waiter.

When Event 4 happens, the response of our system will be to check items from the menu are available (using the Restaurant Rules data store) and to compile an order (on to the Orders data store). The chef is then signalled with Meal Required and Waiter Free is issued, to allow the waiter to be employed for other duties.

Finally, Event 5 causes the system to shut down. The waiter has earned a well deserved rest. So turn off the control flow Waiter Free.

Notice the close correlation between the event list and the context diagram.

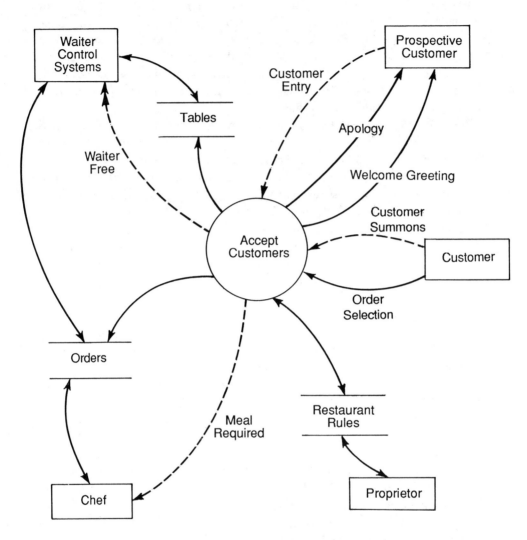

Figure A1.2 Context diagram for Accept Customers.

Effectively they are different sides of the same coin. Often used in conjunction with, or instead of, these two tools is an entity relationship diagram (ERD). An example is shown in Figure A1.3. Stored data is shown in somewhat unstructured fashion on the context diagram. The ERD serves to explore and develop a structure for stored data. This is a map of the stored data structure required to support the system, in terms of categories of information known as entities (shown as boxes) and associations of interest between entities known as relationships (shown as diamonds).

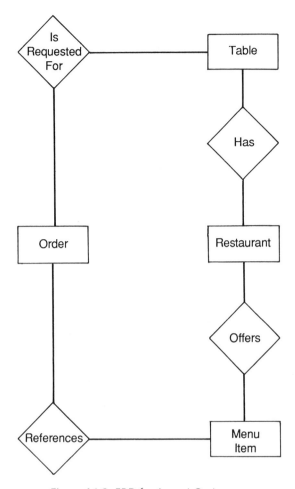

Figure A1.3 ERD for Accept Customers.

What does the ERD tell us? Firstly, we need to keep information about the restaurant itself; for example, the opening time and closing time; so we model Restaurant as an entity. Secondly, we need to keep descriptions and prices of each item on the menu; so we model Menu Item as an entity. Thirdly we need to record the fact that the restaurant offers such menu items; so we model Offers as a relationship . . . and so on.

Thus far we have confined ourselves to graphic symbols. What about the specific data items that actually live in the flows and entities that we have modelled? Textual support is supplied using a data dictionary; the reader should refer to Section A1.3 at this point and examine some of the entries and compare them with the diagrams. Together, the data dictionary and diagrams are said to form a *model*. In fact, what we are doing here is modelling the system scope.

The data dictionary also forms a point of contact between elements from different diagram types. For example, data stores are defined in terms of corresponding entities (not actually listed in Section A1.3), or groups of entities and relationships (for example, see the definition for Restaurant Rules).

The essence of modelling is to raise salient questions with the objective of illuminating the problem. The models make assumptions public: for example, the system:

☐ Depends upon restaurant rules supplied by the proprietor.
☐ Takes priority over all other systems utilising the waiter.
☐ Involves a single waiter.
☐ Requires the waiter to not be available for any other activity whilst the customer is deliberating over what to order.
☐ Is not concerned with payments.

The reader is invited to list other assumptions at this point. There will be many. These assumptions should be questioned: that is the essence of exploring system scope. However, given that they are correct, we now start to develop our understanding of requirements. This will involve refining the ERD, which we have not done here. It will also involve building a state transition diagram (STD), if appropriate, and a data flow diagram (DFD).

The STD models changes of system behaviour over time. An example is shown in Figure A1.4. States (shown as elongated boxes) are time windows through which behaviour is constant until something happens to cause a transition (shown as an arrowed line) to a different state. For example, the system stays in the state Idle until the restaurant opens which causes a transition to Waiting for Customer. The cause of change is known as a condition and is shown above a horizontal line, below which is the system response(s) known as an action. Notice, conditions are associated with events and actions are associated with activation of responses to events. For example, the condition Customer Summons Waiter is associated with Event 3. We have seen that the response to this event is to turn off the Waiter Free control flow (shown on the STD as 'L' for 'Lower') and to activate the system to take order (shown on the STD as 'E' for 'Enable' the response Take Order). Notice also that transitions may be recursive; Waiting for Customer has one of these.

(Whilst not wishing to digress into a technical discussion on activation types at this point, it will be important to understand the other action abbreviations: 'D' = 'Disable'; 'T' = 'Trigger'; 'R' = 'Raise'; 'S' = 'Signal'. A full discussion of these is provided in Section 4.4, if the reader finds this necessary. On first reading however this is not recommended as the main aim is to obtain an intuitive grasp of the toolset.)

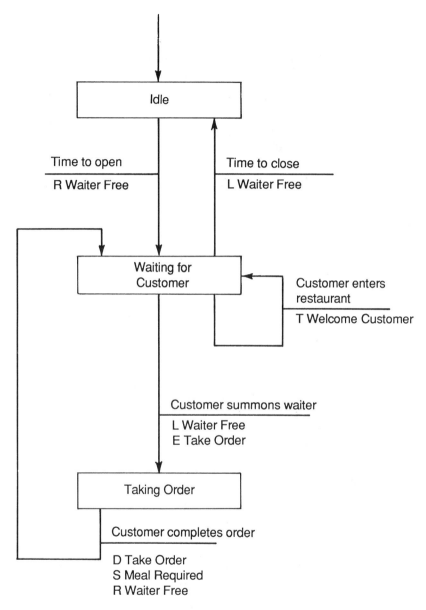

Figure A1.4 STD for Control Customer Acceptance.

We have seen that the STD is intimately related to the event list. Indeed, it is usually developed from it. Again the essence of the exercise is to raise questions. Notice, we are not only tracking the effects of events on admissable system

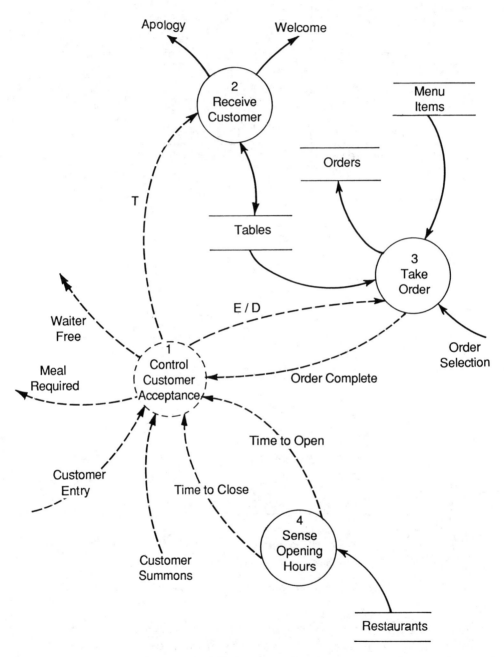

Figure A1.5 DFD for Accept Customers.

behaviour we are also in effect stating when an event is actually allowed to cause a response. For example, the STD states if the event 'Customer enters restaurant' occurs when the system is in the Taking Order state nothing will actually happen! Again we need to examine this assumption. For example, does this mean that on return to the Waiting for Customer state the waiter ignores the customer until he or she issues another Customer Entry flow, presumably by reopening the door? If so then maybe we need to restructure the diagram.

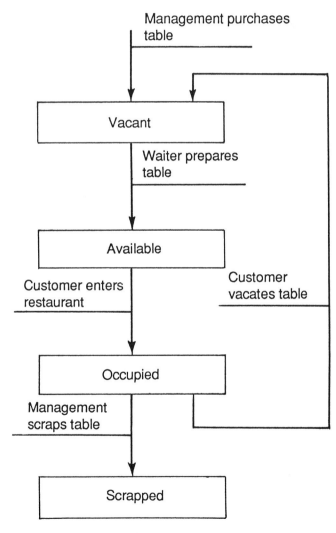

Figure A1.6 ESTD for Occupation Status of Table.

A DFD models the flow of data and control around a system. An example is shown in Figure A1.5. The symbols are essentially the same as for the context diagram with the following exceptions:

☐ Terminators are not usually shown.

☐ A dashed bubble is used as a short-hand representation of an STD, and may be thought of as a manager bubble who controls and co-ordinates all worker bubbles (shown as solid circles); the manager bubble deals only in dashed flows. Incoming dashed flows correspond to conditions and outgoing dashed flows correspond to actions on the associated STD.

The diagram illuminates basic system responsibilities in relation to one another. For example, there is a bubble Receive Customer that is triggered by the manager as a response to Event 2. It decides whether or not there is a vacant table, issues a welcome or apology as appropriate, and if necessary, updates the table as occupied.

Finally, we might also want to model changes of state of an entity, using an entity state transition diagram (ESTD). An example ESTD is shown in Figure A1.6. The notation is the same as for an STD. Again, notice that conditions are associated with events. However, whereas an STD focusses on events from the same system, with the ESTD they may come from different systems. For example, the events 'Management purchases table', 'Waiter prepares table', 'Customer vacates table', and 'Management scraps table' do not appear on the earlier event list; they appertain to different systems. What we are doing here then is to track the effects of events upon an entity across systems.

Notice the actions are left blank at this stage: they will be filled in once we have organized our understanding of requirements. Finally, because an ESTD can involve events from different systems it is said to be, like the ERD, an enterprise modelling tool, in contrast to a system modelling tool.

Once assumptions have been clarified and agreed, our understanding of requirements would be refined and eventually organized into a requirement specification. This would include process specifications for bubbles like Receive Customer which have not been included here, as we are still piecing together our understanding of requirements.

Verification of requirements, though particularly important to confirm the requirements specification, should in actuality be an on-going activity. In this connection, the criticality of user involvement is a subject which is discussed in its own right in Section 2.10.

A1.3 Data dictionary

The following data dictionary report is produced with the '+' symbol implied in all listed items, repeating groups enclosed in curly brackets and optional items enclosed in round brackets.

ENTITIES

Menu Item	=	A dish listed on the Morgan Tandoori menu
Identifier	=	Number
Attributes	=	Description
		Price

Order	=	A record of a customer's request for menu items including the progressing of that request
Identifier	=	Date
		Number
Attributes	=	Customer Name
		Time.Taken
		Progress.Status
		Waiter.Name
		(Payment.Type)
		(Tax.Due)

Restaurant	=	Premises where the very best in specialized tandoori cooking offered by Mr Morgan may be had
Identifier	=	Name
Attributes	=	Address
		Opening.Time
		Closing.Time
		Tax.Code
		License.Number

Table	=	Eating surface approved by the proprietor
Identifier	=	Number
Attributes	=	Size
		Occupation.Status

RELATIONSHIPS

Has	=	A record of the fact that a table is sited in the restaurant
		One restaurant *must* have *one* or *more* tables
		One table *must* be sited in *one* restaurant

Is Required For	= The linking of an order with target table(s)
	One order *must be* required for *one* or *more* tables
	One table *may* require *one* or *more* orders

Offers	= Notice that a dish is on the menu
	One restaurant *must* offer *one* or *more* menu items
	One menu item *must be* offered by *one* restaurant

References	= A record of the fact that a menu item has been ordered
	Note: may occur more than once for the same order and menu item
	One order *must* reference *one* or *more* menu items
	One menu item *may be* referenced by *one* or *more* orders

PACKAGED STORES

Restaurant Rules	= {Table
	Restaurant
	Menu Item}

CONTROL FLOWS

Customer Entry	= Event 2
Persistence	= Discrete

Customer Summons	= Event 3
Persistence	= Discrete

Order Complete	= Event 4
Persistence	= Discrete

Time to Open	= Event 1
Persistence	= Discrete

Time to Close	= Event 5
Persistence	= Discrete

Meal Required	= A signal to the chef that an order is waiting
Persistence	= Discrete

Waiter Free	= If raised the waiter is free to assume other duties. If lowered the waiter is busy
Persistence	= Continuous

DATA FLOWS

Apology	= A waiter's announcement to a customer that, regretfully, the restaurant is full

Persistence	=	Discrete
	=	Announcement
Order Selection	=	Notification by a customer of an order by specific menu items
Persistence	=	Discrete
	=	Waiter.Name
		Table.Number
		{Menu.Item.Number
		Quantity}
Welcome	=	A waiter's greeting to a customer indicating pleasure to serve
Persistence	=	Discrete
	=	Greeting
		Table.Number

Wellbrian Player Administration System

□ □ □ □ □ □ □ □ □ □ □ □ □ □ □ □ □

A2.1 Background

A2.1.1 Systems strategy

The Player Administration System was identified as a candidate context within the systems strategy; the scoped global ERD for this system is included in Figure A.2.1. Systems reconnaissance was subsequently initiated with Mr Mick Blough, the chairman of the Wellbrian Soccer Federation, as executive sponsor. The resulting preliminary DFD is shown in Figure A2.2. The current system profile (excluding cost-benefit analysis) is described in Section A2.2. Notes from the original interview with Mr Blough are included below.

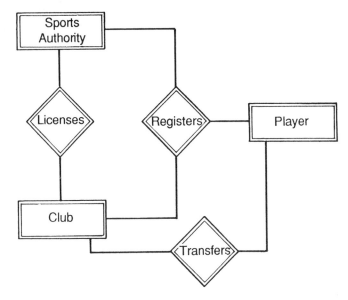

Figure A2.1 Scoped global ERD for Player Administration System.

The reader should note that the detail on some of the models in this appendix differs from that on diagrams within Part Two which confines itself to the system perspective with no benefit of systems or systems reconaissance.

A2.1.2 Interview with Mr Mick Blough

First take your hands out of your pockets and pin back your ears, because I will say this only once:

WSF controls several Sports Authorities each with their own unique name

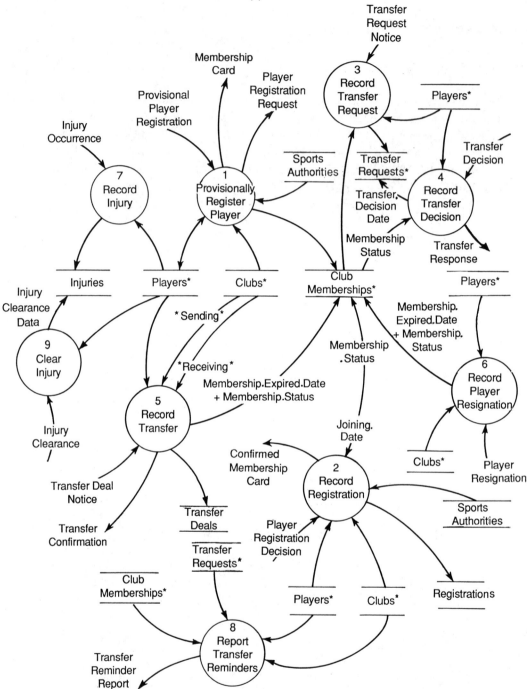

Figure A2.2 Preliminary DFD for Player Administration System.

and address, and responsible for licensing clubs falling in its territory. Each club has a unique name and we hold the address of its ground together with other details, which I am not going to go into here. In any case PAS will be supplied with this information by the WSF Licensing System.

The clubs themselves are responsible for the maintenance of player details (for example, address and date of birth), for recording basic injury details as below, and also for recording a player's membership of that club, and recording transfer detail information. The Sports Authorities are responsible for the registration of players, and it is the player's membership of a club that is registered (not the player himself).

We also need the facility to be able to view a player's career historically, by seeing which clubs he has been a member of, when he was registered, transferred and so on. Now, although PAS is not responsible for displaying such details on request, it must create a data structure that permits other systems to do this. The PAS must support both the club membership side and the registration side of things. Now let's get down to the details. . . .

When a club wishes to take a player on to its books it must first register that player's membership with the Sports Authority. First, the player is registered with the club as a provisional member, a unique membership number is created and recorded along with date of joining and the player's name, address and date of birth, and a request for full registration sent to the Sports Authority. At that stage the player receives no official confirmation, and his membership status is marked 'provisional'. He does, however, receive a membership card which shows the following details:

- ☐ Player id.
- ☐ Player name and address.
- ☐ Player date of birth.
- ☐ Club name and address.
- ☐ Membership number.
- ☐ Date of joining.
- ☐ Membership status.

After the Sports Authority have made a decision as to whether to allow registration a letter is sent to the club by the authority, denoting the decision on the player's membership status as follows:

- ☐ Accepted: Club membership is now formally registered with the Sports Authority. The registration number and date are recorded and printed on a new membership card showing membership status as 'confirmed'.
- ☐ Rejected: Membership status is marked 'rejected'. The player is entitled to keep his card and remain a provisional member.

☐ Deferred: Membership status is marked 'deferred', pending further discussion. In a case like this it is usually a medical query that has to be cleared. Again the player's membership card remains unaltered.

The registration number and date are formally notifed by the Sports Authority for recording within the system, and are shown on a revised membership card.

Players do, from time to time, become restless and make transfer requests. Any player who has a membership status of 'accepted' may be transferred between clubs who have made a deal and agreed terms with the player concerned. However, if that player has made a previous *request* to be transferred this will have an adverse effect on his 'cut' of the fee agreed. Therefore, a player is required to submit such a request on a transfer request notice showing player id, club membership number and date; clearly it is important to record such requests, which assume a status of 'pending' until a decision has been made.

The club are bound to make a decision on a transfer request by 5 pm on the Friday of the week following the week in which the request is made. Therefore it is necessary to report reminders two days in advance so that the club has no excuse for shirking its obligations. The club's decision on a transfer request must be recorded as accepted/rejected, along with the date of the decision.

Providing a player has membership status of 'accepted', he may be transferred between clubs who have agreed a deal. The authority require that the membership card is forfeited and that the sending club record the following details of the transfer deal on a transfer deal notice:

☐ Fee agreed.
☐ Date of agreement.
☐ Player id.
☐ Sending and receiving club names.

On submission of the transfer deal the player's membership of the 'sending' club expires, entailing an expired date and membership status = 'transferred' to be recorded against membership. The membership itself is not deleted as the authority require a history to be kept. The receiving club are sent a transfer confirmation containing the same details as submitted on the transfer deal (as above). It is then up to the receiving club to register the player in the normal way.

On a less happy note players do occasionally suffer injuries. Where the injury is deemed 'serious' the club doctor submits injury details which must be recorded, though it is not permitted to go into great detail (on ethical grounds). Such injuries fall into the following stipulated types:

☐ Fracture.
☐ Strain.

☐ Illness.

☐ Miscellaneous.

The player id, date incurred and type of injury are suffcient to identify an individual injury. Therefore if a player incurred a thigh strain, broke his arm, damaged his eye, and caught 'flu in the same day there would be four occurrences of injury. Injury details may also include a doctor's comment.

Once the doctor is satisfied that the player is fit again, an injury clearance is submitted indicating date of clearance and method of treatment code, which I will not go into here.

Finally, players may resign, either for personal reasons or more commonly because although the spirit is willing the flesh is no longer strong enough. In this case the player hands in his membership card and his membership status is marked 'resigned' and the expiry date recorded.

A2.2 System profile

SYSTEM TITLE
Player Administration System.

STATEMENT OF PURPOSE
The purpose of the Player Administration System is to support the Wellbrian Soccer Federation and its member clubs in the registration and transfer of players and the recording of all injury details.

BACKGROUND
The PAS is to be developed to support the Wellbrian Soccer Federation and its member clubs in administration of soccer player details. This includes registration and outward transfer of players and the recording of a limited amount of player data, including injury data. It should be understood that PAS will eventually be developed as part of a much larger integrated collection of systems to support the whole range of activities of the WSF and its clubs. Therefore, although terms of reference for this more limited exercise of building an essential model for PAS exclude the examples listed below, the analysis must bear in mind that PAS will collect information which may be used by other systems. Also, the analysis must be flexible enough to cater for other team games with similar infrastructures so that the system can be targeted at other markets later on. For example, both the Jollysticks Hockey Authority and Rugby Associated Team Services (RATS for short) have expressed an interest.

PROVISOS
☐ Transfers inward.
☐ Fixture scheduling.
☐ Match administration.
☐ Team selection and support.
☐ Club licensing.
☐ Competition control.
☐ *Ad hoc* enquiries.

CONSTRAINTS
Existing hardware, DBMSs, operating and TP systems to be used:

1. Club PCs:

☐ Online recording of all information with respect to an individual club.
☐ Daily production of membership cards, transfer confirmation and weekly reporting of transfer reminders.

☐ Refreshing of club information (uploaded from WSF mini).
☐ Downloading of player information from club database to WSF mini, using floppy disk(s).

2. Sports Authority minis:

☐ Recording of registrations.

3. WSF mini:

☐ Refreshing of player information to the WSF database (uploaded from club PC).
☐ Downloading of club information from WSF database to club PC, using floppy disk(s).

Existing clerical resources to be used:

1. Club clerical staff:

☐ Input of all transactions.
☐ Sending of registration requests to appropriate Sports Authority.
☐ Sending of responses to transfer requests to players.

2. Sports Authority registrar:

☐ Receipt of registration requests.
☐ Making decisions on registrations, entering to Sports Authority mini and sending decisions to clubs.

DEVELOPMENT STRATEGY

1. To date:

☐ Rigorous requirements specification in procedral language.
☐ External design.
☐ Primitive prototypes on WSF mini.

2. Proposed:

☐ Decision support prototyping on WSF mini.
☐ Event prototyping (on Alexandra United's Club PC).

MODELS
As enclosed.

A2.3 Requirements specification

Note: The convention adopted here is to suppress all error messages on diagrams.

A2.3.1 Context diagram

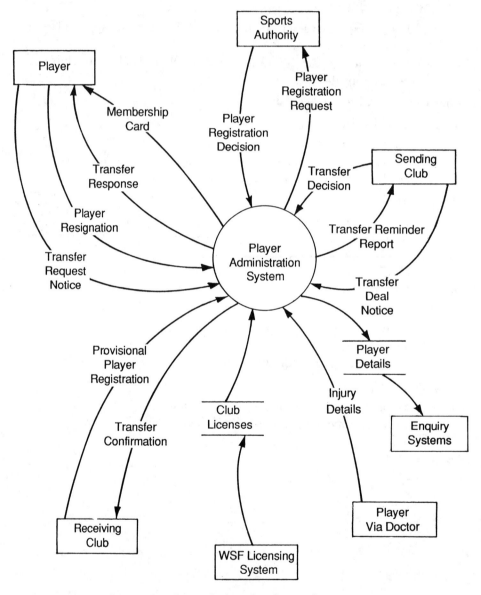

Figure A2.3 Context diagram for Player Administration System.

A2.3.2 Event list

1. Club registers player provisionally (D).
2. Sports Authority makes decision on player registration (D).
3. Player requests transfer (D).
4. Club makes decision on transfer request (D).
5. Club transfers player (D).
6. Player resigns from club (D).
7. Doctor submits player's injury details (D).
8. Time to report transfer reminders (DT).
9. Doctor submits clearance of injury (D).

Figure A2.4 Event list for Player Administration System.

A2.3.3 Levelled set of DFDs

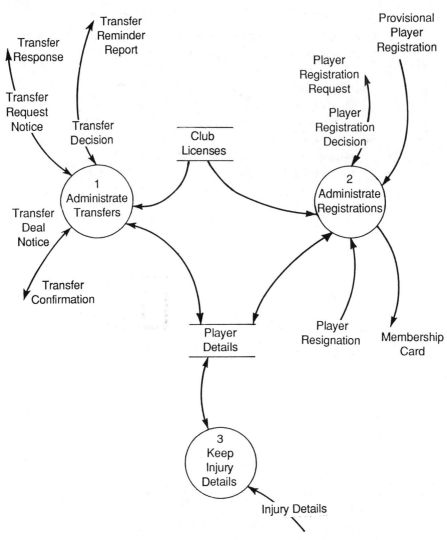

Figure A2.5(a) Figure 0: Player Administration System.

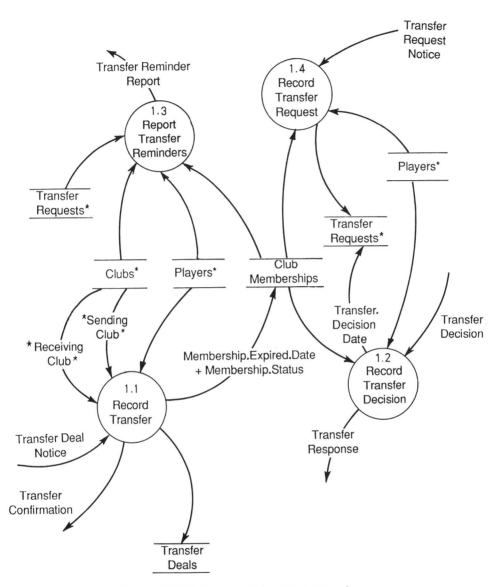

Figure A2.5(b) Figure 1: Administrate Transfers.

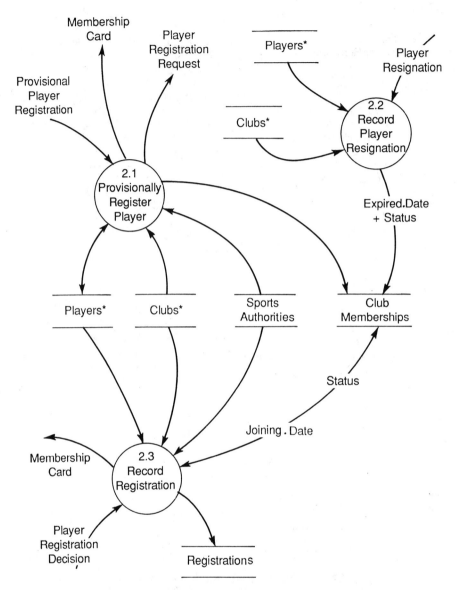

Figure A2.5(c) Figure 2: Administrate Registrations.

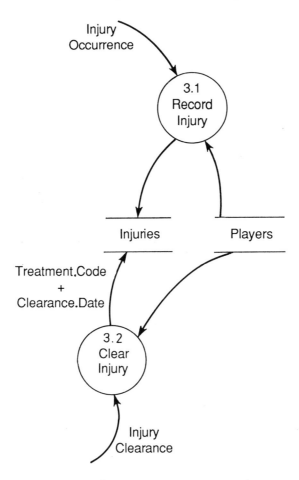

Figure A2.5(d) Figure 3: Keep Injury Details.

A2.3.4 System ERD

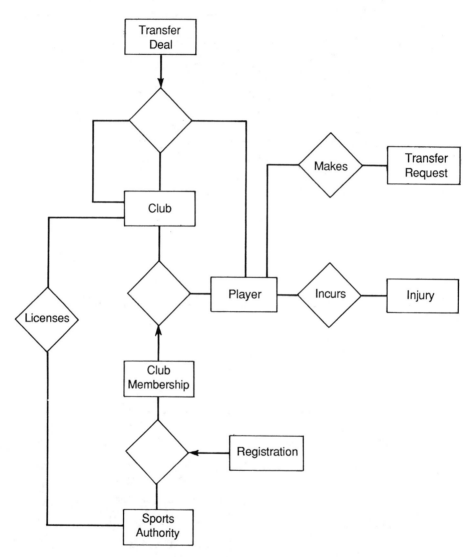

Figure A2.6 ERD for Player Administration System.

A2.3.5 Process descriptions and specifications

Note: Data dictionary items have been capitalised.

1.1 RECORD TRANSFER

Process objective. To set up a transfer deal, set up a new membership for the receiving club, and expire the membership of the sending club. Also produce transfer confirmation.

Process views

    Flows in: TRANSFER DEAL NOTICE

    Flows out: TRANSFER CONFIRMATION

    Entities: PLAYER (*Read*)

          CLUB (*Read*)

    Associative entities: CLUB MEMBERSHIP (*Update*)

                  TRANSFER DEAL (*Create*)

    Relationships: None

Process specification

For each TRANSFER DEAL NOTICE

    Read PLAYER using PLAYER.ID

    If not found

        Issue Error Message = 'Player Not Found'

        Exit

    Read [Sending] CLUB using CLUB.NAME = SENDING.CLUB.NAME from TRANSFER DEAL NOTICE

    If [Sending] CLUB not found

        Issue Error Message = 'Sending Club Not Found'

        Exit

    Read CLUB MEMBERSHIP which references PLAYER and [Sending] CLUB

    If not found or CLUB.MEMBERSHIP.STATUS not = 'Accepted'

        Issue Error Message = 'Invalid Sending Club Membership'

        Exit

    Read [Receiving] CLUB using CLUB.NAME = RECEIVING.CLUB.NAME from TRANSFER DEAL NOTICE

    If not found

        Issue Error Message = 'Receiving Club Not Found'

        Exit

Create TRANSFER DEAL referencing PLAYER and [Sending] Club and
[Receiving] Club with DATE and FEE from TRANSFER DEAL
NOTICE

Update CLUB MEMBERSHIP with STATUS = 'transferred' and
EXPIRED.DATE = DATE from TRANSFER DEAL NOTICE

Issue TRANSFER CONFIRMATION

1.2 RECORD TRANSFER DECISION

Process objective. To record details of transfer decision and produce a transfer
response.

Process views

Flows in: TRANSFER DECISION

Flows out: TRANSFER RESPONSE

Entities: PLAYER (*Read*)
  TRANSFER REQUEST (*Update*)

Associative entities: CLUB MEMBERSHIP (*Read*)
Relationships: PLAYER *MAKES* TRANSFER REQUEST (*Read*)

Process specification

For each TRANSFER DECISION

Read PLAYER using PLAYER.ID
If not found
  Issue Error Message = 'Player Not Found'
  Exit
If no matching CLUB MEMBERSHIP using CLUB.MEMBERSHIP.
NUMBER from TRANSFER DECISION
  Issue Error Message = 'Club Membership Not Found'
  Exit

Read TRANSFER REQUEST referencing PLAYER with STATUS =
'pending'
If not found
  Issue Error Message = 'No Transfer Request Pending'

Update TRANSFER REQUEST with STATUS, DECISION.DATE from
  TRANSFER DECISION

Issue TRANSFER RESPONSE

1.3 REPORT TRANSFER REMINDERS

Process objective. **To report all transfer requests undealt with from previous week.**

Process views

    Flows In: None

    Flows Out: TRANSFER REMINDER REPORT

    Entities: PLAYER (*Read*)
           TRANSFER REQUEST (*Read*)
           CLUB (*Read*)

    Associative Entities: CLUB MEMBERSHIP (*Read*)

    Relationships: PLAYER *MAKES* TRANSFER REQUEST (Read)

Process specification

Set TRANSFER.REMINDER.REPORT.DATE = TODAYS.DATE

For each CLUB

    Set Next CLUB.NAME in TRANSFER REMINDER REPORT

    For each PLAYER with CLUB MEMBERSHIP referencing CLUB

        For each TRANSFER REQUEST referencing PLAYER with STATUS
        = 'pending' and DATE < TODAYS DATE – 2
           Set Next PLAYER.ID
                PLAYER.NAME
                CLUB.MEMBERSHIP.NUMBER
                TRANSFER.REQUEST DATE
                in TRANSFER REMINDER REPORT

Issue TRANSFER REMINDER REPORT

1.4 RECORD TRANSFER REQUEST

Process objective. To record transfer request details.

Process views

    Flows in: TRANSFER REQUEST NOTICE

    Flows out: None

    Entities: PLAYER (*Read*)

           TRANSFER REQUEST (*Create*)

Associative entities: CLUB MEMBERSHIP (*Read*)

Relationships: PLAYER *MAKES* TRANSFER REQUEST (*Create*)

Process specification

For each TRANSFER REQUEST NOTICE

Read PLAYER using PLAYER.ID
If not found
    Issue Error Message = 'Player Not Found'
    Exit

If no matching CLUB MEMBERSHIP using CLUB.MEMBERSHIP.
NUMBER from TRANSFER DECISION
    Issue Error Message = 'Club Membership Not Found'
    Exit

Create TRANSFER REQUEST referencing PLAYER with
    STATUS = 'pending'
    REQUEST.DATE from TRANSFER REQUEST

2.1 PROVISIONALLY REGISTER PLAYER

Process objective. To set up provisional membership and produce a membership card and registration request for a player joining a club.

Process views

Flows in: PROVISIONAL PLAYER REGISTRATION

Flows out: PLAYER REGISTRATION REQUEST
        MEMBERSHIP CARD

Entities: CLUB (*Read*)
      PLAYER (*Read, Create*)
      SPORTS AUTHORITY (*Read*)

Associative entities: CLUB MEMBERSHIP (*Create*)

Relationships: SPORTS AUTHORITY *LICENSES* CLUB (*Read*)

Algorithms

Allocate Player.Id

Allocate Club.Number

Process specification

For each PROVISIONAL PLAYER REGISTRATION

> Read CLUB using CLUB.NAME from PROVISIONAL PLAYER REGISTRATION
> If not found
>> Issue Error Message = 'Club Not Found'
>> Exit
>
> If matching SPORTS AUTHORITY referencing CLUB
>> Next Statement
> Else
>> Issue Error Message = 'Licensing Sports Authority Not Found'
>> Exit
>
> If PROVISIONAL PLAYER REGISTRATION has PLAYER.ID present
>> Read PLAYER using PLAYER.ID
>> If not found
>>> Issue Error Message = 'Player Not Found'
>>> Exit
>> Else
>>> Next Statement
> Else
>> Create PLAYER with ID set using Allocate Player.Id
>>> NAME, BIRTH.DATE, ADDRESS from
>>> PROVISIONAL PLAYER REGISTRATION
>
> Create CLUB MEMBERSHIP referencing PLAYER and CLUB with
>> NUMBER set using Allocate Club.Number
>> JOINING.DATE from PROVISIONAL PLAYER REGISTRATION
>> STATUS = 'provisional'
>
> Issue PLAYER REGISTRATION REQUEST
>
> Issue MEMBERSHIP CARD

PROCESS DESCRIPTION FOR 2.2 RECORD PLAYER RESIGNATION

Process objective. To resign a player's club membership.

Process views

> Flows in: PLAYER RESIGNATION
> Flows out: None

Entities: CLUB (*Read*)
PLAYER (*Read*)

Associative entities: CLUB MEMBERSHIP (*Update*)

Relationships: None

Process specification

For each PLAYER RESIGNATION

Read CLUB using CLUB.NAME from PLAYER RESIGNATION
If not found

Issue Error Message = 'Club Not Found'
Exit

Read PLAYER using PLAYER.ID from PLAYER RESIGNATION
If not found

Issue Error Message = 'Player not Found'
Exit

Read CLUB MEMBERSHIP referencing PLAYER and CLUB using CLUB.
MEMBERSHIP.NUMBER from PLAYER RESIGNATION
If not found

Issue Error Message = 'Club Membership Not Found'
Exit

Update CLUB MEMBERSHIP with
EXPIRED.DATE from PLAYER RESIGNATION
STATUS = 'expired'

2.3 RECORD REGISTRATION

Process Objective. To update membership in line with registration decision, and to produce membership card where the decision is to accept registration.

Process views

Flows in: PLAYER REGISTRATION DECISION

Flows out: MEMBERSHIP CARD

Entities: Player (*Read*)
CLUB (*Read*)
SPORTS AUTHORITY (*Read*)

Associative entities: CLUB MEMBERSHIP (*Update*)
REGISTRATION (*Create*)

Relationships: SPORTS AUTHORITY *LICENSES* CLUB (*Read*)

Process specification

For each PLAYER REGISTRATION DECISION

Read Club using CLUB.NAME from PLAYER REGISTRATION
DECISION
If not found
Issue Error Message = 'Club Not Found'
Exit

If matching SPORTS AUTHORITY referencing CLUB
Next Statement
Else
Issue Error Message = 'Licensing Sports Authority Not Found
Exit

Read PLAYER using PLAYER.ID from PLAYER REGISTRATION
DECISION
If not found
Issue Error Message = 'Player Not Found'
Exit

Read CLUB MEMBERSHIP referencing PLAYER and CLUB
If not found
Issue Error Message = 'Incorrect Club Membership Number'
Exit

If PLAYER.REGISTRATION.DECISION.STATUS = 'accepted'
Update CLUB MEMBERSHIP with STATUS = 'confirmed'
Next Statement
Else
Update CLUB MEMBERSHIP with STATUS from
PLAYER REGISTRATION DECISION
Exit

Create REGISTRATION referencing CLUB MEMBERSHIP and SPORTS
AUTHORITY with
NUMBER, DATE from PLAYER REGISTRATION DECISION

Issue Membership Card

3.1 RECORD INJURY

Process objective. To record details of an injury to a player.

Process views

    Flows in: INJURY OCCURRENCE

    Flows out: None

    Entities: PLAYER (*Read*)
            INJURY (*Create*)

    Associative entities: None

    Relationships: PLAYER *INCURS* INJURY (*Create*)

Process specification

For each INJURY OCCURRENCE

    Read PLAYER using PLAYER.ID from INJURY OCCURRENCE
    If not found
        Issue Error Message = 'Player Not Found'
        Exit

    Create INJURY referencing PLAYER with
        TYPE, INCURRED.DATE and DOCTORS.COMMENT from
        INJURY OCCURRENCE

3.2 CLEAR INJURY

Process objective. To record details of clearance of injury to a player.

Process views

    Flows in: INJURY CLEARANCE

    Flows out: None

    Entities: PLAYER (*Read*)
            INJURY (*Update*)

    Associative entities: None

    Relationships: PLAYER *INCURS* INJURY (*Read*)

Process specification

For each INJURY CLEARANCE

Read PLAYER using PLAYER.ID from INJURY CLEARANCE
If not found
    Issue Error Message = 'Player Not Found'
    Exit

If matching INJURY referencing PLAYER and with TYPE and INCURRED.
DATE matching INJURY CLEARANCE
    Update INJURY with
        TREATMENT.CODE and CLEARANCE.DATE from
        INJURY CLEARANCE
Else
    Issue Error Message = 'Injury Not Found'

A2.3.6 Data dictionary

The following data dictionary report is produced using an adaptation of BNF; the '+' symbol is implied in all listed items.

ENTITIES

Club	=	Organization whose purpose is to run teams participating in sports governed by the WSF
Identifier	=	Name
Attributes	=	Ground.Address
Player	=	Individual participating in sports governed by the WSF
Identifier	=	Id
Attributes	=	Name
		Address
		Birth.Date
Injury	=	A medical condition likely to affect a player's capacity to perform to expectations
Identifier	=	Reference to Player
		Type
		Incurred.Date
Attributes	=	(Doctors.Comment)
		(Treatment.Code)
		(Clearance.Date)
Sports Authority	=	Body set up by WSF to regulate the activity of clubs and their players under Section 19 of the Sports Act

Identifier	=	Name
Attributes	=	Address

Transfer Request	=	A record of a player's formal request to be transferred and of the resulting decision made by the club
Identifier	=	Reference to Player
		Date
Attributes	=	Status
		(Decision.Date)

ASSOCIATIVE ENTITIES

Club Membership	=	Formal statement of a player being on a club's books
Cardinality	=	Single
Participation	=	A Player MUST *have been a member of* ONE or MORE Clubs
		A Club MAY *have had as members* ONE or MORE Players
Identifier	=	Number
Attributes	=	Joining.Date
		Status
		(Expired.Date)

Registration	=	The WSF's recognition of a player's club membership conferring rights under Reg 243
Cardinality	=	Single
Participation	=	A Club Membership MAY *be registered* with ONE Sports Authority
		A Sports Authority MAY *have registered* ONE or MORE Club Memberships
Identifier	=	Number
Attributes	=	Date

Transfer Deal	=	A record of signature of agreement between two clubs and a player on the movement of that player from one club to the other as under WSF Reg 256
Cardinality	=	Single
Participation	=	A Player May *be transferred from* a [Sending] Club *to* ONE or MORE [Receiving] Clubs

		A [Sending] Club MAY *transfer* to a [Receiving] Club ONE or MORE Players

A [Sending] Club MAY *transfer* to a
[Receiving] Club ONE or MORE Players
A Player MAY *be transferred* to a
[Receiving] Club *from* ONE or MORE
[Sending] Clubs

Identifier = Reference to Player
Reference to [Sending] Club
Reference to [Receiving] Club

Attributes = Date
Fee

RELATIONSHIPS

Incurs = Reflection of doctor's judgment that a player has received an injury.

    Participation = A Player MAY *incur* ONE or MORE Injuries
An Injury MUST *be incurred by* ONE Player

Licenses = A record of a Sports Authority's decision to grant a license to a Club

    Participation = A Sports Authority MAY *license* ONE or MORE Clubs
ONE Club MUST BE *licensed by* ONE Sports Authority

Makes = The submission of a transfer request by a specific player

    Participation = A Player MAY *make* ONE OR MORE Transfer Requests
A Transfer Request MUST BE *made by* ONE Player

PACKAGED STORES

Club Licenses = {Club}
{Sports Authority}

Player Details = {Club}
{Player}
{Injury}
{Club Membership}
{Registration}
{Transfer Deal}
{Transfer Request}

DISCRETE DATA FLOWS

Injury Clearance	=	A doctor's submission of clearance of injury
Attributes	=	Player.Id
		Type
		Incurred.Date
		Treatment.Code
		Clearance.Date

Injury Occurrence	=	A doctor's submission of diagnosis relating to a player's incapacity to perform to expectations
Attributes	=	Player.Id
		Type
		Incurred.Date
		(Doctors.Comment)
		(Treatment.Code)
		(Clearance.Date)

Membership Card	=	A player's documentation of club membership
Attributes	=	Club.Membership.Number
		Club.Membership.Joining.Date
		(Club.Membership.Expired.Date)
		Club.Membership.Status
		Player.Id
		Player.Name
		Player.Birth.Date
		Club.Name
		Club.Address

Player Registration Decision	=	Sports Authority's notification to a club of decision as to whether or not a player's club membership is to be registered
Attributes	=	Player.Id
		Club.Name
		Sport.Authority.Name
		Status
		(Registration.Number)
		(Registration.Date)

Player Registration Request	=	A request made by a club to a Sports Authority for registration of a player's membership

Attributes	=	Player.Id
		Player.Name
		Club.Name
		Club.Membership.Number
		Sports.Authority.Name

Player Resignation	=	Formal notice from a player of retirement from the game
Attributes	=	Player.Id
		Club.Name
		Club.Membership.Number
		Expired.Date

Provisional Player Registration	=	Notification of player initially joining club
Attributes	=	(Player.Id)
		Player.Name
		Player.Address
		Player.Birth.Date
		Club.Name
		Joining.Date

Transfer Confirmation	=	Notice to the receiving club that transfer of a player is completed but awaiting registration
Attributes	=	Player.Id
		Player.Name
		[Sending] Club.Name
		[Receiving] Club.Name
		Transfer.Deal.Date
		Transfer.Deal.Fee

Transfer Deal Notice	=	Notice of signature of agreement between two clubs and a player for that player's membership to be transferred between clubs
Attributes	=	Player.Id
		Sending.Club.Name
		Receiving.Club.Name
		Date
		Fee

Transfer Decision	=	Club's formal decision as to whether a transfer request is to be granted. *
Attributes	=	Club.Membership.Number Player.Id Status Decision.Date

Transfer Request Notice	=	A player's formal request to be transferred to another club
Attributes	=	Player.Id Club.Membership.Number Date

Transfer Reminder Report	=	A report produced Wednesday 5 pm each week showing transfer requests for which decisions are outstanding
Attributes	=	Report.Date {Club.Name {Player.Id Player.Name Club.Membership.Number Transfer.Request.Date}}

Transfer Response	=	Notification to a player of a club's decision regarding his transfer request *
Attributes	=	Player.Id Player.Name Club.Membership.Number Transfer.Request.Date Transfer.Decision.Date Transfer.Decision.Status

PACKAGED FLOWS

Injury Details	=	(Injury Occurrence) (Injury Clearance)

A2.4 External design extract

A2.4.1 Allocation of processes to processors

Club PC

Essential processes:
1. Administrate transfers
2. Administrate registrations
3. Keep injury details

Envisaged implementation:
- ☐ Online data capture for all essential processes
- ☐ Daily reporting system for membership cards and transfer confirmations
- ☐ Weekly reporting system for transfer reminders

Implementation processes:
- ☐ Load receiving clubs (On request)
- ☐ Download database (Weekly)

Sports Authority mini

Essential processes:
    2.3. Record registrations; minus Issue Membership Card.

Envisaged implementation:
- ☐ Online data capture

Implementation processes:
- ☐ None

WSF mini

Essential processes:
- ☐ None

Implementation processes:
- ☐ Create receiving club updates (on request)
- ☐ Format and upload database updates (from club PC)

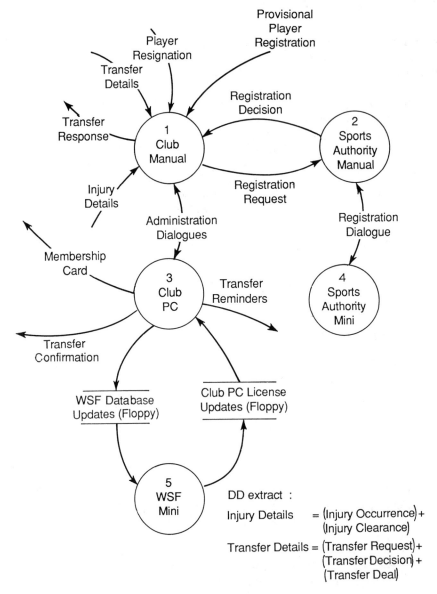

Figure A2.7 Wellbrian Players Administration System: processor DFD: Figure 0.

A.2.4.2 Allocation of data to processors

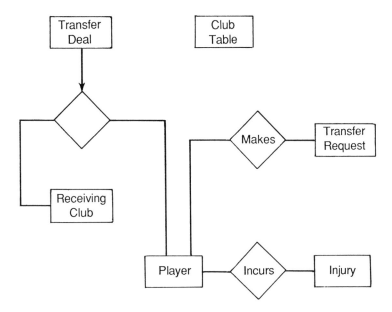

Note: Registration and Club Membership attributes held against Player,
host Club and Sports Authority attributes held in single row Club Table.

Figure A2.8 Processor ERD for club PC.

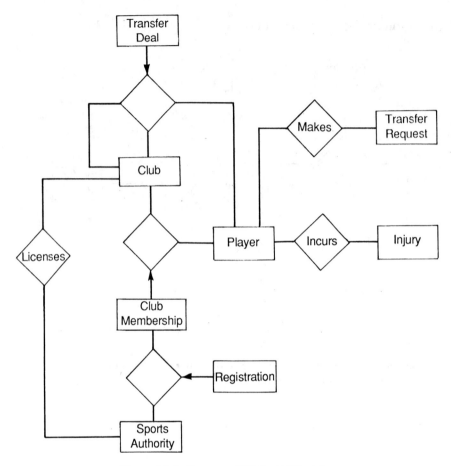

Figure A2.9 Processor ERD for WSF mini.

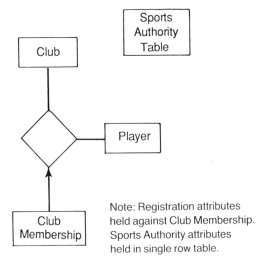

Note: Registration attributes
held against Club Membership.
Sports Authority attributes
held in single row table.

Figure A2.10 Processor ERD for Sports Authority mini.

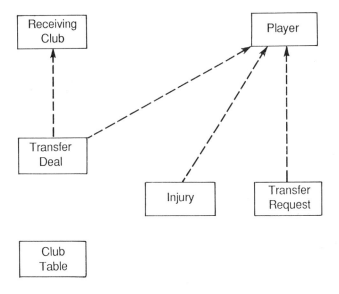

Figure A2.11 Logical data structure diagram for club PC.

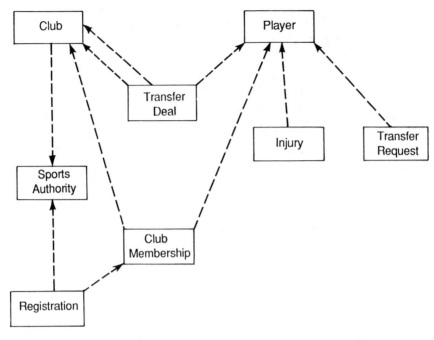

Figure A2.12 Logical data structure diagram for WSF mini.

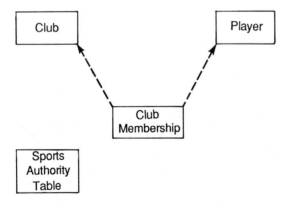

Figure A2.13 Logical data structure diagram for Sports Authority mini.

Superdeal Petrol Sale Control System

□ □ □ □ □ □ □ □ □ □ □ □ □ □ □ □ □

A3.1 Background

A3.1.1 Systems strategy

Unlike many oil companies Superdeal make their own pumps including microchip control software. The Petrol Sale Control System was identified as a candidate context within the system strategy; the scoped global ERD for this system is included in Figure A3.1. The reader will note from this that the scope of the systems strategy confined itself to the filling station subsidiary, which might be considered a sub-enterprise within the business of Superdeal as a whole. This was for reasons of cost, the board expressing its willingness to release further funds for strategic work in other areas on the condition that this exercise progressed successfully.

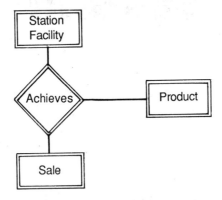

Figure A3.1 Scoped global ERD for Petrol Sale Control System.

A systems analysis project was subsequently initiated with Ms Betty Goodgas, the chairwoman of Superdeal Filling Stations, as executive sponsor. The current system profile (excluding cost-benefit analysis) is described in Section A3.2. Notes from the original interview with Ms Goodgas's chief engineer, Phil Tank are included below.

A3.1.2 Interview with Mr Phil Tank

Each petrol pump dispenses four blends of petrol: 2 star leaded, 2 star unleaded, 4 star leaded and 4 star unleaded. Customers serve their own petrol as follows. The required blend of petrol is selected by pressing the appropriate button and the pump gun is lifted from its catch. Before petrol is dispensed it is necessary to set the pump register to zero. This is requested by the cashier who presses a reset button, provided the previous customer has paid. Once the register is reset petrol is dispensed by squeezing the gun trigger, the register displaying running totals of the cost (to the nearest penny) and quantity purchased (in litres and centilitres). The dispenser has a sensor which indicates the purchase of each centilitre of petrol, the cost of which must be rounded up to the nearest penny.

Once the gun is replaced in its catch, that concludes the sale and a receipt is produced for the customer showing the pump number, petrol blend description, volume purchased (in litres) and amount due. A receipt is similarly produced for accounts except the petrol blend type (e.g. '4L') is printed instead of the full description (e.g. '4 Star Leaded') and the volume purchased is shown in centilitres. The station name and address and VAT number are pre-printed on both types of receipt. The reset button is then activated for the cashier to subsequently press on payment by the customer.

The following details are held in a microchip for each pump.

☐ The type, description and price of each blend of petrol, authorized by Product Management.

☐ Pump details authorized by Equipment Control. These include a unique identifier and the date of last maintenance service.

☐ Station facilities details maintained by the system itself: both current sale and grand totals of the cost and volume of petrol dispensed since the date of last maintenance service for each pump.

A3.2 System profile

SYSTEM TITLE
Petrol Sale Control System.

STATEMENT OF PURPOSE
The purpose of the Petrol Sale Control System is to manage the selling process for an individual pump. This includes calculating cost, maintaining pump registers and ensuring the integrity of each sale.

BACKGROUND
Although the system pertains to an individual pump it must nevertheless be compatible with strategic information requirements.

In order to maintain integrity, the register must only be zeroed once the cashier has had the chance to verify that the correct payment has been made.

PROVISOS
The storage tank capacity and level are maintained by a separate system which monitors petrol flow. The system will not be responsible for control of the petrol flow itself; the dispenser will, however, need to be made aware of when a sale is started. The system will not be responsible for storing payment details.

CONSTRAINTS
    1. Pump hardware specification: 'Superpump Chip Mark 1.5'.
    2. Existing cashier clerical resources to be used.

DEVELOPMENT STRATEGY
    1. To date:
        ☐ Rigorous requirements specification for normal processing in non-procedural language.
    2. Proposed:
        ☐ Event prototyping.
        ☐ Requirements specification to include error processing.

MODELS
As enclosed.

A3.3 Requirements specification

A3.3.1 Context diagram

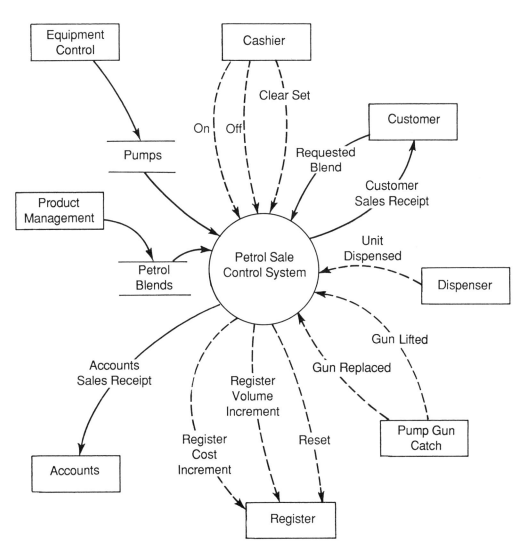

Figure A3.2 Context diagram for Petrol Sale Control System.

A3.3.2 Event list

> 1 Cashier switches pump on (C)
> 2. Cashier switches pump of (C)
> 3. Customer lifts petrol gun (C)
> 4. Cashier requests to clear register (C)
> 5. Customer replaces gun (CD)
> 6. Customer selects blend (D)
> 7. Dispenser reports unit dispensed (D)

Figure A3.3 Event list for Petrol Sale Control System.

A3.3.3 System ERD

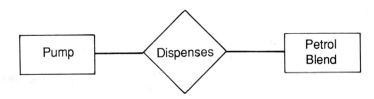

Figure A3.4 ERD for Petrol Sale Control System.

Note

☐ The entity Pump is part of the global entity Station Facility and is single
occurrence relative to each pump's system.

☐ The entity Petrol is part of the global entity Product.

☐ The relationship Dispenses is part of the global relationship Achieves. (The
global relationship Achieves contains another relationship (Stocks) and an
associative entity (Sale), both of which are outside the scope of the system.)

A3.3.4 STD

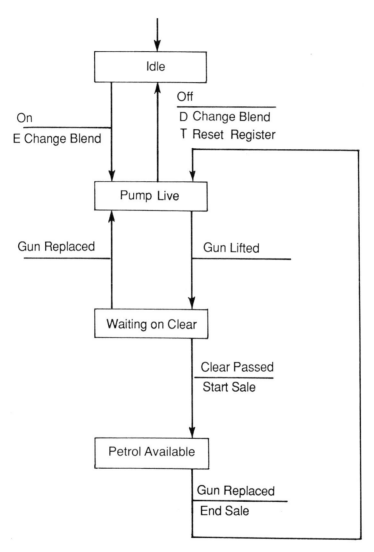

Figure A3.5 STD for Figure 1 Control Petrol Sale.

A3.3.5 DFD

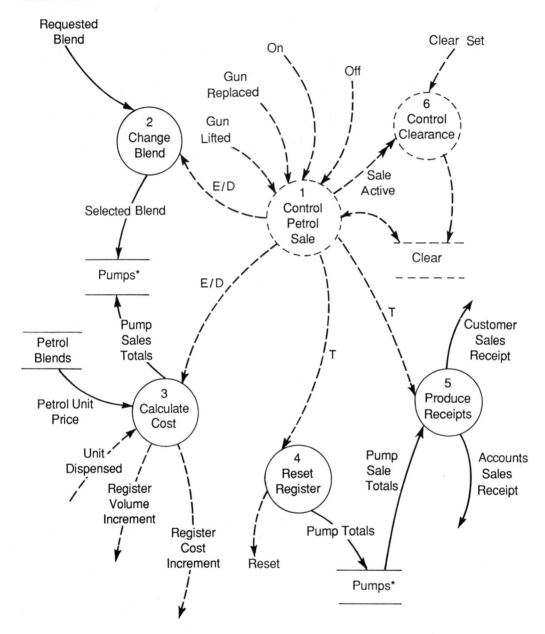

Figure A3.6 DFD Figure 0 for Petrol Sale Control System.

A3.3.6 Process descriptions and specifications

The following specifications itemize the normal pre- and post-condition only. Data dictionary items have been capitalized.

2 CHANGE BLEND

Process objective. To record which blend is currently to be dispensed by a pump.

Process views
> Flows in: REQUESTED BLEND
> Flows out: None
> Entities: PETROL BLEND (*Read*)
>> PUMP (*Read*)
> Associative entities: None
> Relationships: PUMP *DISPENSES* PETROL BLEND (*Update*)

Process specification

Pre-condition 1: A REQUESTED BLEND occurs with matching PETROL BLEND

Post-condition 1: PUMP references matching PETROL BLEND

3 CALCULATE COST

Process objective. To calculate and record cost of each unit of petrol dispensed and to signal the register on cost and volume increments.

Process views
> Flows in: UNIT DISPENSED
> Flows out: REGISTER COST INCREMENT
>> REGISTER VOLUME INCREMENT
> Entities: PETROL BLEND (*Read*)
>> PUMP (*Update*)
> Associative entities: None
> Relationships: PUMP *DISPENSES* PETROL BLEND (*Read*)

Algorithms
> Calculate nearest penny

Process specification

Pre-condition 1: A UNIT DISPENSED occurs
There is a PETROL BLEND referencing PUMP

Post-condition 1: A REGISTER VOLUME INCREMENT is issued
1 is added to PUMP.CURRENT.VOLUME.
For every penny worth of petrol dispensed
(as indicated by Calculate Nearest Penny, using
PETROL.BLEND.UNIT.PRICE)
A REGISTER COST INCREMENT is issued
1 is added to PUMP.CURRENT.SALE.AMOUNT

4 RESET REGISTER

Process objective. To signal register for reset and to zero pump totals.

Process views
Flows in: None
Flows out: RESET
Entities: PUMP (*Update*)
Associative entities: None
Relationships: None

Process specification

Pre-condition 1: None

Post-condition 1: A RESET is issued
PUMP.CURRENT.VOLUME and PUMP.CURRENT.SALE.
AMOUNT are zeroed

5 PRODUCE RECEIPTS

Process objective. To accumulate current pump totals and to produce receipts for customer and for accounts.

Process views
Flows in: None
Flows out: CUSTOMER SALES RECEIPT
ACCOUNTS SALES RECEIPT

Entities: PUMP (*Update*)
        PETROL BLEND (*Read*)
Associative entities: None
Relationships: PUMP *DISPENSES* PETROL BLEND

Process specification

Pre-condition 1: There is a PETROL BLEND referencing PUMP

Post-condition 1: A CUSTOMER SALES RECEIPT is produced with
        LITRE.PRICE = PETROL.BLEND.UNIT.PRICE X 100
        An ACCOUNTS SALES RECEIPT is produced
        PUMP.CURRENT.VOLUME is added to PUMP.TOTAL.
        VOLUME.
        PUMP.CURRENT.SALE.AMOUNT is added to PUMP.
        TOTAL.SALE.AMOUNT

A3.3.7 Data dictionary

The following data dictionary report is produced using an adaptation of BNF; the '+' symbol is implied in all listed items.

ENTITIES

Pump	= Device approved by Superdeal for the dispensing of petrol and registering of sales
Identifier	= Id
Attributes	= Totals Last.Service.Date

Petrol Blend	= A classification of petrol for retail purposes
Identifier	= Type
Attributes	= Description Unit.Price

RELATIONSHIPS

Dispenses	= Reflection of the fact that a pump is currently able to supply given blends of petrol
Participation	= A Pump MAY *dispense* ONE Blend A Blend MAY *be dispensed by* ONE or MORE Pumps

COMPOSITE ATTRIBUTES

Pump.Totals	= Current.Sale.Amount
	Total.Sale.Amount
	Current.Volume
	Total.Volume

DISCRETE CONTROL FLOWS

Clear Set	= Event 4
Gun Lifted	= Event 3
Gun Replaced	= Event 5
Off	= Event 2
On	= Event 1
Register Cost Increment	= A signal to the register that a unit of cost has been dispensed
Register Volume Increment	= A signal to the register that a unit of retail volume has been dispensed
Reset	= A signal to the register to indicate that all counters be set to zeros
Unit dispensed	= Event 7

CONTINUOUS CONTROL FLOWS

Sale Active	= If raised this indicates that a sale is in progress and therefore it is not allowed to clear the register and to start a new sale

DISCRETE DATA FLOWS

Accounts Sales Receipt	= Confirmation for book keeping purposes that a sale has taken place
Attributes	= Pump.Id
	Date
	Time
	Petrol.Blend.Type

Petrol.Blend.Unit.Price
Pump.Current.Sale.Amount
Pump.Current.Volume

Customer Sales Receipt = Confirmation to the customer that a sale has taken place
    Attributes = Pump.Id
Date
Time
Petrol.Blend.Description
Litre.Price
Pump.Current.Sale.Amount
Pump.Current.Volume

Requested Blend = A request made for a given pump to dispense a specific blend of petrol
    Attributes = Petrol.Blend.Type

ACTION SPECIFICATIONS

Start Sale = Do in order:
T Reset register
D Change blend
E Calculate cost
R Sale active

End Sale = Do in order:
D Calculate cost
T Produce receipts
E Change blend
L Sale active

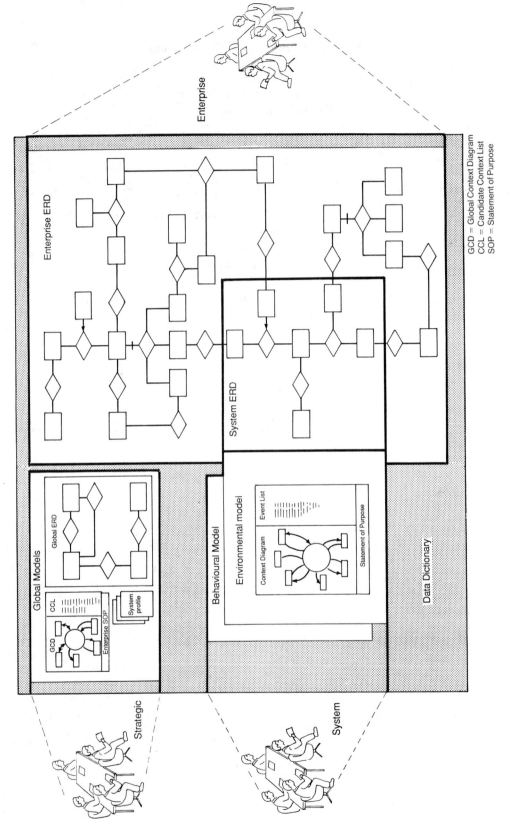

Figure D Perspectives for Effective Systems.

GLOSSARY

Glossary of terms

Balancing rules. Rules for ensuring consistency between diagrams of different types.

Behavioural model. A set of graphic and textual tools for modelling and documenting the essential characteristics of system behaviour. The model is projected from the Environmental Model and consists of the following components:

- ☐ Data flow diagrams (DFDs).
- ☐ State transition diagrams (STDs).
- ☐ System entity relationship diagram (system ERD).
- ☐ Data dictionary (textual support for above diagrams).
- ☐ Process specifications (for lowest level bubbles).

Candidate context list. A list, applied at strategic level, of those functions which are necessary to support the enterprise in its environment.

Context diagram. A graphic tool for modelling the boundary between the system under study and the rest of the world and for documenting the system scope. In effect it is a data flow diagram with a single bubble and terminators included.

Data dictionary. A definitive statement of all textual information used in all models.

Data flow diagram (DFD). A graphical tool for modelling a system's functional behaviour in terms of flow of data and control.

Decision support prototyping. A sub-class of essential prototyping which seeks to verify underlying data structure as flexible enough to meet a wide range of ad hoc enquiries, typically at executive level.

Design prototyping. A class of prototyping, designed to elicit how best to support requirements for a system, which falls into two sub-classes:

- ☐ User interface.
- ☐ Technical.

Enterprise data model. The collective term for EERM and EDBM.

Enterprise database model (EDBM). The collective term for all of the following appertaining to the enterprise's database:

- ☐ Database structure diagrams (logical and physical versions).
- ☐ Schema definitions (logical and physical versions).
- ☐ Database transaction validation tables.

Enterprise ERD. An ERD applied, across systems, for a whole enterprise.

Enterprise entity relationship model (EERM). The enterprise ERD plus its supporting data dictionary definitions.

Enterprise statement of purpose. A concise description of the area of the business to be addressed by strategic modelling. This will include a broad description of business functions and definition of the audience for whom the models are being built.

Entity relationship diagram (ERD). A graphical tool for modelling the essential structure of stored data, aside from considerations of processing or control.

Entity state transition diagram (ESTD). A graphic tool for modelling and documenting significant changes of state of an entity with respect to events.

Environmental model. A set of graphic and textual tools for modelling the boundary between the system under study and the rest of the world. It forms documentation of system scope in terms of:

- ☐ Statement of purpose.
- ☐ Scoped global ERD.
- ☐ Context diagram.
- ☐ Event list.
- ☐ Data dictionary (entries for flows from context diagram).

Essential model. A set of models describing system requirements regardless of technology used to implement those requirements. It is the collective term for the environmental and behavioural models.

Essential prototyping. A class of prototyping designed to elicit essential requirements for a system, which falls into four sub-classes:

- ☐ Primitive.
- ☐ Event.
- ☐ Decision support.
- ☐ Object oriented.

Event. A stimulus or happening which must satisfy each of the following criteria:

- ☐ It occurs in the system environment.
- ☐ It occurs at a specific point in time.
- ☐ Requires the system to make a response.

Event list. A textual tool for modelling the boundary between the system under study and the rest of the world. It forms a catalogue of all events, which are numbered, relevant to the system under study.

Event prototyping. A sub-class of essential prototyping which seeks to resolve uncertainty over specific event responses from the behavioural model.

Global context diagram. A graphic tool applied at strategic level for modelling the boundary between the enterprise and its business environment.

Global DFD. A high-level version of a DFD applied at strategic level for modelling the interfaces between candidate contexts and between candidate contexts and the business environment.

Global ERD. A high-level version of an ERD applied at strategic level.

Global ESTD. A high-level version of an ESTD applied at strategic level to a global entity (instead of an entity).

Global event list. An event list applied to an enterprise.

Global modelling. The building of an initial hazy view of the enterprise in terms of global models and the mapping out system scopes in terms of system profiles.

Levelling rules. Rules for ensuring consistency between different diagrams of the same type.

Logical data structure diagram (LDSD). A graphic tool for modelling and documenting the organization of data into record types (or tables) according to DBMS architectural constraints but independently of physical characteristics. Textual support is normally expressed in Data Description Language (DDL).

Model. A collective term for a diagram (or set of diagrams) plus supporting text.

Object. 'An abstraction of data and exclusive processing on that data, reflecting the capabilities of a system to keep information about or interact with something in the real world' (Coad and Yourdon, 1990).

Object oriented prototyping. A sub-class of essential prototyping which seeks to integrate facts and rules to develop objects.

Organic lifecycle. An approach to systems development founded upon growth and in which systems strategy, analysis and prototyping are seen as iterative activities which are performed at project level with the aim of reducing uncertainty regarding the requirements definition for a system. Two important features of this are as follows. Firstly, projects do not start with a 'clean slate' every time, they need to be selected and initiated in the context of what has already been learnt. Secondly, what we have already learnt in earlier phases is subject to subsequent review as new found knowledge is consolidated. All other systems development activities are also ultimately controlled in this way. Although the organic approach shares an important feature of the waterfall model in that it aims to produce deliverables, it is inherently different in that it views the underlying models as living documents.

Primitive prototyping. A sub-class of essential prototyping which has a two-fold purpose:

- To confirm a chosen portion of the EERM.
- To construct primitive database modules to create/read/update/delete tables (or records) on the database.

Process description. A summary of objectives and required components for a lowest level process (from the behavioural model DFDs).

Process specification. A rigorous description of business logic of a lowest level process (from the behavioural model DFDs).

Project profile. A repository of all relevant information from the point of view of a project, which should include the following:

- ☐ Project name.
- ☐ Project type (Strategic Planning/Global Modelling/Systems Reconnaissance/Systems Analysis/Prototyping)
- ☐ Executive sponsor.
- ☐ Project plan:
  project organization, reporting structure, team members, roles etc.,
  schedule, budget,
  cost-benefit analysis,
  priority,
  risk assessment.
- ☐ System profile.

This is not meant to be an exhaustive list: it is rather meant as a check list of necessary pre-conditions for project initiation. Typically organizational needs will vary according to circumstances. For example, it is often useful to include a short description of objectives, which may include a cost-benefit analysis for the project (as opposed to the system).

Prototyping. A lifecycle of the following activities designed to elicit useful information about the system under study, through the use of working models:

- ☐ Creation.
- ☐ Evaluation.
- ☐ Modification.
- ☐ Completion.

Prototyping may be classed as essential or design prototyping.

Prototyping, evolutionary. The employment of prototyping as a strategy for building systems (as well as eliciting useful information) in which the prototype itself evolves into the finished system.

Provisional Specification. The set of information used to drive event prototyping.

Requirements specification. The name which is customarily given to a document which describes the essential model in terms of a deliverable for sign-off or approval.

Simulation. See 'Technical prototyping'.

State transition diagram (STD). A graphical tool for modelling a system's dynamic behaviour over time.

Statement of purpose. A concise textual statement of rationale of the system which forms the point of departure for building the context diagram and event list. It should answer the question. '*Why* are we building a system?'

Strategic perspective. An attitude or disposition toward systems development which is influenced by the dominant need for systems which are *holistic* and which is *politically sound* in that it is underwritten by top management commitment. The systems development approach itself must be *responsive* and *flexible*.

Strategic modelling. A collective term for:

- ☐ Strategic planning.
- ☐ Global modelling.
- ☐ Systems reconnaissance.

Strategic planning. The setting out and co-ordination of all other activities with respect to the needs of the enterprise as a whole. Activities (including global modelling and systems reconnaissance projects themselves) are commissioned on a short-term project basis thus reducing difficulties in measuring progress, endemic to architectural approaches.

System ERD. An ERD applied at system level. In effect it is the portion of the enterprise ERD which is relevant with respect to a specific system's behaviour.

System profile. A repository of all relevant information from the point of view of a specific system. Four components are included:

- ☐ Statement of purpose.
- ☐ Systems development strategy.
- ☐ Constraints.
- ☐ Models.
- ☐ Cost-benefit analysis.

The very minimum we would expect here would be a statement of purpose. Most importantly, however, from the point of view of this book, any models developed from previous work will be consolidated within the system profile. The type and number of models included will vary according to the stage at which the system is being developed.

Systems reconnaissance. Modelling which provides advance information by scouting ahead to glean more information about those areas about which we are most uncertain. A systems reconnaissance project is a deliberately short-term intensive affair which may operate at either system or enterprise level. The results of systems reconnaissance are saved for consolidation within the appropriate system profile.

Systems strategy. A term which covers both strategic modelling and developing the technical and migration strategies.

Systems Strategy Report. The collective name for documentation which includes:

- ☐ Strategic models:
  global models
  system profiles.
- ☐ Strategic development plan:
  transition plans
  project profiles.
- ☐ Technical strategy.
- ☐ Migration strategy.

Technical prototyping (or 'simulation'). A sub-class of design prototyping which is performed in detailed systems design in order to determine the adequacy of a solution from a performance viewpoint.

User interface prototyping. A sub-class of design prototyping which seeks to establish how the interface between the user and computer system will look and behave.

Glossary of symbols

Symbol name	*Symbol*	*Diagram (page reference)*
Action	Action name	STD (92) ESTD (243) Global ESTD (204)
Associative entity		System ERD (95)
Candidate context		Global DFD (199)
Condition	Condition name	STD (90) ESTD (243) Global ESTD (204)
Control flow (continuous)		Context diagram (65) DFD (85)
Control flow (discrete)		Context diagram (65) DFD (85)
Control process		DFD (85)
Control store		Context diagram (65) DFD (87)

Symbol name	*Symbol*	*Diagram (page reference)*
Data flow (continuous)		Context diagram (65) DFD (85)
Data flow (discrete)		Context diagram (65) DFD (82) Global Context Diagram (180) Global DFD (199)
Data store		Context diagram (65) DFD (85)
Embedded (foreign) key		LDSD (245)
Entity		System ERD (93) Enterprise ERD (234)
Entity state (including global entity)		ESTD (241) GESTD (203)
Entity state transition (including global entity)		ESTD (243) GESTD (203)
Entity supertype/subtype		System ERD (96) Enterprise ERD (240)

Symbol name	Symbol	Diagram (page reference)
External terminator		Global DFD (199)
Global entity		Global ERD (175)
Global relationship		Global ERD (175)
Process (including context process and enterprise)		Context diagram (64) DFD (82) Global Context Diagram (180) Global DFD (199)
Relationship		System ERD (94) Enterprise ERD (234)
State		STD (88)
State transition		STD (90)
Table		LDSD (245)
Terminator		Context diagram (65) DFD (82) Global Context Diagram (180) Global DFD (199)

BIBLIOGRAPHY

Albrecht, A.J., October 1979, 'Measuring Application Development Productivity', *Proceedings of IBM Application Development Symposium*, CA.

Allen, C.P., August 1987, 'Visions and Traps in Software Engineering', *Proceedings of Twelfth Structured Methods Conference*, Chicago, Illinois.

Anthony, R.N., 1965, *Planning and Control Systems: A Framework for Analysis*, Harvard University Press, Cambridge, Mass.

ANSI/X3/SPARC (American National Standards Institute/Standards Planning and Requirements Committee), 1978, DBMS Framework, '*Report of the Study Group on Database Management Systems*', ed. Dennis Tsichritzis and Anthony Klug, University of Toronto, Canada, AFIPS Press.

Blanchard, B.S. and Fabrycky, W.J., 1984, *Systems Engineering and Analysis*, Prentice Hall, Englewood Cliffs, N.J.

Boar, B.H., 1984, *Application Prototyping*, Wiley, New York.

Bennis, W. and Schein, E., 1965, *Personal and Organisational Change Through Group Methods*, Wiley, New York.

Boehm, 1976, 'Software Engineering'. *IEEE Transactions on Computers*, Vol. C-25, No 12, December 1976, pp. 1226–41.

Boehm, B.W., 1981, *Software Engineering Economics*, Prentice Hall, Englewood Cliffs, N.J.

Boehm, B.W., 1986, 'A Spiral Model of Software Development and Enhancement', in *ACM Sigsoft Software Engineering Notes*, Vol 11, no 4, pp. 14–23.

Brooks, F.P., 1975, *The Mythical Man Month*, Addison Wesley, Reading, Mass.

Chen, P., March 1976, The Entity-Relationship Model – 'Toward a Unified View of Data', *ACM Transactions on Database Systems*, Vol 1, No 1.

Coad, P. and Yourdon, E., 1990, *Object Oriented Analysis*, Prentice Hall (Yourdon Press).

Codd, E.F., June 1970, 'A Relational Model of Data for Large Shared Data Banks'. *Comm. ACM Transactions on Database Systems*. Vol 13, No 6, pp. 377–87.

Codd, E.F., 1972, 'Further Normalisation of the Data Base Relational Model'. *Courant Computer Science Series*, 6, (pp. 33–64), Prentice Hall, Englewood Cliffs, N.J.

Connell, J.L. and Shafer, L.B., 1989, *Structured Rapid Prototyping*, Prentice Hall (Yourdon Press).

Connor, D.A., 1988, *Computer Systems Development, Strategic Resource Information Planning and Execution – STRIPE*, Prentice Hall, Englewood Cliffs, N.J.

Constantine, L., Summer 1989, Object Oriented and Structured Methods: 'Toward Integration', *American Programmer*, Vol 2, Nos 7–8.

Date, C.J., 1982, *An Introduction to Database Systems: Vol 1*, Addison-Wesley, Reading, Mass.

De Marco, T., 1978, *Structured Analysis and System Specification*, Prentice Hall (Yourdon Press).

De Marco, T., 1982, *Controlling Software Projects*, Prentice Hall (Yourdon Press).

Dijkstra, E.W., 1965, 'Programming Considered as a Human Activity', *Proceedings of 1965 IFIP Conference*, North Holland.

Dijkstra, E.W., 1968, 'Cooperating Sequential Processes', *Programming Languages*, F. Genuys (ed.), Academic Press, New York.

Doyle, M. and Straus, D., 1976, *How to Make Meetings Work*, Berkley/Jove, New York.

Fagin, R., September 1977, Multivalued Dependencies and a New Normal Form for Relational Databases, *ACM Transactions on Database Systems*, No. 3.

Fisher, A.S., 1988, *CASE: Using Software Development Tools*, Wiley, New York.

Flavin, M., 1981, *Fundamental Concepts of Information Modelling*, Prentice Hall, (Yourdon Press).

Floyd, C., 1984, 'A Systematic Look at Prototyping', in: Budde, R., Kuhlenkamp, K., Mathiassen, L. and Zullighoven, H., (eds), *Approaches to Prototyping*, pp. 1–19, Springer-Verlag, Berlin.

Gane, C., 1989, *Rapid System Development Using Structured Techniques and Relational Technology*, Prentice Hall, Englewood Cliffs, N.J.

GUIDE Publication GPP–147, 1986, *Joint Application Design*, Chicago: GUIDE International.

Gremillion, L.L. and Pyburn, P., 1983, 'Breaking the Systems Bottleneck', *Harvard Business Review*, March–April.

Hatley, D.J. and Pirbhai, I.A., 1987, *Strategies for Real-Time System Specification*, Dorset House, New York.

Henderson, C., Rockart, J.F. and Sifonis, J.G., September 1984, 'A Planning Methodology for Integrating Management Support Systems', *Centre for Information Systems Research Working Paper 116*, Sloan School of Management, MIT, Cambridge, Mass.

Hewett, J. and Durham, T., 1987, *Computer-aided Software Engineering: Commercial Strategies*, Ovum.

Houtchens, S. and Pollock, J., 1987, 'Developing Real-Time Software without Writing Source Code', *Internal Report*, Integrated Systems, Inc., Santa Clara, California.

Howe, D., 1989, *Data Analysis for Database Design*, 2nd edn, Arnold, London.

Inmon, W.H., 1984, *Information Systems Architecture*, Prentice Hall, Englewood Cliffs, N.J.

Inmon, W.H., 1988, *Information Engineering for the Practitioner*, Prentice Hall (Yourdon Press).

Jacky, J., January 1985, 'The Star Wars Defense Won't Compute', in *Atlantic Monthly*.

Jones, C., 1986, *Programming Productivity*, McGraw-Hill, New York.

Knuth, D., 1973, *The Art of Computer Programming*, Vol 1, Addison-Wesley, Reading, Mass.

Kowal, J.A., 1988, *Analysing Systems*, Prentice Hall, Englewood Cliffs, N.J.

Martin, J., 1975, *Computer Data-Base Organisation*, Prentice Hall, Englewood Cliffs, N.J.

Martin, J., 1982, *Application Development without Programmers*, Prentice Hall, Englewood Cliffs, N.J.

Martin, J., 1988, *The Justification for Information Engineering*, Savant.

Martin, J. and McClure, C., 1985, *Action Diagrams: Clearly Structured Program Design*, Prentice Hall, Englewood Cliffs, N.J.

McClure, C., 1989, *CASE is Software Automation*, Prentice Hall, Englewood Cliffs, N.J.

McMenamin, S.M. and Palmer, J.F., 1984, *Essential Systems Analysis*, Prentice Hall (Yourdon Press).

Meyer, B., 1989, *Object Oriented Software Construction*, Prentice Hall, Hemel Hempstead.

Neumann, P., January 1985, 'Some Computer Related Disasters and Other Egrarious Horrors', in *ACM Sigsoft Software Engineering Notes*.

Page-Jones, M., 1985, *Practical Project Management: Restoring Quality to DP Projects and Systems*, Dorset House, New York.

Page-Jones, M., 1988, *The Practical Guide to Structured Systems Design*, 2nd edn, Prentice Hall (Yourdon Press).

Parikh, G., 19 February 1986, 'Restructuring Your COBOL Programs', *Computer World Focus*.

Parker, M. and Benson, R., 1985, 'Enterprise-Wide Information Management – An Introduction to Concepts', *IBM Los Angeles Scientific Centre Report G320–2768*.

Parnas, D.L., December 1972, 'On the Criteria to Be Used in Decomposing Systems into Modules', *Communications of the ACM*, Vol 5, No 2, pp. 1053–58.

Peters, T., 1987, *Thriving on Chaos*, MacMillan, London.

Porter, M.E., 1980, *Competitive Strategy*, Free Press, New York.

Porter, M.E., 1985, *Competitive Advantage*, Free Press, New York.

Putnam, L., 1978, 'A General Empirical Solution to the Macro Software Sizing and Estimating Problem', *IEEE Transactions on Software Engineering*, Vol 4, No 4.

Roberts, M.L., August/September 1989, 'Enterprise Engineering: Old Goals. New Techniques', *System Builder*.

Rockart, J.F., March–April 1979, 'Chief Executives Define Their Own Data Needs', *Harvard Business Review*.

Sanders, N., 1978, *The St Merino Solution*, Associated Business Programs Ltd.

Steiner, G., 1979, *Strategic Planning*, New York Press.

Sullivan, L., March 1896, 'The Tall Office Building Artistically Considered', in *Lippinscott's Magazine*.

Ward, P.T. and Mellor, S.J., 1985, *Structured Development for Real Time Systems*, Prentice Hall (Yourdon Press).

Veryard, R., 1984, *Pragmatic Data Analysis*, Blackwell, Oxford.

Vonk, R., 1990, *Prototyping, The Effective Use of CASE Technology*, Prentice Hall International (UK) Ltd, Hemel Hempstead.

Weinberg, G.M., 1985, *The Secrets of Consulting*, Dorset House, New York.

Weinberg, G.M., 1988, *Rethinking Systems Analysis and Design*, Dorset House, New York.

Wetherbe, J.C. and Leitheiser, R.L., 1985, 'Information Centres: A Survey of Services, Decisions, Problems and Successes', *Journal of Information Systems Management*, Summer 3–10.

Wiseman, C., 1988, *Strategic Information Systems*, Irwin, Homewood, Illinois.

Yourdon, E., 1986(a), *Managing the Structured Techniques*, 3rd edn, Prentice Hall (Yourdon Press).

Yourdon, E., 1986(b), *Nations at Risk*, Prentice Hall (Yourdon Press).

Yourdon, E., 1988, *Managing the System Life Cycle*, 2nd edn, Prentice Hall (Yourdon Press).

Yourdon, E., 1989, *Modern Structured Analysis*, Prentice Hall (Yourdon Press).

Zachman, J.A., 1986, 'A Framework for Information Systems Architecture', *IBM Los Angeles Scientific Centre*.

General reference books

Dictionary of Computing, 1986, Oxford University Press.

INDEX

*Folios in **bold** numerals indicate an especially significant reference.*